# PRENTICE HALL

# The READER'S JOURNEY

## STUDENT EDITION

## GRADE SEVEN

**HARVEY DANIELS**
**GRANT WIGGINS**

PEARSON

Upper Saddle River, New Jersey • Boston, Massachusetts • Chandler, Arizona • Glenview, Illinois

**Go Online**
About the Author
Visit: PHSchool.com
Web Code: exe-7101

Whenever you see a box like this, go to PHSchool.com and enter the Web code given. This will link you directly to extra online helps.

To look at a list of the online helps, enter the following code: exk-7000.

Acknowledgments appear on page 545, which constitutes an extension of this copyright page.

**Cover Design:** Judith Krimski, Judith Krimski Design, Inc.

ISBN-13: 978-0-13-363596-6
ISBN-10: 0-13-363596-1
12 13 14 15 16   V011   16 15 14 13 12

**PEARSON**

# Contributing Authors

The contributing authors guided the direction and philosophy of Prentice Hall *The Reader's Journey*. Their work helped to inform the pedagogical integrity of the program and to ensure its relevance for today's teachers and students.

**Harvey Daniels, Ph.D.,** has been a classroom teacher, writing project director, author, and university professor. Also known as "Smokey," Daniels serves as an international consultant to schools, districts, and educational agencies. Daniels is known for his work on student-led book clubs, as recounted in *Literature Circles: Voice and Choice in Book Clubs and Reading Groups* and his newer title, *Mini-lessons for Literature Circles.* He has authored or co-authored eleven other books. Recent works include *Subjects Matter: Every Teacher's Guide to Content-Area Reading* and *Content Area Writing: Every Teacher's Guide.* Daniels is on the faculty of National-Louis University in Chicago, and is Founding Director of the Walloon Institute.

**Grant Wiggins, Ed.D.,** is the President of Authentic Education in Hopewell, New Jersey. He earned his Ed.D. from Harvard University and his B.A. from St. John's College in Annapolis. Grant consults with schools, districts, and state education departments on a variety of reform matters; organizes conferences and workshops; and develops print materials and Web resources on curricular change. He is the co-author, with Jay McTighe, of *Understanding By Design* and *The Understanding By Design Handbook*, the award-winning and highly successful materials on curriculum published by ASCD. His work has been supported by the Pew Charitable Trusts, the Geraldine R. Dodge Foundation, and the National Science Foundation.

# Program Advisory Board

The following educators helped shape the program from the very beginning. As classroom practitioners and advocates of a novel-based approach to the teaching of the language arts, they helped to conceptualize the program, lending their advice to the Student Work Text, the Teacher's Guide, and the Anchor Book library alike.

**Linda Banas**
Department of Learning
and Instruction at SUNY Buffalo
Buffalo, New York

**Diane Boni**
Director of Language Arts
Greece Central School District
Rochester, New York

**Heidi Driscoll**
English Language Arts
Curriculum Supervisor, 7-12
Taunton Public Schools
Taunton, Massachusetts

**Laurie Herriges**
Language Arts Instructor
Morgan Butler Middle School
Waukesha, Wisconsin

**Sharon Hiller, Ed.D.**
Director of Curriculum and
Educational Services
Richmond Community Schools
Richmond, Michigan

**Darlene Groves Musso**
English Department Chairperson
Broward County School District
Plantation, Florida

**Deborah Nevill**
Language Arts Instructor
Granite Valley Middle School
Monson, Massachusetts

**Helen Shiffer**
English Department chairperson
Carmel School District
Carmel, Indianas

**Ginny White**
Language Arts Instructor
Fernandina Beach Middle School
Fernandina Beach, Florida

# Teacher Reviewers

The program reviewers provided ongoing input throughout the development of *The Reader's Journey*. Their valuable insights ensure that the perspectives of the teachers throughout the country are represented within this language arts series.

**Ella Briand**
Humanities Field Coordinator
Syracuse City Schools
Syracuse, New York

**Julia A. Delahunty**
English Department Head
Edison Township Public Schools
Edison, New Jersey

**Sharon S. Hoff**
La Quinta High School
Desert Sands Unified School District
La Quinta, California

**Marilyn Kline**
Senior Research Associate
David C. Anchin Center
University of South Florida
Tampa, Florida

**Kathleen Oropallo, Ph.D.**
National Educational Consultant
Zephyrhills, Florida

**Elizabeth Primas, Ed.D.**
Director of Literacy
District of Columbia Public Schools
Washington, D.C.

**Ellin Rossberg**
Language Arts Consultant
Westchester County
New York, New York

**Helen Turner**
English-Language Arts Teacher
Bancroft Middle School
San Leandro, California

**Charles Youngs**
Language Arts Curriculum Facilitator
Bethel Park High School
Bethel Park, Pennsylvania

# A Novel Way to Learn!

## Learning Through Reading Books

This program is like no other you have studied from. You will get to read lots of interesting books of all sorts, from novels to nonfiction. In each unit, your teacher will assign a book for you to read (your **Anchor Book**). Later in the unit you get to choose another book on your own (your **Free-Choice Book**).

## How Does The Program Work?

You start in the Student Work Text.

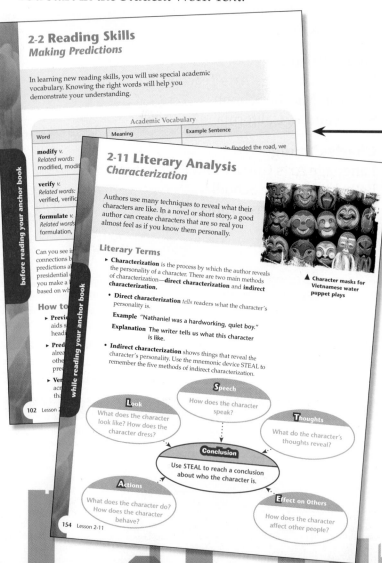

before reading your anchor book

### 2-2 Reading Skills
*Making Predictions*

In learning new reading skills, you will use special academic vocabulary. Knowing the right words will help you demonstrate your understanding.

#### Academic Vocabulary

| Word | Meaning | Example Sentence |
|---|---|---|
| **modify** v. *Related words:* modified, modi | | |
| **verify** v. *Related words:* verified, verific | | |
| **formulate** v. *Related words:* formulation, | | |

while reading your anchor book

### 2-11 Literary Analysis
*Characterization*

Authors use many techniques to reveal what their characters are like. In a novel or short story, a good author can create characters that are so real you almost feel as if you know them personally.

▲ Character masks for Vietnamese water puppet plays

#### Literary Terms

▶ **Characterization** is the process by which the author reveals the personality of a character. There are two main methods of characterization—**direct characterization** and **indirect characterization.**

• **Direct characterization** *tells* readers what the character's personality is.

**Example** "Nathaniel was a hardworking, quiet boy."

**Explanation** The writer tells us what this character is like.

• **Indirect characterization** shows things that reveal the character's personality. Use the mnemonic device STEAL to remember the five methods of indirect characterization.

**S**peech
How does the character speak?

**L**ook
What does the character look like? How does the character dress?

**T**houghts
What do the character's thoughts reveal?

**Conclusion**
Use STEAL to reach a conclusion about who the character is.

**A**ctions
What does the character do? How does the character behave?

**E**ffect on Others
How does the character affect other people?

154 Lesson 2-11

## Before Reading Your Anchor Book

You will learn reading strategies and how to set up your **Reader's Journal**.

## While Reading Your Anchor Book

Along the way you will learn lots of other skills that will help you too.

From time to time you will get to talk about your Anchor Book and your ideas in special **Literature Circles**.

In the following selection, the author uses flashback and foreshadowing. *Guiding Question:* How does Clyde's mother resolve a conflict so that both she and her son can get what they want?

## Trombones and Colleges
### by Walter Dean Myers

**Background** The following selection is a chapter from the novel *Fast Sam, Cool Clyde, and Stuff.* The author, Walter Dean Myers, writes about the experience of modern teens growing up in his old neighborhood, Harlem, New York.

### Vocabulary Builder

**Before you read,** you will discuss the following words. In the Vocabulary Builder box in the margin, use a vocabulary building strategy to make the words your own.

**commercial    nonchalant    colander**

**As you read,** draw a box around unfamiliar words you could add to your vocabulary. Use context clues to unlock their meaning.

*Marking the Text*

**Flashback and Foreshadowing**

**As you read,** *underline details that indicate flashback and foreshadowing. Write notes in the margin explaining how these techniques help develop the characters and the plot.*

It was a dark day when we got our report cards. The sky was full of gray clouds and it was sprinkling rain. I was over to Clyde's house and Gloria and Kitty were there. Sam probably would have been there too, only he had got a two-week job in the afternoons helping out at Freddie's. Actually he only did it so that his mother would let him be on the track team again. Sam and his mother had this little system going. He would do something good-doing and she'd let him do something that he wanted to.

Clyde's report card was on the kitchen table and we all sat around it like it was some kind of a big important document. I had got a pretty good report card and had wanted to show it off

130 Lesson 2-6

## Learn to Mark Texts Too!
Here is what is really cool about this Work Text. It's *yours.* You will get to interact with the text by marking passages while you read—underlining important phrases, marking vocabulary words, and making notes in the margins.

## Now It's Your Turn to Choose
In the middle of the unit you will get to pick a Free-Choice Book. How does it compare to your Anchor Book?

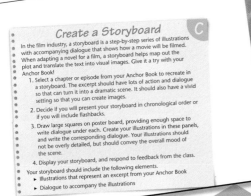

### Create a Storyboard  C

In the film industry, a storyboard is a step-by-step series of illustrations with accompanying dialogue that shows how a movie will be filmed. When adapting a novel for a film, a storyboard helps map out the plot and translate the text into visual images. Give it a try with your Anchor Book!

1. Select a chapter or episode from your Anchor Book to recreate in a storyboard. The excerpt should have lots of action and dialogue so that can turn it into a dramatic scene. It should also have a vivid setting so that you can create images.

2. Decide if you will present your storyboard in chronological order or if you will include flashbacks.

3. Draw large squares on poster board, providing enough space to write dialogue under each. Create your illustrations in these panels, and write the corresponding dialogue. Your illustrations should not be overly detailed, but should convey the overall mood of the scene.

4. Display your storyboard, and respond to feedback from the class.

Your storyboard should include the following elements.
▶ Illustrations that represent an excerpt from your Anchor Book
▶ Dialogue to accompany the illustrations

after reading

## After Reading Your Anchor Book
You will get to do some fun projects based on your Anchor Book. Which project you choose is up to you.

## So are you ready for The Reader's Journey?

# Unit 1  What is the best way to find the *truth*?

## Genre Focus: Fiction and Nonfiction

### Unit Book Choices

*With this unit you will read a book (your Anchor Book) as you learn unit skills. Here are six books that complement the unit well.*

- The Outsiders
- Journey of the Sparrows
- Rosa Parks: My Story
- The Lottery Rose
- Guys Write for Guys Read
- The Glory Field

### Free-Choice Book

*Enrich and extend your learning with a free-choice book.*

# Unit 2  Does every *conflict* have a winner?

## Genre Focus: The Novel

 **Unit Book Choices**
*With this unit you will read a book (your Anchor Book) as you learn unit skills. Here are six books that complement the unit well.*

- Let the Circle Be Unbroken
- Heat
- Hatchet
- A Step from Heaven
- Between Madison and Palmetto
- Fast Sam, Cool Clyde, and Stuff

**Free-Choice Book**
*Enrich and extend your learning with a free-choice book.*

## After Reading Your Anchor Book

# Unit 3  What should we *learn*?

## Genre Focus: Types of Nonfiction

**Unit Book Choices**
*With this unit you will read a book (your Anchor Book) as you learn unit skills. Here are six books that complement the unit well.*

- Farewell to Manzanar
- Oddballs
- Who Moved My Cheese?
- Zlata's Diary
- They Led the Way
- Promises to Keep

**Free-Choice Book**
*Enrich and extend your learning with a free-choice book.*

# Unit 4  What is the best way to *communicate*?

## Genre Focus: Prose and Poetry

 **Unit Book Choices**
*With this unit you will read a book (your Anchor Book) as you learn unit skills. Here are six books that complement the unit well.*

- Restless Spirit
- Crazy Loco
- Eyes on the Prize
- Someone Is Hiding on Alcatraz Island
- Within Reach: My Everest Story
- Touching Spirit Bear

**Free-Choice Book**
*Enrich and extend your learning with a free-choice book.*

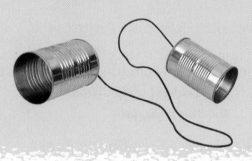

# Unit 5

 **Do others** *see* **us more clearly than we** *see* **ourselves?**

## Genre Focus: Drama

 **Unit Book Choices**
*With this unit you will read a book (your Anchor Book) as you learn unit skills. Here are six books that complement the unit well.*

- **The Yellow Boat**
- **Novio Boy**
- **Doors**
- **Lost in Yonkers**
- **Our Town**
- **Flowers for Algernon**

 **Free-Choice Book**
*Enrich and extend your learning with a free-choice book.*

# Unit 6  *Community* or *Individual:*
## Which is more important?

### Genre Focus: The Research Process

**Unit Book Choices**
*With this unit you will read a book (your Anchor Book) as you learn unit skills. Here are six books that complement the unit well*

- Portraits of African-American Heroes
- The Kid Who Invented the Popsicle
- Dr. Jenner and the Speckled Monster
- Micromonsters
- Sea Otter Rescue
- Gandhi

**Free-Choice Book**
*Enrich and extend your learning with a free-choice book.*

# What is the best way to find the *truth*?

## Unit 1 Genre focus:
# Fiction and Nonfiction

### Your Anchor Book
There are many good books that would work well to support both the Big Question and the genre focus of this unit. In this unit you will read one of these books as your Anchor Book. Your teacher will introduce the book you will be reading.

### Free-Choice Reading
Later in this unit you will be given the opportunity to choose another book to read. This is called your free-choice book.

# Thinking About What You Already Know

Regardless of whether they are telling true or made-up stories, good storytellers use the same techniques. The more you read, the more you will find yourself recognizing these techniques.

Think about differences between fiction and nonfiction and record them below. You will complete the chart with a partner after you have read the excerpts in this unit. Using what you already know, read the selections and think about whether they are fiction or nonfiction (or whether they could be either). Then, discuss your conclusions with a partner.

| Similarities | Differences |
|---|---|
| | |

## Fiction

### from "The Talk" by Gary Soto

My best friend and I knew that we were going to grow up to be ugly. On a backyard lawn—the summer light falling west of the mulberry tree where the house of the most beautiful girl on the street stood—we talked about what we could do: shake the second-base dirt from our hair, wash our hands of frog smells and canal water, and learn to smile without showing our crooked teeth. We had to stop spitting when girls were looking and learn not to pile food onto a fork and into a fat cheek already churning hot grub.

We were twelve, with lean bodies that were beginning to grow in weird ways. First, our heads got large, but our necks wavered, frail as crisp tulips. The eyes stayed small as well, receding into pencil dots on each side of an unshapely nose that cast remarkable shadows when we turned sideways. It seemed that Scott's legs sprouted muscle and renegade veins, but his arms, blue with ink markings, stayed short and hung just below his waist. My gangly arms nearly touched my kneecaps. In this way, I was built for picking up grounders and doing cartwheels, my arms swaying just inches from the summery grass.

**Nonfiction**

## from *"Nisei Daughter"* by Monica Sone

Our bus idled a moment at the traffic signal and we noticed at the left of us an entire block filled with neat rows of low shacks, resembling chicken houses. Someone commented on it with awe, "Just look at those chicken houses. They sure go in for poultry in a big way here." Slowly the bus made a left turn, drove through a wire-fenced gate, and to our dismay, we were inside the over-sized chicken farm. The bus driver opened the door, the guard stepped out and stationed himself at the door again. Jim, the young man who had shepherded us into the buses, popped his head inside and sang out, "Okay, folks, all off at Yokohama, Puyallup."

We stumbled out, stunned, dragging our bundles after us. It must have rained hard the night before in Puyallup, for we sank ankle deep into gray, glutinous mud. The receptionist, a white man, instructed us courteously, "Now, folks, please stay together as family units and line up. You'll be assigned your apartment."

**Fiction**

## from *"Bronx Masquerade"* by Nikki Grimes

I ain't particular about doing homework, you understand. My teachers practically faint whenever I turn something in. Matter of fact, I probably got the longest list of excuses for missing homework of anyone alive. Except for my homey Tyrone. He tries to act like he's not even interested in school, like there's no point in studying hard, or dreaming about tomorrow, or bothering to graduate. He's got his reasons. I keep on him about going to school, though, saying I need the company. Besides, I tell him, if he drops out and gets a J.O.B., he won't have any time to work on his songs. That always gets to him. Tyrone might convince everybody else that he's all through with dreaming, but I know he wants to be a big hip-hop star. He's just afraid he won't live long enough to do it. Me, I hardly ever think about checking out. I'm more worried about figuring what I want to do if I live.

## Partner Activity

Discuss similarities shared by these fiction and nonfiction excerpts with a partner, and add your answers to the chart on the previous page.

Reading nonfiction can be just as entertaining as reading fiction. As you read a variety of works from both genres throughout the year, pay attention to how the authors use many of the same techniques to engage their audience.

# 1-1 Understanding the Big Question

## What is the best way to find the truth?

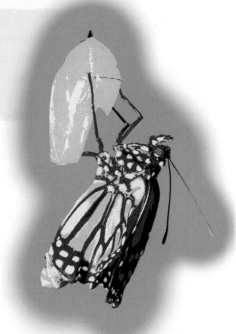

Some things you know for certain are not true. You know that a genie doesn't come out of a bottle. Other things you can prove are true, but first you must identify the best way to find the truth.

Truth can be found in different places. Think of stories you read. Sometimes imagined stories share ideas that are "true." A fable might teach a lesson that is true. A love story might not have real characters, but it could show true emotions because they are feelings many people share.

Where you find the truth depends upon what kind of truth you are looking for. What do the words *true, truth,* or *truthful* mean to you?

**Directions** Think about and discuss the following three words with a partner. Then, complete the graphic organizer. Brainstorm words and phrases you associate with each word. Then, write a sentence using the word.

**True**

> **Words and Phrases I Associate With the Word**
>
> **My Sentence** _____
> _____

**Truth**

> **Words and Phrases I Associate With the Word**
>
> **My Sentence** _____
> _____

**Truthful**

> **Words and Phrases I Associate With the Word**
>
> **My Sentence** _____
> _____

*before reading your anchor book*

Truth is usually thought of as a statement that has been proven to be true. However, sometimes it is based upon facts we *accept* to be true but which we cannot prove.

**Directions** With a partner, complete the chart. Discuss how the following truths are expressed in different content areas.

| Truth | Can it be proven? | Where could you find evidence for this kind of truth? |
|---|---|---|
| All plants need water to survive. (*Science*) | | |
| The nightly news reports the facts without bias. (*Current Events*) | | |
| Hurricane force winds can be devastating. (*Science*) | | |
| A photograph can reveal emotion. (*Art/Humanities*) | | |

 In this book, you will see questions that are labeled "The Big Question." These questions appear at the end of certain lessons. As you read, remember that fiction and nonfiction present different kinds of truth.

**Getting Ready for Your Anchor Book**

*You will start reading your Anchor Book soon. The next few pages in this book give you some background information plus a reading skill.*

# Introduction to
# Fiction and Nonfiction

What is real and what is imaginary? In many cases, you can tell in an instant—a dog is real, but a dragon is imaginary. Other times, such as when your friend tells you a far-fetched story, it's not so obvious. The difference between real and imaginary is what makes fiction different from nonfiction.

A work of **fiction** is a story that is imagined. It may tell about impossible events, such as time travel or vampires, or it may tell about things that could be true, like a boy who makes a new friend. It can also take place during a real historical event.

Works of **nonfiction** are true. They contain facts and ideas that really happened. They might also include thoughts and opinions, but they leave out anything that is untrue.

## Elements of Fiction

Fiction has been around as long as people have been able to tell stories. The first stories were told to entertain people and pass down information from generation to generation. Here are some things you can find in all fiction.

▶ All fictional stories are about a problem, or **conflict.** The whole story is about how this conflict builds and affects the characters. The way the story develops is called the **plot.**

▶ Every story has **characters**—people, animals, or other creatures that play a role in the story.

▶ The time and place where the events in the story occur is called the **setting.** The setting can affect the action and the characters.

▶ Almost all fiction has a **theme.** This is a big message that the author is trying to communicate.

*before reading your anchor book*

# Elements of Nonfiction

▶ Some nonfiction stories can have the same elements as fiction, such as plot, characters, and setting.

▶ Nonfiction includes facts and characters that are real.

▶ Nonfiction can be written for many purposes. It can be written to inform, to persuade, or to entertain the reader. It can also be written to reflect on an experience or event.

## Fiction Versus Nonfiction

With a partner, compare the features and purposes of two books you use in your classes. Compare a book of fiction, a novel or a short story collection with a nonfiction book or a textbook from your science, math, or social studies class. For example, you might compare how the features of a novel, such as the chapters and the chapter titles, convey information about the novel's plot or theme and how the headings in a textbook communicate information about the topic. Record the title of each book, as well as the features and purposes, in the chart below.

| Kind of Text | Features | Purposes |
|---|---|---|
| Fiction: _____ |  |  |
| Nonfiction: _____ |  |  |

**Evaluate** What are the merits of each kind of text? How do they help you learn about the world? Discuss your answers with a partner.

### Strategies for Reading Fiction and Nonfiction

As you read both fiction and nonfiction, self-monitor and self-correct when you encounter the following situations.

**Reread the Text** If you feel lost while reading, go back to where you felt you understood the text. Then, slowly reread that section.

**Mark the Text** Check your understanding by marking the text, summarizing, and using graphic organizers, such as tables and webs.

**Read Aloud** You might also try reading difficult sections aloud to help you self-monitor for comprehension. As you read aloud, work to use a rhythm, flow, and meter that sounds like everyday speech.

# 1-2 Reading Skills
## Context Clues

In learning new reading skills, you will use special academic vocabulary. Knowing the right words will help you demonstrate your understanding.

### Academic Vocabulary

| Word | Meaning | Example Sentence |
|------|---------|------------------|
| **clarify** *v.* <br> *Related words:* <br> clarified, clarification | to make clearer | Could you please *clarify* what you mean? |
| **verify** *v.* <br> *Related words:* <br> verified, verification | to confirm | Your birth certificate will *verify* your date and place of birth. |
| **context** *n.* <br> *Related words:* <br> contextual | the part of a text or statement that surrounds a word | I could tell what he meant by the *context* that surrounded his statement. |

When you come across a word you don't know, what do you do? You can look it up or ask someone what it means. You can also look at the **context**—the words and ideas that surround a word. These words and ideas are clues that can help you identify and **verify** a word's meaning.

Here are some questions you might ask yourself to find the meaning of a word by using **context clues.**

Are there any words that mean the same thing?

Are there any words that mean the opposite?

Do other parts of the sentence give clues about how the word is used?

Is the word defined in another part of the sentence?

Is there another word I could put in place of the word to make the sentence clear?

Are there headings, pictures, or charts that help to clarify the meaning?

**Directions** Read the following excerpt from a poem. Look at how a student drew a box around unfamiliar words and underlined context clues.

**Student Model: Marking the Text**

*When I Was One-and-Twenty* by A. E. Housman

Go Online
**About the Author**
Visit: PHSchool.com
Web Code: exe-7101

When I was one-and-twenty    person's past age?
I heard a wise man say,
'Give crowns and pounds and guineas
But not your heart away;
Give pearls away and rubies    valuable
But keep your fancy free.'
But I was one-and-twenty,
No use to talk to me.

**1** **Identify** What do you think "crowns and pounds and guineas" are? What clues help **clarify** what these words mean?

_____

_____

_____

**2** **Infer** What kind of information might you expect to find after the phrase "When I was…"? How does this help you understand what "one-and-twenty" means?

_____

_____

_____

**Directions** Read the following sentences, then use context clues to complete the chart.

| Sentence | Meaning | How I Know |
|---|---|---|
| The teacher asked us to *refrain* from talking while she was speaking. | *Refrain* means "not to do something." | A teacher would probably ask you not to talk while she is speaking. |
| I went to the *optometrist* to have my eyes examined. | | The phrase "have my eyes examined" is a clue that the speaker is going to see someone who studies eyes. |
| To *initiate* planting the trees, the leader gave volunteers shovels. | | |

Practice using context clues when you read this passage. When you encounter a word you do not know, read the paragraph the word appears in aloud and see if you can identify context clues to help you with the word's meaning. *Guiding Question:* **How could you prove that the ideas stated in the article are true?**

# AFTER THE
# TSUNAMI

**by Greg Stone**

*A team of scientist-divers predicts quick recovery for most reefs pounded by killer waves.*

The word *tsunami* comes from the Japanese for *harbor* and *wave*. Tsunamis are devastating tidal waves that are triggered by underwater movement of the earth or underwater volcanoes. When sudden motion happens underwater, a powerful wave shoots out across the ocean at tremendous speed. When the wave reaches shallow water, the tsunami becomes one of the deadliest forces of nature.

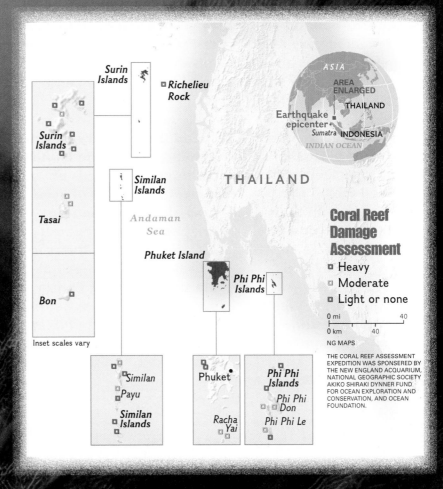

Surin
Islands

□ *Richelieu
Rock*

□ *Surin
Islands*

ASIA

AREA
ENLARGED

THAILAND

Earthquake
epicenter
*Sumatra*   INDONESIA

*INDIAN OCEAN*

□ *Similan
Islands*

THAILAND

*Tasai*

*Andaman
Sea*

### Coral Reef Damage Assessment

□ Heavy

□ Moderate

□ Light or none

*Bon*

*Phuket Island*

□ *Phi Phi
Islands*

0 mi                    40

0 km          40

NG MAPS

Inset scales vary

THE CORAL REEF ASSESSMENT
EXPEDITION WAS SPONSERED BY
THE NEW ENGLAND ACQUARIUM,
NATIONAL GEOGRAPHIC SOCIETY
AKIKO SHIRAKI DYNNER FUND
FOR OCEAN EXPLORATION AND
CONSERVATION, AND OCEAN
FOUNDATION.

□ *Similan*

□ *Payu*

□ *Phuket*

□ *Phi Phi
Islands*

□ *Similan
Islands*

□ *Phi Phi
Don*

□ *Racha
Yai*

*Phi Phi Le*

**W**hen a submarine earthquake sent monster waves surging through the Indian Ocean and Andaman Sea on December 26, 2004, there was no mistaking the toll on land: more than 225,000 people dead; homes, farms, fishing boats destroyed. Three and a half months later I joined seven other biologists and set off on a two-week research cruise along the coast of Thailand to survey a less obvious toll—the damage to the coral reefs. Priceless for their biological diversity, Thailand's reefs are a lifeline for hundreds of thousands of people who catch fish spawned there or work in the dive-tourism industry. In some places the reefs may also have helped blunt the tsunami's force as it hit land.

After more than 500 dives at 56 sites, we found plenty of damage but even more reason for optimism. In the open ocean the tsunami's fast-moving waves were only a few feet high and posed little hazard to deepwater reefs. But in the shallows they slowed, piled up, and unleashed thousands of tons of force. Large bays, which can intensify the waves, were hit especially hard, with table corals big enough for a family dinner scattered and broken, and massive coral heads toppled and smothered in silt. Development on shore often worsened the damage by providing an ample supply of debris, including refrigerators, cars, and roofing, which battered the reefs as it was swept out to sea. And near the earthquake's epicenter off Indonesia—far from our survey—the seafloor was heaved up by an estimated 16 feet, lifting some coral clear out of the water.

Overall, though, our survey of the Andaman

Sea coast and islands of southern Thailand (map) revealed very light damage or none at all at 36 percent of the study sites and moderate damage at another 50 percent. Only 14 percent had severe damage. Except for localized kills, reef fish also seemed to have fared well. "The tsunami shook up their world like mad for a few minutes, but there are still plenty of fish around," concluded fish expert Gerry Allen of the Western Australian Museum.

Much of the damage will heal quickly, re-creating vibrant habitats. Broken and toppled coral can continue to grow. Even dead reefs can recover, providing they haven't been buried, as coral larvae drift in and recolonize them.

We also saw efforts to speed the recovery. In the Similan Islands the tsunami dislodged hundreds of delicate, decades-old sea fans, dooming them to drift around and eventually die. We watched divers in a project led by the Phuket Marine Biological Center swimming in pairs, holding six-foot sea fans between them like chandeliers and reattaching them to rocks using masonry nails and cement.

The project is a rare case of humans affecting reefs for the better. Throughout our survey we saw the opposite—the effects of overfishing, development, and global warming, which can raise water temperatures and cause fatal coral bleaching. "For reefs, in the fullness of time, this tsunami was just another bad day," says Australian coral expert Charlie Veron. But human impacts are unrelenting, and reefs may not be able to shrug them off so easily.

Uplifted more than five feet by the undersea earthquake that spawned the tsunami, dead coral reefs span seventy miles of coast off Simeulue Island near Sumatra, Indonesia.

# Thinking About the Selection
## After the Tsunami

**1** **Define** Use context clues from the selection to help you define the words in the chart. Complete the chart, adding the meanings and explaining how you knew the answers.

| Word | Meaning | How I Know |
|---|---|---|
| submarine (first paragraph) | | |
| debris (second paragraph) | | |
| habitats (fourth paragraph) | | |
| dooming (fifth paragraph) | | |

**2** **Distinguish** In the second paragraph, the writer uses the phrase "far from our survey." How does the meaning of the word *survey* change when it is used in the sentence "I took a survey of favorite names in my class"?

_____

_____

_____

**3** **Interpret** What does the phrase "shrug them off" mean at the end of the selection? How can you tell?

_____

**Write** Answer the following question on a separate piece of paper.

 **4** **Evaluate** How could you prove that the ideas stated in the article are true?

# 1-3 Vocabulary Building Strategies
## *Suffixes*

There are many times when we are reading a selection or book and come across a word we don't know. One of the benefits of reading is learning how to unlock the meaning of a word and expand our vocabulary. There are many tools and strategies to help us. Identifying word parts, such as suffixes, is just one of these strategies.

## Unlocking Word Meanings

Here are some strategies for discovering the meaning of a word.

If you come across a word you don't know, skip it! See if you come across the meaning later.

Sound out each syllable of the word. This can help trigger your memory of it.

Read the word and its surrounding context aloud. Look at the words around the word you don't know. Do they provide any clues as to its meaning?

Think about how the word connects to the topic of your reading.

What part of speech is the word? Knowing whether it's a noun, verb, or adjective can help provide clues to the word's meaning.

Look at the word root, prefix, or suffix of the word if it has any. Make connections to familiar words that have these word parts.

Get handy and use a tool! Use a dictionary, glossary, thesaurus, or online resource to help you identify the word's meaning, part of speech, and pronunciation. Restate the word and its meaning to remember it.

A **suffix** is one or more syllables that follows a word root. Every suffix has a meaning. Once you learn to recognize a suffix, you can use its meaning to help you understand and remember the meanings of words that end with the suffix.

| Suffix | Definition | Fiction Narrative |
|--------|-----------|-------------------|
| *-ize* | to cause to be; to become | idol*ize*: to admire greatly |
| *-tion* | an expression of action or state of being | revolu*tion*: a process of great change, often against an accepted norm |
| *-able* | capable of; fit to be | read*able*: easily read, pleasing to read |

**Directions** Rewrite each word using the suffix *-ize, -tion,* or *-able* on each line to form a word that fits the definition.

**1** material _____ : to become real or to come into existence

**2** manage _____ : easily managed

**3** confuse _____ : state of being confused

**Directions** Look through your work text and find an unfamiliar word that contains a suffix. Fill in the graphic organizer below to help you make the word your own.

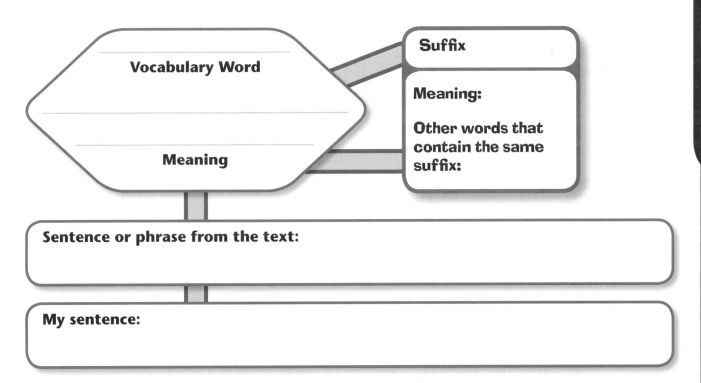

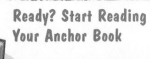

## 1-4  Writing About Your Anchor Book
### Reader's Journal

**while reading your anchor book**

**Introduction** You will keep a Reader's Journal for your Anchor Book. Use your journal for the following purposes.

▶ To develop personal reading goals and keep a record of your accomplishments

▶ To answer questions from lessons in this work text

▶ To record what you think and feel and make connections to yourself, to the text, and to the world

▶ To answer questions you or your teacher have

▶ To write informal notes, questions, and ideas

**How to Set Up Your Reader's Journal**

Organize your Reader's Journal like this student model. Type your journal entries on a computer, or write them neatly using print or cursive in a notebook.

**Student Model: Reader's Journal Response**

| | |
|---|---|
| Bryce Johnson | March 12 |

*A Tree Grows in Brooklyn* by Betty Smith

**Question:** Explain how a flashback reveals information about a character or characters in your Anchor Book.

**Answer:** A flashback describes the lives of Francie's parents, Katie and Johnny Nolan, before Francie was born. The flashback shows they had a hard time making money and that they both worked as janitors to support themselves. We also learn that her parents were in love and willing to go through hard times with each other.

Score the student model response on the previous page and explain your scores in the "Comments" column.

| RUBRIC FOR READER'S JOURNAL RESPONSES | | |
|---|---|---|
| Your response . . . | 1 (Can Do Much Better)<br>2 (Okay)<br>3 (Nice Work)<br>4 (Excellent Job) | Comments |
| shows proof of deep thinking about what you are reading. | | |
| shows evidence that you are applying what you have learned about analyzing literature. | | |
| is long enough to explain your ideas fully. | | |

Sometimes your teacher will ask you to write less formal responses to your Anchor Book. These informal notes and ideas can be the basis of discussions of your Anchor Book. The student model below shows you what your informal responses could look like.

**Student Model: Reader's Journal Response**

Bryce Johnson                                          March 12

*A Tree Grows in Brooklyn* by Betty Smith

Notes and Ideas

Confused about:

-Why does Francie have trouble making friends?

-Why does Uncle Flittman run away?

Seems important:

-The Tree of Heaven – It grows without water, light, or soil. Maybe the tree is a

symbol for Francie since she thrives in harsh surroundings.

# 1-5 Literary Analysis
## *Narrative Texts*

A **narrative** is a story. It can be about anyone or anything, real or imagined—it could be a story about yourself, an alien creature, or a made-up person who is just like you.

Most fiction and nonfiction narrative texts include the same elements.

| Element | Definition | Fiction Narrative |
| --- | --- | --- |
| Character | who the story is about | Elastic Man |
| Setting | time and place where the events take place | New York, 2042 |
| Conflict | a problem which the characters must face and overcome | evil genius threatens the world |
| Plot | series of events that take place as the characters deal with conflict | tells how Elastic Man takes steps to save the world |

## Marking the Text

Have you ever read something, and afterward had no idea what you read? One good strategy to help you remember more information and better understand what it is you are reading is marking the text.

When you mark the text, you write down comments, questions, and ideas after you read and reflect upon a short portion of text. You can make connections between the text and class discussions, or other books, or even your own experiences.

## Guidelines for Marking a Text

Throughout this book, you will be asked to read and mark a variety of texts with different purposes. Mark the text using the following guidelines.

- ▶ **Underline** Underline important details and dialogue.

- ▶ **Use margins** Write comments, questions, and ideas in the margins. Explain why you think details are important.

- ► **Circle** Circle new vocabulary or unfamiliar words. Use context clues to determine the word's meaning, or find its definition in a dictionary.

- ► **Create symbols** Instead of writing complete sentences, use symbols to create your own "code".

| | |
|---|---|
| ? | What does this mean? |
| ! | This must be important! |
| ✔ | I knew that. OR I agree. |
| ✗ | I disagree. |
| | |
| | |
| | |

**Directions** Complete the chart to the right. Create three of your own symbols and their meanings. Then, mark the text below with one of your own symbols.

**Student Model: Marking the Text**

**About the Author**
Visit: PHSchool.com
Web Code: exe-7102

### from *"The Talk"* by Gary Soto

<u>My best friend and I knew that we were going to grow up to be</u> <u>ugly. On a backyard lawn</u>—the summer light falling west of the mulberry tree where the house of the most beautiful girl on the street stood—we talked about what we could do: shake the second-base dirt from our hair, wash our hands of frog smells and canal water, and learn to smile without showing our crooked teeth. We had to stop spitting when girls were looking and learn not to pile food onto a fork and into a fat cheek already churning hot grub.

   <u>We were twelve</u>, with lean bodies that were beginning to grow in weird ways. First, our heads got large, but our necks wavered, frail as crisp tulips. <u>The eyes stayed small as well, receding into pencil</u> <u>dots on each side</u> of an unshapely nose that cast remarkable shadows when we turned sideways. It seemed that Scott's legs sprouted muscle and renegade veins, but his arms, blue with ink markings, stayed short and hung just below his waist. My gangly arms nearly touched my kneecaps. In this way, I was built for picking up grounders and doing cartwheels, my arms swaying just inches from the summery grass.

*character*
*— best friend and*
*narrator*

*setting*
*— summer on a*
*backyard lawn*

*conflict*
*— growing*
*up in*
*weird ways*

*plot*
*— What will*
*happen*
*to the boys?*

**Directions** Now it's your turn. Read the following excerpt. This excerpt is a section from a longer fictional narrative. As you read, mark the text according to the guidelines. Then complete the graphic organizer.

**Go Online**

**About the Author**
Visit: PHSchool.com
Web Code: exe-7103

## from "The Medicine Bag"
### by Virginia Driving Hawk Sneve

My kid sister Cheryl and I always bragged about our Sioux grandpa, Joe Iron Shell. Our friends, who had always lived in the city and only knew about Indians from movies and TV, were impressed by our stories. Maybe we exaggerated and made Grandpa and the reservation sound glamorous, but when we'd return home to Iowa after our yearly summer visit to Grandpa we always had some exciting tale to tell.

We always had some authentic Sioux article to show our listeners. One year Cheryl had new moccasins that Grandpa had made. On another visit he gave me a small, round, flat, rawhide drum which was decorated with a painting of a warrior riding a horse. He taught me a real Sioux chant to sing while I beat the drum with a leather-covered stick that had a feather on the end. Man, that really made an impression.

We never showed our friends Grandpa's picture. Not that we were ashamed of him, but because we knew that the glamorous tales we told didn't go with the real thing. Our friends would have laughed at the picture, because Grandpa wasn't tall and stately like TV Indians. His hair wasn't in braids, but hung in stringy, gray strands on his neck and he was old. He was our great-grandfather, and he didn't live in a tipi, but all by himself in a part log, part tar-paper shack on the Rosebud Reservation in South Dakota. So when Grandpa came to visit us, I was so ashamed and embarrassed I could've died.

I got up and walked to the curb to see what the commotion was. About a block away I saw a crowd of little kids yelling, with the dogs yipping and growling around someone who was walking down the middle of the street.

I watched the group as it slowly came closer and saw that in the center of the strange procession was a man wearing a tall black hat. He'd pause now and then to peer at something in his hand and then at the houses on either side of the street. I felt cold and hot at the same time as I recognized the man. "Oh, no!" I whispered. "It's Grandpa!"

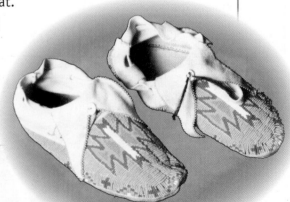

**1** **Interpret** Complete the graphic organizer with what you know about "The Medicine Bag."

| Narrative Element | Question | Details of the Story |
|---|---|---|
| Character(s) | Who was involved? | |
| Setting | Where and when do the events(s) take place? | |
| Conflict | What is the problem or obstacle? | |
| Plot | What happens? | |

**2** **Assess** What cultural differences do the narrator and her grandfather face? How do these differences affect the narrative?

_____

_____

_____

**3** **Take a position** Do you think it is acceptable that the main character in this narrative is "ashamed and embarrassed" by the grandfather? Explain your position.

_____

_____

_____

**4** **Evaluate** Compare your marked text with one marked by a classmate. Notice that there is no one correct way to mark the text. Discuss what questions you had about the selection. How did marking the text help you better understand the selection?

_____

_____

_____

Now look for narrative elements as you read this nonfiction narrative about Monica Sone. *Guiding Question:* **How could the narrator prove what she describes is true?**

# from Nisei Daughter
## by Monica Sone

**Background** *During World War II, the United States was at war with both Germany and Japan. In the United States, people of Japanese descent—most of them American citizens—were forced out of their homes and taken to camps. There, they were shocked to find they would be living under armed guard, behind barbed-wire fences. In this selection, Monica Sone tells of her family's internment in one of the camps.*

## Vocabulary Builder

**Before you read,** *you will discuss the following words. In the Vocabulary Builder box in the margin, use a vocabulary building strategy to make the words your own.*

**palled    glutinous    laconically    harrowing**

**As you read,** *draw a box around unfamiliar words you could add to your vocabulary. Use context clues to unlock their meaning.*

### Marking the Text

**Narrative Texts**

**As you read,** *analyze the text for elements of narrative. Underline words and phrases about the setting, conflict, plot, and characters. Write any questions you have in the margins.*

When our bus turned a corner and we no longer had to smile and wave, we settled back gravely in our seats. Everyone was quiet except for a chattering group of university students who soon started singing college songs. A few people turned and glared at them, which only served to increase the volume of their singing. Then suddenly a baby's sharp cry rose indignantly above the hubbub. The singing stopped immediately, followed by a guilty silence. Three seats behind us, a young mother held a wailing red-faced infant in her arms, bouncing it up and down. Its angry little face emerged from multiple layers of kimonos, sweaters and blankets, and it, too, wore the white pasteboard tag pinned to its blanket. A young man stammered out an apology as the mother gave him a wrathful look. She hunted frantically for a bottle of milk in a shopping bag, and we all relaxed when she had found it.

We sped out of the city southward along beautiful stretches of farmland, with dark, newly turned soil. In the beginning we devoured every bit of scenery which flashed past our window and admired the massive-muscled work horses plodding along the edge of the highway, the rich burnished copper color of a browsing herd of cattle, the vivid spring green of the pastures, but eventually the sameness of the country landscape **palled** on us. We tried to sleep to escape from the restless anxiety which kept bobbing up to the surface of our minds. I awoke with a start when the bus filled with excited buzzing. A small group of straw-hatted Japanese farmers stood by the highway, waving at us. I felt a sudden warmth toward them, then a twinge of pity. They would be joining us soon.

About noon we crept into a small town. Someone said, "Looks like Puyallap, all right." Parents of small children babbled excitedly, "Stand up quickly and look over there. See all the chick-chicks and fat little piggies?" One little boy stared hard at the hogs and said tersely, "They're *bachi*—dirty!"

Our bus idled a moment at the traffic signal and we noticed at the left of us an entire block filled with neat rows of low shacks, resembling chicken houses. Someone commented on it with awe, "Just look at those chicken houses. They sure go in for poultry in a big way here." Slowly the bus made a left turn, drove through a wire-fenced gate, and to our dismay, we were inside the over-sized chicken farm. The bus driver opened the door, the guard stepped out and stationed himself at the door again. Jim, the young man who had shepherded us into the busses, popped his head inside and sang out, "Okay, folks, all off at Yokohama, Puyallup."

### Critical Viewing ▶
How do these photographs help describe the conflict of this narrative?

### Marking the Text

## Vocabulary Builder

**palled**
(pôld) *v.*

**Meaning**

We stumbled out, stunned, dragging our bundles after us. It must have rained hard the night before in Puyallup, for we sank ankle deep into gray, **glutinous** mud. The receptionist, a white man, instructed us courteously, "Now, folks, please stay together as family units and line up. You'll be assigned your apartment."

We were standing in Area A, the mammoth parking lot of the state fairgrounds. There were three other separate areas, B, C, and D, all built on the fair grounds proper near the baseball field and the race tracks. This camp of army barracks was hopefully called Camp Harmony.

We were assigned to apartment 2-1-A, right across from the bachelor quarters. The apartments resembled elongated, low stables about two blocks long. Our home was one room, about 18 by 20 feet, the size of a living room. There was one small window in the wall opposite the one door. It was bare except for a small, tinny wood-burning stove crouching in the center. The flooring consisted of two-by-fours laid directly on the earth, and dandelions were already pushing their way up through the cracks. Mother was delighted when she saw their shaggy yellow heads. "Don't anyone pick them. I'm going to cultivate them."

Father snorted, "Cultivate them! If we don't watch out, those things will be growing out of our hair."

Just then Henry stomped inside, bringing the rest of our baggage. "What's all the excitement about?"

Sumi replied **laconically**, "Dandelions."

Henry tore off a fistful. Mother scolded, "Arra! Arra! Stop that. They're the only beautiful things around here. We could have a garden right in here."

"Are you joking, Mama?"

I chided Henry, "Of course, she's not. After all, she has to have some inspiration to write poems, you know, with all the 'nali keli's[1].' I can think of a poem myself right now:

Oh, Dandelion, Dandelion,
Despised and uprooted by all,
Dance and bob your golden heads
For you've finally found your home
With your yellow fellows, nali keli, amen!"

Henry said, thrusting the dandelions in Mother's black hair, "I think you can do ten times better than that, Mama."

Sumi reclined on her seabag and fretted, "Where do we sleep? Not on the floor, I hope."

"Stop worrying," Henry replied disgustedly.

Mother and Father wandered out to see what the other folks were doing and they found people wandering in the mud, wondering what other folks were doing. Mother returned shortly,

---

[1] **nali keli's** *n.* Japanese expression used to convey wonder and awe.

## Vocabulary Builder

**glutinous**
(glo͞ot'n əs) *adj.*

**Meaning**

**laconically**
(lə-kän'i-klē) *adv.*

**Meaning**

her face lit up in an ecstatic smile, "We're in luck. The latrine is right nearby. We won't have to walk blocks."

We laughed, marveling at Mother who could be so poetic and yet so practical. Father came back, bent double like a woodcutter in a fairy tale, with stacks of scrap lumber over his shoulder. His coat and trouser pockets bulged with nails. Father dumped his loot in a corner and explained, "There was a pile of wood left by the carpenters and hundreds of nails scattered loose. Everybody was picking them up, and I hustled right in with them. Now maybe we can live in style with tables and chairs."

The block leader knocked at our door and announced lunchtime. He instructed us to take our meal at the nearest mess hall. As I untied my seabag to get out my pie plate, tin cup, spoon and fork, I realized I was hungry. At the mess hall we found a long line of people. Children darted in and out of the line, skiing in the slithery mud. The young stood impatiently on one foot, then the other, and scowled, "The food had better be good after all this wait." But the Issei[2] stood quietly, arms folded, saying very little. A light drizzle began to fall, coating bare black heads with tiny sparkling raindrops. The chow line inched forward.

Lunch consisted of two canned sausages, one lob of boiled potato, and a slab of bread. Our family had to split up, for the hall was too crowded for us to sit together. I wandered up and down the aisles, back and forth along the crowded tables and benches, looking for a few inches to squeeze into. A small Issei woman finished her meal, stood up and hoisted her legs modestly over the bench, leaving a space for one. Even as I thrust myself

---

[2] **Issei** *n.* Japanese for "first generation"; first-generation immigrants from Japan.

◄ **Good to Know!**
Henry Sugimoto, a Japanese American artist alive at the time of World War II, was ordered to an internment camp. There, he created numerous works of art that depict the difficult conditions in the camp and the perseverance of those living there. In this painting, entitled *Documentary, Our Mess Hall,* from 1942, Mr. Sugimoto portrays a group of people seated for a meal.

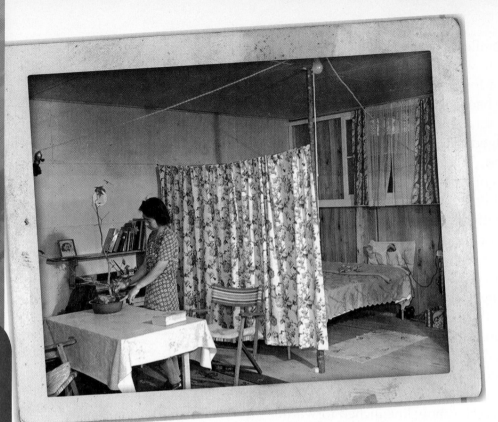

◀ **Critical Viewing**
How does this
photograph match
your idea of the living
conditions the narrator
describes?

into the breach, the space had shrunk to two inches, but I worked myself into it. My dinner companion, hooked just inside my right elbow, was a bald headed, gruff-looking Issei man who seemed to resent nestling at mealtime. Under my left elbow was a tiny, mud-spattered girl. With busy runny nose, she was belaboring her sausages, tearing them into shreds and mixing them into the potato gruel which she had made with water. I choked my food down.

We cheered loudly when trucks rolled by, distributing canvas army cots for the young and hardy, and steel cots for the older folks. Henry directed the arrangement of the cots. Father and Mother were to occupy the corner nearest the wood stove. In the other corner, Henry arranged two cots L shape and announced that this was the combination living room-bedroom area, to be occupied by Sumi and myself. He fixed a male den for himself in the corner nearest the door. If I had had my way, I would have arranged everyone's cots in one neat row as in Father's hotel dormitory.

We felt fortunate to be assigned to a room at the end of the barracks because we had just one neighbor to worry about. The partition wall separating the rooms was only seven feet high with an opening of four feet at the top, so at night, Mrs. Funai next door could tell when Sumi was still sitting up in bed in the dark, putting her hair up. "Mah, Sumi-chan," Mrs. Funai would say through the plank wall, "are you curling your hair tonight again? Do you put it up every night?" Sumi would put her hands on her hips and glare defiantly at the wall.

*Marking the Text*

# Literature in Context

## Why Were There Relocation Camps?

Link to Social Studies

On December 7, 1941, Japan attacked Pearl Harbor in Hawaii. People in the United States were stunned. Many people started to doubt the loyalty of all Japanese people. In February, 1942, President Franklin D. Roosevelt ordered the military to exclude people from certain areas of the country in the interest of national defense. By the end of the year, 120,000 people of Japanese ancestry had been removed from their West Coast homes and sent to one of ten relocation camps.

### Imprisoned under Armed Guard

Two-thirds of the people in the camps were citizens of the United States. Many of them had family members fighting for the United States against Japan during World War II. In fact, 25,000 Japanese Americans fought on the side of the United States. Still, their relatives were imprisoned in relocation camps where they were kept under armed guard for as long as four years. The people in the camps lived in military-style barracks. The barracks were too hot in the summer and too cold in the winter. They had little privacy.

### Life in the Camps

Still, the people in the camps struggled to live as normal a life as possible. They worked at farming or other jobs for low pay. They had Boy Scout troops and Parent-Teacher Associations. They held religious observances and put on plays and athletic competitions. And most of them remained loyal to the United States throughout their ordeal.

The block monitor, an impressive Nisei[3] who looked like a star tackle with his crouching walk, came around the first night to tell us that we must all be inside our room by nine o'clock every night. At ten o'clock, he rapped at the door again, yelling, "Lights out!" and Mother rushed to turn the light off not a second later.

Throughout the barracks, there were a medley of creaking cots, whimpering infants and explosive night coughs. Our attention was riveted on the intense little wood stove which glowed so violently I feared it would melt right down to the floor. We soon learned that this condition lasted for only a short time, after which it suddenly turned into a deep freeze. Henry and Father took turns at the stove to produce the **harrowing** blast which

### Vocabulary Builder

**harrowing**
(har'ō i[ng]) *adj.*

**Meaning**

---

[3] **Nisei** *n.* Japanese for "second generation"; the American-born children of people who emigrated from Japan.

all but singed our army blankets, but did not penetrate through them. As it grew quieter in the barracks, I could hear the light patter of rain. Soon I felt the "splat! splat!" of raindrops digging holes into my face. The dampness on my pillow spread like a mortal bleeding, and I finally had to get out and haul my cot toward the center of the room. In a short while Henry was up. "I've got multiple leaks, too. Have to complain to the landlord first thing in the morning."

All through the night I heard people getting up, dragging cots around. I stared at our little window, unable to sleep. I was glad Mother had put up a makeshift curtain on the window for I noticed a powerful beam of light sweeping across it every few seconds. The lights came from high towers placed around the camp where guards with Tommy guns kept a twenty-four hour vigil. I remembered the wire fence encircling us, and a knot of anger tightened in my breast. What was I doing behind a fence like a criminal? If there were accusations to be made, why hadn't I been given a fair trial? Maybe I wasn't considered an American anymore. My citizenship wasn't real, after all. Then what was I? I was certainly not a citizen of Japan as my parents were. On second thought, even Father and Mother were more alien residents of the United States than Japanese nationals for they had little tie with their mother country. In their twenty-five years in America, they had worked and paid their taxes to their adopted government as any other citizen.

Of one thing I was sure. The wire fence was real. I no longer had the right to walk out of it. It was because I had Japanese ancestors. It was also because some people had little faith in the ideas and ideals of democracy. They said that after all these were but words and could not possibly insure loyalty. New laws and camps were surer devices. I finally buried my face in my pillow to wipe out burning thoughts and snatch what sleep I could.

## Vocabulary Builder

**After you read,** *review the words you decided to add to your vocabulary. Write the meaning of words you have learned in context. Look up the other words in a dictionary, glossary, thesaurus, or electronic resource.*

# Thinking About the Selection

## Nisei Daughter

Go Online

**About the Author**
Visit: PHSchool.com
Web Code: exe-7104

**1**   **Apply** Complete the graphic organizer below for this selection.

| Narrative Element | Question | Details of the Story |
|---|---|---|
| Character(s) | Who was involved? | |
| Setting | Where and when do the event(s) take place? | |
| Conflict | What is the problem or obstacle? | |
| Plot | What happens? | |

**2**   **Describe** How do the narrative elements of the selection contribute to its meaning?

_____

_____

_____

**3**   **Infer** Does the main character of the story consider herself Japanese or American? Use clues from the text to support your answer.

_____

_____

**Write** Answer the following questions in your Reader's Journal.

**4**   **Analyze** Monica Sone describes experiences that happened to her as a girl many years before. How can she prove the truth of what she describes?

**5**   **Apply** Copy the graphic organizer above in your Reader's Journal. Fill it in with information about your Anchor Book.

# 1-6 Literary Analysis
## Conflict

Has anyone ever asked you, "What's your problem?" Well, in fiction, it is the main character's problem, or conflict, that sets the story in motion.

## Literary Terms

**Conflict** is a struggle between opposing forces. A character who wants something is struggling against someone or something that is getting in the way. The action of the story shows how the conflict is worked out, or **resolved**.

There are two main types of conflict. An **external conflict** is a struggle between two characters or between a character and an outside force, such as nature, society, or fate. An **internal conflict** is a struggle within the mind of a character. For example, a character might be torn between conflicting feelings, desires, or beliefs.

**Directions** Read the following examples of different types of conflict. Then write your own example of each type of conflict.

while reading your anchor book

| EXTERNAL CONFLICT | |
|---|---|
| character struggles against another character | **Example** Joe wants to be class president, but so does Kim. <br> **My example** |
| character struggles against nature | **Example** A hurricane destroys a family's home. <br> **My example** |
| character struggles against society | **Example** Sarah wants to get a job, but the law says she's too young. <br> **My example** |
| INTERNAL CONFLICT | |
| character struggles against something inside his or her own mind | **Example** Derek wants to go to college, but he's afraid of failing. <br> **My example** |

**Directions** Read the following fable. Underline details that reveal the conflict, and then answer the questions.

**Go Online**

**About the Author**
Visit: PHSchool.com
Web Code: exe-7105

## The Father and His Sons *by Aesop*

**Background** *A fable is a short narrative that illustrates a useful truth or concept.*

A certain father had a family of sons, who were forever quarreling among themselves. No words he could say did the least good, so he cast about in his mind for some very striking example that should make them see that discord would lead them to misfortune. One day, when the quarreling had been much more violent than usual and each of the sons was moping in a surly manner, he asked one of them to bring him a bundle of sticks. Then handing the bundle to each of his sons in turn he told them to try to break it. But although each one tried his best, none was able to do so. The father then untied the bundle and gave the sticks to his sons to break one by one. This they did very easily. "My sons," said the father, "do you not see how certain it is that if you agree with each other and help each other, it will be impossible for your enemies to injure you? But if you are divided among yourselves, you will be no stronger than a single stick in that bundle."

In unity is strength.

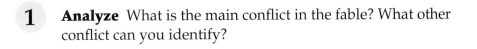

1  **Analyze** What is the main conflict in the fable? What other conflict can you identify?

_____

_____

_____

2  **Classify** Is the main conflict external or internal? Explain your answer.

_____

_____

_____

In the following short story, a conflict emerges between an artist and other people in the neighborhood.

*Guiding Question:* **What truth do the narrator and the other people in the neighborhood discover about the artist?**

# The War of the Wall

## by Toni Cade Bambara

**Background** *"The War of the Wall" presents an age-old story: A stranger comes to town and stirs things up. In this case, a mysterious woman arrives in a Southern community where everyone knows everybody else. The narrator and the other kids in the neighborhood see her presence as a threat to their community until they finally discover the truth about why she is there.*

## Marking the Text

### Conflict

**As you read,** *underline details that identify and explain the conflict. In the margin, write notes explaining what these details tell you about the story.*

### Vocabulary Builder

**Before you read,** *you will discuss the following words. In the Vocabulary Builder box in the margin, use a vocabulary building strategy to make the words your own.*

**integration    concentration    beckoned    liberation**

**As you read,** *draw a box around unfamiliar words you could add to your vocabulary. Use context clues to unlock their meaning.*

Me and Lou had no time for courtesies[1]. We were late for school. So we just flat out told the painter lady to quit messing with the wall. It was our wall, and she had no right coming into our neighborhood painting on it. Stirring in the paint bucket and not even looking at us, she mumbled something about Mr. Eubanks, the barber, giving her permission. That had nothing to do with it as far as we were concerned. We've been pitching pennies against that wall since we

---

[1] **courtesies** (kʉrt'ə sēs) *n.* politeness, such as kind words or gestures.

were little kids. Old folks have been dragging their chairs out to sit in the shade of the wall for years. Big kids have been playing handball against the wall since so-called **integration** when the crazies 'cross town poured cement in our pool so we couldn't use it. I'd sprained my neck one time boosting my cousin Lou up to chisel Jimmy Lyons's name into the wall when we found out he was never coming home from the war in Vietnam to take us fishing.

"If you lean close," Lou said, leaning hipshot against her beat-up car, "you'll get a whiff of bubble gum and kids' sweat. And that'll tell you something—that this wall belongs to the kids of Taliaferro Street." I thought Lou sounded very convincing. But the painter lady paid us no mind. She just snapped the brim of her straw hat down and hauled her bucket up the ladder.

"You're not even from around here," I hollered up after her. The license plates on her old piece of car said "New York." Lou dragged me away because I was about to grab hold of that ladder and shake it. And then we'd really be late for school.

When we came from school, the wall was slick with white. The painter lady was running string across the wall and taping it here and there. Me and Lou leaned against the gumball machine outside the pool hall and watched. She had strings up and down and back and forth. Then she began chalking them with a hunk of blue chalk.

The Morris twins crossed the street, hanging back at the curb next to the beat-up car. The twin with the red ribbons was hugging a jug of cloudy lemonade. The one with yellow ribbons was holding a plate of dinner away from her dress. The painter lady began snapping the strings. The blue chalk dust measured off halves and quarters up and down and sideways too. Lou was about to say how hip it all was, but I dropped my book satchel on his toes to remind him we were at war.

Some good aromas were drifting our way from the plate leaking pot likker[2] onto the Morris girl's white socks. I could tell from where I stood that under the tinfoil was baked ham, collard greens, and candied yams. And knowing Mrs. Morris, who sometimes bakes for my mama's restaurant, a slab of buttered cornbread was probably up under there too, sopping up some of the pot likker. Me and Lou rolled our eyes, wishing somebody would send us some dinner. But the painter lady didn't even turn around. She was pulling the strings down and prying bits of tape loose.

Side Pocket came strolling out of the pool hall to see what Lou and me were studying so hard. He gave the painter lady the once-over, checking out her paint-spattered jeans, her chalky T-shirt, her floppy-brimmed straw hat. He hitched up his pants and glided over toward the painter lady, who kept right on with what she was doing.

---

[2] **pot likker** (pät' lik' ər) *n.* the juice from boiled collard greens and ham.

"Whatcha got there, sweetheart?" he asked the twin with the plate.

"Suppah," she said all soft and countrylike.

"For her," the one with the jug added, jerking her chin toward the painter lady's back.

Still she didn't turn around. She was rearing back on her heels, her hands jammed into her back pockets, her face squinched[3] up like the masterpiece she had in mind was taking shape on the wall by magic. We could have been gophers crawled up into a rotten hollow for all she cared. She didn't even say hello to anybody. Lou was muttering something about how great her **concentration** was. I butt him with my hip, and his elbow slid off the gum machine.

"Good evening," Side Pocket said in his best ain't-I-fine voice. But the painter lady was moving from the milk crate to the step stool to the ladder, moving up and down fast, scribbling all over the wall like a crazy person. We looked at Side Pocket. He looked at the twins. The twins looked at us. The painter lady was giving a show. It was like those old-timey music movies where the dancer taps on the tabletop and then starts jumping all over the furniture, kicking chairs over and not skipping a beat. She didn't even look where she was stepping. And for a minute there, hanging on the ladder to reach a far spot, she looked like she was going to tip right over.

"Ahh," Side Pocket cleared his throat and moved fast to catch the ladder. "These young ladies here have brought you some supper."

"Ma'am?" The twins stepped forward. Finally the painter turned around, her eyes "full of sky," as my grandmama would say. Then she stepped down like she was in a trance. She wiped her hands on her jeans as the Morris twins offered up the plate and the jug. She rolled back the tinfoil, then wagged her head as though something terrible was on the plate.

"Thank your mother very much," she said, sounding like her mouth was full of sky too. "I've brought my own dinner along." And then, without even excusing herself, she went back up the ladder, drawing on the wall in a wild way. Side Pocket whistled one of those oh-brother breathy whistles and went back into the pool hall. The Morris twins shifted their weight from one foot to the other, then crossed the street and went home. Lou had to drag me away, I was so mad. We couldn't wait to get to the firehouse to tell my daddy all about this rude woman who'd stolen our wall.

All the way back to the block to help my mama out at the restaurant, me and Lou kept asking my daddy for ways to run the painter lady out of town. But my daddy was busy talking about the trip to the country and telling Lou he could come too because Grandmama can always use an extra pair of hands on the farm.

Later that night, while me and Lou were in the back doing our chores, we found out that the painter lady was a liar. She came

## Vocabulary Builder

**concentration**
(kän′sən trā′ shən) *n.*

**Meaning**

---

[3] **squinched** (skwinchd) *adj.* squeezed.

into the restaurant and leaned against the glass of the steam table, talking about how starved she was. I was scrubbing pots and Lou was chopping onions, but we could hear her through the service window. She was asking Mama was that a ham hock in the greens, and was that a neck bone in the pole beans, and were there any vegetables cooked without meat, especially pork.

"I don't care who your spiritual leader is," Mama said in that way of hers. "If you eat in the community, sistuh, you gonna eat pig by-and-by, one way or t'other."

Me and Lou were cracking up in the kitchen, and several customers at the counter were clearing their throats, waiting for Mama to really fix her wagon[4] for not speaking to the elders when she came in. The painter lady took a stool at the counter and went right on with her questions. Was there cheese in the baked macaroni, she wanted to know? Were there eggs in the salad? Was it honey or sugar in the iced tea? Mama was fixing Pop Johnson's plate. And every time the painter lady asked a fool question, Mama would dump another spoonful of rice on the pile. She was tapping her foot and heating up in a dangerous way. But Pop Johnson was happy as he could be. Me and Lou peeked through the service window, wondering what planet the painter lady came from. Who ever heard of baked macaroni without cheese, or potato salad without eggs?

"Do you have any bread made with unbleached flour?[5]" the painter lady asked Mama. There was a long pause, as though everybody in

▲ **Critical Viewing**
What does the picture reveal about the story's conflict?

◀ **Good to Know!**
**Dialect** is the language spoken by people in a particular location or group. **Colloquialisms** are local or regional expressions.

*Marking the Text*

---

[4] **fix her wagon** to scold or get even with her.

[5] **unbleached flour** flour that has not been processed to make it whiter.

## Literature in Context
## The Vietnam War

Link to Social Studies

The conflict known in the United States as the Vietnam War (and in Vietnam as the American War) lasted from 1954 through 1975 and cost the lives of more than 58,000 Americans and millions of Vietnamese. What began as a civil war developed into an international conflict with the United States supporting South Vietnam, while the Soviet Union and China sided with North Vietnam. In the late 1960s, a growing antiwar movement demanded an end to U.S. involvement. In 1973, the United States withdrew from Vietnam, and in 1975, North Vietnam defeated South Vietnam. By 1995, diplomatic relations between the United States and Vietnam had resumed.

▲ U.S. combat troops arrived in Vietnam in 1961 and reached more than 500,000 in 1969.

*while reading your anchor book*

the restaurant was holding their breath, wondering if Mama would dump the next spoonful on the painter lady's head. She didn't. But when she set Pop Johnson's plate down, it came down with a bang.

When Mama finally took her order, the starving lady all of a sudden couldn't make up her mind whether she wanted a vegetable plate or fish and a salad. She finally settled on the broiled trout and a tossed salad. But just when Mama reached for a plate to serve her, the painter lady leaned over the counter with her finger all up in the air.

"Excuse me," she said. "One more thing." Mama was holding the plate like a Frisbee, tapping that foot, one hand on her hip. "Can I get raw beets in that tossed salad?"

"You will get," Mama said, leaning her face close to the painter lady's, "whatever Lou back there tossed. Now sit down." And the painter lady sat back down on her stool and shut right up.

All the way to the country, me and Lou tried to get Mama to open fire on the painter lady. But Mama said that seeing as how she was from the North, you couldn't expect her to have any manners. Then Mama said she was sorry she'd been so impatient with the woman because she seemed like a decent person and was simply trying to stick to a very strict diet. Me and Lou didn't want to hear that. Who did that lady think she was, coming into our neighborhood and taking over our wall?

"Wellllll," Mama drawled, pulling into the filling station so Daddy could take the wheel, "it's hard on an artist, ya know. They can't always get people to look at their work. So she's just doing her work in the open, that's all."

**Marking the Text**

Me and Lou definitely did not want to hear that. Why couldn't she set up an easel downtown or draw on the sidewalk in her own neighborhood? Mama told us to quit fussing so much; she was tired and wanted to rest. She climbed into the back seat and dropped down into the warm hollow Daddy had made in the pillow.

All weekend long, me and Lou tried to scheme up ways to recapture our wall. Daddy and Mama said they were sick of hearing about it. Grandmama turned up the TV to drown us out. On the late news was a story about the New York subways. When a train came roaring into the station all covered from top to bottom, windows too, with writings and drawings done with spray paint, me and Lou slapped five. Mama said it was too bad kids in New York had nothing better to do than spray paint all over the trains. Daddy said that in the cities, even grown-ups wrote all over the trains and buildings too. Daddy called it "graffiti." Grandmama called it a shame.

We couldn't wait to get out of school on Monday. We couldn't find any black spray paint anywhere. But in a junky hardware store downtown we found a can of white epoxy[6] paint, the kind you touch up old refrigerators with when they get splotchy and peely. We spent our whole allowance on it. And because it was too late to use our bus passes, we had to walk all the way home lugging our book satchels and gym shoes, and the bag with the epoxy.

When we reached the corner of Taliaferro and Fifth, it looked like a block party or something. Half the neighborhood was gathered on the sidewalk in front of the wall. I looked at Lou, he looked at me. We both looked at the bag with the epoxy and

---

[6] **epoxy** (ē päk'sē) *n.* a type of thick paint.

wondered how we were going to work our scheme. The painter
lady's car was nowhere in sight. But there were too many people
standing around to do anything. Side Pocket and his buddies
were leaning on their cue sticks, hunching each other. Daddy was
there with a lineman[7] he catches a ride with on Mondays. Mrs.
Morris had her arms flung around the shoulders of the twins on
either side of her. Mama was talking with some of her customers,
many of them with napkins still at the throat. Mr. Eubanks came
out of the barbershop, followed by a man in a striped poncho,
half his face shaved, the other half full of foam.

"She really did it, didn't she?" Mr. Eubanks huffed out his
chest. Lots of folks answered right quick that she surely did when
they saw the straight razor in his hand.

Mama **beckoned** us over. And then we saw it. The wall. Reds,
greens, figures outlined in black. Swirls of purple and orange.
Storms of blues and yellows. It was something. I recognized some
of the faces right off. There was Martin Luther King, Jr. and there
was a man with glasses on and his mouth open like he was laying
down a heavy rap. Daddy came up alongside and reminded us
that that was Minister Malcolm X[8]. The serious woman with a rifle
I knew was Harriet Tubman[9] because my grandmama has pictures

---

**Marking the Text**

---

**Vocabulary Builder**

**beckon**
(bek'ən) v.

**Meaning**

---

[7] **lineman** (līn'mən) n. a worker who installs or repairs telephone or power lines or railroad tracks.

[8] **Minister Malcolm X** (1925–1965) African American political activist and religious leader.

[9] **Harriet Tubman** (1819–1913) former slave who helped other slaves to escape
    to Canada on the Underground Railway (see page 214).

To The People of Taliaferro Street
I Dedicate This Wall of Respect
Painted in Memory of My Cousin
Jimmy Lyons

of her all over the house. And I knew Mrs. Fannie Lou Hamer[10] 'cause a signed photograph of her hangs in the restaurant next to the calendar.

Then I let my eyes follow what looked like a vine. It trailed past a man with a horn, a woman with a big white flower in her hair, a handsome dude in a tuxedo seated at a piano, and a man with a goatee[11] holding a book. When I looked more closely, I realized that what had looked like flowers were really faces. One face with yellow petals looked just like Frieda Morris. One with red petals looked just like Hattie Morris. I could hardly believe my eyes.

"Notice," Side Pocket said, stepping close to the wall with his cue stick like a classroom pointer. "These are the flags of **liberation**," he said in a voice I'd never heard him use before. We all stepped closer while he pointed and spoke. "Red, black, and green," he said, his pointer falling on the leaflike flags of the vine. "Our liberation flag. And here Ghana, there Tanzania. Guinea-Bissau, Angola, Mozambique[12]." Side Pocket sounded very tall, as though he'd been waiting all his life to give this lesson.

Mama tapped us on the shoulder and pointed to a high section of the wall. There was a fierce-looking man with his arms crossed against his chest guarding a bunch of children. His muscles bulged, and he looked a lot like my daddy. One kid was looking

▲ **Critical Viewing**
Why does the artist include people from the community in the mural?

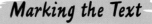

Marking the Text

**Vocabulary Builder**

**liberation**
(lib'ərā'shən) n.

**Meaning**

---

[10] **Mrs. Fannie Lou Hamer** (1918–1977) politician and civil rights activist.

[11] **goatee** (gō tē') n. a beard covering just the chin.

[12] **Ghana . . . Mozambique** various African nations.

at a row of books. Lou hunched[13] me 'cause the kid looked like me. The one that looked like Lou was spinning a globe on the tip of his finger like a basketball. There were other kids there with microscopes and compasses. And the more I looked, the more it looked like the fierce man was not so much guarding the kids as defending their right to do what they were doing.

Then Lou gasped and dropped the paint bag and ran forward, running his hands over a rainbow. He had to tiptoe and stretch to do it, it was so high. I couldn't breathe either. The painter lady had found the chisel marks and had painted Jimmy Lyons's name in a rainbow.

"Read the inscription, honey," Mrs. Morris said, urging little Frieda forward. She didn't have to urge much. Frieda marched right up, bent down, and in a loud voice that made everybody quit oohing and ahhing and listen, she read,

> *To the People of Taliaferro Street*
> *I Dedicate This Wall of Respect*
> *Painted in Memory of My Cousin*
> *Jimmy Lyons*

---

[13] **hunched** *v.* pushed; shoved.

## Vocabulary Builder

**After you read,** *review the words you decided to add to your vocabulary. Write the meaning of words you have learned in context. Look up the other words in a dictionary, glossary, thesaurus, or electronic resource.*

# Toni Cade Bambara (1939-1995)

Although she grew up in New York City, Toni Cade Bambara often wrote about African Americans living in the South, as in "The War of the Wall." Born with the last name "Cade," she adopted the name "Bambara" to honor her great-grandmother after finding the name on a sketchbook in her attic. Bambara's fiction frequently reflects her political activism and interest in social justice for African Americans and women. Bambara is best known for her compelling portraits of everyday African American life in her short story collections *Gorilla, My Love* (1972) and *The Sea Birds Are Still Alive* (1977), and in her novels *The Salt Eaters* (1980) and *If Blessing Comes* (1987).

*while reading your anchor book*

## Thinking About the Selection

### The War of the Wall

Go Online

About the Author
Visit: PHSchool.com
Web Code: exe-7106

**1** **Analyze** What is the main conflict in the story? Is this conflict internal or external? Explain.

_____

_____

_____

**2** **Analyze** What assumptions do the narrator and the other children make about the artist?

_____

_____

_____

_____

**3** **Speculate** Why do you think the artist chooses not to reveal her purpose until the mural is finished?

_____

_____

_____

**4** **Analyze** How does the author's biography help you understand the meaning of the story?

_____

_____

**Write** Answer the following questions in your Reader's Journal.

**5** **Interpret** What truth do the narrator and the other people in the neighborhood discover about the artist? How does their discovery resolve the story's conflict?

**6** **Describe** What is the conflict in your Anchor Book? How does this conflict affect certain characters?

while reading your anchor book

Conflict **41**

# 1-7 Analyzing an Informational Text
## Step-by-Step Instructions

Following step-by-step instructions can help you learn new skills. Being able to follow them correctly could even save a life.

Read the following step-by-step instructions about providing first aid for a choking victim. Analyze the way the information is presented. Ask yourself if the information is presented in the best way.

---

# First Aid for the Choking Victim

## Abdominal Thrusts

If a choking victim can speak or cough, encourage the victim to keep coughing, in an effort to cough up the object. If the person cannot cough up the object, call 911. Then follow these steps about using abdominal thrusts. For the following procedures, you should assume that the victim has no spinal injuries and is sitting or standing.

## What to Look For in the Victim

**1** Cannot speak or breathe   **2** Skin turns blue   **3** Collapses

## With the Victim Standing or Sitting

1 Stand behind the victim or behind the victim's chair if he or she is sitting. Wrap your arms around the victim's waist. **(Fig. A)**

2 Place the thumb side of your fist against the victim's abdomen, above the navel and below the rib cage. Do not allow your forearms to touch the victim's ribcage. **(Fig. B)**

3 Grab your fist with the other hand, and give 5 quick inward and upward thrusts into the abdomen. Repeat this cycle of 5 abdominal thrusts until the victim (a) coughs up the object, (b) begins to breathe or cough forcefully, or (c) becomes unconscious.

4 If the victim is sitting, stand behind the victim's chair and perform the procedure the same way.

5 After the object is dislodged, the victim should see a doctor for follow-up care.

**NOTE:** If you are alone and start to choke, press your abdomen onto a firm object, such as a counter, desk, or table.

**Universal Sign of Choking**

This is a universally recognizable sign that someone is choking.

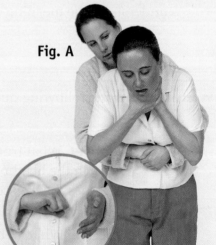

Fig. A

Fig. B

Always check for notes that may provide alternative instructions for different situations.

while reading your anchor book

## Thinking About the Selection

# First Aid for the Choking Victim

**1** **Explain** Why do you think the universal sign for choking has been illustrated?

**2** **Analyze** Why is the order of the steps important when you help a choking victim?

**3** **Evaluate** How do the pictures support the meaning of the text?

**4** **Evaluate** What other information might be useful to provide?

**Workplace Documents** You might see a poster like this informational text in your place of work. There are other kinds of informational applications associated with the workplace, such as the following contract.

> The Contract is considered legal and binding in all countries. If there should be any legal dispute, the laws of the state of Indiana shall apply.
>
> I. The Employee hereby agrees with the Company that:
>
>     A. The Employee will agree to work 80 hours/week.
>
>     B. The Company will not prohibit the Employee from working without pay.
>
> This representations contained herein are true on the date of the signing of this contract.
>
> Employee's Signature: _____ Date: _____

**5** **Evaluate** Based on what you read in the contract, would you agree to take the job it describes? Explain why or why not.

**Partner Activity** How good are you at giving and following instructions? Find an image from a magazine. Do not show it to your partner. Sit with your back to your partner. Your partner should have a pen or pencil and a blank sheet of paper.

Instruct your partner on how to draw the image without using words that will let the partner guess what the object is. When you have finished, see how your partner did at following instructions and how well you did at giving them. Then, switch roles and repeat the activity.

## Show, Don't Tell

As a writer, you need to provide details that support what you want your readers to believe. Telling your readers that someone is a wonderful person, a talented musician, or a fool is not enough. You must **show** them.

**Learn More**
Visit: PHSchool.com
Web Code: exp-7101

**TELLING**    Marissa felt terrible about lying to her mother.

**SHOWING**    "Oh, no!" Marissa put her head in her hands, tears stinging her eyes. "How could I have lied to my mom?"

In the "showing" example, the writer uses specific details to create an image in the reader's head. The following chart shows important elements in revealing the personality of your character.

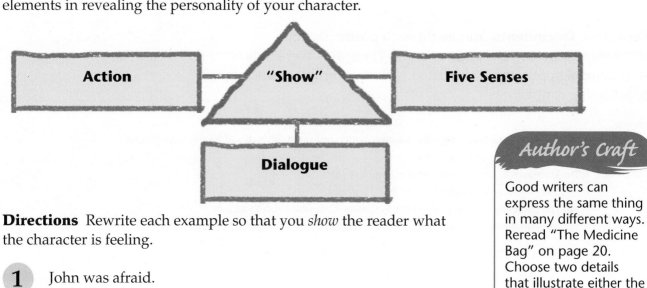

**Directions** Rewrite each example so that you *show* the reader what the character is feeling.

**1** John was afraid.

_____

_____

_____

**2** Chiara was excited.

_____

_____

**3** Emilio was confused.

_____

_____

_____

### Author's Craft

Good writers can express the same thing in many different ways. Reread "The Medicine Bag" on page 20. Choose two details that illustrate either the technique of action, of the five senses, or of dialogue. Add your own details to the story, using one of the techniques.

# Transitions

**Transitions** are words and phrases that help explain the relationships between ideas. Think of transitions as road signs or directions to help the driver (your reader) know where to go.

Transitions also help you, the writer, organize your ideas. When writing a draft, do not worry about overusing transitions. Be overly specific at first — you can always cut them later.

**Directions** Some kinds of transitions and examples are shown below. In the lines provided, write a story. Each sentence must use a transition from one of the categories at the left.

**Go Online**

**Learn More**
Visit: PHSchool.com
Web Code: exp-7102

**Author's Craft**

Transitions show how writers think. If an author is focused on the order of events, time transitions are best. If an author is focused on how some events cause others, cause-and-effect transitions are best. Turn to "The War of the Wall" that begins on page 32. Which types of transition would you add to show how the author thinks?

**Time**

> as soon as
> after
> meanwhile

**Addition**

> then
> furthermore

**Example**

> for instance
> in particular

**Comparison**

> likewise
> similarly

**Contrast**

> on the contrary
> on the other hand

**Cause**

> because
> for that reason

**Effect**

> consequently
> therefore

In this workshop, you will write a descriptive essay that allows your reader to "experience" the people, places, and things that you describe.

Your descriptive essay should feature these elements.

▶ Vivid sensory details (sight, taste, touch, sound, and smell)

▶ Sentences that show characters' thoughts and emotions

▶ Error-free writing

▶ Consideration of your intended audience

**Purpose** To write a descriptive essay that creates a picture in your reader's mind

**Audience** You, your teacher, and your classmates

Read through the rubric at the end of the lesson to preview the criteria for your descriptive essay. You may wish to add your own criteria, such as an aspect of descriptive writing you wish to focus on.

## Prewriting—Plan It Out

To select what you want to describe, use the following steps. One good way to help you plan and organize your writing is to keep a writer's notebook.

**Choose your topic.** Compile a list of special events, places, or times that are important to you. Think of topics that you remember clearly.

**Narrow it down.** Narrow your list to two or three topics, then select the one you can describe most vividly or compare to another topic. Which selection do you feel the most comfortable writing about in great detail?

**Collect details.** Fill in the chart with details (vivid verbs, descriptive adjectives, specific nouns) that you remember. Choose details that help create a specific mood and tone.

| SIGHT | SOUND | SMELL | TOUCH | TASTE |
|---|---|---|---|---|
| bright flowers | lawn mower engine | smell of cut grass | sun beating down on face | sweet lemonade |

| SIGHT | SOUND | SMELL | TOUCH | TASTE |
|---|---|---|---|---|
| | | | | |

# Drafting–Get It on Paper

Now that you have important details, it's time to arrange them in an order that gives a logical flow and rhythm to your writing. Use one of the following methods of organization.

| | |
|---|---|
| **Spatial Order** | When describing an object or place, present your details in the order in which they relate to one another physically. Use transitions such as *through, next to,* and *in front of*. |
| **Chronological Order** | When describing an event, present your details in the order they occur. |
| **Order of Importance** | When your details show the importance of your subject, begin with your least important details and build up to the most significant ones. |

**Provide elaboration.** Focus on providing vivid details such as descriptions of, or comparisons to, your subject's movements, gestures, and expressions.

## Revising—Make It Better

You've written the first draft of your descriptive essay, using vivid details and appropriate organization. Now make sure that it's ready to be shared.

**Revise depth of description.** Make certain your descriptions are vivid and effective. Use a thesaurus to find varied, creative language.

| Dull | Vivid |
|---|---|
| I had to cut the grass. | My chore on this hot and humid Saturday was to mow the front and back lawns and rake up every single blade of cut grass. |
| Spring vacation was fun. | I spent every day of spring vacation hiking through the woods behind my cousin's house. |

Now, try creating a vivid sentence of your own.

| Dull | Vivid |
|---|---|
| I played a game. | |

***Peer Review*** Ask a partner to read and respond to your descriptive essay. Based on your partner's response, revise to achieve the reaction you had intended.

**Directions** Read this student descriptive essay as a model for your own.

**Student Model: Writing**

**Go Online**

**Student Model**
Visit: PHSchool.com
Web Code: exr-7101

*Charity Jackson, Fort Wayne, IN*

## Spring Into Spring

Spring is the perfect time to get outdoors and get active. The spring season brings the freshness of a new beginning. If you've been cooped up all winter, the perfect start to spring is a brisk walk. If you walk during the day, you will feel the sunshine warming up the pavement; a breeze may ruffle your hair; you'll hear the songs of birds that you'd almost forgotten about over the winter. If you walk in the early evening, in the purple-gray dusk, you may even hear the "spring peepers," little frogs that become suddenly vocal around April. You might mistake them for crickets, because they have that same high-pitched monotonous chirping sound, but peepers are more shrill and persistent. Any one of these sensations by itself is enough to raise a little hope that winter is over. If you're lucky enough to experience them all at once on your first spring walk, you'll feel uplifted and energized by the knowledge that soon that stuffy old winter coat can be put in storage for many months. During the rest of the season, if you continue to walk, you will experience new additions to the spring line-up. Not long after you've heard the peepers, you'll start to smell the earth. The scent of warm earth says "spring" the way the scent of pine says "winter." Because the ground is warming up, the smell of flowers can't be far behind! The first flowers of spring, though, are more a treat for the eyes than the nose. The brilliant yellow forsythia don't have much of an aroma, but they're so bright, they don't really need one to announce their arrival! The shy hyacinth, which blooms shortly after, is not as easily spotted, but your nose will tell you that the strong perfume in the air means a hyacinth is hiding somewhere nearby. Neighbors working their gardens—some of whom you may not have seen all winter—will call a friendly hello. Everyone seems friendlier at the beginning of spring.

Sensory details about sunshine, breezes, and bird songs appeal to the senses of sight, touch, and hearing.

The writer reinforces the overall impression of lightness and energy to contrast with the stuffy winter coat.

The description is organized in chronological order—new details are introduced in the order in which they appear as spring progresses.

The writer includes feelings and reactions to show the importance of what is described.

# Editing—Be Your Own Language Coach

Review your essay for language convention errors. Be careful if you are typing on a computer: *Always* double-check your work. Use a grammar reference, style book, or online source to edit your work. Ask a teacher to check your work, and paraphrase your teacher's suggestions to make sure you understand any corrections that need to be made.

# Publishing—Share It!

Consider one of the following ideas to share your writing.

**Create an album.** Find photographs that reflect the images you've described in your essay, and put them in an album with your work.

**Show the world.** Post your work on your school Web site, in another online publication, or on a message board.

**Keep a portfolio.** Save all your finished writing in a folder. In your portfolio, record suggestions from your conversations with peers and your teacher on how to improve your writing through organization, sentence structure, and diction.

# Reflecting on Your Writing

**Rubric for Self-Assessment** Assess your essay.

| CRITERIA | RATING SCALE | | | | |
|---|---|---|---|---|---|
| | NOT VERY | | | | VERY |
| IDEAS Is your essay clear and focused with rich details? | 1 | 2 | 3 | 4 | 5 |
| ORGANIZATION How well do you employ a clear and logical organization? | 1 | 2 | 3 | 4 | 5 |
| VOICE Is your writing lively and engaging? | 1 | 2 | 3 | 4 | 5 |
| WORD CHOICE Do your readers experience your topic as if they are actually there? | 1 | 2 | 3 | 4 | 5 |
| SENTENCE FLUENCY How smooth and rhythmic is your writing, and how varied is its sentence structure? | 1 | 2 | 3 | 4 | 5 |
| CONVENTIONS How correct is your grammar, especially your use of transitions? | 1 | 2 | 3 | 4 | 5 |
| ADD YOUR OWN CRITERIA | 1 | 2 | 3 | 4 | 5 |

**Introduction** A Literature Circle consists of students who meet as a group to share their thoughts about what they are reading. In your Literature Circle, you will talk about topics and work together to complete activities related to your Anchor Books.

## PART 1: Open Discussion

Participation in a Literature Circle involves two skills: listening and speaking. When you speak, you should not only say what you think, but also ask other group members to explain what they think about their Anchor Books. Use the Discussion Guidelines on the next page to help keep your Literature Circles productive.

Ready? The best way to get started is to look back at what you have written in your Reader's Journal about your Anchor Book.

► First, look through your recent Reader's Journal entries for what you think is your best insight about the Anchor Book.

► Take turns sharing your insights with your Literature Circle.

► After each group member has shared an insight, the group should make connections as to what the group member said or ask questions to help push the group member's ideas further.

► Take it back to the text. If the discussion seems vague or unfocused, find passages from your Anchor Book that support or contradict the discussion.

In the space below, record a good insight, question, and passage shared in your Literature Circle discussion.

| Insight About the Anchor Book | Question | Passage |
|---|---|---|
| | | |

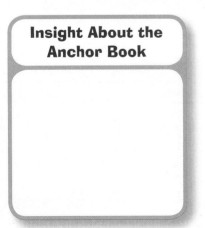

while reading your anchor book

## DISCUSSION GUIDELINES

**1 LISTEN**

Be courteous. When a classmate shares his or her ideas with your Literature Circle, listen carefully and respectfully. Do not interrupt.

**2 BUILD**

Think about how you might build on what has already been said. Provide examples that support what another member has said.

**Sentence Starters for Building Discussion**

- **When Kayla pointed** out the reasons for the prediction she made about her Anchor Book, **I thought about** how I might change the prediction I had made in my Anchor Book.
- **When Jorge observed that** . . . **it reminded me of** . . .

**3 QUESTION**

Sometimes you might be confused by a classmate's comment, or disagree with it. Ask specific questions to get members to clarify and expand upon their ideas.

**Sentence Starters for Asking Questions**

- **My opinion is different from yours.** Does it seem possible that the setting in your Anchor Book affected the characters in a different way?
- **I don't understand what you meant when you said** . . . **Could you explain this in more detail?**

## PART 2: Discuss—Active Listening

How successful was your first Literature Circle? Identify three ways your group demonstrated active listening. Then, identify a goal for making your next discussion more productive. Write your goal in your Reader's Journal.

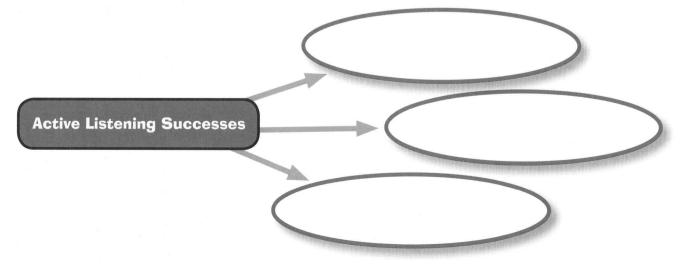

Active Listening Successes

## Reading Skills: Context Clues

Read the following passage. Then answer the questions.

> Sarah had nearly finished her physical therapy training, and everywhere she went, she seemed to find eager patients fervently awaiting her completion of the program. Sarah had had the best training, her skills were exemplary, and she couldn't wait to open her own practice. The local health club seemed too haughty for her tastes. She wanted an office where people were friendly and polite, not stuck-up and superficial.

**1** Using context clues, the best word to define **haughty** is _____.

   **A.** poor

   **B.** conceited

   **C.** glamorous

   **D.** unaware

**2** A word that means the opposite of **exemplary** is _____.

   **F.** ordinary

   **G.** perfect

   **H.** complete

   **J.** indisputable

**3** From the clues in the text, you could best define **fervently** as _____.

   **A.** lazily

   **B.** enthusiastically

   **C.** angrily

   **D.** painfully

**4** Which word provides clues to the meaning of the word **haughty?**

   **F.** exemplary

   **G.** friendly

   **H.** fervently

   **J.** stuck-up

**5** Which words help you find the meaning of **exemplary?**

   **A.** couldn't wait

   **B.** friendly and polite

   **C.** best training

   **D.** physical therapy

**6** A word that helps you define **fervently** is _____.

   **F.** haughty

   **G.** patients

   **H.** seemed

   **J.** eager

# Literary Analysis: Elements of Fiction and Nonfiction

Read the following passage. Then answer the questions.

> The farmer took great pride in his vegetables. But he was not the only fan of his labors. A family of rabbits also appreciated the farmer's gardening skills. One day, the farmer noticed that his carrot crop was shrinking! He rushed toward the rabbit he saw in his carrot plot, screaming, "What are you doing? Those are mine!"
>
> "I only take just enough to feed my family," replied the rabbit.
>
> "But these aren't for my family," responded the frustrated farmer. "I sell these to local produce markets so I can afford to maintain my farm!"
>
> "Then it appears," responded the rabbit, "we both need these carrots."

**7** What is the **conflict** between these two characters?

   **A.** The farmer and the rabbit both want to live on the same farm.

   **B.** The farmer's wife is afraid of rabbits.

   **C.** They both need the carrots for their welfare.

   **D.** The rabbit's family is larger than the farmer's.

**8** The **conflict** between the farmer and the rabbit can be identified as _____.

   **F.** universal

   **G.** unpredictable

   **H.** internal

   **J.** external

**9** What is a suitable **resolution** for both parties in the conflict above?

   **A.** The farmer moves to another town.

   **B.** The farmer grows enough extra carrots for the rabbit's family.

   **C.** The farmer changes what crops he grows.

   **D.** The farmer's wife overcomes her fear of rabbits.

**10** What is the **setting** of the passage?

   **F.** the carrot plot

   **G.** the farmer's home

   **H.** the produce market

   **J.** the rabbit's burrow

## Timed Writing: Compare–and–Contrast

Consider the conflict between the rabbit and the farmer in the story above. Look at the conflict in the story "The War of the Wall." How are these two conflicts similar? How are they different? Use information from both stories to support your answers.
**(20 minutes)**

# 1-11 Reading Skills
## Author's Purpose

In learning new reading skills, you will use special academic vocabulary. Knowing the right words will help you to demonstrate your understanding.

### Academic Vocabulary

| Word | Meaning | Example Sentence |
|---|---|---|
| **establish** v.<br>*Related word:*<br>established | to prove or create | James *established* that his prediction was correct. |
| **convince** v.<br>*Related word:*<br>convinced | to cause someone to agree | The candidate *convinced* the crowd that she was the best choice to be the governor. |
| **interpret** v.<br>*Related word:*<br>interpreted | to explain or provide the meaning of | Our teacher taught us how to *interpret* the poem. |

An **author's purpose** is his or her main reason for writing. An author must **establish** a purpose that matches the subject and audience. Authors use tools, such as theme, to communicate their purpose. Examine the following chart to see the clues for each purpose.

| Author's Purpose | Clues | Types of Writing |
|---|---|---|
| **to inform** | author includes facts, statistics, and details | newspaper articles, encyclopedia articles, manuals |
| **to persuade** | favors one side of an issue, author tries to **convince** the reader of his or her point of view | editorials, opinion essays, advertisements |
| **to entertain** | author uses humor, suspense, or exciting language | poems, plays, short stories, novels, narrative nonfiction |
| **to reflect** | author provides personal comments about the meaning of an experience or an event | autobiographies, diaries, memoirs, essays |

**Directions** Read the newspaper article. Underline the clues in the text that hint at the author's purpose. Then, answer the questions.

09

# One Out Away!

Few people who saw today's softball game will ever forget it. Monica Bradshaw came within one pitch of a no-hitter. In each inning, she eliminated each of the opposing hitters, striking out every single batter. Then, with two outs in the ninth inning and Bradshaw's team up 1-0, she walked Luisa Miller. That brought Karen Wilson to the plate. Bradshaw had struck Wilson out twice previously.

After two pitches, she had two strikes on Wilson—but on the last pitch of the game, Wilson put a good swing on a Bradshaw fastball. Everyone at the game watched the ball sail over the left-field fence for a game-winning home run. Monica Bradshaw was one pitch away from a 1-0 victory and a no-hitter. Instead, Karen Wilson gave her team a victory of 2-1.

**Karen Wilson homered to give her team a victory.**

1  **Identify** What is the topic of this article? What happened in the article that makes the writer think this is worthy of the reader's attention?

_____

_____

_____

2  **Analyze** What is the author's main purpose for writing this selection? What clues convince you that this is the purpose?

_____

_____

3  **Interpret** Does the author have a second purpose? Explain.

_____

_____

_____

Now that you have learned about the reading skill author's purpose, read this article and look for clues that support the purpose. *Guiding Question:* **Is the writer concerned with proving whether his argument is true?**

# LAPTOPS VS. LEARNING

## by David Cole

*In this article, author David Cole argues that technology—often thought of as an essential learning tool—can sometimes get in the way of learning.*

### Could you repeat the question?

In recent years, that has become the most common response to questions I pose to my law students at Georgetown University. It is usually asked while the student glances up from the laptop screen that otherwise occupies his or her field of vision. After I repeat the question, the student's gaze as often as not returns to the computer screen, as if the answer might magically appear there. Who knows, with instant messaging, maybe it will.

Some years back, our law school, like many around the country, wired its classrooms with Internet hookups. It's the way of the future, I was told. Now we are a wireless campus, and incoming students are required to have laptops. So my first-year students were a bit surprised when I announced at the first class this year that laptops were banned from my classroom.

I did this for two reasons, I explained. Note-taking on a laptop encourages verbatim transcription. The note-taker tends to go into stenographic[1] mode and no longer processes information in a way that is conducive to the give-and-take of classroom discussion. Because taking notes the old-fashioned way, by hand, is so much slower, one actually has to listen, think and prioritize the most important themes.

In addition, laptops create temptation to surf the Web, check e-mail, shop for shoes, or instant-message friends. That's not only distracting to the student who is checking Red Sox statistics but for all those who see him, and many others, doing something besides being involved in class. Together, the stenographic mode and Web surfing make for a much less engaged classroom, and that affects all students (not to mention me).

I agreed to permit two volunteers to use laptops to take notes that would be made available to all students. And that first day I allowed everyone to use the laptops they had with them. I posed a question, and a student volunteered an answer. I answered her with a follow-up question. As if on cue, as soon as I started to respond, the student went back to typing—and then asked, "Could you repeat the question?"

When I have raised with my colleagues the idea of cutting off laptop access, some accuse me of being paternalistic[2], authoritarian, or worse.

We daydreamed and did crosswords when we were students, they argue, so how can we prohibit our students, who are adults after all, from using their time in class as they deem fit?

A crossword hidden under a book is one thing. With the aid of [the Web], we have effectively put at every seat a library of magazines, a television and the opportunity for real-time side conversations and invited our students to check out whenever they find their attention wandering.

I feel especially strongly about this issue because I'm addicted to the Internet myself. I checked my e-mail at least a dozen times while writing this op-ed. I've often resolved, after a rare and liberating weekend away from e-mail, that I will wait till the end of the day to read e-mail at the office. Yet, almost as if it is beyond my control, e-mail is the first thing I check when I log on each morning. As for multitasking, I don't buy it. Attention diverted is attention diverted.

But this is all theory. How does banning laptops work in practice? My own sense has

---

1  **stenographic** (ste nŏ′graf fik) *adj.* taking notes literally, word-for-word.

2  **paternalistic** (pə tur′nəl ist′ik) *adj.* treating adults as if they were children.

been that my class is much more engaged than recent past classes. I'm biased[3], I know. So I conducted an anonymous survey of my students after about six weeks — by computer, of course.

The results were striking. About 80 percent reported that they are more engaged in class discussion when they are laptop-free. Seventy percent said that, on balance, they liked the no-laptop policy. And perhaps most surprising, 95 percent admitted that they use their laptops in class for "purposes other than taking notes, such as surfing the Web, checking e-mail, instant messaging and the like." Ninety-eight percent reported seeing fellow students do the same.

I am sure that the Internet can be a useful pedagogical tool in some settings and for some subjects. But for most classes, it is little more than an attractive nuisance. Technology has outstripped us on this one, and we need to reassess its appropriate and inappropriate role in teaching. The personal computer has revolutionized our lives, in many ways for the better. But it also threatens to take over our lives. At least for some purposes, unplugging may still be the best response.

---

[3] **biased** (bī'əsd) *adj.* having a prejudiced opinion.

# Thinking About the Selection

## Laptops vs. Learning

**1** **Evaluate** What is the author's main purpose for writing this essay? How does he achieve this purpose?

_____

_____

_____

**2** **Analyze** Complete this chart.

| Cause | Effect |
|---|---|
| Why the professor banned laptops in his classroom | |

**3** **Speculate** Do you think the author is against using computers in the classroom for such purposes as researching or writing a paper? Explain your answer.

_____

_____

_____

**4** **Respond** What's your opinion? On a separate piece of paper, write a letter to your school board expressing your opinion of whether laptops should appear in the classroom.

**Write** Answer the following questions in your Reader's Journal.

 **5** **Analyze** Is the writer concerned with proving whether his argument is true? Explain.

 **6** **Deduce** What is the author's purpose in your Anchor Book? Use details to support your answer.

 **Ready for a Free-Choice Book?** _Your teacher may ask you if you would like to choose another book to read on your own. Select a book that fits your interest and that you'll enjoy. As you read, think about how your new book compares with your Anchor Book._

# 1-12 Literary Analysis
## Character

When you can't stop reading a book or a story, it is usually because you have become involved in the lives of its **characters.** They start to feel like real people, with real personalities and problems.

## Literary Terms

► A **character** is someone who takes part in the action of a narrative. Most characters are people, but they might also be animals—or even robots or aliens.

► **Major characters** are the most important characters in a narrative. **Minor characters** are less important characters who are not the main focus of the action.

► The **protagonist** is the main character. The protagonist's conflict—what he or she wants—is what sets the story in motion. The **antagonist** is a character or force that is in conflict with the protagonist.

► A **dynamic character** is someone who changes and learns something as a result of what happens during the narrative. A **static character** does not change or develop.

► A **round character** is a complex, fully developed character with many different personality traits, both good and bad. A **flat character** is one-sided—someone with just one or two personality traits.

**Directions** Look at the photo to the right and read the caption underneath it. Then, answer the following question.

**1** What literary terms on this page could you use to describe what you know about *The Strange Case of Dr. Jekyll and Mr. Hyde?*

_____

_____

_____

_____

_____

▲ **Good to Know!**
*The Strange Case of Dr. Jekyll and Mr. Hyde* a book by Robert Louis Stevenson, features a main character, Dr. Jekyll, who keeps changing into another personality—the violent Mr. Hyde. Written in 1886, it was an instant success, and has been adapted many times for the stage and screen. A "Jekyll and Hyde" has come to mean a person with wildly changeable behavior.

**Directions** Read the following passage. Underline details that provide information about the narrator and his friend Tyrone. Then answer the questions that follow.

Go Online

**About the Author**
Visit: PHSchool.com
Web Code: exe-7107

## from *Bronx Masquerade*

### *by Nikki Grimes*

I ain't particular about doing homework, you understand. My teachers practically faint whenever I turn something in. Matter of fact, I probably got the longest list of excuses for missing homework of anyone alive. Except for my homey Tyrone. He tries to act like he's not even interested in school, like there's no point in studying hard, or dreaming about tomorrow, or bothering to graduate. He's got his reasons. I keep on him about going to school, though, saying I need the company. Besides, I tell him, if he drops out and gets a J.O.B., he won't have any time to work on his songs. That always gets to him. Tyrone might convince everybody else that he's all through with dreaming, but I know he wants to be a big hip-hop star. He's just afraid he won't live long enough to do it. Me, I hardly ever think about checking out. I'm more worried about figuring what I want to do if I live.

**1** **Summarize** Summarize what this passage reveals about the character of Tyrone.

_____

_____

**2** **Compare and Contrast** How is the narrator similar to Tyrone? How are these two characters different?

_____

_____

_____

_____

**3** **Predict** Do you think Tyrone will turn out to be a dynamic character—someone who changes? Explain your answer.

_____

_____

_____

_____

# Point of View

Imagine that you have just watched your sister's basketball game. When you get home, both of you tell your parents all about the game. Your account is probably going to be different from that of your sister. That's because you were an observer, while she was part of the action.

## Literary Terms

**Point of view** is the perspective from which a literary work is told. The **narrator** is the voice that is telling the narrative.

▶ When a narrative is told from the **first-person point of view,** the narrator is a character who is part of the action and uses the first-person pronouns *I, me,* and *my.* The reader sees everything through this character's eyes.

▶ When a narrative is told from the **third-person point of view,** the narrator is someone outside the action, rather than a character. There are two types of third-person points of view.

• With **omniscient third-person point of view,** the narrator is an all-knowing observer who can relate what every character thinks and feels.

• With the **limited third-person point of view,** the narrator relates some thoughts and feelings of only one character—but that character is not actually telling the story.

**Directions** Read the following passage, and then answer the questions.

**Go Online**

**About the Author**
Visit: PHSchool.com
Web Code: exe-7108

### *from* Travel Team *by Mike Lupica*

He knew he was small.

He just didn't *think* he was small.

*Big* difference.

Danny had known his whole life how small he was compared to everybody in his grade, from the first grade on. How he had been put in the front row, front and center, of every class picture taken. Been in the front of every line marching into every school assembly, first one through the door. Sat in the front of every classroom. Hey, little man. Hey, little guy. He was used to it by now. They'd been studying DNA in science

while reading your anchor book

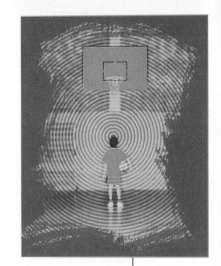

lately; being small was in his DNA. He'd show up for soccer, or Little League baseball tryouts, or basketball, when he'd first started going to basketball tryouts at the Y, and there'd always be one of those clipboard dads who didn't know him, or his mom. Or his dad.

Asking him: "Are you sure you're with the right group, little guy?" Meaning the right age group.

It happened the first time when he was eight, back when he still had to put the ball up on his shoulder and give it a heave just to get it up to a ten-foot rim. When he'd already taught himself how to lean into the bigger kid guarding him, just because there was always a bigger kid guarding him, and then step back so he could get his dopey shot off.

This was way back before he'd even tried any fancy stuff, including the crossover.

He just told the clipboard dad that he was eight, that he was little, that this was his right group, and could he have his number, please? When he told his mom about it later, she just smiled and said, "You know what you should hear when people start talking about your size? Blah blah blah."

He smiled back at her and said that he was pretty sure he would be able to remember that.

**1** **Identify** What point of view is used in this passage? How can you tell?

_____

_____

_____

**2** **Speculate** What feelings do you think Danny has about how people react to his size? Use details from the selection to support your answer.

_____

_____

_____

**3** **Infer** How might the passage be different if it were told from the first-person point of view?

_____

_____

In the following story, the first-person point of view allows you to get inside the narrator's head.
*Guiding Question:* **Does the main character believe he is telling the truth? How do you know?**

# Stolen Day

## by Sherwood Anderson

**Background** *In this story, the adult narrator describes an incident from his childhood. The main character convinces himself that he has "inflammatory rheumatism." Today this condition is called rheumatoid arthritis. It is a disease that attacks the joints and causes pain, swelling, and stiffness.*

### Vocabulary Builder

**Before you read,** *you will discuss the following words. In the Vocabulary Builder box in the margin, use a vocabulary building strategy to make the words your own.*

**solemn          presently          pitch**

**As you read,** *draw a box around unfamiliar words you could add to your vocabulary. Use context clues to unlock their meaning.*

### Marking the Text

**Character and Point of View**

**As you read,** *underline details that reveal what the adult narrator was like as a young boy. In the margin, explain the adult narrator's point of view.*

It must be that all children are actors. The whole thing started with a boy on our street named Walter, who had inflammatory rheumatism. That's what they called it. He didn't have to go to school.

Still he could walk about. He could go fishing in the creek or the waterworks pond. There was a place up at the pond where in the spring the water came tumbling over the dam and formed a deep pool. It was a good place. Sometimes you could get some big ones there.

I went down that way on my way to school one spring morning. It was out of my way but I wanted to see if Walter was there.

He was, inflammatory rheumatism and all. There he was, sitting with a fish pole in his hand. He had been able to walk down there all right.

It was then that my own legs began to hurt. My back too. I went on to school but, at the recess time, I began to cry. I did it when the teacher, Sarah Suggett, had come out into the schoolhouse yard.

She came right over to me.

"I ache all over," I said. I did, too.

I kept on crying and it worked all right.

"You'd better go on home," she said.

So I went. I limped painfully away. I kept on limping until I got out of the schoolhouse street.

Then I felt better. I still had inflammatory rheumatism pretty bad but I could get along better.

I must have done some thinking on the way home.

"I'd better not say I have inflammatory rheumatism," I decided. "Maybe if you've got that you swell up."

I thought I'd better go around to where Walter was and ask him about that, so I did—but he wasn't there.

"They must not be biting today," I thought.

I had a feeling that, if I said I had inflammatory rheumatism, Mother or my brothers and my sister Stella might laugh. They did laugh at me pretty often and I didn't like it at all.

"Just the same," I said to myself, "I have got it." I began to hurt and ache again.

I went home and sat on the front steps of our house. I sat there a long time. There wasn't anyone at home but Mother and the two little ones. Ray would have been four or five then and Earl might have been three.

It was Earl who saw me there. I had got tired sitting and was lying on the porch. Earl was always a quiet, **solemn** little fellow.

He must have said something to Mother for **presently** she came.

"What's the matter with you? Why aren't you in school?" she asked.

I came pretty near telling her right out that I had inflammatory rheumatism but I thought I'd better not. Mother and Father had been speaking of Walter's case at the table just the day before.

## Vocabulary Builder

**solemn**
(säl'əm) adj.

**Meaning**

**presently**
(prez'ənt lē) adv.

**Meaning**

"It affects the heart," Father had said. That frightened me when I thought of it. "I might die," I thought. "I might just suddenly die right here; my heart might stop beating."

On the day before I had been running a race with my brother Irve. We were up at the fairgrounds after school and there was a half-mile track.

"I'll bet you can't run a half-mile," he said. "I bet I could beat you running clear around the track."

And so we did it and I beat him, but afterwards my heart did seem to beat pretty hard. I remembered that lying there on the porch. "It's a wonder, with my inflammatory rheumatism and all, I didn't just drop down dead," I thought. The thought frightened me a lot. I ached worse than ever.

"I ache, Ma," I said. "I just ache."

She made me go in the house and upstairs and get into bed.

It wasn't so good. It was spring. I was up there for perhaps an hour, maybe two, and then I felt better.

I got up and went downstairs. "I feel better, Ma," I said.

Mother said she was glad. She was pretty busy that day and hadn't paid much attention to me. She had made me get into bed upstairs and then hadn't even come up to see how I was.

I didn't think much of that when I was up there but when I got downstairs where she was, and when, after I said I felt better and she only said she was glad and went right on with her work, I began to ache again.

I thought, "I'll bet I die of it. I bet I do."

I went out to the front porch and sat down. I was pretty sore at Mother.

"If she really knew the truth, that I have the inflammatory rheumatism and I may just drop down dead any time, I'll bet she wouldn't care about that either," I thought.

I was getting more and more angry the more thinking I did. "I know what I'm going to do," I thought; "I'm going to go fishing."

I thought that, feeling the way I did, I might be sitting on the high bank just above the deep pool where the water went over the dam, and suddenly my heart would stop beating.

And then, of course, I'd **pitch** forward, over the bank into the pool and, if I wasn't dead when I hit the water, I'd drown sure.

They would all come home to supper and they'd miss me.

"But where is he?"

Then Mother would remember that I'd come home from school aching.

She'd go upstairs and I wouldn't be there. One day during the year before, there was a child got drowned in a spring. It was one of the Wyatt children.

Right down at the end of the street there was a spring under a birch tree and there had been a barrel sunk in the ground.

## Vocabulary Builder

**pitch**
(pich) *v.*

**Meaning**

Everyone had always been saying the spring ought to be kept covered, but it wasn't.

So the Wyatt child went down there, played around alone, and fell in and got drowned.

Mother was the one who had found the drowned child. She had gone to get a pail of water and there the child was, drowned and dead.

This had been in the evening when we were all at home, and Mother had come running up the street with the dead, dripping child in her arms. She was making for the Wyatt house as hard as she could run, and she was pale.

She had a terrible look on her face, I remembered then.

"So," I thought, "they'll miss me and there'll be a search made. Very likely there'll be someone who has seen me sitting by the pond fishing, and there'll be a big alarm and all the town will turn out and they'll drag[1] the pond."

I was having a grand time, having died. Maybe, after they found me and had got me out of the deep pool, Mother would grab me up in her arms and run home with me as she had run with the Wyatt child.

I got up from the porch and went around the house. I got my fishing pole and lit out for the pool below the dam. Mother was busy—she always was—and didn't see me go. When I got there I thought I'd better not sit too near the edge of the high bank.

By this time I didn't ache hardly at all, but I thought.

---

[1] **drag** (drag) *v.* search a body of water with a net or other device.

▲ **Critical Viewing** How do these images reflect the main character's point of view?

"With inflammatory rheumatism you can't tell," I thought. "It probably comes and goes," I thought.

I had got my line into the pool and suddenly I got a bite. It was a regular whopper. I knew that. I'd never had a bite like that.

I knew what it was. It was one of Mr. Fenn's big carp.

Mr. Fenn was a man who had a big pond of his own. He sold ice in the summer and the pond was to make the ice. He had bought some big carp[2] and put them into his pond and then, earlier in the spring when there was a freshet[3], his dam had gone out.

So the carp had got into our creek and one or two big ones had been caught—but none of them by a boy like me.

The carp was pulling and I was pulling and I was afraid he'd break my line, so I just tumbled down the high bank holding onto the line and got right into the pool. We had it out, there in the pool. We struggled. We wrestled. Then I got a hand under his gills[4] and got him out.

He was a big one all right. He was nearly half as big as I was myself. I had him on the bank and I kept one hand under his gills and I ran.

I never ran so hard in my life. He was slippery, and now and then he wriggled out of my arms; once I stumbled and fell on him, but I got him home.

*Marking the Text*

---

[2] **carp** (kärp)  *n.* a kind of freshwater fish that includes the goldfish.

[3] **freshet** (fresh′it) *n.* a great rise or overflowing of a stream caused by heavy rains or melted snow.

[4] **gills** (gils) *n.* organs through which fish get oxygen, usually in chambers on the sides of the head.

So there it was. I was a big hero that day. Mother got a washtub and filled it with water. She put the fish in it and all the neighbors came to look. I got into dry clothes and went down to supper—and then I made a break that spoiled my day.

There we were, all of us, at the table, and suddenly Father asked what had been the matter with me at school. He had met the teacher, Sarah Suggett, on the street and she had told him how I had become ill.

"What was the matter with you?" Father asked, and before I thought what I was saying I let it out.

"I had the inflammatory rheumatism," I said—and a shout went up. It made me sick to hear them, the way they all laughed.

It brought back all the aching again, and like a fool I began to cry.

"Well, I *have* got it—I *have*, I *have*," I cried, and I got up from the table and ran upstairs.

I stayed there until Mother came up. I knew it would be a long time before I heard the last of the inflammatory rheumatism. I was sick all right, but the aching I now had wasn't in my legs or in my back.

## Vocabulary Builder

**After you read,** *review the words you decided to add to your vocabulary. Write the meaning of words you have learned in context. Look up other words in a dictionary, glossary, thesaurus, or electronic resource.*

## Sherwood Anderson
### (1876–1941)

Born in Camden, Ohio, Sherwood Anderson moved often as a child. He never finished high school and worked for years as a laborer at a number of different jobs. It was not until later in life that he turned his hand to writing. He was over forty by the time his first book was published, and it was not until his fourth book, *Winesburg, Ohio* (1919), that he became widely known. His works about ordinary people struggling in the face of change influenced a number of important writers of the time.

# Thinking About the Selection

## Stolen Day

**Go Online**

**About the Author**
Visit: PHSchool.com
Web Code: exe-7109

**1**    **Recall**   Is Walter a major or minor character? How do you know?

_____

_____

**2**    **Analyze**   Is the main character a dynamic character? If so, how does he change, or what does he learn, over the course of the story?

_____

_____

_____

**3**    **Identify**   Complete the chart below by giving an example from the selection in which the narrator shares his thoughts and feelings about a situation.

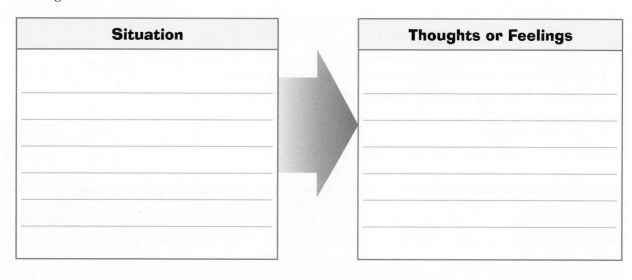

| Situation | Thoughts or Feelings |
|---|---|
| | |

**4**    **Interpret**   Throughout the story, the narrator keeps his belief that he has inflammatory rheumatism to himself. Does this make his life easier or more difficult? Explain.

_____

_____

_____

_____

while reading your anchor book

**5**  What are three details that could have been included if the mother had been the narrator?

**Detail 1**

**Detail 2**

**Detail 3**

**6**  **Interpret**  Why is first-person a good point of view for this story?

_____

_____

_____

_____

_____

**Write**  Answer the following questions in your Reader's Journal.

**7**  **Infer**  Does the narrator believe that he is telling the truth? How do you know?

**8**  **Analyze**  What point of view does the author use in your Anchor Book? How would the story be different if it were told from a different point of view?

# 1-13 Comparing Literary Works
## Setting and Mood

Have you ever seen a movie or TV show that retells a familiar story, but then sets it in a completely different place or time period? How much does this change in **setting** affect the meaning and impact of the story?

## Literary Terms

▶ The **setting** is the time and place of the action. In some narratives, setting serves only as a backdrop. In other stories, setting is more important, affecting how characters think and behave.

▶ **Mood** is the overall feeling of a literary work. The mood of a work might be gloomy, cheerful, peaceful, scary, or thoughtful. Setting details and word choice help create mood.

▶ **Imagery** is language that appeals to the five senses: sight, sound, smell, taste, and touch. Writers use **images,** or **sensory details,** to bring a setting to life and convey a mood.

**Directions** The following chart includes the five senses. Think about your favorite place to be, then fill in each row of the chart with details about that place.

| Sense | Imagery |
|-------|---------|
| Sight |  |
| Sound |  |
| Smell |  |
| Touch |  |
| Taste |  |

**Partner Activity** Read aloud the imagery of each sense to a partner and ask him or her to name the setting and mood you described. Then have your partner do the same.

**Directions** Read the passage on the next page. Underline imagery that reveals the setting and mood. Then, answer the questions that follow.

*from* **Heart of a Chief** *by Joseph Bruchac*

It's hard to see it through the mist, but it's right out there across the bay. The island. Where I'm sitting, you can get a good view of it when the clouds clear away. Or, as Doda would say, when the fog walks back across the wide lake to sleep in the marshy lands near the sunset.

This is a good place to sit. I'm comfortable now, even though rain is falling and I'm all wet. But I was already wet before I came to sit here. This rock was shaped long ago to make a seat big enough for two people: one to tell the story and one to listen. It wasn't made by a person, at least not in the way you'd understand that word, person, in English. But it was shaped by someone, a very ancient someone called Gluskabe by my people, as a place to rest and listen and look out at the island. So I'm going to sit here in Gluskabe's Seat and tell you this story.

**1** **Describe** Fill in the following imagery chart with details from the selection. Then, briefly describe the setting.

| Sense | Imagery |
|-------|---------|
| Sight | |
| Sound | |
| Smell | |
| Touch | |
| Taste | |

................................................................

................................................................

................................................................

**2** **Analyze** What mood does the imagery convey? Which details are most important in creating this mood?

................................................................

................................................................

................................................................

while reading your anchor book

Earlier in this unit, you read "The War of the Wall." Now, read the excerpt from *An American Childhood* to compare the setting and mood of these two selections. *Guiding Question:* **How do the setting and the mood make these stories "true" for the reader?**

From

# An American Childhood

## By Annie Dillard

**Background** *In this excerpt from her autobiography, Annie Dillard recalls a day in her childhood when her quiet Pittsburgh suburb became the setting for an exciting adventure.*

*(sidebar)* while reading your anchor book

### Vocabulary Builder

**Before you read,** *you will discuss the following words. In the Vocabulary Builder box in the margin, use a vocabulary building strategy to make the words your own.*

**solitude**       **translucent**       **mazy**

**As you read,** *draw a box around unfamiliar words you could add to your vocabulary. Use context clues to unlock their meaning.*

**Marking the Text**

**Setting and Mood**

**As you read,** *underline words that help you to see, hear, and feel the story's setting. In the margin, explain how these details help create the mood.*

Some boys taught me to play football. This was fine sport. You thought up a new strategy for every play and whispered it to the others. You went out for a pass, fooling everyone. Best, you got to throw yourself mightily at someone's running legs. Either you brought him down or you hit the ground flat out on your chin, with your arms empty before you. It was all or nothing. If you hesitated in fear, you would miss and get hurt: you would take a hard fall while the kid got away, or you would get kicked in the face while the kid got away. But if you flung yourself wholeheartedly at the back of his knees—if you gathered and joined body and soul and pointed them diving fearlessly—then you likely wouldn't get hurt, and you'd stop the ball. Your fate, and your team's score, depended on your concentration and courage. Nothing girls did could compare with it.

Boys welcomed me at baseball, too, for I had, through enthusiastic practice, what was weirdly known as a boy's arm. In winter, in the snow, there was neither baseball nor football, so the boys and I threw snowballs at passing cars. I got in trouble throwing snowballs, and have seldom been happier since.

On one weekday morning after Christmas, six inches of new snow had just fallen. We were standing up to our boot tops in snow on a front yard on trafficked Reynolds Street, waiting for cars. The cars traveled Reynolds Street slowly and evenly; they were targets all but wrapped in red ribbons, cream puffs. We couldn't miss.

I was seven; the boys were eight, nine, and ten. The oldest two Fahey boys were there—Mikey and Peter—polite blond boys who lived near me on Lloyd Street, and who already had four brothers and sisters. My parents approved Mikey and Peter Fahey. Chickie McBride was there, a tough kid, and Billy Paul and Mackie Kean too, from across Reynolds, where the boys grew up dark and furious, grew up skinny, knowing, and skilled. We had all drifted from our houses that morning looking for action, and had found it here on Reynolds Street.

It was cloudy but cold. The cars' tires laid behind them on the snowy street a complex trail of beige chunks like crenellated[1] castle walls. I had stepped on some earlier; they squeaked. We could have wished for more traffic. When a car came, we all popped it one. In the intervals between cars we reverted to the natural **solitude** of children.

I started making an iceball—a perfect iceball, from perfectly white snow, perfectly spherical, and squeezed perfectly **translucent** so no snow remained all the way through. (The Fahey boys and I considered it unfair actually to throw an iceball at somebody, but it had been known to happen.)

I had just embarked on the iceball project when we heard tire chains come clanking from afar. A black Buick was moving toward us down the street. We all spread out, banged together some regular snowballs, took aim, and, when the Buick drew nigh, fired.

A soft snowball hit the driver's windshield right before the driver's face. It made a smashed star with a hump in the middle.

Often, of course, we hit our target, but this time, the only time in all of life, the car pulled over and stopped. Its wide black door opened; a man got out of it, running. He didn't even close the car door.

He ran after us, and we ran away from him, up the snowy Reynolds sidewalk. At the corner, I looked back; incredibly, he was

---

[1] **crenellated** (cren'el lat'ed) *adj.* having protective barriers.

## Vocabulary Builder

**solitude**
(säl'ə tood') *n.*

**Meaning**


**translucent**
(trans loo' sənt) *adj.*

**Meaning**

still after us. He was in city clothes: a suit and tie, street shoes. Any normal adult would have quit, having sprung us into flight and made his point. This man was gaining on us. He was a thin man, all action. All of a sudden, we were running for our lives.

Wordless, we split up. We were on our turf; we could lose ourselves in the neighborhood backyards, everyone for himself. I paused and considered. Everyone had vanished except Mikey Fahey, who was just rounding the corner of a yellow brick house. Poor Mikey, I trailed him. The driver of the Buick sensibly picked the two of us to follow. The man apparently had all day.

He chased Mikey and me around the yellow house and up a backyard path we knew by heart: under a low tree, up a bank, through a hedge, down some snowy steps, and across the grocery store's delivery driveway. We smashed through a gap in another hedge, entered a scruffy backyard and ran around its back porch and tight between houses to Edgerton Avenue; we ran across Edgerton to an alley and up our own sliding woodpile to the Halls' front yard; he kept coming. We ran up Lloyd Street and wound through **mazy** backyards toward the steep hilltop at Willard and Lang.

He chased us silently, block after block. He chased us silently over picket fences, through thorny hedges, between houses, around garbage cans, and across streets. Every time I glanced back, choking for breath, I expected he would have quit. He must have been as breathless as we were. His jacket strained over his body. It was an immense discovery, pounding into my hot head with every sliding, joyous step, that this ordinary adult evidently knew what I thought only children who trained at football knew: that you have to fling yourself at what you're doing, you have to point yourself, forget yourself, aim, dive.

## Vocabulary Builder

**mazy**
(māʹzē) *adj.*

**Meaning**

Mikey and I had nowhere to go, in our own neighborhood or out of it, but away from this man who was chasing us. He impelled us forward; we compelled him to follow our route. The air was cold; every breath tore my throat. We kept running, block after block; we kept improvising, backyard after backyard, running a frantic course and choosing it simultaneously, failing always to find small places or hard places to slow him down, and discovering always, exhilarated, dismayed, that only bare speed could save us—for he would never give up, this man—and we were losing speed.

He chased us through the backyard labyrinths of ten blocks before he caught us by our jackets. He caught us and we all stopped.

We three stood staggering, half blinded, coughing, in an obscure hilltop backyard: a man in his twenties, a boy, a girl. He had released our jackets, our pursuer, our captor, our hero: he knew we weren't going anywhere. We all played by the rules. Mikey and I unzipped our jackets. I pulled off my sopping mittens. Our tracks multiplied in the backyard's new snow. We had been breaking new snow all morning. We didn't look at each other. I was cherishing my excitement. The man's lower pants legs were wet; his cuffs were full of snow, and there was a prow of snow beneath them on his shoes and socks. Some trees bordered the little flat backyard, some messy winter trees. There was no one around: a clearing in a grove, and we the only players.

It was a long time before he could speak. I had some difficulty at first recalling why we were there. My lips felt swollen; I couldn't see out of the sides of my eyes; I kept coughing.

"You stupid kids," he began perfunctorily[2].

We listened perfunctorily indeed, if we listened at all, for the chewing out was redundant, a mere formality, and besides the point. The point was that he had chased us passionately without giving up, and so he had caught us. Now he came down to earth. I wanted the glory to last forever.

But how could the glory have lasted forever? We could have run through every backyard in North America until we got to Panama. But when he trapped us at the lip of the Panama Canal, what precisely could he have done to prolong the drama of the chase and cap its glory? I brooded about this for the next few years. He could only have fried Mikey Fahey and me in boiling oil, say, or dismembered us piecemeal, or staked us to anthills. None of which I really wanted, and none of which any adult was likely to do, even in the spirit of fun. He could only chew us out there in the Panamanian jungle, after months or years of exalting pursuit. He could only begin, "You stupid kids," and continue in his ordinary Pittsburgh accent with his normal righteous anger and the usual common sense.

---

[2] **perfunctorily** (per func′to rily) *adv.* without much thought.

◀ **Critical Viewing**
How does this image help communicate the mood of the chase?

If in that snowy backyard the driver of the black Buick had cut off our heads, Mikey's and mine, I would have died happy, for nothing has required so much of me since as being chased all over Pittsburgh in the middle of winter—running terrified, exhausted—by this sainted, skinny, furious red-headed man who wished to have a word with us. I don't know how he found his way back to his car.

*Marking the Text*

## Vocabulary Builder

**After you read,** *review the words you decided to add to your vocabulary. Write the meaning of words you have learned in context. Look up the other words in a dictionary, glossary, thesaurus, or electronic resource.*

# Annie Dillard

Annie Dillard grew up in Pittsburgh, Pennsylvania, the setting of this narrative. Her parents encouraged her creativity and her love of reading. After college, she spent a year living on a secluded creek. Her journal from that period formed the basis for her first award-winning book, *Pilgrim at Tinker Creek.*

# Thinking About the Selections

*from* An American Childhood *and*
The War of the Wall

**Go Online**

**About the Author**
Visit: PHSchool.com
Web Code: exe-7111

**1** **Analyze** When and where does the excerpt from *An American Childhood* take place? How important is this setting to the events of the narrative?

_____

_____

_____

**2** **Analyze** What is the setting of "The War of the Wall" on page 32? How important is this setting to the events of the narrative?

_____

_____

_____

_____

**3** **Compare and Contrast** Both selections feature young people in conflict with an unknown adult. In what way does this conflict affect the mood of each selection?

_____

_____

_____

**4** **Explain** What does the author of *An American Childhood* mean when she says the passing cars were "targets all but wrapped in red ribbons, creampuffs"?

_____

_____

_____

**Write** Answer the following questions in your Reader's Journal.

 **5** **Evaluate** How do the setting and the mood make these stories "true" for the reader?

 **6** **Evaluate** How is the historical setting of your Anchor Book important to the story?

## Subject-Verb Agreement

There is one main rule for subject-verb agreement—a verb must agree with its subject in number. Following this rule will make your writing more effective.

A **singular subject** must have a **singular verb**. A **plural subject** must have a **plural verb.**

**Go Online**

**Learn More**
Visit: PHSchool.com
Web Code: exp-7103

| Singular and Plural Verbs | |
|---|---|
| **Singular** | **Plural** |
| The dog barks. | The dogs bark. |
| I am hungry. | We are hungry. |
| This was a wonderful day. | Those were wonderful days. |

**Directions** Read the paragraph below from a student essay. Circle the errors and rewrite the paragraph correctly.

**1** My summer vacation are amazing! I visited my uncle Rinaldo in Florida, and we swam with dolphins. They is interesting because they is not fish but mammals, even though they look like fish to me. My uncle Rinaldo and I is very close. We talks together for hours. I loves visiting him.

_____

_____

_____

**Author's Craft**

One common mistake writers make with subject-verb agreement is to choose a verb that agrees with another noun or pronoun in the sentence rather than the subject. Turn to "Stolen Day" on page 64. Choose one paragraph and underline all of the nouns and pronouns. Then, circle the subjects.

**Directions** Write a sentence in which the subject and verb agree.

**2** Singular Subject and Singular Verb

_____

**3** Plural Subject and Plural Verb

_____

# Singular and Plural Pronouns

**Nouns** are used to replace people, places, or things. **Personal pronouns** are used to replace people, places, things, and ideas. Personal pronouns refer to the person speaking (first person), the person spoken to (second person), or the person, place, or thing, spoken about (third person). They are either **singular** or **plural**.

Go Online

Learn More
Visit: PHSchool.com
Web Code: exp-7104

| Personal Pronouns | | |
|---|---|---|
| | **Singular** | **Plural** |
| **First Person** | I, me, my, mine | we, us, our, ours |
| **Second Person** | you, your, yours | you, your, yours |
| **Third Person** | he, him, his, she, hers, it, its | they, them, their, theirs |

When using a personal pronoun, make sure it agrees in number with the noun it replaces.

**Directions** In each sentence, circle the italicized personal pronoun that is used incorrectly. Write the correct pronoun above it.

**1** Juan gave *me* the two pens *them* found.

**2** The girls like *your* picture and *she* want to know if *they* can have a copy.

**Directions** Personal pronouns make writing less awkward. Replace any repeated nouns with personal pronouns.

**3** Yuri did not want to miss the bus, so Yuri walked quickly.

_____

**4** The dog likes to run away, so the dog must be on a leash when the dog goes for a walk.

_____

**5** Charlene woke up, then Charlene went to the market. Charlene decided to drive to Charlene's friend's house.

_____

> **Author's Craft**
>
> Scan "Laptops vs. Learning" on page 56. Which type of pronoun does the writer use most: first person, second person, or third person? What does that tell you about the passage?

**Go Online**

**Learn More**
Visit: PHSchool.com
Web Code: exp-7105

# Possessive Pronouns and Pronoun-Antecedent Agreement

**Possessive pronouns** are personal pronouns used to show ownership of an object. *Mine, ours, yours, his, hers, theirs, its,* and *whose* are possessive pronouns.  Some possessive pronouns are used alone. Some possessive pronouns are used before nouns.

A **pronoun** takes the place of a noun or nouns. An **antecedent** is the word or words to which a pronoun refers. An antecedent may appear before or after the pronoun. Sometimes the antecedent is not in the same sentence as the pronoun.

> **Example**  My <u>brother's</u> gloves are thick. <u>His</u> hands
> stay warm.

It is important that readers be able to tell what the antecedent for each pronoun is. Words such as *neither, either, everyone,* or *everything* are singular, so they must be paired with singular pronouns such as *his, her,* or *its.*

**Directions**  Write each sentence. Replace the underlined word with a possessive pronoun.

**1**  I like the <u>twins'</u> knitted hats.

_____

**2**  Tomas's new suit is gray. <u>Tomas's</u> shoes match.

_____

**3**  A dog sits outside a store. The <u>dog's</u> owner is inside.

_____

**Directions**  Rewrite the following paragraph, replacing the italicized antecedents with the correct pronouns.

> The more Luisa practiced, the better *Luisa* became at pitching. Her team played so well that *the team* won the championship game. Monique and Jordan decided to invite everyone over to *Monique and Jordan's* house for a victory party.  Coach Glen said this has been *Coach Glen's* best coaching experience.

_____

_____

_____

# Indefinite Pronouns and Use of *Who* and *Whom*

**Go Online**
**Learn More**
Visit: PHSchool.com
Web Code: exp-7106

An **indefinite pronoun** refers to a person, place, or thing that is not specifically named. Some indefinite pronouns are singular, while others are plural. Still others can be either singular or plural. Use an apostrophe and *s* with an indefinite pronoun to show possession.

| Indefinite Pronouns | | | | |
|---|---|---|---|---|
| **Singular** | | | **Plural** | **Singular or Plural** |
| another | everybody | nothing | both | all |
| anybody | everything | one | few | any |
| anyone | little | other | many | more |
| anything | much | somebody | others | most |
| each | nobody | someone | several | none |
| either | no one | something | | some |

**Who or Whom** When to use *who* or *whom* can sometimes confuse even experienced writers. As a general rule, the pronoun *who* is used as a subject, and *whom* is used as an object—so *whom* will be used with a preposition, for example, *to whom, for whom, with whom*, and so on.

One way to check if you have used who or whom correctly is rewrite the sentence, replacing *who* or *whom* with *he-she* or *him-her*.

▶ Who took the bus? Replace *who* with *he* or *she*. <u>He</u> took the bus.

▶ To whom will you tell the story? Replace *whom* with *him* or *her*. You will tell the story to <u>her</u>.

If the sentence still makes sense, you have chosen correctly!

**Directions** Rewrite each sentence as a question using *who* or *whom*.

**1** He never got a chance to see the band perform live.

_____

**2** You are going to study with her.

_____

**Directions** Read the paragraph. Circle indefinite pronouns that are used incorrectly. Then rewrite the paragraph correctly.

**3** Several of the computers in the lab were missing its cable modems. The computer teacher was not sure whom took them, but everyone was upset.

_____

> ### Author's Craft
>
> Sometimes authors use second person pronouns and indefinite pronouns so that readers can imagine themselves or people they know inside of a scene. Read the first paragraph of "An American Child-hood" on page 74. Why do you think the author wants you to imagine yourself tackling someone?

In a **how-to essay,** you explain how to do or make something. First, you arrange the process in a series of logical steps. Then, you explain the steps in the correct order. Follow the steps outlined in this workshop to write your own how-to essay.

Your how-to essay should include the following elements.

- ▶ A focused topic that can be fully explained

- ▶ Multi–step directions that are explained in order

- ▶ Transitional words and phrases to make the order clear

- ▶ Terms specific to your topic

- ▶ Error-free writing, including correct use of pronouns and subject–verb agreement

**Purpose** To write a how-to essay about a process that you know well

**Audience** You, your teacher, and your classmates

## Prewriting—Plan It Out

**Choose your topic.** On your own or with a partner, create a list of topic ideas—for example, making paper airplanes, tying shoelaces, or cooking something. Choose a topic from your list.

**Gather details.** In the **idea web** below, note facts about your topic. Use the small model web to the right as a guide.

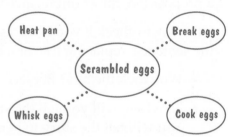

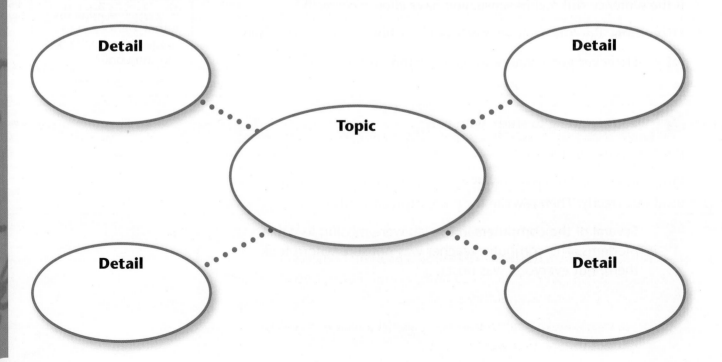

# Drafting—Get It on Paper

Using your idea web as an outline, write your draft. You may wish to look at technical, instruction, or procedure manuals as models.

**Shape your writing.** Organize your directions in sequential order. On a separate sheet of paper, create a list to help arrange the steps. Use the list of transitions below as a guide.

| First, you | find a "practice" volleyball. |
|---|---|
| Then, you | begin working on your toss. |
| Next, | practice repeatedly until your toss is perfect, straight up, and not too low. |
| After that, | work on hitting the ball over the net. |
| Finally, | practice with a regular volleyball. |

**Provide elaboration.** Be as precise as possible when laying out your steps. Offer details that show specific amounts, lengths of time, or how to complete a step.

# Revising—Make It Better.

Vary your transitional words. Insert transitions that show specific timing to help clarify the order of events. They include such words and phrases as *first, later, next, finally,* and *in about an hour.*

**Student Model: Inserting Transitions**

> **To start off,**
> Use a volleyball that is heavier than normal. It will be
> ^
> harder at the beginning, but when you finally get your serve
> over…

*The writer added a transition to show time order.*

On the lines provided, rewrite two sentences from your draft so that they each include a transition.

_____

_____

_____

**Check for specific vocabulary.** Double-check that when you describe necessary materials, you avoid general descriptions and use specific terms whenever possible.

*Peer Review* Ask for a partner's response to your how-to essay. Revise to clarify steps that were unclear.

**Directions** Read this student's how-to essay as a model for your own.

**Student Model: Writing**

**Go Online**

**Student Model**
Visit: PHSchool.com
Web Code: exr-7102

*Danielle Spiess, LaPorte, IN*
## How to Serve Overhand in Volleyball

Volleyball is one of the most popular sports around. Knowing how to serve overhand will be useful if you ever decide to try out for a team. If you have ever seen anyone serve, it may look pretty easy, but it is not as easy as it looks. It takes a lot of practice!

To practice, you'll need a volleyball, a practice ball that is heavier than regulation balls, and a net.

1. To start off, use a volleyball that is heavier than normal. It will be more difficult at the beginning, but when you finally get your serve over, it will be a lot stronger. The regular volleyball is lighter, so you won't have to put as much force into your serve during games.

2. Next is the toss, probably the most important part of the serve. Throw the volleyball into the air so it goes as high as possible. If your toss is too low or off to one side, the ball will not go over the net the way you want it to when you hit it. It might also go too far in front of you or behind you. If this happens, catch the volleyball and start over...

3. The final step is hitting it over. You can either use an open or a closed hand. Using an open hand is easier because when a closed hand is used, you sometimes hit the volleyball off your knuckles. After you toss the ball, wait until your toss reaches its peak, and then hit it. The volleyball may not go over the first time, but soon you will get it.

In volleyball, serving takes a lot of practice and a lot of effort, but it is a key skill for any serious player. As with any other athletic skill, set a goal for yourself. Then, just keep with it and don't give up!

> The writer focuses her essay on how to serve a volleyball.

> The writer provides a list to identify key items.

> Steps for tossing the ball are presented in the order they should be done.

> The conclusion reinforces the value of completing the process.

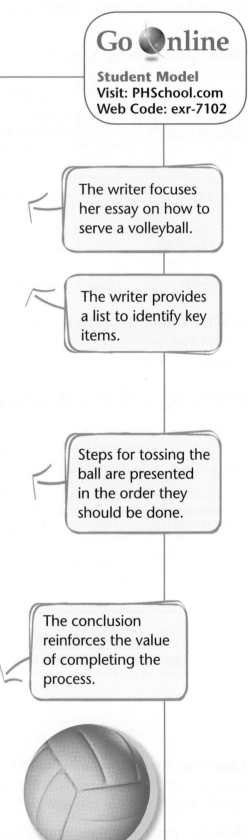

# Editing—Be Your Own Language Coach

Review your essay for language convention errors. Pay special attention to your correct use of pronouns, apostrophes for plural possessives, and subject-verb agreement. Also, correct any **double-negatives**. For example, *"Don't not throw the volleyball high in the air"* is confusing. Instead, say, *"Don't throw the volleyball high in the air."*

# Publishing—Share It!

When you publish a work, you produce it for a specific audience. Consider one of the following ideas to share your writing.

**Give a demonstration.** Demonstrate your topic by using props to show how to perform a process step by step.

**Make an instructional anthology.** Use word processing or publishing software to combine your work with that of your classmates to create an instructional booklet of various tasks or activities. You could send your anthology to a local publishing company or display it in your school or local library.

# Reflecting on Your Writing

**Rubric for Self-Assessment** Assess your essay. For each question, circle a rating.

| CRITERIA | RATING SCALE | | | | |
|---|---|---|---|---|---|
| | NOT VERY | | | | VERY |
| **IDEAS** How well have you focused on your topic? | 1 | 2 | 3 | 4 | 5 |
| **ORGANIZATION** How well do you employ a clear and logical organization? | 1 | 2 | 3 | 4 | 5 |
| **VOICE** How lively and engaging is your writing? | 1 | 2 | 3 | 4 | 5 |
| **WORD CHOICE** How appropriate is the language for your audience? | 1 | 2 | 3 | 4 | 5 |
| **SENTENCE FLUENCY** How varied is your sentence structure? | 1 | 2 | 3 | 4 | 5 |
| **CONVENTIONS** How correct is your grammar, especially your use of pronouns and subject-verb agreement? | 1 | 2 | 3 | 4 | 5 |

Now that you have completed reading your Anchor Book, it is time to get creative! Complete one of the following projects.

**after reading your anchor book**

### Be a News Reporter — A

Television reporters may have topics to cover in a limited amount of time. In this project, you become the reporter.

1. Select an event from your Anchor Book. Write notes about the main idea, details, and how each character is involved.

2. Write out each main idea as a sentence. Then, list supporting details below. Use vivid language and keep your writing exciting.

3. Practice reading your report. Edit for grammar, word choice, and content. Are you using a reporter's voice? What can you change or add to make your report more interesting?

4. Present your report. If you'd like, you can arrange your report on posterboard to use as a teleprompter.

Your project should include the following elements.

▸ A list of details and characters involved in an event

▸ A written report that describes the main idea and important details

▸ Use of voice and language that makes your report exciting to hear

### Map It Out — B

A travel brochure is an advertisement intended to attract people to visit a location. Persuade people to read your Anchor Book by creating a travel brochure with a visual map that brings to life the ideas and images described on the page.

1. Draw a map of your Anchor Book's setting, including all the places where important events occurred.

2. Next to each location, write a brief description of the important events that occurred there.

3. Choose two locations. Write directions from one location to another using ordinal and cardinal directions, landmarks, street names, and distances, and explain their importance. You may add a map key, a compass rose, or a distance scale.

Your brochure project should include the following elements.

▸ A map of the locations

▸ A description of important events that occur in each location

▸ A set of directions and explanation of their importance

## Journey In Time

C

Historic events and people sometimes inspire writers to retell history through a fictionalized perspective. These writers combine real details with invented ones to help their readers imagine the past. If your Anchor Book is a piece of nonfiction, imagine how a writer might create historical fiction based on events and people in your book.

1. Create a character that narrates the story. What is his or her role in history? The character can be based on a real or fictional person.

2. Use first-person point of view to tell the story. What is this narrator's perspective on the historical events and people?

3. Describe your character interacting with historical people and events.

Your project should include the following elements.
▸ Nonfiction facts, details, events, and people from your Anchor Book
▸ Creative details that help the characters, events, and setting seem true to history

## Free-Choice Book Reflection

You have completed your free-choice book. Before you take your test, read the following instructions to write a brief reflection of your book.

My free-choice book is _____ .

The author is _____ .

**1** Would you recommend this book to a friend?  Yes _____    No _____

Why or why not?

_____

_____

**Write and Discuss**  Answer the following question in your Reader's Journal. Then, discuss your answer with a partner.

**2** **Compare and Contrast**  *What is the best way to find the truth?* Compare and contrast how your Anchor Book free-choice book, and your background knowledge from other subjects help you answer this question. Use specific details from both books to support your ideas. To extend, consider how this question might be answered by a scientist, a journalist, or a historian.

## Reading Skills: Context Clues

Read this selection. Then, answer the questions that follow.

> It was one year to the day since Will had accepted the position of team captain for his school's soccer team. He had wanted that honor since he had watched his older brother lead the team to a state finals victory three years earlier. Now that the privilege was his, Will found himself **restive** and unable to sit still. It was only the first game of the season, but Will **envisioned** great things, both for himself and for the rest of his team. After all, this day had been a long time in coming.

**1** Based on the surrounding text, the word **restive** most likely means _____.

A. tired

B. pensive

C. bored

D. restless

**2** A word that means the same as **envisioned** is _____.

F. prevented

G. initiated

H. imagined

J. prayed for

## Reading Skills: Author's Purpose

Read this selection. Then answer the questions that follow.

> The wind was blowing hard as the team took its final time out. The driving rains seemed to be coming sideways. Both teams were exhausted as they dragged themselves back to the field. With just four seconds left on the clock, there was nothing left to do but watch as the football was booted through the air and passed just through the goal post. The crowd roared; the home team had won.

**3** The **author's purpose** for this piece is to _____.

A. persuade

B. entertain

C. inform

D. reflect upon an experience

**4** Clues in the text tell what the **author's purpose** was in writing it. This text contains mostly _____.

F. strong language, favoring one side of an issue

G. facts and details

H. suspenseful and exciting details

J. thoughts and feelings

# Literary Analysis: Elements of Fiction and Nonfiction

Choose the best answer for the following questions.

**5** The **plot** of a story is _____.

    **A.** where and when an event takes place

    **B.** the main character's feelings and thoughts

    **C.** the events that take place as characters deal with the conflict

    **D.** what happens when the conflict is resolved

**6** The sentence *José couldn't choose between joining the football team or the hockey team* is an example of a(n) _____.

    **F.** conflict resolution

    **G.** internal conflict

    **H.** external conflict

    **J.** internal resolution

Read this selection and answer the questions that follow.

> Dillain was an adventurous dog; perhaps it was the pit bull in him, maybe it was the boxer. Whatever lineage was responsible, nothing could stop him from going after that fox that mocked him from across the river. Of course, in spite of all the wonderful things that Dillain had grown to become—great friend, watchdog, protector—he had never become a strong swimmer.
>
> Upon hearing the quick splashing and the slight whimper in his yelps, I quickly hopped up from the hammock and rushed into the frigid water to help my brave but foolish companion. This happens every year when Dillain and I head up the river toward Maine. But he loves the cool rush of the river, and I love him too much to deprive him of that.

**7** From what **point of view** is this selection written?

    **A.** first-person

    **B.** second-person

    **C.** omniscient third-person

    **D.** limited third-person

**8** What clues tell you that Dillain is a **static character?**

    **F.** Dillain is a great friend, watchdog, and protector.

    **G.** This happens every year.

    **H.** Dillain is a poor swimmer.

    **J.** Dillain is an adventurous dog.

**9** What **point of view** provides the reader with the thoughts and feelings of only one character?

    A. round character

    B. limited third–person

    C. omniscient third–person

    D. character motivation

**10** Two characters, or a character and an outside force, in opposition are an example of _____.

    F. external conflict

    G. character motivation

    H. internal conflict

    J. resolution

**11** A **round character** is_____.

    A. someone with just one or two personality traits

    B. the person narrating the story

    C. someone who does not change or develop throughout the story

    D. a complex, fully developed character

**12** Which of the following questions reveals clues to the reader about potential **conflict** in a story?

    F. How many people are involved?

    G. Where does the story take place?

    H. What helps or doesn't help a character make a decision?

    J. Why is this important to the reader?

## Language Skills: Vocabulary

Choose the best answer.

**13** What is one step you should take if you come across an unfamiliar word as you read a story?

    A. Stop reading and move on to another story.

    B. Think of other words that start with the same letter.

    C. See if you come across the meaning later on in the story.

    D. Make a wild guess.

**14** Which word means "to cause to be a victim"?

    F. victim

    G. victimize

    H. victimable

    J. victimhood

**15** The word *realization* probably means _____.

    A. cause to be realized

    B. to avoid being realized

    C. state of being realized

    D. capable of being realized

**16** Which word means "capable of being understood"?

    F. understanding

    G. understands

    H. understandation

    J. understandable

# Language Skills: Grammar

Choose the answer.

**17** Choose the word that best completes the following sentence.

None of the animals in the shelter _____ to anyone.

A. belong

B. are belonging

C. belongs

D. is belonging

**18** Everybody in the classroom _____ ice cream and soda now.

F. is enjoying

G. enjoy

H. are enjoying

J. enjoys

**19** What is the **indefinite pronoun** in the following sentence?

*Everybody likes to receive compliments!*

A. Everybody

B. likes

C. receive

D. compliments

**20** Some examples of **personal pronouns** in the third-person singular are _____ .

F. *he, she, his,* and *her*

G. *you, your,* and *yours*

H. *I, me, my,* and *mine*

J. *they, them,* and *their*

**21** Choose the word that correctly completes the sentence.

Lemonade and grape soda _____ on sale today.

A. is

B. was

C. are

D. am

**22** The painter is putting _____ brushes into the water to soak.

F. its

G. his

H. ours

J. theirs

**23** An **indefinite pronoun** is _____ .

A. a person, place, or thing that IS specifically named

B. a person, place, or thing that IS NOT specifically named

C. always singular

D. always plural

**24** Read the following sentence. Identify the **possessive pronoun.**

My brother is an opera star. His voice is loud.

F. brother

G. my

H. is

J. His

# Does every *conflict* have a winner?

## Unit 2 Genre focus:
# The Novel

### Your Anchor Book
There are many good books that would work well to support both the Big Question and the genre focus of this unit. In this unit you will read one of these books as your Anchor Book. Your teacher will introduce the book you will be reading.

### Free-Choice Reading
Later in this unit you will be given the opportunity to choose another book to read. This is called your free-choice book.

in the clouds
I carefully
a handmade
within
weekend crowd with
board and
tourists

# Thinking About What You Already Know

Why are some stories more interesting than others? You know the ingredients for a story: character, conflict, plot, and setting. These are simple ingredients, but the way authors use and combine them create very different results.

## Group Activity

In a small group, discuss at least three memorable fictional characters and the conflicts they face. Think about why these characters are memorable and how they face their conflicts. Record your conclusions below.

| Memorable Character | Conflict | What makes this character memorable? |
|---|---|---|
| 1. | | |
| 2. | | |
| 3. | | |

Are there common traits that make these characters memorable? Discuss and write your answer below.

_____

_____

_____

Now, let's consider a historical character. What do you know about Harriet Tubman from social studies class?

_____

_____

Social studies textbooks can provide facts about Harriet Tubman, but we do not have records of what she thought and felt at every important moment in her life. Read the following excerpt to see how a writer fictionalizes her leading of the slaves to freedom.

## from *Harriet Tubman: The Railroad Runs to Canada* by Ann Petry

When she knocked on the door of a farmhouse, a place where she and her parties of runaways had always been welcome, always been given shelter and plenty to eat, there was no answer. She knocked again, softly. A voice from within said, "Who is it?" There was fear in the voice.

She knew instantly from the sound of the voice that there was something wrong. She said, "A friend with friends," the password on the Underground Railroad.

The door opened, slowly. The man who stood in the doorway looked at her coldly, looked with unconcealed astonishment and fear at the eleven disheveled runaways who were standing near her. Then he shouted, "Too many, too many. It's not safe. My place was searched last week. It's not safe!" and slammed the door in her face.

She turned away from the house, frowning. She had promised her passengers food and rest and warmth, and instead of that, there would be hunger and cold and more walking over the frozen ground: Somehow she would have to instill courage into these eleven people, most of them strangers, would have to feed them on hope and bright dreams of freedom instead of the fried pork and corn bread and milk she had promised them.

How is what you knew about Harriet Tubman different from what you read about her in this excerpt?

_____

_____

_____

Compare your answers with those of your classmates.

A baseball team wins the World Series. A politician wins an election. Although these conflicts end with a winner, the outcomes of other conflicts may not be as clear.

Conflict comes in many forms and can be found in books, movies, and real life. We frequently think of conflict only in terms of winners and losers, but maybe it's not that simple. For example, if two friends get into an argument and stop talking to each other, who wins?

## Critical Viewing

**Directions** The cartoon below explains the outcome of a conflict. With a partner, discuss what the conflict was and how the cartoon answers the Big Question. Then answer the questions on the following page.

"Jenkins and I worked it out. He can have the office with the window."

before reading your anchor book

**1** **Identify** What was the conflict? How did the two participants choose to resolve it?

_____

_____

**2** **Interpret** What is the cartoon's answer to the Big Question?

_____

_____

_____

**Role Play** Now, with your partner, identify a conflict you have experienced or heard about where there was no winner.

> **Describe the conflict.** _____
>
> _____
>
> _____

> **Explain why there was no winner. Was the conflict resolved in the best way?**
>
> _____
>
> _____
>
> _____
>
> _____

Consider how the conflict might have been resolved differently. You and your partner should each choose a role as participants in the conflict. Brainstorm actions and words that could have changed the outcome. Then, act out a different resolution.

> **My role** _____ **My partner's role** _____
>
> **Actions and words that could have changed the outcome.** _____
>
> _____
>
> _____

As you read your Anchor Book and the related readings, think about how a character's attitudes and expectations impact the outcome of a conflict. How can seeing a conflict only in terms of winning and losing impact its outcome?

**Getting Ready for Your Anchor Book**

*You will start reading your Anchor Book soon. The next few pages in this book give you some background information plus a reading skill.*

# Introduction to the
# Novel

Reading is not only an academic skill, but also a way to experience the world through someone else's eyes. Even after you finish a good book, the experience stays with you and changes the way you see the world.

What kind of book do most people read? The **novel**, a book-length story that both entertains its readers and helps them understand the human experience.

## The Novel: A Kind of Fictional Narrative

The novel is a kind of fictional narrative, as are short stories and drama. All forms of fictional narrative share a number of common elements.

▶ **Characters** help us connect fiction to life. A novel tells a story about characters who are not real people but are like them.

▶ These characters go through a series of actions or events. This chain of events is called the **plot.**

▶ The events occur in a specific place and time, or **setting**. Details of setting help establish the **mood,** or overall feeling of the work.

▶ Details about character, plot, and setting work together to communicate a **theme,** a message about human experience.

## History of the Novel

Poetry and drama existed before people could read. These literary forms were shared orally. An audience listened while a poet sang or chanted a poem and actors performed a play. However, the novel is different. It became a popular literary form in the eighteenth century, when a significant percentage of the population could read. The novel is written to be read silently and on one's own.

*before reading your anchor book*

# Strategies for Reading a Novel

Use these strategies as you read a novel.

**Read Expressively.** Even though you are reading silently, try to read "in your head" with appropriate expression and phrasing.

**Connect With a Character.** Imagine yourself as a specific character in the story. Would you behave in the same way? Try to understand how a character feels and why she or he reacts to events in a certain way.

**Monitor Your Reading.** Keep track of how many pages you need to read each night or week to finish your book on time. Adjust your reading rate if you are reading too quickly to keep track of details, or too slowly to stay engaged with the text.

## The Novel and the Short Story

The novel and the short story are frequently compared. As you read, think about how the two genres are different. Here are some of the important differences between them.

**The Novel**
- ▶ usually consists of more than 100 pages
- ▶ has many subplots and many characters
- ▶ major characters develop throughout the story

**The Short Story**
- ▶ is intended to be read in one sitting
- ▶ produces one strong effect
- ▶ has no subplot
- ▶ has a limited number of characters

**Novellas** are shorter than novels but longer than short stories.

## With a Partner

Great storytelling is universal. Many stories have been the basis for great movies: *Lord of the Rings* and *Holes* are just two examples.

**Directions** Discuss the purpose and characteristics of your favorite book, novella or short story with your partner. How would you make this story into a movie?

Remember a novel usually takes more than two hours to read, while most movies are no longer than two hours. What details, characters, and events from the novel would you include? What would you cut? Whom would you cast to play which characters, and why?

# 2-2 Reading Skills
## Making Predictions

In learning new reading skills, you will use special academic vocabulary. Knowing the right words will help you demonstrate your understanding.

### Academic Vocabulary

| Word | Meaning | Example Sentence |
|---|---|---|
| **modify** *v.* <br> *Related words:* <br> modified, modification | to change | Because the rain flooded the road, we had to *modify* our travel plans. |
| **verify** *v.* <br> *Related words:* <br> verified, verification | to confirm | Your birth certificate will *verify* your date and place of birth. |
| **formulate** *v.* <br> *Related words:* <br> formulation, formulator | to devise, to develop | The scientist worked hard to *formulate* her new theory. |

**Making predictions** helps you make connections between present and future events. When you predict, you make a logical assumption about future actions and outcomes based on what you already know. Use this strategy throughout the reading process. It can help you address confusion by connecting to what you already know.

## How to Make Predictions

► **Preview** the selection by looking at text structures and graphic aids such as the title, chapter titles, captions, photos, and headings. These can provide clues about the selection.

► **Predict** what will happen next by thinking about what you already know. Use personal experiences and knowledge of other selections to help **formulate** your predictions. Make predictions before you read and while you read.

► **Verify** your predictions as you read. **Modify** them if you come across new information requiring a change, or if you discover that they are incorrect.

**Directions** Read the following article. As you read, fill in the boxes to practice predicting. The passage is split into sections so that you can make your predictions in a step-by-step process.

**Preview:** What do the title, subtitle, and photograph suggest this article will be about?

Link to Real Life

# GEOGRAPHIC BEE
## Against the Odds

**GEOGRAPHY** is a snap for **Nicholas Clemons** of California. A voracious reader with an impeccable memory, the San Francisco 14-year-old won his school's National Geographic Bee and placed fifth in his state's competition—without really studying. "It sort of came naturally," explains Nicholas. But not everything has been so easy for this middle schooler.

**My Prediction**

**Why I Think So**

"Nicholas has been in shelters and group homes for most of his life," says his teacher Karen Anzaldo. After winning his school's Bee in front of more than 800 people, the teenager said he felt "on top of the world"—and it showed. "Nick threw his arms into the air. He looked just like Rocky Balboa up on stage," Karen recalls. His teachers then rallied around him to send him to the state Bee in Sacramento to represent his city and his school.

## What Actually Happened?

The triumphs didn't end there. As word spread of his impressive showing at the Bee, the *San Francisco Chronicle* did a story on Nicholas.

## My Prediction

## Why I Think So

This past summer, after demonstrating in the article an uncanny knowledge of San Francisco transit lines, he won an internship with a city transportation office. And Nicholas gained admission to Gateway High School, a charter school for high achievers, after writing about his experience at the Bee in his application. He's now in his freshman year there.

"There has been a huge turnaround in his relationship with himself," says Karen, his teacher, of Nicholas's Bee success. "It's been a life-changing event."

## What Actually Happened?

# Surfing's Dynamic Duo

by Joel K. Bourne Jr.

In the tattooed, slash-and-burn circus that passes for surf culture these days, Harry Richard "Skip" Frye is the sport's Fred Astaire, a quiet, God-fearing surfer and surfboard shaper, whose unmistakable style on and off the water speaks louder than his words. At a time in his life when many of his contemporaries are contemplating bypass surgery, Frye spent his 64th birthday surfing for hours in head-high surf, riding everything from monster 12-foot longboards to short high-speed "fish" designs that he helped immortalize in the 1960s. To anyone who has ever tried to sit on a surfboard, much less paddle one in big surf, the feat was impressive. But what truly impressed the lifeguards, who let him in to San Onofre State Park early, was the hour he spent forgoing the fantastic waves to pick up trash along the beach.

"In Genesis, God lays it out," says Frye as he dusts off his latest creation–an alabaster fish with so many subtle curves da Vinci could appreciate its potential for flight. "We're in charge of Earth, but we have a responsibility to take care of it."

It's a responsibility Frye has been taking seriously for years, going back to the days when he used to pick up garbage around Harry's, the old-school surf shop that he and friend Harry "Hank" Warner ran for years just off the boardwalk at Pacific Beach. The strip of beach shops and bars serves as party central for much of San Diego, hitting a peak on the Fourth of July. July 5 is now officially dubbed by local beach activists the "morning after mess." Says Frye: "It's like they took the landfill, backed it up, and dumped it on the beach. It's the sickest thing you can imagine. I used to get very down on the human race."

DANGER
CONTAMINATED WATER
KEEP OUT

Those are the kinds of thoughts that Skip's wife, Donna–who has more faith in people's ability to clean up their own messes—tries to temper. While Skip has evolved into a quiet role model for many surfers, Donna—loud, proud, and a veteran activist—became galvanized by the clean water issue after she and Skip opened Harry's back in 1990. "People kept coming into the surf shop with a variety of ailments," she recalls. "First I was skeptical. 'Oh, the swell's up, sure you're sick!'" But then in September 1995, Skip came in from surfing in water unusually brown and murky. Normally healthy as a seahorse, Skip felt dizzy and short of breath, and was so weak he couldn't drive home. "I did some research and found out that nearly all the popular surf spots were in front of storm drains or river mouths," Donna says. "We actually mapped them."

Donna explains all this in her husky Lauren Bacall voice. Her deep tan, straight blonde hair, and ready smile give her a surfer-girl façade, but that quickly fades when she starts reeling off TMDLs, BMPs, and other arcane nuances of clean water regulations. What they found in 19 storm drains along some of San Diego's most popular surfing beaches was disgusting: Total coliform bacteria counts— which should be below 1,000 parts per million (ppm) for safe swimming–as high as 240,000. Armed with hard data, Donna launched a tireless campaign to get warning signs posted by the storm drains, fix leaking sewer pipes, require more stringent beach-water monitoring, and divert the worst offending drains into the sewer system.

Her activism eventually catapulted her onto the city council in 2001, one of the few Democrats to win a seat in the largely Republican town. Such is the power of her clean water

message that Donna has twice nearly won the mayor's seat, losing by 8 percent last November to a former police chief. With city hall wracked with scandals and mountains of debt from the previous administration, San Diegans chose the conservative cop over the radical clean water activist.

Donna takes it all in stride. Since she began her campaign in the mid-1990s, the city has experienced 70 percent fewer sewage spills and 60 percent fewer beach closures. The beaches are better, she says, but much more needs to be done, like restoring the San Diego River and upgrading the Point Loma wastewater plant to secondary treatment.

Storm drains, such as this one in San Diego, dump dirty water into public waterways, exposing people to illness-causing bacteria.

**Above:** Skip Frye walks along murky waters as sewage spills into the ocean.
**Below:** Donna and Skip Frye

# Thinking About the Selection
## Surfing's Dynamic Duo

**1** **Connect** Before you read the selection, did you know anything about water pollution? How did your prior knowledge or lack of knowledge affect your predictions?

_____

_____

**2** **Predict** After you previewed the selection, what did you predict the selection was going to be about? As you were reading, what predictions did you make? Why did you make them?

_____

_____

_____

_____

_____

**3** **Evaluate** Were you able to verify your predictions as you kept reading, or did you have to modify them? Explain.

_____

_____

_____

**4** **Assume** What can you assume finally caused Donna Frye to become a clean-water activist?

_____

_____

_____

**Write** Answer the following question in your Reader's Journal.

 **5** **Predict** What can you infer from this passage about the conflict over water pollution? Explain why you think this conflict will or will not ever be resolved. Support your point of view with information from the selection.

# 2-3 Vocabulary Building Strategies
## *Prefixes*

A **prefix** is one or more syllables at the beginning of a word root. Every prefix has a meaning. You can use its meaning to help you understand the meanings of words that begin with the prefix. When you encounter an unknown word, use your knowledge of prefixes as a clue to the word's meaning.

| Prefix | Meaning | Examples |
|--------|---------|----------|
| *con-* | with, together | <u>con</u>vention: an agreement or meeting between people |
| *sub-* | below | <u>sub</u>heading: a caption, title, or heading that occupies a lower postion than another |
| *ob-* | against, blocking | <u>ob</u>jection: a reason or argument presented in opposition |

**Directions** Read each definition. Then write *con-*, *sub-*, or *ob-* on the line to form a word that fits the definition.

**1** _____ ordinate _____ : someone who ranks below others.

**2** _____ clusion _____ : answer found by putting all the clues together.

**3** _____ struction _____ : something that blocks your way.

**Directions** Now, look through the pages of this book. Find as many words as you can that include one of the prefixes you just learned.

_____

_____

## Definition Map

In a dictionary, you are given three components of a word's definition. Look at the following example for the word "retriever."

| What is it? | a type of dog |
|-------------|---------------|
| How would you describe it? | any of several breeds of dogs having a heavy, water-resistant coat, and that can be trained to retrieve |
| What are some examples? | golden retriever, Labrador retriever |

When you learn a new word, it also helps to ask yourself, *What can it be compared to?* For example, a retriever is a medium-sized dog, whereas a pug is a small dog.

**Directions** Choose an unfamiliar word from the list on this page. Make it your own by completing the definition map below. First, use your knowledge of prefixes to guess what it means. Then, using a dictionary, thesaurus, or electronic resource, find answers to the definition map questions. Use drawings and words to complete the definition map.

| Words |
| --- |
| conjunction |
| subhuman |
| obscure |
| consign |
| obstacle |
| subtext |

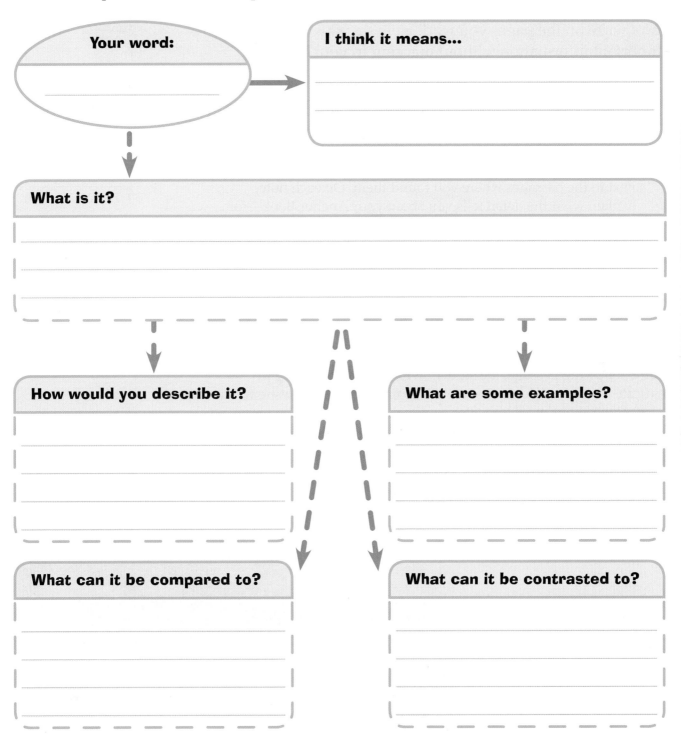

Your word: ____

I think it means... ____

What is it? ____

How would you describe it? ____

What are some examples? ____

What can it be compared to? ____

What can it be contrasted to? ____

**Ready? Start Reading Your Anchor Book**    *It's time to get started. As you learn from this work text, your teacher will also give you reading assignments from your Anchor Book.*

## 2-4 Writing About Your Anchor Book
### Reader's Journal

**Using Self-Stick Notes** Marking the text is a great way to keep track of ideas and important details, but sometimes you can't write on the pages you read. Here's a way to record important information without marking in your book.

**How to Use Self-Stick Notes**  You can use self-stick notes to track details and plan your writing as you read your Anchor Book. You can also use self-stick notes to monitor your comprehension.

> ► **As you read,** track important details by placing self-stick notes next to the passages where you found them. On each note, explain what the detail tells you about your Anchor Book—for example, whether it deals with plot development, character, or setting. You can also jot down ideas and questions, such as predictions, confusing passages, or unfamiliar vocabulary.

> ► **After you read,** review your notes for examples to use in your Reader's Journal response. You can also use notes for other tasks that require you to support your ideas with details from the text, as in informational and persuasive texts.

In the following passage, the student wrote the word *Setting* to indicate the type of detail she referred to on her note. Then she wrote a brief note about the setting along with a question. She also wrote a note about an unfamiliar word and guessed at its meaning.

**Directions**  Read the passage on  the following page, and examine the self-stick note.

### from *The Bracelet* by *Yoshiko Uchida*

I looked around at my empty room. The clothes that Mama always told me to hang up in the closet, the junk piled on my dresser, the old rag doll I could never bear to part with—they were all gone. There was nothing left in my room, and there was nothing left in the rest of the house. The rugs and furniture were gone, the pictures and drapes were down, and the closets and cupboards empty. The house was like a gift box after the nice thing inside was gone; just a lot of nothingness. It was almost time to leave our home, but we weren't moving to a nicer house or a new town. It was April 21, 1942. The United States and Japan were at war, and every Japanese person on the West Coast was being evacuated by the government to a concentration camp. Mama, my sister Keiko, and I were being sent from our home, and out of Berkeley, and eventually out of California.

**Setting**
- description makes story sound sad
- What did they do with their stuff?
- evacuated = moved?

One style of using self-stick notes is to write short phrases, but make sure you write in a way that allows you to remember what the note is about later.

**1** **Justify** What details in the passage support the student's first comment on her self-stick note?

_____

_____

**Directions** Read the passage, and add comments and questions to the blank self-stick note. Then, answer the questions that follow.

**Go Online**

About the Author
Visit: PHSchool.com
Web Code: exe-7201
exe-7202

### from *Treasure Island* by *Robert Louis Stevenson*

The appearance of the island when I came on deck next morning was altogether changed. Although the breeze had now utterly ceased, we had made a great deal of way during the night and were now lying becalmed about half a mile to the southeast of the low eastern coast. Gray-colored woods covered a large part of the surface. This even tint was indeed broken up by streaks of yellow sand-break in the lower lands, and by many tall trees of the pine family, out-topping the others—some singly, some in clumps; but the general coloring was uniform and sad.

**Setting**

**2** **Analyze** How can self-stick notes help you analyze your Anchor Book more deeply?

_____

_____

**while reading your anchor book**

# 2-5 Literary Analysis
## Learning About Plot

Have you ever felt yourself getting lost in a good story—involved in the characters' lives and anxious to know what will happen to them? When a story makes you feel this way, it's because the author has created a narrative with a strong **plot**.

## Literary Terms

As you have learned, the **conflict** in a narrative is a struggle between opposing forces. The **plot** is the sequence of events that shows how the conflict develops and is finally resolved.

The following diagram shows the five parts of a typical plot.

The **climax** is the most exciting moment in the plot, when the conflict is the most intense. The climax is sometimes called the turning point.

**Climax**

The **rising action** introduces the story's main conflict. During the rising action, this conflict grows more intense.

The **falling action** is everything that happens after the climax. During the falling action, the conflict winds down in intensity.

Rising Action

Falling Action

The beginning of the story is called the **exposition**. It introduces the characters, the setting, and the basic situation.

The **resolution** is the end of the story, when the conflict is resolved and all the loose ends are tied up. The resolution is sometimes called the **denouement.**

**PLOT PYRAMID**

**Exposition
(Beginning)**

**Resolution
(Ending)**

The **initiating event** is the incident that introduces the central conflict in a story. It may have occurred before the opening of the story.

As you read a narrative, realize that an author makes choices of which details and events to serve his/her purpose and think about how these choices impact the story.

**Directions** Read the following fable and underline the most important events in the plot. Use the questions in the margin to help you complete the question that follows.

## Go Online

**About the Author**
Visit: PHSchool.com
Web Code: exe-7203

## Androcles and the Lion *by Aesop*

A slave named Androcles once escaped from his master and fled to the forest. As he was wandering about there he came upon a Lion lying down moaning and groaning. At first he turned to flee, but finding that the Lion did not pursue him, he turned back and went up to him. As he came near, the Lion put out his paw, which was all swollen and bleeding, and Androcles found that a huge thorn had got into it, and was causing all the pain. He pulled out the thorn and bound up the paw of the Lion, who was soon able to rise and lick the hand of Androcles like a dog. Then the Lion took Androcles to his cave, and every day used to bring him meat from which to live. But shortly afterwards both Androcles and the Lion were captured, and the slave was sentenced to be thrown to the Lion, after the latter had been kept without food for several days. The Emperor and all his Court came to see the spectacle, and Androcles was led out into the middle of the arena. Soon the Lion was let loose from his den, and rushed bounding and roaring towards his victim. But as soon as he came near to Androcles he recognized his friend, and fawned upon him, and licked his hands like a friendly dog. The Emperor, surprised at this, summoned Androcles to him, who told him the whole story. Whereupon the slave was pardoned and freed, and the Lion let loose to his native forest.

### How to Analyze a Plot

Ask these questions to divide the events in a story into the five main parts of the plot.

1. Which part of the story tells you *who, what, where,* and *when*? That is the **exposition**—the basic situation that sets up the story.

2. When do we learn what the conflict is? What events make it build in intensity? This part of the story is the **rising action**.

3. What is the most exciting moment in the story? Ask yourself, *Is this the point in the story when the main character wins or loses? Lives or dies?* This decisive moment is the **climax**.

4. When does the conflict start to wind down after the climax? This part of the story is the **falling action**.

5. When is the conflict finally resolved? When do we learn how all the loose ends are tied up? This is the **resolution**.

**Classify** Divide the events in the fable into the five main parts of a plot.

**Exposition:**

**Rising Action:**


**Climax:**

**Falling Action:**


**Resolution:**

*while reading your anchor book*

As you read this excerpt from a novel, pay attention to how the plot develops. *Guiding Question:* **Is there a winner in the conflict between Waverly and her mother? Why or why not?**

# RULES of the GAME

## From *The Joy Luck Club* by Amy Tan

**Background** *"Rules of the Game" is one of the stories in* The Joy Luck Club, *a novel that weaves together the tales of four Chinese immigrant mothers and their American-born daughters. In this excerpt from the opening story, the narrator, Waverly Jong, becomes a national chess champion. She defeats many opponents but discovers that her biggest struggle is with her own mother.*

## Vocabulary Builder

**Before you read,** *you will discuss the following words. In the Vocabulary Builder box in the margin, use a vocabulary building strategy to make the words your own.*

**benefactor    ancestral    adversaries    obscured**

**As you read,** *draw a box around unfamiliar words you could add to your vocabulary. Use context clues to unlock their meaning.*

### Marking the Text

**Plot**

**As you read,** *underline the story's most important events. In the margin, jot down brief notes about the importance of these events to the plot.*

My older brother Vincent was the one who actually got the chess set. We had gone to the annual Christmas party held at the First Chinese Baptist Church at the end of the alley. The missionary ladies had put together a Santa bag of gifts donated by members of another church. None of the gifts had names on them. There were separate sacks for boys and girls of different ages.

One of the Chinese parishioners had donned a Santa Claus costume and a stiff paper beard with cotton balls glued to it. I think the only children who thought he was the real thing were too young to know that Santa Claus was not Chinese. When my turn came up, the Santa man asked me how old I was. I thought it was a trick question: I was seven according to the American formula and eight by the Chinese calendar. I said I was born on March 17, 1951. That seemed to satisfy him. He then solemnly asked if I had been a very, very good girl this year and did I believe in Jesus Christ and obey my parents. I knew the only answer to that. I nodded back with equal solemnity.

Having watched the other children opening their gifts, I already knew that the big gifts were not necessarily the nicest ones. One girl my age got a large coloring book of biblical characters, while a less greedy girl who selected a smaller box received a glass vial of lavender toilet water. The sound of the box was also important. A ten-year-old boy had chosen a box that jangled when he shook it. It was a tin globe of the world with a slit for inserting money. He must have thought it was full of dimes and nickels, because when he saw that it had just ten pennies, his face fell with such undisguised disappointment that his mother slapped the side of his head and led him out of the church hall, apologizing to the crowd for her son who had such bad manners he couldn't appreciate such a fine gift.

As I peered into the sack, I quickly fingered the remaining presents, testing their weight, imagining what they contained. I chose a heavy, compact one that was wrapped in shiny silver foil and red satin ribbon. It was a twelve-pack of Life Savers and I spent the rest of the party arranging and rearranging the candy tubes in the order of my favorites. My brother Winston chose wisely as well. His present turned out to be a box of intricate plastic parts; the instructions on the box proclaimed that when they were properly assembled he would have an authentic miniature replica of a World War II submarine. Vincent got the chess set, which would have been a very decent present to get at a church Christmas party, except it was obviously used and, as we discovered later, it was missing a black pawn and a white knight. My mother graciously thanked the unknown **benefactor,** saying, "Too good. Cost too much." At which point, an old lady with fine white, wispy hair nodded toward our family and said with a whistling whisper, "Merry, merry Christmas."

When we got home, my mother told Vincent to throw the chess set away. "She not want it. We not want it," she said, tossing her head stiffly to the side with a tight, proud smile. My brothers had deaf ears. They were already lining up the chess pieces and reading from the dog-eared[1] instruction book. I watched Vincent

---

[1] **dog-eared** *adj.* worn or shabby from overuse.

## Vocabulary Builder

**benefactor**
(ben´ə fak´tər ) *n.*

**Meaning**

and Winston play during Christmas week. The chessboard seemed to hold elaborate secrets waiting to be untangled. The chessmen were more powerful than old Li's magic, herbs that cured **ancestral** curses. And my brothers wore such serious faces that I was sure something was at stake that was greater than avoiding the tradesmen's door to Hong Sing's.

"Let me! Let me!" I begged between games when one brother or the other would sit back with a deep sigh of relief and victory, the other annoyed, unable to let go of the outcome. Vincent at first refused to let me play, but when I offered my Life Savers as replacements for the buttons that filled in for the missing pieces, he relented. He chose the flavors: wild cherry for the black pawn and peppermint for the white knight. Winner could eat both.

As our mother sprinkled flour and rolled out small doughy circles for the steamed dumplings that would be our dinner that night, Vincent explained the rules, pointing to each piece. "You have sixteen pieces and so do I. One king and queen, two bishops, two knights, two castles, and eight pawns. The pawns can only move forward one step, except on the first move. Then they can move two. But they can only take men by moving crossways like this, except in the beginning, when you can move ahead and take another pawn."

"Why?" I asked as I moved my pawn. "Why can't they move more steps?"

"Because they're pawns," he said.

"But why do they go crossways to take other men? Why aren't there any women and children?"

"Why is the sky blue? Why must you always ask stupid questions?" asked Vincent. "This is a game. These are the rules. I didn't make them up. See. Here. In the book." He jabbed a page with a pawn in his hand. "Pawn. P-A-W-N. Pawn. Read it yourself."

## Vocabulary Builder

**ancestral**
(an ses´trəl) *adj.*

**Meaning**

---

*Marking the Text*

---

▼ **Good to Know!**
Chess is the oldest skill game in the world. The invention of chess has been credited to India, China, and Iran.

*a small weekend crowd of Chinese*
*... and tourists would gather*
*my mother would join the crowds*

My mother patted the flour off her hands. "Let me see book," she said quietly. She scanned the pages quickly, not reading the foreign English symbols, seeming to search deliberately for nothing in particular.

"This American rules," she concluded at last. "Every time people come out from foreign country, must know rules. You not know, judge say, Too bad, go back. They not telling you why so you can use their way, go forward. They say, Don't know why, you find out yourself. But they knowing all the time. Better you take it, find out why yourself." She tossed her head back with a satisfied smile.

I found out about all the whys later. I read the rules and looked up all the big words in a dictionary. I borrowed books from the Chinatown library. I studied each chess piece, trying to absorb the power each contained.

I learned about opening moves and why it's important to control the center early on; the shortest distance between two points is straight down the middle. I learned about the middle game and why tactics between two **adversaries** are like clashing ideas; the one who plays better has the clearest plans for both attacking and getting out of traps. I learned why it is essential in the endgame to have foresight, a mathematical understanding of all possible moves, and patience; all weaknesses and advantages become evident to a strong adversary and are **obscured** to a tiring opponent. I discovered that for the whole game one must gather invisible strengths and see the endgame before the game begins.

I also found out why I should never reveal "why" to others. A little knowledge withheld is a great advantage one should store for future use. That is the power of chess. It is a game of secrets in which one must show and never tell.

I loved the secrets I found within the sixty-four black and white squares. I carefully drew a handmade chessboard and pinned it to the wall right next to my bed, where at night I would stare for hours at imaginary battles. Soon I no longer lost any games or Life Savers, but I lost my adversaries. Winston and Vincent decided they were more interested in roaming the streets after school in their Hopalong Cassidy[2] cowboy hats.

On a cold spring afternoon, while walking home from school, I detoured through the playground at the end of our alley. I saw a group of old men, two seated across a folding table playing a game of chess, others smoking pipes, eating peanuts, and watching. I ran home and grabbed Vincent's chess set, which was bound in a cardboard box with rubber bands. I also carefully selected

---

[2] **Hopalong Cassidy** fictional cowboy hero originally featured in books and later in movies, television and radio shows, and comic books during the late 1940s and 1950s.

**Vocabulary Builder**

**adversaries**
(ad´vər ser´ēz) n.

**Meaning**


**obscured**
(əb skyoor´d) v.

**Meaning**

*Marking the Text*

while reading your anchor book

while reading your anchor book

two prized rolls of Life Savers. I came back to the park and approached a man who was observing the game.

"Want to play?" I asked him. His face widened with surprise and he grinned as he looked at the box under my arm.

"Little sister, been a long time since I play with dolls," he said, smiling benevolently.[3] I quickly put the box down next to him on the bench and displayed my retort.

Lau Po, as he allowed me to call him, turned out to be a much better player than my brothers. I lost many games and many Life Savers. But over the weeks, with each diminishing roll of candies, I added new secrets. Lau Po gave me the names. The Double Attack from the East and West Shores. Throwing Stones on the Drowning Man. The Sudden Meeting of the Clan. The Surprise from the Sleeping Guard. The Humble Servant Who Kills the King. Sand in the Eyes of Advancing Forces. A Double Killing Without Blood.

There were also the fine points of chess etiquette.[4] Keep captured men in neat rows, as well-tended prisoners. Never announce "Check" with vanity, lest someone with an unseen sword slit your throat. Never hurl pieces into the sandbox after you have lost a game, because then you must find them again, by yourself, after apologizing to all around you. By the end of the summer, Lau Po had taught me all he knew, and I had become a better chess player.

A small weekend crowd of Chinese people and tourists would gather as I played and defeated my opponents one by one. My mother would join the crowds during these outdoor exhibition games. She sat proudly on the bench, telling my admirers with proper Chinese humility, "Is luck."

A man who watched me play in the park suggested that my mother allow me to play in local chess tournaments. My mother smiled graciously, an answer that meant nothing. I desperately

---

[3] **benevolently** (bə nev′ə lənt lē) adv. kindly; charitably.

[4] **etiquette** (et′i kit) n. proper behavior.

wanted to go, but I bit back my tongue. I knew she would not let me play among strangers. So as we walked home I said in a small voice that I didn't want to play in the local tournament. They would have American rules. If I lost, I would bring shame on my family.

"Is shame you fall down nobody push you," said my mother.

During my first tournament, my mother sat with me in the front row as I waited for my turn. I frequently bounced my legs to unstick them from the cold metal seat of the folding chair. When my name was called, I leapt up. My mother unwrapped something in her lap. It was her chang, a small tablet of red jade which held the sun's fire. "Is luck," she whispered, and tucked it into my dress pocket. I turned to my opponent, a fifteen-year-old boy from Oakland. He looked at me, wrinkling his nose.

As I began to play, the boy disappeared, the color ran out of the room, and I saw only my white pieces and his black ones waiting on the other side. A light wind began blowing past my ears. It whispered secrets only I could hear.

"Blow from the South," it murmured. "The wind leaves no trail." I saw a clear path, the traps to avoid. The crowd rustled. "Shhh! Shhh!" said the corners of the room. The wind blew stronger. "Throw sand from the East to distract him." The knight came forward ready for the sacrifice. The wind hissed, louder and louder. "Blow, blow, blow. He cannot see. He is blind now. Make him lean away from the wind so he is easier to knock down."

"Check," I said, as the wind roared with laughter. The wind died down to little puffs, my own breath.

My mother placed my first trophy next to a new plastic chess set that the neighborhood Tao society[5] had given to me. As she wiped each piece with a soft cloth, she said, "Next time win more, lose less."

"Ma, it's not how many pieces you lose," I said. "Sometimes you need to lose pieces to get ahead."

---

[5] **Tao society** a group that believes in Taoism, a major Chinese religion and philosophy that stresses simplicity, acceptance, and freedom from desire.

Learning About Plot **119**

"Better to lose less, see if you really need."

At the next tournament, I won again, but it was my mother who wore the triumphant grin.

"Lost eight piece this time. Last time was eleven. What I tell you? Better off lose less!" I was annoyed, but I couldn't say anything.

I attended more tournaments, each one farther away from home. I won all games, in all divisions. The Chinese bakery downstairs from our flat displayed my growing collection of trophies in its window, amidst the dust-covered cakes that were never picked up. The day after I won an important regional tournament, the window encased a fresh sheet cake with whipped-cream frosting and red script saying "Congratulations, Waverly Jong, Chinatown Chess Champion." Soon after that, a flower shop, headstone engraver, and funeral parlor offered to sponsor me in national tournaments. That's when my mother decided I no longer had to do the dishes. Winston and Vincent had to do my chores.

"Why does she get to play and we do all the work," complained Vincent. "Is new American rules," said my mother. "Meimei[6] play, squeeze all her brains out for win chess. You play, worth squeeze towel."

By my ninth birthday, I was a national chess champion. I was still some 429 points away from grand-master status, but I was touted[7] as the Great American Hope, a child prodigy[8] and a girl to boot. They ran a photo of me in Life magazine next to a quote in which Bobby Fischer[9] said, "There will never be a woman grand master." "Your move, Bobby," said the caption.

The day they took the magazine picture I wore neatly plaited braids clipped with plastic barrettes trimmed with rhinestones. I was playing in a large high school auditorium that echoed with phlegmy coughs and the squeaky rubber knobs of chair legs sliding across freshly waxed wooden floors. Seated across from me was an American man, about the same age as Lau Po, maybe fifty. I remember that his sweaty brow seemed to weep at my every move. He wore a dark, malodorous[10] suit. One of his pockets was stuffed with a great white kerchief on which he wiped his palm before sweeping his hand over the chosen chess piece with great flourish.

In my crisp pink-and-white dress with scratchy lace at the neck, one of two my mother had sewn for these special occasions,

---

[6] **Meimei** (mā mā) Chinese for "little sister."

[7] **touted** (tout id) *v.* praised.

[8] **prodigy** (präd´ə jē) *n.* a person, often a child, with exceptional talent.

[9] **Bobby Fischer** American chess prodigy who became a grand master in 1958.

[10] **malodorous** (mal ō´dər əs ) *adj.* having a bad smell.

# Literature in Context
## Chinese Immigration

Chinese immigrants began coming to the United States in the middle of the nineteenth century. They came as the American West was being settled, and many hoped to make their fortune during the California Gold Rush. Most Chinese immigrants did not strike it rich and wound up doing hard manual labor. For example, Chinese immigrants did much of the work on the construction of the Transcontinental Railroad. In the late nineteenth century, Chinese immigrants faced discrimination from people who felt that the Chinese immigrants were taking jobs away from them. In response, Congress passed the Chinese Exclusion Act in 1882. This law drastically reduced Chinese immigration by preventing Chinese without family already in the United States from entering the country. In 1943, this law was repealed, and immigration expanded.

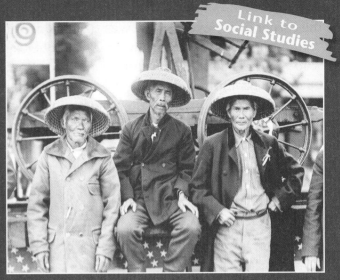

*Link to Social Studies*

**During the 1800s, many Chinese immigrants faced discrimination and hard manual labor.**

During the 1960s, Chinese Americans made significant strides as many entered the fields of medicine, law, politics, and business. Today, Chinese immigration continues to flourish, with most immigrants coming to the United States to pursue economic opportunities or greater freedom.

---

I would clasp my hands under my chin, the delicate points of my elbows poised lightly on the table in the manner my mother had shown me for posing for the press. I would swing my patent leather shoes back and forth like an impatient child riding on a school bus. Then I would pause, suck in my lips, twirl my chosen piece in midair as if undecided, and then firmly plant it in its new threatening place, with a triumphant smile thrown back at my opponent for good measure. I no longer played in the alley of Waverly Place. I never visited the playground where the pigeons and old men gathered. I went to school, then directly home to learn new chess secrets, cleverly concealed advantages, more escape routes.

But I found it difficult to concentrate at home. My mother had a habit of standing over me while I plotted out my games. I think she thought of herself as my protective ally. Her lips would be sealed tight, and after each move I made, a soft "Hmmmmph" would escape from her nose.

"Ma, I can't practice when you stand there like that," I said one day.

She retreated to the kitchen and made loud noises with the pots and pans. When the crashing stopped, I could see out of

*Marking the Text*

the corner of my eye that she was standing in the doorway. "Hmmmmph!" Only this one came out of her tight throat.

My parents made many concessions[11] to allow me to practice. One time I complained that the bedroom I shared was so noisy that I couldn't think. Thereafter, my brothers slept in a bed in the living room facing the street. I said I couldn't finish my rice; my head didn't work right when my stomach was too full. I left the table with half-finished bowls and nobody complained. But there was one duty I couldn't avoid. I had to accompany my mother on Saturday market days when I had no tournament to play. My mother would proudly walk with me, visiting many shops, buying very little. "This my daughter Wave-ly Jong," she said to whoever looked her way.

One day after we left a shop I said under my breath, "I wish you wouldn't do that, telling everybody I'm your daughter." My mother stopped walking. Crowds of people with heavy bags pushed past us on the sidewalk, bumping into first one shoulder, then another.

"Aiii-ya. So shame be with mother?" She grasped my hand even tighter as she glared at me.

I looked down. "It's not that, it's just so obvious. It's just so embarrassing."

"Embarrass you be my daughter?" Her voice was cracking with anger.

"That's not what I meant. That's not what I said."

"What you say?"

I knew it was a mistake to say anything more, but I heard my voice speaking, "Why do you have to use me to show off? If you want to show off, then why don't you learn to play chess?"

My mother's eyes turned into dangerous black slits. She had no words for me, just sharp silence.

I felt the wind rushing around my hot ears. I jerked my hand out of my mother's tight grasp and spun around, knocking into an old woman. Her bag of groceries spilled to the ground.

"Aii-ya! Stupid girl!" my mother and the woman cried. Oranges and tin cans careened[12] down the sidewalk. As my mother stooped to help the old woman pick up the escaping food, I took off.

I raced down the street, dashing between people, not looking back as my mother screamed shrilly, "Meimei! Meimei!" I fled down an alley, past dark, curtained shops and merchants washing the grime off their windows. I sped into the sunlight,

---

[11] **concessions** (kən sesh´əns) *n.* compromises.

[12] **careened** (kə rēn´d) *v.* swerved.

while reading your anchor book

into a large street crowded with tourists examining trinkets and souvenirs. I ducked into another dark alley, down another street, up another alley. I ran until it hurt and I realized I had nowhere to go, that I was not running from anything. The alleys contained no escape routes.

My breath came out like angry smoke. It was cold. I sat down on an upturned plastic pail next to a stack of empty boxes, cupping my chin with my hands, thinking hard. I imagined my mother, first walking briskly down one street or another looking for me, then giving up and returning home to await my arrival. After two hours, I stood up on creaking legs and slowly walked home.

The alley was quiet and I could see the yellow lights shining from our flat like two tiger's eyes in the night. I climbed the sixteen steps to the door, advancing quietly up each so as not to make any warning sounds. I turned the knob; the door was locked. I heard a chair moving, quick steps, the locks turning—click! click! click!—and then the door opened.

"About time you got home," said Vincent. "Boy, are you in trouble."

He slid back to the dinner table. On a platter were the remains of a large fish, its fleshy head still connected to bones swimming upstream in vain escape. Standing there waiting for my punishment, I heard my mother speak in a dry voice.

"We not concerning this girl. This girl not have concerning for us."

Nobody looked at me. Bone chopsticks clinked against the inside of bowls being emptied into hungry mouths.

I walked into my room, closed the door, and lay down on my bed. The room was dark, the ceiling filled with shadows from the dinnertime lights of neighboring flats.

In my head, I saw a chessboard with sixty-four black and white squares. Opposite me was my opponent, two angry black slits. She wore a triumphant smile. "Strongest wind cannot be seen," she said.

Her black men advanced across the plane, slowly marching to each successive level as a single unit. My white pieces screamed as they scurried and fell off the board one by one. As her men drew closer to my edge, I felt myself growing light. I rose up into the air and flew out the window. Higher and higher, above the alley, over the tops of tiled roofs, where I was gathered up by the wind and pushed up toward the night sky until everything below me disappeared and I was alone.

I closed my eyes and pondered my next move.

## Vocabulary Builder

**After you read,** *review the words you decided to add to your vocabulary. Write the meaning of words you have learned in context. Look up the other words in a dictionary, glossary, thesaurus, or electronic resource.*

## Amy Tan (B. 1952)

Born and raised in Oakland, California, and the child of Chinese parents, Amy Tan often writes about mother-daughter relationships. Specifically, she explores the cultural and generational conflicts that can arise between immigrant mothers and their American-born daughters. Tan wrote her first novel, *The Joy Luck Club* (1989), after she returned from a trip to China with her mother. The book became a bestseller and was made into a movie in 1993. Tan's other novels include *The Kitchen God's Wife* (1991), *The Bonesetter's Daughter* (2001), and *Saving Fish From Drowning* (2005).

# Thinking About the Selection

## *from* Rules of the Game *from* The Joy Luck Club

**Go Online**
**About the Author**
Visit: PHSchool.com
Web Code: exe-7204

**1** **Analyze** How does the plot develop? Fill in the diagram below, identifying the most important elements.

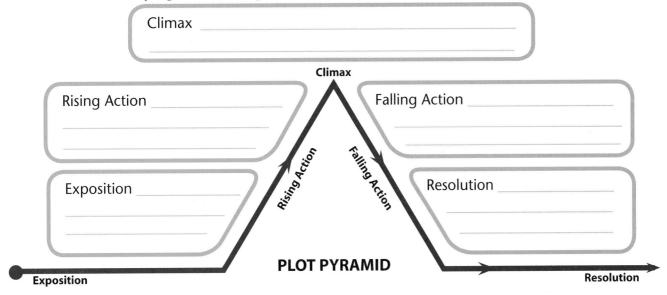

Climax _____

Rising Action _____

Falling Action _____

Exposition _____

Resolution _____

**Climax**

Rising Action

Falling Action

**PLOT PYRAMID**

Exposition

Resolution

**2** **Interpret** What realization does Waverly come to by the end of the story? Does this realization resolve the conflict? Explain.

_____

_____

_____

**3** **Interpret** An **analogy** is a comparison that clarifies something unfamiliar by comparing it to something familiar. Explain the analogy in this story. How does the title of the story help convey this analogy?

_____

_____

_____

**Write** Answer the following questions in your Reader's Journal.

**4** **Interpret** Is there a winner in the conflict between Waverly and her mother? Why or why not?

**5** **Predict** Think about the main conflict in your Anchor Book. How realistic is it? How do you think it will be resolved? Explain your prediction.

# 2-6 Literary Analysis
## Flashback

You are watching a movie and the picture starts to fade—and suddenly you are seeing an event from a character's past. This is a **flashback**.

## Literary Terms

A **flashback** is a scene in a narrative that takes the reader back in time to an event that happened before the story began. A flashback can be a memory of one particular character or it can be a retelling of an event by the narrator or author. Good writers use flashback carefully. Since a flashback interrupts the sequence of the plot, too many flashbacks make a story difficult to follow.

An author may use a flashback for any of these reasons.

| Reason | Example | What It Shows |
| --- | --- | --- |
| to explain why a character acts a certain way | a girl flashing back to a happy time with her grandmother | shows why the character is fighting to improve nursing homes |
| to show how a situation developed | a flashback to a car breaking down on the side of the road | shows how the characters got stranded in a strange place |
| to present information that cannot be shown in other ways | a man flashing back to scenes from different times in his childhood | shows how the character's personality developed over time |

A flashback breaks the order in which the story is told and introduces new details. Something in present time will cause the character to have a flashback, which is often viewed through a character's memory.

**With a Partner**
Insert a flashback in the sentences below.

Harold walked to the store thinking about his plans for tomorrow. The noise of evening traffic interrupted his thoughts. He looked across the street and saw Rita.

**Directions** Read the passage. Notice the details a student underlined about flashback and the notes she wrote in the margin. Then answer the questions that follow.

**Student Model: Marking the Text**

<u>Maricela hugged the blanket to her chest. It was one of the few things she had from her childhood and homeland</u>. The fierce bright geometric pattern had grown dull and soft with age. She held the blanket to her face and breathed in deeply. <u>She is six again, back in the Philippines</u>, running barefoot along a dusty road with her cousins. The air <u>is</u> humid, and her thin dress <u>clings</u> to her small frame. She <u>stops</u> to catch her breath in the shade of the tamarind tree. The sweet fruit <u>hangs</u> in dusty pods that look like her grandmother's swollen fingers. She <u>pulls</u> off a pod and cracks the hard shell by rolling it between her palms. She gently <u>parts</u> the orange veins that surround the deep red fruit and bites down gently, the sweet stickiness filling her mouth.

*beginning of story = past tense*

*blanket makes Maricela remember—*

*triggers flashback*

*flashback begins here*

*flashback = present tense*

1 **Analyze** What information does the flashback provide? Why do you think the writer includes this flashback?

_____

_____

_____

2 **Evaluate** What details in the flashback tell you how much time has passed in the story?

_____

_____

3 **Analyze** How does the amount of detail told in the flashback indicate its affect in Maricela's life?

_____

_____

_____

# Foreshadowing

Have you ever been in the middle of a story and just known that something bad was about to happen? Sometimes the writer gives clues about what will happen. These clues are known as **foreshadowing**.

## Literary Terms

**Foreshadowing** is the use of clues to hint at an event that will occur later in the narrative.

Authors use foreshadowing to create suspense and help the reader predict what will happen next. Have you ever seen a shadow of something before you saw the thing itself? Foreshadowing is the shadow of an action that has not yet happened. Writers use setting details, dialogue, action, and comments by the narrator to foreshadow events to come.

### Group Activity

You are probably most familiar with foreshadowing clues from the movies. For example, a close-up shot of a rope appears, and later that rope is used for the hero's escape.

**Directions** You have started reading your Anchor Book. With your group members, look back at the first three pages of your Anchor Book. If you were going to film a movie about your Anchor Book, what details would you add to the beginning to help foreshadow events to come? Complete the chart with your group.

| Clue for Anchor Book | What They Foreshadow |
| --- | --- |
| | |

On a separate sheet of paper, rewrite the first page with your foreshadowing clues in brackets at the appropriate moments in the text.

**Directions** Read the following passage. Underline details that might foreshadow events to come. Then answer the questions that follow.

I arrived at the house just as it started to rain. The sky had turned yellowish brown, the color of an old bruise. The air was thick and strangely still. Two strips of masking tape in the shape of an *X* covered the doorbell, so I knocked—first timidly and then more insistently. No one answered. I took the crumpled newspaper ad out of my pocket and checked the address. Finally, a woman of about sixty opened the door. She looked at me suspiciously and then glanced at the sky. "Yes?"

"I came about the room. I tried to call but . . . "

"We have no room. Not any more. Go away, if you know what's good for you. I don't want any more trouble."

**1** **Predict** What do the details you underlined seem to foreshadow? Why?

_____

_____

_____

**2** **Respond** How do the details you underlined affect your reading of the passage?

_____

_____

**3** **Analyze** Choose one detail, and explain why it foreshadows what you think it does.

_____

_____

_____

**4** **Analyze** What words in the last sentence are an example of foreshadowing? Explain.

_____

_____

_____

In the following selection, the author uses flashback and foreshadowing. *Guiding Question:* **How does Clyde's mother resolve a conflict so that both she and her son can get what they want?**

# Trombones and Colleges

### by Walter Dean Myers

**Background** *The following selection is a chapter from the novel* Fast Sam, Cool Clyde, and Stuff. *The author, Walter Dean Myers, writes about the experience of modern teens growing up in his old neighborhood, Harlem, New York.*

## Vocabulary Builder

**Before you read,** *you will discuss the following words. In the Vocabulary Builder box in the margin, use a vocabulary building strategy to make the words your own.*

**commercial    nonchalant    colander**

**As you read,** *draw a box around unfamiliar words you could add to your vocabulary. Use context clues to unlock their meaning.*

## Marking the Text

### Flashback and Foreshadowing

**As you read,** *underline details that indicate flashback and foreshadowing. Write notes in the margin explaining how these techniques help develop the characters and the plot.*

It was a dark day when we got our report cards. The sky was full of gray clouds and it was sprinkling rain. I was over to Clyde's house and Gloria and Kitty were there. Sam probably would have been there too, only he had got a two-week job in the afternoons helping out at Freddie's. Actually he only did it so that his mother would let him be on the track team again. Sam and his mother had this little system going. He would do something good-doing and she'd let him do something that he wanted to.

Clyde's report card was on the kitchen table and we all sat around it like it was some kind of a big important document. I had got a pretty good report card and had wanted to show it off but I knew it wasn't the time. Clyde pushed the card toward me and I read it. He had all satisfactory remarks on the side labeled Personal Traits and Behavior. He had also received B's in music and art appreciation. But everything else was either a C or a D except mathematics. His mathematics mark was a big red F that had been circled. I don't know why they had to circle the F when it was the only red mark on the card. In the Teacher's Comments section someone had written that Clyde had "little ability to handle an academic program."

"A little ability is better than none," I said. No one said anything so I figured it probably wasn't the right time to try to cheer Clyde up.

I knew all about his switching from a **commercial** program to an academic program, but I really hadn't thought he'd have any trouble.

"I saw the grade adviser today. He said I should switch back to the commercial program." Clyde looked like he'd start crying any minute. His eyes were red and his voice was shaky. "He said that I had to take mathematics over and if I failed again or failed another required subject I couldn't graduate. The way it is now I'm going to have to finish up in the summer because I switched over."

"I think you can pass it if you really want to," Kitty said. Clyde's sister was so pretty I couldn't even look at her. If I did I started feeling funny and couldn't talk right. Sometimes I daydreamed about marrying her.

Just then Clyde's mother came in and she gave a quick look at Kitty. "Hi, young ladies and young gentlemen." Mrs. Jones was a kind of heavy woman but she was pretty, too. You could tell she was Kitty's mother if you looked close. She put her package down and started taking things out. "I heard you people talking when I first came in. By the way you hushed up I guess you don't want me to hear what you were talking about. I'll be out of your way in a minute, soon as I put the frozen foods in the refrigerator."

"I got my report card today," Clyde said. His mother stopped taking the food out and turned toward us. Clyde pushed the report card about two inches toward her. She really didn't even have to look at the card to know that it was bad. She could have told that just by looking at Clyde. But she picked it up and looked at it a long time. First she looked at one side and then the other and then back at the first side again.

"What they say around the school?" she asked, still looking at the card.

"They said I should drop the academic course and go back to the other one." I could hardly hear Clyde, he spoke so low.

"Well, what you going to do, young man?" She looked up at Clyde and Clyde looked up at her and there were tears in his eyes

Vocabulary Builder

**commercial**
(kə mʉr'shəl) *adj.*

**Meaning**

Flashback and Foreshadowing **131**

and I almost started crying. I can't stand to see my friends cry. "What are you going to do, Mr. Jones?"

"I'm—I'm going to keep the academic course," Clyde said. "You think it's going to be any easier this time?" Mrs. Jones asked.

"No."

"Things ain't always easy. Lord knows that things ain't always easy." For a minute there was a faraway look in her eyes, but then her face turned into a big smile. "You're just like your father, boy. That man never would give up on anything he really wanted. Did I ever tell you the time he was trying to learn to play the trombone?"

"No." Clyde still had tears in his eyes but he was smiling, too. Suddenly everybody was happy. It was like seeing a rainbow when it was still raining.

"Well, we were living over across from St. Nicholas Park in this little rooming house. Your father was working on a job down on Varick Street that made transformers or some such nonsense—anyway, he comes home one day with this long package all wrapped up in brown paper. He walks in and sits it in the corner and doesn't say boo about what's in the bag. So at first I don't say anything either, and then I finally asks him what he's got in the bag, and he says, 'What bag?' Now this thing is about four feet long if it's an inch and he's asking *what* bag." Mrs. Jones wiped the crumbs from Gloria's end of the table with a quick swipe of the dish cloth, leaving a swirling pattern of tiny bubbles. Gloria tore off a paper towel and wiped the area dry.

"Now I look over at him and he's trying to be **nonchalant.** Sitting there, a grown man, and big as he wants to be and looking for all the world like somebody's misplaced son. So I says, 'The bag in the corner.' And he says, 'Oh, that's a trombone I'm taking back to the pawn shop[1] tomorrow.' Well, I naturally ask him what he's doing with it in the first place, and he says he got carried away and bought it but he realized that we really didn't have the thirty-five dollars to spend on foolishness and so he'd take it back the next day. And all the time he's sitting there scratching his chin and rubbing his nose and trying to peek over at me to see how I felt about it. I just told him that I guess he knew what was best. Only the next day he forgot to take it back, and the next day he forgot to take it back, and finally I broke down and told him why didn't he keep it. He said he would if I thought he should.

"So he unwraps this thing and he was just as happy with it as he could be until he tried to get a tune out of it. He couldn't get a sound out of it at first, but then he started oomping and woomping with the thing as best he could. He worked at it and worked at it and you could see he was getting disgusted. I think

## Vocabulary Builder

**nonchalant**
(nän′shə länt′) *adj.*

**Meaning**

---

[1] **pawn shop** (pôn′ shäp′) *n.* a shop where people sell items they own to raise money. Later they can buy back these items if they have not already been sold—but at a higher price.

he was just about to give it up when the lady who lived under us came upstairs and started complaining about the noise. It kept her Napoleon awake, she said. Napoleon was a dog. Little ugly thing, too. She said your father couldn't play, anyway.

"Well, what did she say that for? That man played that thing day and night. He worked so hard at that thing that his lips were too sore for him to talk right sometime. But he got the hang of it."

"I never remembered Pop playing a trombone," said Clyde.

"Well, your father had a streak in him that made him stick to a thing," she said, pouring some rice into a **colander** to wash it off, "but every year his goals got bigger and bigger and he had to put some things down so that he could get to others. That old trombone is still around here some place. Probably in one of them boxes under Kitty's bed. Now, you children, excuse me, young ladies and gentlemen, get on out of here and let me finish supper."

We all went into Clyde's living room.

"That was my mom's good-doing speech," Clyde said. "She gets into talking about what a great guy my father was and how I was like him and whatnot."

Marking the Text

## Vocabulary Builder

**colander**
(kul'ən dər) *n.*

**Meaning**

"You supposed to be like your father," Sam said. "He was the one that raised you, right?"

"She wants me to be like him, and I want to be like him, too, I guess. She wants me to keep on trying with the academic thing."

"What you want to do," Sam asked, "give it up?"

"No. Not really. I guess I want people like my mother to keep on telling me that I ought to do it, really. Especially when somebody tells me I can't do it."

"Boy," Sam said, sticking his thumbs in his belt and leaning back in the big stuffed chair, "you are just like your father."

Then we all went into Clyde's room and just sat around and talked for a while. Mostly about school and stuff like that, and I wanted to tell Clyde that I thought I could help him if he wanted me to. I was really getting good grades in school, but I thought that Clyde might get annoyed if I mentioned it. But then Gloria said that we could study together sometime and that was cool, too.

## Vocabulary Builder

**After you read,** review the words you decided to add to your vocabulary. Write the meaning of words you have learned in context. Look up the other words in a dictionary, glossary, thesaurus, or electronic resource.

## Walter Dean Myers (b. 1937)

Walter Dean Myers was born in West Virginia, but after his mother died, he grew up with foster parents in Harlem—the section of New York City where *Fast Sam, Cool Clyde, and Stuff* takes place. Myers began writing when he was in fifth grade. His teacher required each student to read aloud in front of the class. Because he had a speech impediment, Myers was dreading the experience. However, when his teacher said that students could read their own writing, he relaxed and did fine. Myers started writing poems, using only words he could pronounce, and never stopped writing.

When Myers won a picture-book contest in 1969, his career as an author for young adults and children took off. His most popular books include *Hoops* (1981), *Scorpions* (1988), *Monster* (1999), and *Bad Boy: A Memoir* (2001).

while reading your anchor book

# Thinking About the Selection

## Trombones and Colleges

Go Online

About the Author
Visit: PHSchool.com
Web Code: exe-7205

**1** **Apply** How does the first sentence of the selection foreshadow the results on Clyde's report card? Why is it a "dark day" for Clyde?

_____

_____

_____

**2** **Explain** Briefly describe the flashback in the story. Why do you think the author includes it?

_____

_____

_____

**3** **Infer** Why do you think the author titled this selection "Trombones and Colleges"?

_____

_____

_____

_____

**4** **Analyze** What point of view is used in the selection? How would the selection be different if it were told from Clyde's point of view?

_____

_____

_____

_____

**Write** Answer the following questions in your Reader's Journal.

**5** **Analyze** How does Clyde's mother resolve a conflict so that both she and her son can get what they want?

**6** **Evaluate** Find an example of flashback or foreshadowing in your Anchor Book. Explain its significance to the novel's plot and/or theme.

while reading your anchor book

# 2-7 Language Coach
## Grammar and Spelling

### Active and Passive Voice

A verb is active when its subject performs an action. Sentences written in the **active voice** are clear and easy to understand. The subject of the verb is also the subject of the sentence.

A verb is passive when its subject is acted upon. Sentences written in the **passive voice** have the person or thing doing the action hidden within a prepositional phrase.

**Go Online**

**Learn More**
**Visit: PHSchool.com**
**Web Code: exp-7201**

| Active Voice | Passive Voice |
|---|---|
| The catcher <u>dropped</u> the ball. | The ball <u>was dropped</u> by the catcher. |
| John <u>invented</u> the idea. | The idea <u>was invented</u> by John. |
| He <u>drove</u> the car. | The car <u>was driven</u> by him. |

**Directions** Read the passage, which is written in passive voice. Rewrite it in the active voice and then discuss with a partner which voice is the better choice and why.

> The baseball was thrown by Ian, and the bat was swung by Chester. Through the air toward Ernie's house the ball was flying. The sound of glass breaking was heard by the entire neighborhood. Ernie's living room window was smashed by their baseball. Chester and Ian were reprimanded by Ernie. After their conversation, the broken glass was swept into a pile by Ernie. The window was replaced by Chester and Ian.

**Author's Craft**

Most writing is done in active voice, but at times writers use passive voice to highlight the person or thing acted upon. Scan "Surfing's Dynamic Duo" on page 105. Find one example of active voice and passive voice in the passage. Explain why the voice is appropriate for each.

# Regular and Irregular Verbs

**Regular verbs** form their tenses in a predictable way. **Irregular verbs** do not follow any predictable patterns. It is important to remember these tenses to be able to use them correctly in your writing.

**Learn More**
Visit: PHSchool.com
Web Code: exp-7202

## Regular Verbs

| Present Tense | Present Participle | Past | Past Participle |
|---|---|---|---|
| land | (is) landing | landed | (had) landed |
| rain | (is) raining | rained | (had) rained |

## Irregular Verbs

| Present Tense | Present Participle | Past | Past Participle |
|---|---|---|---|
| know | (is) knowing | knew | (had) known |
| think | (is) thinking | thought | (had) thought |

**Directions** Rewrite each sentence in the tense indicated in parentheses.

**1** Some birds use spider webs and pieces of bark in their nests. (past)

**2** Sasha waited inside the school for her mom to pick her up. (present participle)

**3** I will bring binoculars with me. (past participle)

**Directions** The paragraph should be written in the past tense. Underline the verbs that are in the wrong tense and then rewrite the paragraph correctly.

**4**
> Jonathan is writing a letter to the editor of the local newspaper. He believed that the city should continue to recycle. The city is discussing eliminating recycling due to budgetary issues. Jonathan is thinking that a letter printed in the newspaper would be a great way to spread the news.

**Go Online**

**Learn More**
Visit: PHSchool.com
Web Code: exp-7203

# Verb Tenses

The **tense** of a verb shows time. **Present tense** action takes place now, while **past tense** action took place in the past. **Future tense** action will happen in the future and uses the helping verbs *will* and *shall*. Notice that the form of the verb is modified to reflect grammatical information such as gender, tense, number, or person.

| | |
|---|---|
| **Present tense** | I *sleep* in a tent. |
| **Past tense** | I *slept* in a tent last night. |
| **Future tense** | I *will sleep* in a tent tomorrow. |

**Perfect tenses** show completed action by combining a form of the helping verb *have* with the past participle form of the verb.

| Tense | Expresses Action | Helping Verbs | Example |
|---|---|---|---|
| **Present Perfect** | happened in the past and may still be happening | have, has | Dan <u>has grown</u> a lot. |
| **Past Perfect** | happened before another past action | had | I <u>had thought</u> so. |
| **Future Perfect** | will be finished before a stated time in the future | will have, shall have | By then, it <u>will have been</u> too late. |

Generally writers use one verb tense—a dominant one—throughout a work. Verb tenses show when events happened in relation to one another.

**Directions** Read the paragraph below. Underline all verbs and circle the dominant verb tense.

**1**    Gary built the box for my ant farm. An ant farm shows a community of ants. Ants work very hard. An ant farm is a good way to learn about their community. Tomorrow I will display my ant farm.

        past                present              future

**Directions** Read the paragraph. Replace each underlined word with the form of the word in the parentheses. Cross out the original word and write the new one above it.

**2** Last Saturday, we <u>wash</u> (past tense) cars for charity. The charity <u>needed</u> (present tense) our help again. Next week we <u>did</u> (future tense) it again. We <u>tried</u> (future tense) to raise even more money. I just <u>think</u> (past tense) up a new plan for next week. Super Grocer <u>give</u> (past tense) us permission to wash cars in its parking lot. There <u>are</u> (future tense) hundreds of cars for us to wash then!

**Directions** Complete the table by writing examples for the verb *act*.

| Tense | Helping Verb + Past Participle | Sentence |
|---|---|---|
| Present perfect | | |
| Past perfect | | |
| Future perfect | | |

**Directions** Write *present perfect, past perfect,* or *future perfect* to show the tense of each underlined verb.

**3** We <u>will have learned</u> about southwestern Native Americans.

_____

**4** Navajo and Apaches <u>had lived</u> in the Southwest for hundreds of years.

_____

**5** Arrowheads and other relics <u>have told</u> us about this early life.

_____

**6** Spaniards <u>have played</u> a part in Native American life.

_____

# 2-8 Writer's Workshop
## Narration: Short Story

A work of fiction does not need to be long to be meaningful and engaging. In a few pages, a writer can create exciting, dramatic moments that will leave a lasting impression with a reader. A **short story** is a brief, creative, fictional narrative that usually deals with a central character engaged in some form of conflict. Follow the steps outlined in this workshop to write your own short story about an interesting or original situation.

**Purpose** To write a short story about an interesting or original situation

**Audience** You, your teacher, and your classmates

To be effective, your short story should include the following elements.

▶ One or more well-developed characters

▶ A clear conflict that keeps the reader asking, "What will happen next?"

▶ Effective pacing and a strong plot

▶ Use of vivid language to create interesting characters and setting

▶ Precise vocabulary and error-free grammar, including correct use of verbs and verb tenses

## Prewriting—Plan It Out

To choose the people and action of your story, use these steps.

**Choose your topic.** Use the "What If?" method to get started. Fill in the blanks of a sentence such as the one shown here.

> **What if <u>Daniel</u> (name a person) suddenly <u>got a flat tire on his bike</u> (describe a problem)?**

**Identify a conflict.** Ask yourself questions about the characters that help you identify whether the conflict is internal or external. Use the graphic organizer to help you.

| What does the narrator want? | ⟹ | |
|---|---|---|

| What might get in the character's way? | ⟹ | |
|---|---|---|

| What type of conflict is this? | ⟹ | |
|---|---|---|

**Gather details.** Compile details using these steps.

1. Quickly list everything that comes to mind about a general idea related to your story.

2. Circle the most interesting item on the list and create another list of everything that comes to mind about it.

3. Generate several lists, and look for connections among the circled items. These connections will help you decide which details to include in your story.

**Create the plot.** Use a plot pyramid like the one in Lesson 5 to jot down ideas. Alternatively, you could develop your plot using a story map. Choose the organizational tool that best matches your style.

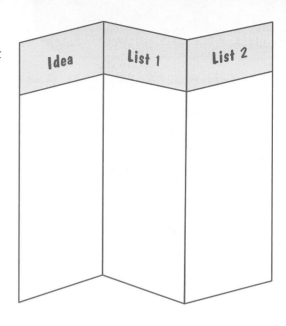

## Drafting—Get It on Paper

Using your plot pyramid as an outline, write your first draft.

**Use literary elements and devices.** Create a strong setting through descriptive words and phrases. Use foreshadowing to create suspense or flashback to provide character motivation. Create strong descriptions and tone by using figurative language.

**Provide elaboration.** Use varied sentence structure to reveal what your characters look like, how they act, and what they think. Develop the setting by incorporating important aspects of the character's environment.

**Enhance your style and tone.** Include effectively developed and complex characters. Rather than telling readers how the characters feel, show how they feel through their gestures, movements, expressions and dialogue.

**Student Model: Show, Don't Tell**

> gripped my father's pendant for reassurance, clenching the jade cross and
> I ~~reassured myself,~~ willing myself to be strong.
>   ^

The writer chooses words that show rather than tell the character's feelings.

**Maintain a consistent point of view and tone.** Decide whether you want your narrator to be a participant or observer of the story. Keep the point of view consistent throughout your story.

Look back at the excerpt "Trombones and Colleges" by Walter Dean Myers in Lesson 2-6. Find sentences in which Myers uses concrete word choices to show how his characters feel and to develop his own voice as a writer. Use these examples as a model for your own writing.

## Revising—Making It Better

Develop clear relationships among your ideas by rearranging paragraphs, sentences, and words. Delete any details that do not match or are inconsistent with your purpose.

**Peer Review** Read your short story aloud to a partner and get feedback. Revise to achieve the reaction and mood you had intended.

**Directions** Read this student short story as a model for your own.

**Student Model: Writing**

**Student Model**
Visit: PHSchool.com
Web Code: exr-7201

*KC Marker, Portland, OR*

### The Leaky Boat

It was a cold September evening. My linen cuffs flapped uncontrollably in a biting wind baring its white teeth of snow. The sun had long since set, and all was quiet on the sea. A cool mist had settled around the bay, sending a sharp chill down my spine. I continued to row; I had seen worse. I could still hear the voice ringing through my head:

"This is it, son. Either you're ready or you're not."

I was ready. . . . I gripped my father's pendant for reassurance, clenching the jade cross and willing myself to be strong. I was ready.

No one dared go out on such a night. Tonight was Friday—the 13th. I was the only one traveling the waters, or so I thought. . . .

Now, I had survived many a boating trip before, but what happened next would become a remarkable memory for the rest of my life.

As I shifted in my seat I could feel it. . . . Rushing water all around me—a storm! It had come slowly at first.

I had not thought much of it, but now it was at its nastiest, and I was in the middle of it! . . . I was violently thrown back and forth in my boat! I turned to the side. How close was I to the rocky shore? . . .

As I struggled to keep upright, a massive wave came up from behind, plunging me into the water. I swam with all my strength to the surface, taking in a big breath of air, and holding tight to my father's pendant.

Descriptive language sets the scene for the story.

The story has a consistent first-person point of view. Readers learn about the narrator from what he thinks and experiences.

The writer develops suspense by foreshadowing something dangerous.

The varied sentence structure makes the pacing of the story's conflict suspenseful.

Vivid details and tension make the reader want to know what is going to happen next.

# Editing—Be Your Own Language Coach

Review your draft for language convention errors. Pay special attention to your use of active and passive voice, regular and irregular verbs, and verb tenses.

# Publishing—Share It!

When you publish a work, you produce it for a special audience. Consider one of the following ideas to share your writing.

**Submit your story.** Offer your story to a school literary magazine, a national publication, an online journal, or a contest.

**Give a reading.** Read your story aloud to your class, to an adult, or to a group.

# Reflecting on Your Writing

**1** On a separate sheet of paper, answer the following questions and hand it in with your final draft. What new insights did you gain about writing a short story? What did you do well? What do you need to work on?

**2** **Rubric for Self-Assessment** Assess your short story. For each question, circle a rating.

| CRITERIA | RATING SCALE | | | | |
|---|---|---|---|---|---|
| | NOT VERY | | | | VERY |
| **IDEAS** How compelling are your plot, characters, setting, and theme? | 1 | 2 | 3 | 4 | 5 |
| **ORGANIZATION** How well is your story organized? How clear and developed are your conflict and climax? | 1 | 2 | 3 | 4 | 5 |
| **VOICE** How well do you set a tone and tell the story in an engaging way? | 1 | 2 | 3 | 4 | 5 |
| **WORD CHOICE** How appropriate is the language for your audience? | 1 | 2 | 3 | 4 | 5 |
| **SENTENCE FLUENCY** How varied is your sentence structure? | 1 | 2 | 3 | 4 | 5 |
| **CONVENTIONS** How correct is your grammar, especially your use of verbs and verb tenses? | 1 | 2 | 3 | 4 | 5 |

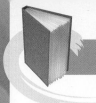

# 2-9 Discussing Your Anchor Book
## Literature Circles

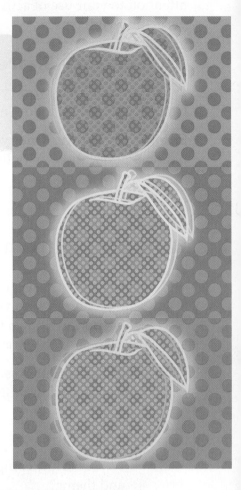

**Connecting to Real Life** Today, your group members will begin with an open discussion, then connect the characters, events, and ideas in your Anchor Book to experiences in real life.

## PART 1: Open Discussion

Begin your open discussion sharing your thoughts, opinions, and questions about your Anchor Book. Use your Reader's Journal and follow-up questions to get group members to elaborate on and support their ideas. If you need help starting your discussion, talk about predictions you made, revised, and verified as you read your Anchor Book. Identify passages that support your predictions.

## PART 2: Discuss—Connecting to Real Life

Just as novelists often draw upon real-life people and events, readers can often relate a novel to their own lives. Select two characters, events, or ideas from your Anchor Book, and tell what aspect of real life they resemble and how.

| Character, Event, or Idea From Your Anchor Book | Character, Event, or Idea From Real Life |
|---|---|
| | |

**How They Are Similar**

*(sidebar)* while reading your anchor book

After you have completed the organizer, share your comparisons with your group. Then discuss the following questions.

**1** **Compare** What connections were the most popular in your group: characters, events, or ideas? Why do you think this is?

_____
_____
_____
_____

**2** **Speculate** Based on what you have read in your Anchor Book, and what you know about its author, do you think the novel "imitates life"? Why or why not?

_____
_____
_____
_____

**3** **Evaluate** Do you think it matters whether the author drew from personal experience? Why or why not?

_____
_____
_____
_____

**4** **Analyze** Does race, religion, gender, wealth, or disabilities play an important role in your Anchor Book? If so, can you relate to any of the conflicts or challenges characters face regarding these issues?

_____
_____
_____
_____

## Reader-on-the-Street Interviews

Reporters frequently interview people on the street about issues that are important to everyone. A novel is like a reporter in that it also tries to connect its readers to issues that are important to everyone. With your Literature Circle, conduct a "reader-on-the-street" interview with one or more adults about why the characters, events, and themes of your Anchor Book are important to people today. Paraphrase their responses.

## Reading Skill: Making Predictions

Read the passage. Then answer the questions.

> *Well, this is a change,* thought Julia Sparks as she raced toward the school auditorium. Usually, she hated to see her name posted in public. This feeling dated back to the first grade when her teacher tried to control class behavior by scribbling names on the board.
>
> Julia pushed open the auditorium doors. A crowd of kids was bunched up in front of the bulletin board. Julia's stomach flipped. For most of her life, she had hated lists. Lists of "Students who have to retake the algebra test" . . . "Kids who need to stay after class" . . . "Players who are cut from the soccer team" . . . But, this was one list that Julia really, truly wanted to be on.
>
> Finally, Julia reached the crowd. One boy was pushing his way out of the throng, his eyes downcast. Up front, two kids were squealing with delight.
>
> Julia knew that her audition had gone well. She had memorized her lines and delivered them with expression. Even the director had told her that her singing was "brilliant." So, what was she waiting for? Julia took a deep breath and began elbowing her way to the front.

**1** From details in paragraph 1, readers can **predict** that this passage _____.

    **A.** provides factual information about classroom behavior

    **B.** describes something unusual that happens to Julia Sparks

    **C.** takes place in the home of Julia Sparks

    **D.** compares and contrasts first graders with high school students

**2** Which of the following BEST describes what readers might ask themselves after reading paragraph 2?

    **F.** What kind of doors does Julia push open?

    **G.** What kinds of lists does Julia hate?

    **H.** What kind of list does Julia want to see her name on?

    **J.** What kind of people are crowded in front of the bulletin board?

**3** On the lines below, make a prediction about what might happen next.

_____

_____

_____

_____

# Literary Analysis: Elements of a Novel

Read the passage. Then answer the questions.

> King Laius, the ruler of Thebes, asked the Delphic oracle about his future. It said that Laius's own son would kill him and marry his mother. Alarmed, Laius bound the baby's feet and left him to die on a mountain.
>
> But the boy did not die. Found by a herdsman, the boy—called Oedipus—was brought to King Polybus of Corinth. Polybus raised Oedipus himself. However, frightening news from another oracle reached Oedipus when he was an adult. This oracle said that he was destined to kill his own father, whom Oedipus believed to be King Polybus. Oedipus loved Polybus and had no intentions of ending the king's life. He left Corinth to keep from fulfilling the prophecy. On his journey, he met a band of travelers—King Laius and his men. A fight ensued, and Oedipus killed King Laius.
>
> Oedipus continued his travels, outwitting the Sphinx that had been plaguing Thebes. Welcomed by Thebes as a brave and clever man, Oedipus took King Laius's place by marrying the widowed queen—Oedipus' own mother.

**4** Which statement is part of the **exposition** of this passage?

    **A.** King Laius is the ruler of Thebes.

    **B.** Oedipus does not die on the mountain.

    **C.** Oedipus kills King Laius.

    **D.** Oedipus marries his mother.

**5** Which **foreshadows** King Laius' death?

    **F.** The Delphic oracle's prophecy.

    **G.** The king's leaving the baby to die.

    **H.** Oedipus' leaving Corinth so he can't kill Polybus.

    **J.** Oedipus' crossing paths with King Laius and his men.

**6** Which sentence contains the **climax** of the passage?

    **A.** "Laius bound the baby's feet and left him to die on a mountain."

    **B.** "He left Corinth."

    **C.** "Oedipus killed King Laius."

    **D.** "Oedipus took Laius's place."

**7** If you were to add a **flashback,** which of the following could you use?

    **F.** Oedipus thinks about the oracle.

    **G.** As he's dying, King Laius declares that Oedipus will meet his fate.

    **H.** King Laius remembers his life before the prophecy.

    **J.** Oedipus wonders whom he killed.

## Timed Writing: Climax

**Directions** Identify the climax in a book or story you have read. Describe the events or rising action leading up to the climax. Also, discuss the impact the climax had on the main character. (20 minutes)

# 2-10 Reading Skills
## Making Inferences

while reading your anchor book

In learning new reading skills, you will use special academic vocabulary. Knowing the right words will help you demonstrate your understanding.

### Academic Vocabulary

| Word | Meaning | Example Sentence |
|---|---|---|
| **infer** *v.* Related words: inferred, inference | to draw conclusions based on facts | I *inferred* from her frown that she was unhappy. |
| **assume** *v.* Related words: assumed, assumption | to suppose something to be a fact | We can *assume* that our class will start when the bell rings. |
| **conclude** *v.* Related words: concluded, conclusion | to decide by reasoning | After hearing his argument, I *concluded* that he was right. |

**Inferences** are the reasonable **conclusions** a person can form based on the evidence provided. When you make an inference you make an **assumption** based on the information provided and what you already know.

**Clues in the Text** + **Your Background Knowledge** = **Inference**

**Directions** Review the following example and fill in the chart with your own inference.

| Clues in the Text (It Says . . . ) | Your Background Knowledge (You Know . . . ) | Inference (And So . . . ) |
|---|---|---|
| After getting off a rollercoaster, a young man is clutching his stomach. | People who clutch their stomachs are in pain, and some people feel sick after they ride a rollercoaster. | The rollercoaster made the young man feel sick to his stomach. |
| A girl has opened a letter from an art school she applied to, and a smile comes across her face. | | |

**Directions** Read the following passage. Notice the details a student underlined. Then complete the graphic organizer to help you make an inference about the last detail she underlined.

**Student Model: Marking the Text**

Raymond was proud of having excelled in his math class all year. <u>He studied the day before each test and received scores that reflected his hard work.</u> However, the day before his last test, <u>Raymond went to his cousin's birthday party at an amusement park rather than study.</u> "Besides," he reasoned, "I know the math formulas pretty well." He had a blast riding the roller coasters and wished the park had stayed open all night. <u>But the next week, after his teacher returned his math test, Raymond wished that the amusement park had closed a lot earlier than it had.</u>

| Clues in the Text (It Says . . . ) | Your Background Knowledge (You Know . . . ) | Inference (And So . . . ) |
|---|---|---|
| does well because of studying<br><br>goes to the amusement park rather than studying<br><br>wished the park closed earlier | | |

**1**  **Analyze** What information was not provided in the text?

_____

_____

**2**  **Explain** How did you figure out the answer to the previous question?

_____

_____

_____

Remember that graphic organizers, like the chart above, can help you address confusion as you read.

Asking yourself questions can help you make inferences. As you read, ask yourself questions about important facts and details in the reading. A good reader is a good detective. He or she looks at the clues—facts and details—and considers what they mean.

## Partner Activity

Imagine that you and your partner are detectives analyzing clues in your Anchor Book. You have the facts and details from your Anchor Book, but what do they really mean?

**Directions** With your partner, look for clues in your Anchor Book. Use the Question Stem chart below to create specific questions and then see what inferences the facts and details lead you to make. Record the facts, details, and your inferences in the chart.

| Question Stems for Making Inferences About Novels |
| --- |
| A prediction is a kind of inference. <br> • What will [character] do? <br> • What would happen if [plot event]? |
| You can identify the importance and meaning of certain facts and details. <br> • What does [character's action] tell me about [him/her]? <br> • What might the central message or theme of the book be? How are characters, plot events, and setting details related to the theme? |

| Inferences About Our Anchor Book | Facts and Details That Support Them |
| --- | --- |
|  |  |
|  |  |
|  |  |
|  |  |

You are about to read a nonfiction article. Asking questions will help you make inferences about nonfiction, too. As you read, ask yourself, *What can I conclude from the facts and details in the text?*

Now, practice the skill making inferences on this science article. *Guiding Question*: **How can two people's different memories of the same situation lead to conflict?**

**Link to Science**

# What Are MEMORIES Made Of?

**Fast Fact**
Neurons, or brain cells, communicate with each other at speeds up to 270 miles per hour!

Do you think you have the memory of an elephant or a sieve? Can you recall the first day of kindergarten perfectly but remember nothing from last Thursday? If so, your memory is working just the way it should.

## Nerve Cells and Chemicals

Your brain has more than 100 billion nerve cells, called neurons. A neuron is made up of a cell body, plus fibers, or threads, that stretch outward from it. One fiber, the axon, carries signals away from the cell. Other nerve fibers, called dendrites, carry signals toward the cell.

When information about the world comes in through your five senses, the brain goes into action. Chemical messengers flood across certain neurons, making new connections between them.

When information is repeated, these chemical connections are reinforced, or made stronger. When that happens, the signals pass more quickly. This process is how your brain forms memories. A memory is the result of chemical changes in your neurons.

Experiments have shown the importance of chemicals in memory. In one experiment, a group of laboratory rats were given extra doses of a certain brain chemical. These rats learned a path through a maze to find food very quickly.

A second group of rats had a normal amount of the brain chemical. They had a much harder time learning the route. A third group of rats was not given any of the brain chemical. They were unable to learn or remember the route at all.

## Not Like a Computer

People sometimes compare the brain to a computer. A computer organizes information neatly in separate files. Nothing is ever forgotten. The human brain, however, is far more fallible, or likely to make mistakes. That is because the brain scatters its memories in many different places. One group of nerve cells is activated, or put to use, when we say certain types of words. Other groups let us remember different types of words. One group of neurons helps us see an object's color. Another group lets us remember the same object's use.

The brain is more creative than a computer. Often one piece of information can trigger many different groups of neurons. The smell of a certain food, for example, might cause you to remember a party where you ate that food. In your mind, you might also see the people at the party, or hear the music, or remember the gifts.

151

# Studying the Brain

Scientists use special machines to take pictures of the brain. At present, however, these machines cannot distinguish, or tell apart, the regions of the brain where different memories lie. They are too slow to catch the flash of chemicals racing across the brain's neurons. Much of what we know about memory, therefore, comes from patients with brain injuries.

When one part of the brain is injured, a person may lose part of his or her memory. By noting where the injury is and what kind of memory loss occurs, scientists can figure out what that part of the brain does.

One part of the brain is called the hippocampus. When it is damaged, patients cannot form new memories. They can remember everything that happened before their injury, but nothing that happens after the injury. Scientists think that the hippocampus is the "hub" of memory. That means that all new experiences must pass through the hippocampus in order to become memories.

Another small section of the brain is called the amygdala. When it is damaged, patients cannot recall emotions. That is, they cannot remember how they feel or have felt.

We all know how complicated our memories are. Even perfectly normal brains can play tricks on people. We might easily remember some useless bit of information from an old TV commercial. At the same time, we might forget a key fact or an important name that we really need to remember.

## Different Kinds of Memory

There are three major types of memory. **Short-term memory** lasts for only 15 or 20 seconds. That's just long enough to keep a telephone number in your mind as you dial it. Short-term memory is very handy. It keeps our brains from getting clogged up with information we no longer need. After all, you wouldn't want to remember every phone number you ever dialed for the rest of your life.

**Working memory** is a special type of short-term memory that lasts a little longer. Usually, it lasts as long as you need it. You might use it to work a math problem or to talk with friends. After the problem is solved or the conversation is over, you have a general memory of the experience, but can forget many of the details.

**Long-term memory** lasts a long time, perhaps for your entire lifetime. Your knowledge of language, important events in your life, and motor skills such as riding a bike are all part of your long-term memory.

> ## fast Fact
> Because the structure and function of a sheep's brain are similar to that of a human brain, scientists often study the brains of sheep to answer questions about human memory.

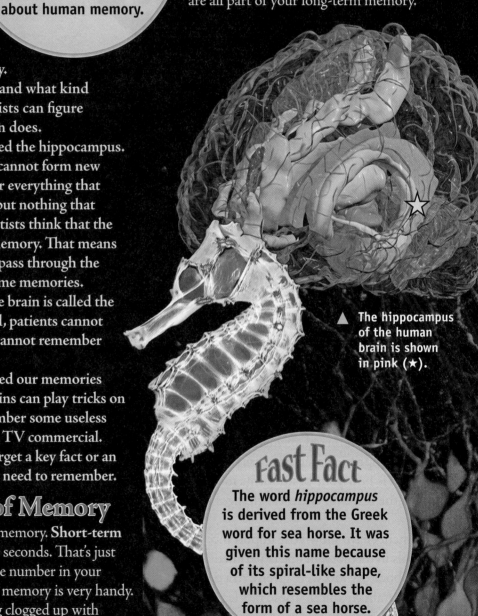

▲ The hippocampus of the human brain is shown in pink (★).

> ## fast Fact
> The word *hippocampus* is derived from the Greek word for sea horse. It was given this name because of its spiral-like shape, which resembles the form of a sea horse.

# Thinking About the Selection

## What Are Memories Made Of?

**1**   **Infer**  What can you infer about the regions of the brain where memories lie? Reread the first few sentences under the heading "Studying the Brain." Underline details that help support your answer.  Then complete the chart.

| Clues in the Text (It Says . . . ) | Your Background Knowledge (I Know . . . ) | Inference (And So . . . ) |
| --- | --- | --- |
| "Scientists use special machines to take pictures of the brain. At present, however, these machines cannot distinguish, or tell apart, the regions of the brain where different memories lie." | | |

**2**   **Conclude**  What can you conclude from the article about how scientists know where certain memories are stored?

_____

_____

_____

**3**   **Explain**  What do the idioms "memory like an elephant or a sieve" mean?

_____

_____

**Write**  Answer the following questions in your Reader's Journal.

**4**   **Analyze**  How can two people's different memories of the same situation lead to conflict?  Is there a clear winner in this conflict?

**5**   **Infer**  Select a passage from your Anchor Book and make an inference about a character or an event in the passage. What information led you to make your inference?

**Ready for a Free-Choice Book?**   *Your teacher may ask you if you would like to choose another book to read on your own. Select a book that fits your interest and that you'll enjoy. As you read, think about how your new book compares with your Anchor Book.*

# 2-11 Literary Analysis
## *Characterization*

In a novel or short story, a good author can create characters that are so real you almost feel as if you know them personally.

▲ **Character masks for Vietnamese water puppet plays**

## Literary Terms

▶ **Characterization** is the process by which the author reveals the personality of a character. There are two main methods of characterization.

- **Direct characterization** *tells* readers what the character's personality is.

  **Example** "Nathaniel was a hardworking, quiet boy."

- **Indirect characterization** shows things that reveal the character's personality. Use the mnemonic device STEAL to remember the five methods of indirect characterization.

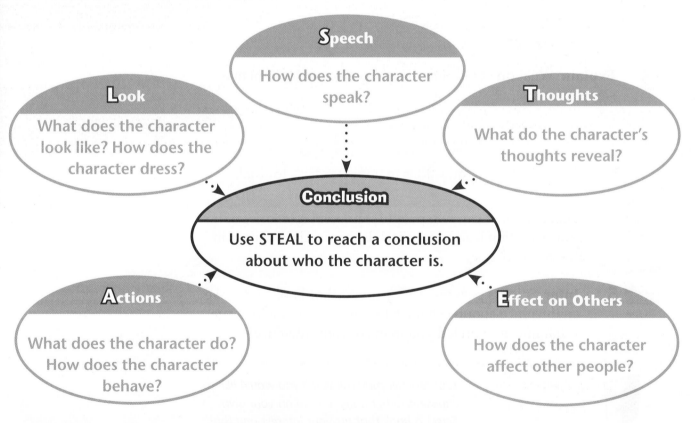

**S**peech
How does the character speak?

**L**ook
What does the character look like? How does the character dress?

**T**houghts
What do the character's thoughts reveal?

**Conclusion**
Use STEAL to reach a conclusion about who the character is.

**A**ctions
What does the character do? How does the character behave?

**E**ffect on Others
How does the character affect other people?

When a character changes, the author recalls those changes through **dynamic characterization.** When a character stays the same the author characterizes him/her the same way, through **static characterization.**

**Directions** Read the following passage. Underline details that reveal Mary's character traits, either directly or indirectly. Then, complete the STEAL device below it and answer the questions that follow.

**Go Online**

**About the Author**
Visit: PHSchool.com
Web Code: exe-7205

## from *The Secret Garden* by *Frances Hodgson Burnett*

When Mary Lennox was sent to Misselthwaite Manor to live with her uncle, everybody said she was the most disagreeable-looking child ever seen. It was true, too. She had a little thin face and a little thin body, thin light hair and a sour expression. Her hair was yellow, and her face was yellow because she had been born in India and had always been ill in one way or another. Her father had held a position under the English Government and had always been busy and ill himself, and her mother had been a great beauty who cared only to go to parties and amuse herself. . . . She had not wanted a little girl at all, and when Mary was born she handed her over to the care of an Ayah,[1] who was made to understand that . . . she must keep the child out of sight as much as possible. So when she was a sickly, fretful, ugly little baby she was kept out of the way, and when she became a sickly, fretful, toddling thing she was kept out of the way also. She never remembered seeing familiarly anything but . . . her Ayah and the other native servants, and as they always obeyed her and gave her her own way in everything, . . . by the time she was six years old she was as tyrannical and selfish a little pig as ever lived.

[1] **Ayah** (ä'yə) *n.* nursemaid in India.

Ellipsis points show us that unimportant text has been left out. When reading, skip over the dots and keep your reading rate steady.

**1** **Analyze** Using the mnemonic device STEAL, jot down observations about Mary Lennox. If part of the mnemonic device does not apply, write *none*.

**S**peech _____

**T**houghts _____

**E**ffect on others _____

**A**ctions _____

**L**ook _____

**2** **Draw Conclusions** What conclusion can you draw about Mary Lennox? Why do you think she behaves as she does?

_____

_____

_____

while reading your anchor book

Characterization **155**

# Understanding Irony

A woman comes home from a long day at work and finds the kitchen sink full of dirty dishes and her teenage son watching TV. "Thanks for cleaning up, honey!" she says cheerfully. "It's so nice to know I can always count on you to help out around the house." Is the woman truly pleased? Of course not! She is trying to make a point by being **ironic,** deliberately saying the opposite of what she really means.

## Literary Terms

**Irony** is a contrast or contradiction between appearance and reality, between what was expected and what actually happened, or between meaning and intention. There are three types of irony.

| Type of Irony | Definition | Example |
|---|---|---|
| Verbal Irony | A writer or character says something that is the opposite of what that person really means. | Your younger brother lets out an enormous burp at dinner, and you say, "I see you've been working on your table manners." |
| Situational Irony | Something happens that contradicts what the reader, a character, or the audience expects to happen. | A character's enemy ends up being the person who saves him when he gets trapped in a cave during a camping trip. |
| Dramatic Irony | The reader or audience knows something that a character does not. | The audience knows that a character in a movie is a liar, but his girlfriend believes everything he tells her. |

**Directions** Complete this chart with examples of each type of irony.

| Type of Irony | Example |
|---|---|
| Verbal Irony | |
| Situational Irony | |
| Dramatic Irony | |

**Directions** Read the cartoon, and then answer the questions that follow.

1   **Identify** What type of irony is the cartoon showing—verbal, dramatic, or situational?

_____

2   **Analyze** Explain why the cartoon is ironic.

_____

_____

_____

3   **Identify** What type of irony does each of the following show?

| A brave hero who has saved his kingdom from an invading army is afraid of the dark. | The narrator in a novel insists that she has gotten over her ex-boyfriend, but readers realize that she still loves him. |
|---|---|
| Type of irony: _____ | Type of irony: _____ |

4   **Apply** With a partner, choose one type of irony and an example of it. Present your example by writing about it, drawing a picture of it, or acting it out for an audience.

Read the following short story and examine how the author uses characterization and irony. *Guiding Question:* **How does the way Arturo intends to deal with any future conflicts in his life differ from the way his grandfather has dealt with conflicts in his life?**

**Background** *Born in Puerto Rico, Judith Ortiz Cofer moved with her family to Paterson, New Jersey, when she was a child. Her writing explores the Puerto Rican experience in America, as in this story about a teenage boy who reluctantly visits his grandfather in a nursing home. Abuelo is Spanish for "grandfather." (For English translations of other Spanish words that are not defined within the story, see "Literature in Context: Spanish Words," page 162.)*

## Vocabulary Builder

**Before you read,** *you will discuss the following words. In the Vocabulary Builder box in the margin, use a vocabulary building strategy to make the words your own.*

### parchment     ammunition

**As you read,** *draw a box around unfamiliar words you could add to your vocabulary. Use context clues to unlock their meaning.*

### Marking the Text

**Characterization and Irony**

**As you read,** *underline details that indicate characterization. Also underline details that strike you as ironic. In the margin, explain the significance of the details in the story.*

"Just one hour, *una hora*, is all I'm asking of you, son." My grandfather is in a nursing home in Brooklyn, and my mother wants me to spend some time with him, since the doctors say that he doesn't have too long to go now. I don't have much time left of my summer vacation, and there's a stack of books next to my bed I've got to read if I'm going to get into the AP[1] English class I want. I'm going stupid in some of my classes, and Mr. Williams, the principal at Central, said that if I passed some reading tests, he'd let me move up.

Besides, I hate the place, the old people's home, especially the way it smells like industrial-strength ammonia and other stuff I won't mention, since it turns my stomach. And really the Abuelo always has a lot of relatives visiting him, so I've gotten out of going out there except at Christmas, when a whole vanload of grandchildren are herded over there to give him gifts and a hug. We all make it quick and spend the rest of the time in the recreation area, where they play checkers and stuff with some of the old people's games, and I catch up on back issues of *Modern Maturity*. I'm not picky, I'll read almost anything.

Anyway, after my mother nags me for about a week, I let her drive me to Golden Years. She drops me off in front. She wants me to go in alone and have a "good time" talking to Abuelo. I tell her to be back in one hour or I'll take the bus back to Paterson. She squeezes my hand and says, "*Gracias, hijo,*" in a choked-up voice like I'm doing her a big favor.

I get depressed the minute I walk into the place. They line up the old people in wheelchairs in the hallway as if they were about to be raced to the finish line by orderlies[2] who don't even look at them when they push them here and there. I walk fast to room 10, Abuelo's "suite." He is sitting up in his bed writing with a pencil in one of those old-fashioned black hardback notebooks. It has the outline of the island of Puerto Rico on it. I slide into the hard vinyl chair by his bed. He sort of smiles and the lines on his face get deeper, but he doesn't say anything. Since I'm supposed to talk to him, I say, "What are you doing, Abuelo, writing the story of your life?"

It's supposed to be a joke, but he answers, "*Sí,* how did you know, Arturo?"

His name is Arturo too. I was named after him. I don't really know my grandfather. His children, including my mother, came to New York and New Jersey (where I was born) and he stayed on the Island[3] until my grandmother died. Then he got sick, and since nobody could leave their jobs to go take care of him, they brought him to this nursing home in Brooklyn. I see him a couple of times a year, but he's always surrounded by his sons and

---

[1] **AP** abbreviation for "Advanced Placement," a rigorous high school course that can lead to college credit.

[2] **orderlies** (ôr'dər lēz) *n.* attendants in a hospital or nursing home.

[3] **the Island** Puerto Rico.

daughters. My mother tells me that Don Arturo had once been a teacher back in Puerto Rico, but had lost his job after the war.[4] Then he became a farmer. She's always saying in a sad voice, "Ay, *bendito!* What a waste of a fine mind." Then she usually shrugs her shoulders and says, "*Así es la vida.*" That's the way life is. It sometimes makes me mad that the adults I know just accept whatever is thrown at them because "that's the way things are." Not for me. I go after what I want.

Anyway, Abuelo is looking at me like he was trying to see into my head, but he doesn't say anything. Since I like stories, I decide I may as well ask him if he'll read me what he wrote.

I look at my watch: I've already used up twenty minutes of the hour I promised my mother.

Abuelo starts talking in his slow way. He speaks what my mother calls book English. He taught himself from a dictionary, and his words sound stiff, like he's sounding them out in his head before he says them. With his children he speaks Spanish, and that funny book English with us grandchildren. I'm surprised that he's still so sharp, because his body is shrinking like a crumpled-up brown paper sack with some bones in it. But I can see from looking into his eyes that the light is still on in there.

"It is a short story, Arturo. The story of my life. It will not take very much time to read it."

"I have time, Abuelo." I'm a little embarrassed that he saw me looking at my watch.

"Yes, *hijo*. You have spoken the truth. *La verdad.* You have much time."

Abuelo reads: " 'I loved words from the beginning of my life. In the *campo* where I was born one of seven sons, there were few books. My mother read them to us over and over: the Bible, the stories of Spanish conquistadors and of pirates that she had read as a child and brought with her from the city of Mayagüez; that was before she married my father, a coffee bean farmer; and she taught us words from the newspaper that a boy on a horse brought every week to her. She taught each of us how to write on a slate with chalks that she ordered by mail every year. We used those chalks until they were so small that you lost them between your fingers.

" 'I always wanted to be a writer and a teacher. With my heart and my soul I knew that I wanted to be around books all of my life. And so against the wishes of my father, who wanted all his sons to help him on the land, she sent me to high school in Mayagüez. For four years I boarded with a couple she knew. I paid my rent in labor, and I ate vegetables I grew myself. I wore my clothes until they were thin as **parchment.** But I graduated

---

[4] **after the war** World War II ended in 1945.

Vocabulary Builder

**parchment**
(pärch'mənt) *n.*

**Meaning**

▲ **Critical Viewing** What does this picture reveal about Abuelo's character?

at the top of my class! My whole family came to see me that day. My mother brought me a beautiful *guayabera*, a white shirt made of the finest cotton and embroidered by her own hands. I was a happy young man.

" 'In those days you could teach in a country school with a high school diploma. So I went back to my mountain village and got a job teaching all grades in a little classroom built by the parents of my students.

" 'I had books sent to me by the government. I felt like a rich man although the pay was very small. I had books. All the books I wanted! I taught my students how to read poetry and plays, and how to write them. We made up songs and put on shows for the parents. It was a beautiful time for me.

" 'Then the war came,⁵ and the American President said that all Puerto Rican men would be drafted. I wrote to our governor and explained that I was the only teacher in the mountain village. I told him that the children would go back to the fields and grow up ignorant if I could not teach them their letters. I said that I

*Marking the Text*

---

⁵ **Then the war came . . .** The United States entered World War II in 1941, after the Japanese bombed Pearl Harbor.

## Literature in Context
## Spanish Words

Throughout the story, Arturo's mother and grandfather sprinkle Spanish words and phrases into their conversation. Some are defined within the story. Here are English translations of those that are not.

- **Gracias, hijo** (grä'sē äs', ē'hō') Thank you, son. Hijo also means "child."
- **Sí** (sē) *adv.* Yes.
- **bendito** (ben'dē'tō) *n.* kind soul; simple soul (literally, "blessed").
- **campo** (käm'pō) *n.* open country; countryside.
- **conquistadors** (kän kēs'tə dor'z) *n.* conquerors; specifically, leaders of the Spanish conquest of the Americas in the 16th century.
- **Nueva** (nwā'və) *n.* new. Nueva York means "New York."
- **Poemas de Arturo** Arturo's poems

### ▲ Good to Know!

Spanish is widely spoken in many United States communities. Here, voters have the option of reading either English or Spanish signs.

thought I was a better teacher than a soldier. The governor did not answer my letter. I went into the U.S. Army.

"'I told my sergeant that I could be a teacher in the army. I could teach all the farm boys their letters so that they could read the instructions on the **ammunition** boxes and not blow themselves up. The sergeant said I was too smart for my own good, and gave me a job cleaning latrines.[6] He said to me there is reading material for you there, scholar. Read the writing on the walls. I spent the war mopping floors and cleaning toilets.

"'When I came back to the Island, things had changed. You had to have a college degree to teach school, even the lower grades. My parents were sick, two of my brothers had been killed in the war, the others had stayed in *Nueva* York. I was the only one left to help the old people. I became a farmer. I married a good woman who gave me many good children. I taught them all how to read and write before they started school.'"

---

[6] **latrines** (lə trēnz) *n.* communal toilets used in military barracks or camps.

---

### Vocabulary Builder

**ammunition**
(am'yoo nish'ən) *n.*

**Meaning**

*Marking the Text*

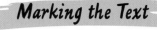

Abuelo then puts the notebook down on his lap and closes his eyes.

"*Así es la vida* is the title of my book," he says in a whisper, almost to himself. Maybe he's forgotten that I'm there.

For a long time he doesn't say anything else. I think that he's sleeping, but then I see that he's watching me through half-closed lids, maybe waiting for my opinion of his writing. I'm trying to think of something nice to say. I liked it and all, but not the title. And I think that he could've been a teacher if he had wanted to bad enough. Nobody is going to stop me from doing what I want with my life. I'm not going to let *la vida* get in my way. I want to discuss this with him, but the words are not coming into my head in Spanish just yet. I'm about to ask him why he didn't keep fighting to make his dream come true, when an old lady in hot-pink running shoes sort of appears at the door.

She is wearing a pink jogging outfit too. The world's oldest marathoner, I say to myself. She calls out to my grandfather in a flirty voice, "Yoo-hoo, Arturo, remember what day this is? It's poetry-reading day in the rec room! You promised us you'd read your new one today."

I see my abuelo perking up almost immediately. He points to his wheelchair, which is hanging like a huge metal bat in the open closet. He makes it obvious that he wants me to get it. I put it together, and with Mrs. Pink Running Shoes's help, we get him in it. Then he says in a strong deep voice I hardly recognize, "Arturo, get that notebook from the table, please."

while reading your anchor book

I hand him another map-of-the-Island notebook—this one is red. On it in big letters it says, *POEMAS DE ARTURO*.

I start to push him toward the rec room, but he shakes his finger at me.

"Arturo, look at your watch now. I believe your time is over." He gives me a wicked smile.

Then with her pushing the wheelchair—maybe a little too fast—they roll down the hall. He is already reading from his notebook, and she's making bird noises. I look at my watch and the hour *is* up, to the minute. I can't help but think that my abuelo has been timing *me*. It cracks me up. I walk slowly down the hall toward the exit sign. I want my mother to have to wait a little. I don't want her to think that I'm in a hurry or anything.

### Vocabulary Builder

**After you read,** *review the words you decided to add to your vocabulary. Write the meaning of words you have learned in context. Look up the other words in a dictionary, glossary, thesaurus, or electronic resource.*

while reading your anchor book

# Judith Ortiz Cofer (born 1952)

Born in Puerto Rico, Judith Ortiz Cofer moved to the United States when she was a young child because her father joined the navy. In her stories, essays, poems, and novels, Ortiz Cofer often explores her bicultural roots, reflecting on her experiences growing up in a Puerto Rican family living in Paterson, New Jersey. Her books include *Silent Dancing: A Partial Remembrance of a Puerto Rican Childhood, The Latin Deli: Prose and Poetry,* and *A Love Story Beginning in Spanish.* Ortiz Cofer is the author of several novels for young adults, including *The Meaning of Consuelo* and *Call Me Maria.* "An Hour With Abuelo" is one of the stories in her collection *An Island Like You: Stories of the Barrio.* Ortiz Cofer has received many awards for her writing and is a professor of English and Creative Writing at the University of Georgia.

# Thinking About the Selection

## An Hour with Abuelo

**About the Author**
Visit: PHSchool.com
Web Code: exe-7207

**1** **Analyze** Which method of characterization—direct or indirect—does the author use most often to reveal what Arturo and Abuelo are like? Support your character analysis with evidence from the story.

_____

_____

_____

**2** **Infer** What did Arturo think about Abuelo when he arrived at the nursing home? How did Arturo change his mind?

_____

_____

_____

_____

**3** **Interpret** Why is Arturo's visit with his grandfather ironic? Is this irony primarily situational, verbal, or dramatic? Explain.

_____

_____

_____

_____

_____

**4** **Evaluate** How does the story's ironic ending affect its meaning and impact on the reader?

_____

_____

_____

**Write** Answer the following questions in your Reader's Journal.

**5** **Compare and Contrast** How does the way Arturo intends to deal with any future conflicts in his life differ from the way his grandfather has dealt with conflicts?

**6** **Evaluate** Pick a character from your Anchor Book who undergoes change. How does the way the author characterizes the character develop to reflect change?

**while reading your anchor book**

# 2-12 Comparing Literary Works
## *Theme*

We read literature not just for entertainment, but also for insights about life. In studying the central message, or **theme,** of a literary work, we learn more about ourselves and the world.

## Literary Terms

▶ The **theme** of a literary work is the central message or insight it reveals about life or human nature. All the elements of a novel, story, poem, essay, or play work together to communicate its theme. Theme is different from the topic (or subject) of the work. For instance, the topic of a story may be friendship or conflict. Theme goes beyond the topic to reveal a broader insight— perhaps a comment about loyalty or about sacrifice. There are two categories of themes.

| Direct Theme | Implied Theme |
|---|---|
| Sometimes, an author directly states the theme. For example, fables often end with a moral that tells the reader exactly what the message is, such as "One good turn deserves another." | Most themes are implied. The reader has to analyze all the different elements in the text for clues about the author's meaning and then make an inference about the work's theme. |

▶ The theme of a literary work often reflects the issues and concerns of its historical time period. However, there are some **universal themes** that appear in the literature and folklore of many different cultures, over many different time periods. Here are some examples of these recurring themes.

- Be loyal to your friends.

- Show courage in the face of danger.

- Be true to yourself despite what others say or do.

**Activity**

Find a news article that addresses the same universal theme as your Anchor Book. Write an explanation of how the two different genres (a newspaper article and a novel) use their different forms to address the same theme. Be prepared to discuss your article and theme with the class.

**Directions** Read the folk tale, then answer the questions that follow.

## The Stonecutter: A Japanese Folk Tale

Once upon a time there lived a stonecutter, who cut slabs of rock to build houses. He knew all about which rocks worked for which purposes, and he had lots of customers. For a long time, he was a happy man. Then one day, he went to the house of a rich man and saw many beautiful things. The stonecutter said to himself, "Oh, if only I were a rich man, how happy I would be!"

A mountain spirit heard his wish. To his surprise, the stonecutter heard a voice answer him. "Your wish is granted. You will be a rich man!" When the stonecutter returned home, he was amazed to see that his simple wooden hut was now a palace with splendid furniture.

For a while the stonecutter was happy, and then one day, he saw a prince who rode in a carriage and had a golden umbrella to protect him from the sun's rays. It was a hot day, and the stonecutter wished that he were a prince, with a carriage and an umbrella to protect him from the sun. Once again, his wish was granted.

Things continued in this way. The stonecutter decided that the sun was even more powerful than a prince, and wished he were the sun. When he became the sun, he wished that he were a cloud, which blocks the sun. Finally he wished he were a rock, which even a heavy rain could not move.

But one day, the stonecutter-who-was-a-rock realized that another stonecutter was about to cut him into pieces. "Oh," he wished, "if only I were a stonecutter again. Then I would be truly happy!"

Once more, the mountain spirit granted his wish.

The stonecutter again toiled at his work. He lived in a wooden hut and had plain furniture, but he had learned to be happy with what he had. He never again asked for things that he did not have.

**1** **Interpret** What is the theme of this folk tale? Cite details.

_____

_____

**2** **Analyze** Is this theme directly stated or implied? Explain.

_____

Earlier in this unit, you read the story "An Hour With Abuelo." Now read "The Luckiest Time of All" to compare the themes of the two selections. *Guiding Question:* **Is there a clear winner in the conflict in each selection?**

The Luckiest Time of All

by Lucille Clifton

while reading your anchor book

**Background** *This selection is from* The Lucky Stone, *a novel about a girl who enjoys listening to her great-grandmother's stories about a stone that has brought luck to each of its owners for more than 100 years. Notice how Clifton uses southern African American dialect to capture the cultural and regional flavor of the storytelling.*

### Vocabulary Builder

**Before you read,** *you will discuss the following words. In the Vocabulary Builder box in the margin, use a vocabulary building strategy to make the words your own.*

**plaited     acquainted**

**As you read,** *draw a box around unfamiliar words you could add to your vocabulary. Use context clues to unlock their meaning.*

*Marking the Text*

**Theme**

**As you read,** *underline details that hint at the theme, and take notes in the margin about the details you mark. Remember that you may need to read between the lines to make inferences.*

Mrs. Elzie F. Pickens was rocking slowly on the porch one afternoon when her great-granddaughter, Tee, brought her a big bunch of dogwood blooms, and that was the beginning of a story.

"Ahhh, now that dogwood reminds me of the day I met your Great-granddaddy, Mr. Pickens, Sweet Tee.

"It was just this time, spring of the year, and me and my best friend Ovella Wilson, who is now gone, was goin to join the Silas Greene. Usta be a kinda show went all through the South, called it the Silas Greene show.[1] Somethin like the circus. Me and Ovella wanted to join that thing and see the world. Nothin wrong at

---

[1] **Silas Greene show** (usually spelled Green) a traveling vaudeville show that was written, and performed by African Americans. The show toured much of the South from 1904 to the mid-1900s, providing comedy and musical entertainment for both black and white audiences.

home or nothin, we just wanted to travel and see new things and have high times. Didn't say nothin to nobody but one another. Just up and decided to do it.

"Well, this day we **plaited** our hair and put a dress and some things in a crokasack[2] and started out to the show. Spring day like this.

"We got there after a good little walk and it was the world, Baby, such music and wonders as we never had seen! They had everything there, or seemed like it.

"Me and Ovella thought we'd walk around for a while and see the show before goin to the office to sign up and join.

"While we was viewin it all we come up on this dancin dog. Cutest one thing in the world next to you, Sweet Tee, dippin and movin and head bowin to that music. Had a little ruffly skirt on itself and up on two back legs twistin and movin to the music. Dancin dancin dancin till people started throwin pennies out of they pockets.

"Me and Ovella was caught up too and laughin so. She took a penny out of her pocket and threw it to the ground where that dog was dancin, and I took two pennies and threw 'em both.

"The music was faster and faster and that dog was turnin and turnin. Ovella reached in her sack and threw out a little pin she had won from never being late at Sunday school. And me, laughin and all excited, reached in my bag and threw out my lucky stone!

"Well, I knew right off what I had done. Soon as it left my hand it seemed like I reached back out for it to take it back. But the stone was gone from my hand and Lord, it hit that dancin dog right on his nose!

"Well, he lit out after me, poor thing. He lit out after me and I flew! Round and round the Silas Greene we run, through every place me and Ovella had walked before, but now that dancin dog was a runnin dog and all the people was laughin at the new show, which was us!

"I felt myself slowin down after a while and I thought I would turn around a little bit to see how much gain that cute little dog was makin on me. When I did I got such a surprise! Right behind me was the dancin dog and right behind him was the finest fast runnin hero in the bottoms of Virginia.

"And that was Mr. Pickens when he was still a boy! He had a length of twine in his hand and he was twirlin it around in the air just like the cowboy at the Silas Greene and grinnin fit to bust.

"While I was watchin how the sun shined on him and made him look like an angel come to help a poor sinner girl, why, he twirled that twine one extra fancy twirl and looped it right around one hind leg of that dancin dog and brought him low.

---

[2] **crokasack** (krō'kər sak) (usually spelled croker sack) *n.* bag made of burlap or similar material.

**plaited**
(plāt'ed) *v.*

**Meaning**

*Marking the Text*

"I stopped then and walked slow and shy to where he had picked up that poor dog to see if he was hurt, cradlin him and talkin to him soft and sweet. That showed me how kind and gentle he was, and when we walked back to the dancin dog's place in the show he let the dog loose and helped me to find my stone. I told him how shiny black it was and how it had the letter A scratched on one side. We searched and searched and at last he spied it!

"Ovella and me lost heart for shows then and we walked on home. And a good little way, the one who was gonna be your Great-granddaddy was walkin on behind. Seein us safe. Us walkin kind of slow. Him seein us safe. Yes." Mrs. Pickens' voice trailed off softly and Tee noticed she had a little smile on her face.

"Grandmama, that stone almost got you bit by a dog that time. It wasn't so lucky that time, was it?"

Tee's Great-grandmother shook her head and laughed out loud.

"That was the luckiest time of all, Tee Baby. It got me **acquainted** with Mr. Amos Pickens, and if that ain't luck, what could it be! Yes, it was luckier for me than for anybody, I think. Least mostly I think it."

Tee laughed with her Great-grandmother though she didn't exactly know why.

"I hope I have that kind of good stone luck one day," she said.

"Maybe you will someday," her Great-grandmother said.

And they rocked a little longer and smiled together.

**Marking the Text**

### Vocabulary Builder

**After you read,** *review the words you decided to add to your vocabulary. Write the meaning of words you have learned in context. Look up the other words in a dictionary, glossary, thesaurus, or electronic resource.*

### Vocabulary Builder

**acquainted**
(ə kwānt'ed) *adj.*

**Meaning**

# Thinking About the Selections

## An Hour With Abuelo *and* The Luckiest Time of All

**About the Author**
Visit: PHSchool.com
Web Code: exe-7208

**1** **Analyze** In "The Luckiest Time of All," how does the lucky stone turn out to be lucky for Tee's great-grandmother in an unexpected way?

_____

_____

_____

**2** **Compare and Contrast** Both selections are about different cultures and topics, but they convey similar themes. What is the topic of each selection? What shared insight about life do they express? Support your interpretation.

_____

_____

_____

_____

**3** **Evaluate** Do you think that this shared theme is a valid (true) and important one? In your opinion, which selection expresses its theme in a more compelling way? Support your evaluation with evidence.

_____

_____

_____

**4** **Synthesize** How does the conflict in each selection help convey its theme?

_____

_____

_____

**Write** Answer the following questions in your Reader's Journal.

**5** **Explain** Is there a clear winner in the conflict in each selection? Why or why not?

**6** **Interpret** What is the theme of your Anchor Book? Cite details from the book to support your answer.

# 2-13 Listening and Speaking Workshop
## Reader's Theater

A good story is dramatic—filled with action and emotion. Reader's Theater is an activity in which you adapt a piece of literature into a dramatic performance.

## Your Task

You and your group members will create a script for an important passage of three to five pages from your Anchor Book. There will be no full stage sets, costumes, or memorization. Instead, you and your group members will read the script aloud so that your audience learns the importance of the passage and is entertained.

## Organize Your Presentation

**1** Choose a passage that is important to the story. Look for a passage that is simple and lively, with lots of dialogue or action. The passage should not contain too many scenes or characters. The passage should provide important information about characters, the central conflict, or theme.

**2** Identify the roles each group member will play: narrator or character. Make cuts and changes in the passage that will make your script easier to understand and perform (as well as more entertaining). Do not make changes that alter the meaning of the passage. Not everything in the passage needs to become dialogue. Some parts can become stage directions for the characters.

**3** Create a script that is easy to read. Readers will need to look up often from their scripts. You may want to mark up the text with reminders about how each section of the script should be read.

**4** Rehearse your presentation. Speak clearly and effectively. Use appropriate expression and pacing, making frequent eye contact with your audience. Move! If your character completes an action, act it out. Or, you can move to communicate the feelings and emotions in your role. With your group, brainstorm different ways of communicating the story through movement.

**5** Be prepared to answer questions about why your group interpreted the passage the way it did and what the passage's importance is.

**Directions** Assess your presentation and your role as an audience. For each question, circle a rating.

## SPEAK: Rubric for Reader's Theater

| CRITERIA | RATING SCALE | | | | |
|---|---|---|---|---|---|
| | NOT VERY | | | | VERY |
| CONTENT How well did you match the message and vocabulary to the audience and purpose? | 1 | 2 | 3 | 4 | 5 |
| ORGANIZATION How well did you present clear ideas and logical organization? | 1 | 2 | 3 | 4 | 5 |
| DELIVERY How well did you demonstrate its purpose through appropriate eye contact, pacing, and tone? | 1 | 2 | 3 | 4 | 5 |
| DELIVERY How well did you demonstrate effective use of tone, expression, and correct use of grammar to communicate ideas? | 1 | 2 | 3 | 4 | 5 |
| COMMUNICATION How well did the audience understand your presentation? | 1 | 2 | 3 | 4 | 5 |

## LISTEN: Rubric for Audience Self-Assessment

| CRITERIA | RATING SCALE | | | | |
|---|---|---|---|---|---|
| | NOT VERY | | | | VERY |
| ACTIVE LISTENING How well did you focus your attention on the speakers? Did you ask questions at the end? | 1 | 2 | 3 | 4 | 5 |
| ACTIVE LISTENING How well did you demonstrate active listening with appropriate silence, responses, and body language? | 1 | 2 | 3 | 4 | 5 |

**Evaluate** What did you learn about the characters, conflict, theme, and mood in your Anchor Book by adapting it for Reader's Theater?

_____

_____

_____

_____

## Adjectives and Articles

An **adjective** describes a noun or pronoun. Adjectives often answer the questions *What kind? How many? Which one?* or *Whose?* An **adjective clause** is a group of words that serve the same purpose as an adjective: to describe. For example, in the sentence "The journalist who wrote about forest fires received an award for her work," the clause "who wrote about forest fires" is an adjective clause.

Good writers choose adjectives that describe a precise quality—and avoid those that add unnecessary or irrelevant details. They also stay away from "empty" adjectives like *a lot* and *very*. For instance, *hundreds of people* conveys a clearer picture than *a lot of people*.

**Directions**  Rewrite each adjective to be more precise.

**1**  very tired _____

**2**  really big _____

**Directions**  Write an adjective clause to complete the sentence.

**3**   On every visit, Julius, _____, tells us a dramatic yarn or recites a sad poem.

**Articles**—*a, an,* and *the*—are adjectives that come before nouns and answer the question *Which one? A* and *an* are indefinite and refer to something general, such as "a girl" or "an eagle." *The* is definite and refers to something specific, such as "the ant." Use *a* if the first sound in the noun it modifies is a consonant. Use *an* if the first sound is a vowel.

**Directions**  Edit the following paragraph to show the correct use of *a* or *an*. Place a line through the incorrect article and write the correct article above it.

> Yesterday, I went to a amusement park with Calvin, an friend of mine. We each got to drive a bumper car, ride an roller coaster, and eat a ice cream cone. I rode a Ferris wheel by myself, because riding it gives Calvin an nervous feeling in his stomach. Afterwards, we were exhausted and just wanted to go home and take an long nap!

Go Online

**Learn More**
Visit: PHSchool.com
Web Code: exp-7204

*Author's Craft*

How important are articles, anyway? To find out, go to "What Are Memories Made Of?" on page 151. Choose a paragraph from the text below the heading "Studying the Brain". Cross out all the articles. Read your revised paragraph aloud to a partner. Listen as your partner reads another revised paragraph to you. Does removing the articles change the meaning of the paragraph? How?

# Adverbs

**Go Online**

**Learn More**
Visit: PHSchool.com
Web Code: exp-7205

An **adverb** describes a verb, an adjective, or another adverb. It answers the questions *How? When? Where? For what purpose?* or *To what extent?* An adverb may be a single word, phrase, or clause. In the chart below, all the adverbs answer the question *When?*, but the adverb clause has a subject and verb.

| Adverb | I went to the game *yesterday*. |
|---|---|
| Adverb Phrase | I went to the game *on Friday*. |
| Adverb Clause | I went to the game *after I had dinner*. |

**Directions** Underline the adverb, adverb phrase, or adverb clause in each sentence. Then explain what information is added, using *how, when, where, for what purpose,* or *to what extent*.

**1**  The Wright brothers formerly owned a bicycle business in Ohio.

_____

**2**  Their first attempts at flight ended quickly.

_____

**3**  Before I played basketball, I finished my homework.

_____

## Scrambled Eggs

To make scrambled eggs, first break 5 eggs into a bowl. Add 1 tablespoon of water. Beat the eggs and water with a fork until they are foaming. Pour the egg mixture into a frying pan over low heat. Stir gently so the eggs will become firm.

**Directions** Rewrite the recipe so that it does not include adverbs or adverb phrases.

**4**  _____

_____

**5**  How did removing the adverbs and adverb phrases affect the meaning of the recipe?

_____

## Degrees of Adjectives and Adverbs

Both adjectives and adverbs have three forms to show comparison. They are the **positive form,** the **comparative form,** and the **superlative form**. Writers use these forms to add emphasis and detail to their descriptions. When an incorrect form is used, the description loses impact, which is the opposite of what is intended. Notice the endings and words that are used in building each of these forms.

**Go Online**

**Learn More**
Visit: PHSchool.com
Web Code: exp-7206

|  | Positive | Comparative | Superlative |
|---|---|---|---|
| **Adjectives** | big<br>speedy | bigger<br>speedier | biggest<br>speediest |
| **Adverbs** | soon<br>seriously | sooner<br>more seriously | soonest<br>most seriously |

The adjectives and adverbs shown below do not follow the usual rules.

|  | Positive | Comparative | Superlative |
|---|---|---|---|
| **Adjectives** | good<br>bad | better<br>worse | best<br>worst |
| **Adverbs** | well<br>badly | better<br>worse | best<br>worst |

**Directions** On a separate sheet of paper, rewrite the following paragraph, inserting adjectives and adverbs where appropriate. Use the positive, comparative, and superlative forms at least once each.

> Kyle saw a fork in the road. Both led to haunted houses. One was not as big as the other, but it was more scary. Curtis dared Kyle to walk into one of the houses. He decided to do it because he wanted Angela to think he was the most brave of everyone in his class. Walking up the road was the most scary experience he'd ever had. He felt a breeze on the back of his neck and felt goose bumps rise on his arms.

# Spelling Tricky or Difficult Words

Some words contain letters that are not heard when the word is pronounced. Because these words do not look like the way they sound, they are often tricky, or difficult, to spell.

**Go Online**

**Learn More**
Visit: PHSchool.com
Web Code: exp-7207

**Directions** Underline the correct word in each sentence.

**1** Who (thoght, thought) of going to the beach?

**2** You must be (ambishus, ambitious) to climb Mt. Everest.

**3** The Aztec Indians had a fascinating (culcher, culture).

**4** The mathematics teacher came up with a humorous (example, exampul) to help his students understand the lesson.

**5** Who (browt, brought) the beautiful flowers?

To eliminate confusion when spelling tricky words, consult a dictionary for the correct spellings. If you have difficulty with particular words, try one of the following.

▶ In a notebook, write words you don't know how to spell by sounding out each syllable. Then, write each word on a note card after looking it up in the dictionary. Check the note cards against the spellings in your notebook.

▶ Before spelling a tricky word on paper, visualize it in your mind.

▶ Trace the letters of the word in the air as you spell it aloud.

▶ Keep a list of difficult-to-spell words when writing and editing your own work.

▶ Use memory aids to help remember difficult words.

**Examples** It is *wise* to *exercise.*
Will you *hand* me a *handkerchief?*

**Directions** Work with a partner to come up with at least five words that are spelled differently from the way they are pronounced. You may use a dictionary to locate words. Afterward, write possible misspellings with a brief explanation of why each word might be misspelled. Partners may share some of their words with the class for discussion.

# 2-15 Writer's Workshop
## *Workplace Writing: Business Letter*

Have you ever wanted to know how your favorite video game was created? A great way to find out is to write a letter to the software company and ask. People write **business letters** to provide or request information, to express an opinion, or to complain. Follow the steps outlined in this workshop to write a one-page business letter requesting information from an organization.

**Purpose** To write a business letter requesting information from an organization

**Audience** People in the organization

To be effective, your letter should include the following elements.

▶ Standard business letter format

▶ A clear statement of your request, supported by details

▶ Formal and polite language

▶ An appropriate organizational structure

▶ Error-free writing, including proper use of adjectives and adverbs

## Prewriting—Plan It Out

**Brainstorm** Work with a partner to identify organizations to contact for information. Consider your audience and purpose when choosing the most desirable option. If you are addressing concerns about the quality of a product, you may wish to use a warranty or consumer info as a source of information.

**Gather details.** Organize the facts of your letter. Use the library, the Internet, or a customer service department to locate the appropriate contact information.

| Organization | Purpose for Writing | Contact Information | Details |
|---|---|---|---|
| City Hall | to voice concern about potholes damaging bicycle tires | Mayor Sarah Williams 1 City Hall Plaza Boston, MA 02201 | I want to know when the potholes on Main St. will be repaired. |

| Organization | Purpose for Writing | Contact Information | Details |
|---|---|---|---|
| | | | |

# Drafting—Get It on Paper

Using your chart as an outline, write your draft. The following steps will make your letter organized and effective.

**Shape your writing.** Use an appropriate format and write in a direct, focused voice. In the first paragraph, state your purpose. In the following paragraphs, include supporting information. Conclude by thanking the recipient and restating your purpose in a polite tone.

| Block format | Each part of the letter begins at the left margin. |
|---|---|
| Modified block format | The heading, the closing, and the signature are indented to the center of the page. |

**Provide elaboration.** Using your knowledge of workplace writing, develop your request by including appropriate details.

## Parts of a Business Letter

**Heading:** the writer's name, address, phone number, e-mail address, and the date

**Inside Address:** the name and address of the recipient

**Salutation:** the greeting to the recipient, followed by a colon

> *Examples:* Dear Mr. Davies:
>
> Dear Sir or Madam:

**Body:** the main part of the letter, which presents the writer's purpose and the information that supports it

**Closing:** begins with a capital letter and ends with a comma

> *Example:* Sincerely,

**Signature:** the writer's name, typed below the closing. Between the closing and the typed name, the writer adds a handwritten signature.

# Revising—Make It Better

Make sure your ideas are organized logically. Delete unnecessary information and modify wordy or repetitive passages by consulting a dictionary or thesaurus.

**Directions** Revise the text. Draw a line through details that are repetitive, extraneous (irrelevant), or inconsistent with your purpose.

```
I am writing you concerning financing for the trip that

my classmates and I are taking to London. I am going to

London with my class. I see it as a great educational

opportunity to learn about a different culture, history,

and way of life. My best friend went to London last

summer and loved it.
```

**Revise sentence structure.** Make your writing engaging by varying your sentence structures and using interesting adjectives and adverbs.

*Peer Review* Ask a classmate, a family member, or your teacher to proofread your letter. Revise to achieve your intended reaction.

**Directions** Read this student letter as a model for your own.

**Student Model: Writing**

Go **O**nline

**Student Model**
Visit: PHSchool.com
Web Code: exr-7202

*Melissa Gornto, Houston, TX*

Melissa Gornto
1436 Any Street
Houston, TX 77001
melissa.gornto@email.com
(555) 123-4567

September 23, 20XX

Corwood Industries
P.O. Box 15375
Houston, TX 77220

Dear Sir or Madam:

I am writing to you concerning financing for the trip that my classmates and I are taking to London. I see it as a great educational opportunity to learn about a different culture, history, and way of life. We do not know much about the British society, and this is a chance for us to find out the real information.

If you were to help us with the monetary grant, a weight would be lifted off our shoulders concerning the money issue. Using the money, we would be able to go to London, where we could see many things. We would be able to go to Buckingham Palace, the Tower of London, and Big Ben. This is also a great educational opportunity because it allows us to see the English way of life, including the exchange of money, and the difference in speech. They may speak English, but that doesn't mean the words have the same sound or definition. So, if you will, look at this as a once-in-a-lifetime opportunity to learn many different things that aren't taught in schools.

Thank your for your time regarding this matter. Please take this trip into consideration and help us out. If you do, you won't have to worry about us not being grateful. This is an adventure my fellow classmates and I would love to go on. Once again, thank you for your time.

Sincerely,

*Melissa Gornto*
Melissa Gornto

> The writer includes a heading and an inside address.

> The writer uses block format, setting all elements at the left margin.

> The writer clearly states her purpose.

> By adding these details, the writer supports her request.

> In the closing, the writer uses friendly, yet formal language.

> The writer includes her typed name and handwritten signature.

# Editing—Be Your Own Language Coach

With a classmate or your teacher, review for language convention errors. Make sure that you have followed the correct format for a business letter and used a variety of adjectives and adverbs.

# Publishing—Share It!

When you publish a work, you produce it for a specific audience. Consider one of the following ideas to share your writing.

**Swap letters.** Trade letters with a classmate and read the letter carefully. Write a response to the request for information.

**Send your letter.** Send your request to the recipient via e-mail or standard mail.

# Reflecting On Your Writing

**Respond** to the following questions on a separate sheet of paper and hand it in with your final draft.

**1** On a separate sheet of paper, answer the following questions and hand it in with your final draft. What new insights did you gain about writing a business letter? What did you do well? What do you need to work on?

**2** **Rubric for Self-Assessment** Assess your business letter. For each question, circle a rating.

| CRITERIA | RATING SCALE |
|---|---|
| | NOT VERY       VERY |
| IDEAS Is your letter clear and focused? | 1   2   3   4   5 |
| ORGANIZATION How logical and consistent is your organization? | 1   2   3   4   5 |
| VOICE Is your writing lively and engaging, drawing the reader in? | 1   2   3   4   5 |
| WORD CHOICE How appropriate is the language for your audience? | 1   2   3   4   5 |
| SENTENCE FLUENCY How varied is your sentence structure? | 1   2   3   4   5 |
| CONVENTIONS How correct is your grammar, especially your use of adjectives and adverbs? | 1   2   3   4   5 |

Now that you have finished reading your Anchor Book, get creative!
Complete one of the following projects.

## Make a Collage

A collage is an artistic grouping of materials, such as photographs, newspaper and magazine clippings, cartoons, and even three-dimensional objects.

1. Select an important theme, character, or event from your Anchor Book that you would like to represent through a collage. Think about images, text, colors, patterns, shapes, and textures that might help you convey your idea visually.

2. Collect materials, including paper or poster board, glue, and newspapers and magazines in which you might find images for your collage. You can also search for images online.

3. Glue or assemble your images and objects to create your collage. You can also create a digital collage using design software.

4. Write a statement explaining your visual interpretation.

Your collage project should include the following elements.

▶ Images, words, and even objects that represent an aspect of your Anchor Book

▶ A brief explanation of the ideas behind your collage

## Hold a Debate

In a debate, two sides present and defend opposing viewpoints, using arguments supported by evidence. By defending a position, regardless of your opinion, you learn to think more clearly and argue more persuasively.

1. With your group, choose a character from your Anchor Book who is involved in a conflict. Identify the conflict you will debate.

2. Divide the group in two teams. One team will support the character's decisions, while the other team will oppose them.

3. Work together with your team to prepare arguments and find details from the text to support your position. Choose a debate leader, although all members should participate in the discussion and planning.

4. Listen respectfully while the other side presents its arguments so that you are prepared with your rebuttal, or counterarguments.

Your debate should include the following elements.

▶ Strong opening, rebuttal, and closing arguments

▶ Evidence and reasons to support each position

## Create a Storyboard

In the film industry, a storyboard is a step-by-step series of illustrations with accompanying dialogue that shows how a movie will be filmed. When adapting a novel for a film, a storyboard helps map out the plot and translate the text into visual images.

1. Select a chapter or episode from your Anchor Book to recreate in a storyboard. The excerpt should have lots of action and dialogue so that you can turn it into a dramatic scene. It should also have a vivid setting so that you can create images.

2. Decide if you will present your storyboard in chronological order or if you will include flashbacks.

3. Draw large squares on poster board. Create your illustrations in these panels, and write the corresponding dialogue underneath. Your illustrations should not be overly detailed, but should convey the overall mood of the scene.

4. Display your storyboard, and respond to feedback from the class.

Your storyboard should include the following elements.
  ▶ Illustrations that represent an excerpt from your Anchor Book
  ▶ Dialogue to accompany the illustrations

## Free-Choice Book Reflection

You have completed your free-choice book. Before you take your test, read the following instructions to write a brief reflection of your book.

My free-choice book is _____ .

The author is _____ .

**1**    Would you recommend this book to a friend? Yes _____ No _____

Briefly explain why.

_____

_____

**Write and Discuss** Answer the following question in your Reader's Journal. Then, discuss your answer with a partner.

**2**    **Compare and Contrast** Great novels ask us to consider the answers to recurring thematic questions, such as, *Does every conflict have a winner?* Compare and contrast how your Anchor Book and free-choice book answer this question. Use specific details from both books to support your ideas. To extend, consider the influence of conflict in other subjects, such as sports, history, or science.

Answer the questions to check your understanding of this unit's skills.

## Reading Skills: Predicting

Read this selection. Then answer the questions that follow.

Benny Chavez had discovered the secret to mastering a math test. He'd completed all the homework assignments. He'd written important formulas on flashcards and studied with a friend. Last night, he had gone to bed early, and this morning, he'd eaten a good breakfast. But Benny had always done these things. Now, he had a secret weapon: yoga. For the past month, Benny had been attending yoga classes after school. He liked how strong and flexible his body had become. Most of all, he loved how yoga trained him to relax his mind and focus his concentration.

   With confidence, Benny turned over his test paper and looked at the questions. He felt a stab of panic. His mind had gone blank.

**1** Which detail leads you to anticipate that Benny will do better on this test than he has on previous exams?

   **A.** He'd completed all the homework assignments.

   **B.** Last night, he had gone to bed early.

   **C.** He had been attending yoga classes after school.

   **D.** This morning, he'd eaten a good breakfast.

**2** Which of the following statements BEST **predicts** what will happen next?

   **F.** Benny will relax his mind and refocus his attention on the test.

   **G.** Benny will leave his test paper blank.

   **H.** Benny will get the answers from another student.

   **J.** Benny will answer most of the items incorrectly.

## Reading Skills: Making Inferences

Read this selection. Then answer the questions that follow.

Excitement raced through Kim's veins as she looked out the car window. She had been waiting for this day since the age of five. And she had followed through on everything her parents had asked. First, she had raised a series of pet goldfish. The summer after fifth grade, she had taken care of the class iguana. She helped Mrs. Loggins next door with her old cat. Last summer, she had earned money walking other people's dogs. As her dad drove toward the dog adoption agency, Kim marveled that this day had finally arrived.

**3** Which statement BEST describes Kim's character?

    **A.** Kim likes dogs better than cats.

    **B.** Kim is smart about earning money.

    **C.** Kim knows how to focus energy toward a goal.

    **D.** Kim always gets her dad to say yes.

**4** When you **infer** you _____.

    **F.** predict what will happen

    **G.** make a conclusion based on given evidence

    **H.** reflect on the past

    **J.** pass judgment on a person or character

**5** You can **infer** that Kim will be what kind of pet owner?

    **A.** absent-minded

    **B.** neglectful

    **C.** responsible

    **D.** unhappy

**6** Which detail from the passage supports your answer to question 5?

    **F.** Kim feels excitement racing through her veins.

    **G.** Kim has followed through on all her commitments.

    **H.** Kim's dad is driving to the dog adoption agency.

    **J.** Kim marvels that this day has finally come.

## Literary Analysis: Elements of the Novel

Read this selection. Then answer the questions that follow.

---

Nadira stood by her friend Lindsey's fitting room, adjusting the folds of her khimaar around her face while she waited. Nadira had agreed to accompany Lindsey to the mall so Lindsey could shop for a new summer dress.

Lindsey muttered something from behind the curtain.

"What?" Nadira said.

Lindsey flung open the curtain and stepped out, twirling in front of the mirror. "What do you think?" Lindsey asked, admiring the cut of the dress.

Nadira couldn't tell Lindsey that she would never be caught dead in clothing so revealing, or that she was embarrassed at the exposed skin. Nadira wanted to pull Lindsey aside—as her own mother had done to her when they first arrived in America—to protect her, to warn her. "Nadira," her mother had said, "it will be different here. Remember your studies and your roots." Though her mother's reminder seemed like a scolding, Nadira had felt proud of her family's Islamic traditions. Then her mother had added, "We also came here because our own customs would be accepted." I have to learn to accept differences, too, Nadira thought, amused, watching Lindsey pose.

"If you like it," Nadira said, grinning, "buy it."

---

**7** The author uses **flashback** in this passage to _____.

   **A.** help explain why Nadira decides to act the way she does

   **B.** explain why the story is at the point it is right now

   **C.** let the reader know that Nadira's religion is Islam

   **D.** introduce another character

**8** What is **exposition?**

   **F.** the beginning of a story

   **G.** the telling of a story

   **H.** the ending of a story

   **J.** the author's purpose

**9** When does the plot of a story reach its highest point?

   **A.** rising action

   **B.** falling action

   **C.** climax

   **D.** resolution

**10** Discuss in one paragraph how the **theme** of the story above applies to your life or the world around you.

_____

_____

_____

_____

_____

## Language Skills: Vocabulary

Choose the best answer.

**11** The prefix *ob-* means _____.

   **A.** against, blocking

   **B.** within

   **C.** in favor of

   **D.** opposite

**12** Which word means "to speak against"?

   **F.** diction

   **G.** contrary

   **H.** contradict

   **J.** dictator

**13** Which prefix would you add to the word *merge* to make it mean "to put under water"?

   **A.** con-

   **B.** sub-

   **C.** pre-

   **D.** ob-

**14** The word *obscure* probably means _____.

   **F.** to move

   **G.** to open

   **H.** to scare

   **J.** to block

## Language Skills: Spelling

Circle the letter of the word that completes each sentence correctly.

**15** Jill did not want to _____ that her soccer team was the underdog in today's match.

A. consede

B. concede

C. conseed

D. conceed

**16** This spring, the town has an _____ supply of water.

F. abundant

G. abundent

H. abondant

J. abondent

## Language Skills: Grammar

Choose the best answer.

**17** Which sentence uses the **active voice?**

A. Julia seems tired today.

B. My sister is a first grader.

C. Matt rides his bike to school.

D. I am proud of my performance.

**18** Identify the correct form of the **irregular verb.**

Celia has _____ an e-mail announcing Saturday's car wash.

F. wrote

G. written

H. writ

J. writed

**19** In which sentence does the verb appear in the **present perfect tense?**

A. Nolan will have reached the airport by now.

B. Sue has two dogs and four goldfish.

C. Ms. Walker has given us lots of helpful research tips.

D. I had lived in Chicago for almost ten years.

**20** Read the following sentence.

Molly the poodle slurped noisily, spilling gravy all over the clean floor.

Which word from the sentence is an **adjective?**

F. slurped

G. noisily

H. spilling

J. clean

**21** Read the following sentence.

Kyle thought his best friend Sam ran too slowly to win the race.

Which word from the sentence is an **adverb?**

A. thought

B. best

C. slowly

D. win

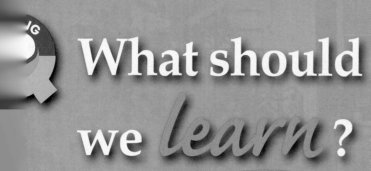

# What should we *learn*?

t 3 Genre focus:

## ɔes of Nonfiction

### ꞏnchor Book

ꞏe many good books that
ꞏvork well to support both
ꞏQuestion and the genre
ꞏ this unit. In this unit you
ꞏ one of these books as
ꞏchor Book. Your teacher
ꞏ ɔduce the book you will
ꞏng.

### Free-Choice Reading

Later in this unit you will be
given the opportunity to choose
another book to read. This is
called your free-choice book.

# Thinking About What You Already Know

No matter what you read—e-mails, textbooks, novels, text messages—you know that the author had a purpose in writing it. Thinking about *what* it means can help you to understand *why* the author wrote it.

## Partner Activity

Reading the passage aloud to emphasize the meaning of the text can make the author's voice come alive and help you understand the text. Read through each passage silently. Then, take turns reading each passage aloud as if you were the author. Discuss and answer the questions.

### from *"All Together Now"* by Barbara Jordan

Today the nation seems to be suffering from compassion fatigue, and issues such as race relations and civil rights have never gained momentum.

Those issues, however, remain crucial. As our society becomes more diverse, people of all races and backgrounds will have to learn to live together. If we don't think this is important, all we have to do is look at the situation in Bosnia today.

How do we create a harmonious society out of so many kinds of people? The key is tolerance—the one value that is indispensable in creating community.

If we are concerned about community, if it is important to us that people not feel excluded, then we have to do something. Each of us can decide to have one friend of a different race or background in our mix of friends. If we do this, we'll be working together to push things forward.

Why do you think the author created this text?

_____

_____

What impact does she want to have on the reader?

_____

_____

## from *"Cyber Chitchat"* by Cindy Kauffman

One day last week, I stood and watched my thirteen-year-old "chat" with some friends via e-mail. I thought I'd take the opportunity to monitor the electronic conversation being passed between these preteens—who long ago decided the telephone wasn't good enough for them.

Looking over her shoulder, I very quickly found that I needed a translator to decipher what was being said. Squinting down at the monitor, I asked my daughter, "What kind of atrocious spelling is that? And what does it mean?"

Peeved at the interruption, she kept typing and answered, "Wat duz WAT mean?"

Why do you think the author created this text?

_____

_____

What is the author's attitude toward this subject?

_____

_____

_____

_____

As you read the selections in this unit, do not just think about what a selection means but also about how the author communicates his or her ideas. When you read and think about an author's purpose, you are aware that the author is a writer who makes choices in order to reach his or her audience. Paying attention to how authors achieve this purpose will make you a better writer and reader.

THE BIG ?

# 3-1 Understanding the Big Question
## What should we learn?

Advancements in technology and the Internet make information available to us twenty-four hours a day, seven days a week. With all of this information so accessible, the question is, "What should we learn?"

It's impossible to learn everything in a lifetime—you have to choose. Some things you need to learn, such as how to read and write; some things you should learn, such as how to ride a bicycle; and other things you would like to learn, such as how to make a movie.

What would you like to learn? Look at the following skills you could learn. Choose five skills and list them in the chart. Then explain why you would like to learn these skills.

**I'd like to learn how to . . .**

scuba dive

survive in the wilderness

speak a new language

play the guitar

drive a car

cook a meal

perform CPR

care for a pet

paint a portrait

build a Web site

get along well with others

| Skill | Why You'd Like to Learn It |
|---|---|
|  |  |
|  |  |
|  |  |
|  |  |
|  |  |

before reading your anchor book

## Partner Activity

How did you choose the skills on your list? Are they skills that are essential for living your life, or are they skills that you would simply like to have? With a partner, talk about the skills you need to learn, should learn, and would like to learn. You might choose skills from the previous page or choose some of your own. Write them in the circles.

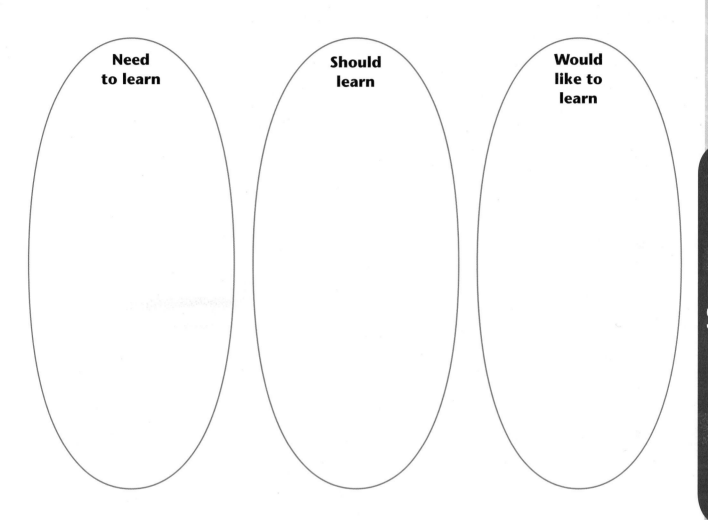

**Need to learn**

**Should learn**

**Would like to learn**

before reading your anchor book

Now talk with your partner about how you created each list. How would your life be different if you didn't learn the skills on each list? Why might different people have different skills on their "Need to learn" list? Are there skills that you might need to know later in life that you don't need to know now?

 As you read your Anchor Book and the related readings, think about why the ideas it contains are important to learn. Also, think about what you already know about the topic and what new information you have learned.

**Getting Ready for Your Anchor Book**

*You will start reading your Anchor Book soon. The next few pages in this book give you some background information plus a reading skill.*

# Introduction to
# Nonfiction

Nonfiction writing can be about almost anything—as long as the information is true. It can tell about new inventions, heroic feats, or strange creatures. It can also tell about everyday events and ideas, such as the author's most embarrassing moment.

**before reading your anchor book**

## Types of Nonfiction

There are four types of nonfiction writing that you will read in this unit.

**Type:** **Narrative**     **Purpose:** to entertain

**Narrative writing** is writing that tells a true story. Unlike fiction, it focuses on events. This type of writing can include a plot full of events that took place, and real-life characters who deal with a conflict.

**Examples:** biography, autobiography

**Type:** **Expository**     **Purpose:** to explain or inform

**Expository writing** is writing that gives information about a topic. This writing might discuss or describe the process of making chocolate. The purpose of expository writing is to explain or inform.

**Examples:** news articles, how-to writing, encyclopedia entries

**Type:** **Persuasive**     **Purpose:** to persuade

**Persuasive writing** is writing that attempts to convince the reader to agree with a certain point of view. Persuasive writing includes facts and opinions that support the author's position.

**Examples:** editorials, advertisements, speeches

*BUY ME!*

*NEW AND IMPROVED!*

**Type:** **Reflective**     **Purpose:** to reflect

**Reflective writing** is writing in which the author thinks about certain ideas or experiences. This type of writing might focus on what the writer learned from something or why the idea matters.

**Examples:** memoirs, letters, journals

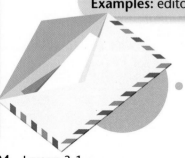

Not all nonfiction includes just one type of writing. Some narratives reflect on the importance of a certain event. Expository writing can include parts that tell a story. Nonfiction writing of any kind can be humorous, descriptive, or analytical.

## Organizing Nonfiction

Nonfiction writing can be organized in a number of ways.

Nonfiction is often organized by the **main idea** and **supporting details.** The main idea is supported by details that tell more about that idea.

- ▶ **Chronological order** is a way of organizing by the order in which events occur.

- ▶ **Cause-and-effect organization** shows how one event leads to another.

- ▶ **Compare-and-contrast organization** is used to show how two or more things are the same and different.

**Directions** With a partner, find the nonfiction selections in Units 1 and 2. Complete the following table by listing the name and page numbers for each selection. Then, identify the type of nonfiction of each selection.

| Name of Selection | Page(s) | Type of Nonfiction |
|---|---|---|
|  |  |  |
|  |  |  |
|  |  |  |
|  |  |  |
|  |  |  |

**Strategies for Reading Nonfiction** Use this strategy as you read nonfiction.

**Scan and Skim** Before you begin reading, **scan** the title, headings, and any pictures. Think about what you know about the topic and what type of writing it is. Then, **skim** the text for key words that give an idea of what you will read.

# 3-2 Reading Skills
## Fact and Opinion

In learning new reading skills, you will use special academic vocabulary. Knowing the right words will help you demonstrate your understanding.

### Academic Vocabulary

| Word | Meaning | Example Sentence |
|---|---|---|
| **evaluate** *v.* <br> *Related word:* value | to decide the value of | I try to *evaluate* all my choices before I make a decision. |
| **investigate** *v.* <br> *Related word:* investigation | to study closely | The detectives arrived to *investigate* the crime. |
| **credible** *adj.* <br> *Related word:* credibility | believable | Telling me that your dog ate your homework is not a *credible* story. |

When you read, you must decide whether the information is a fact or an opinion. A **fact** is something that you can prove. It is **objective**—that is, it actually exists and is not based on someone's beliefs or feelings. "My hat is green" is a fact.

An **opinion**, however, cannot be proved. It is **subjective**, or based on beliefs or feelings. Two people can have a different opinion about the same topic or situation, which you can **evaluate** to see if you agree with it. "My hat is better than your hat" is an opinion. If information is **biased,** it is only being presented in a one-sided way.

**FACT**
*something that can be proved
*not up for debate
*objective—determined by fact instead of beliefs or feelings

**OPINION**
*based on judgment or belief
*open to debate
*subjective—determined by feelings instead of fact

**Directions** Read the following statements and decide if they are facts or opinions. Write *F* if the statement is a fact and *O* if it is an opinion.

**1** _____ My brother is fifteen years old.

**2** _____ My brother is the best football player.

**3** _____ I wish it wouldn't rain.

**4** _____ The game was canceled because of rain.

**5** **Evaluate** In the advertisement above, which facts or opinions did you find most persuasive? Why?

_____

_____

**6** **Investigate** Advertisements like these are a kind of **propaganda**—they present some facts and not others to create a response in the reader. How did the creators of this ad use information and text features to influence the reader? What facts might they have left out to create the response they wanted? Is it biased?

_____

_____

Now that you've learned about fact and opinion, read the following newspaper editorial. Determine what information is factual and what is not. *Guiding Question:* **What can you learn about cell phones from the opinions in the article?**

# Hanging Up On Cell Phones

## by Mark DeLong

The Warren School Board has decided to ban cell phones at school, leading to a heated debate among students. While most students disagreed with the decision, some said cell phones were distracting, and they were glad to get rid of them.

The decision was made after teachers complained that cell phones were getting in the way of class work. Many students would receive calls during class, leading them to either answer the phone or listen to the message. In other cases, students would send text messages to one another during class.

Marcie Bader, a seventh grader, felt that the ban on cell phones was unnecessary and unjust.

"It's not fair," Marcie said. "Only a few people were using them in class. That doesn't give them the right to take them away from everybody."

Other students said that cell phones should be allowed because they can be essential in emergencies.

"What if something happened where my parents needed me to come home right away? They could reach me faster on my cell phone," said Mark Fisher, an eighth grader. Fisher pointed out that just last year, students were able to use their cell phones to call home when they were stuck at school because of a blizzard.

A few students, however, felt that the ban on cell phones was a good thing. They noted

**The use of cell phones during class time is becoming more common.**

that some students had been using them to play games during study hall, distracting them from their work.

"I can't concentrate when people are always goofing around or talking on the phone," said eighth grader Jamal Tinsley.

Under the new rules, students can leave their cell phones at the office at the beginning of the day and pick them back up when they leave. School officials estimate that up to 60 percent of students have cell phones.

"This new rule is an inconvenience, but it will lead to a better learning environment," said school Principal Ted Sullivan.

before reading your anchor book

# Thinking About the Selection
## Hanging Up On Cell Phones

**1** **Distinguish** In the following chart, write three facts and three opinions from the article.

| Facts | Opinions |
|---|---|
|  |  |
|  |  |
|  |  |

**2** **Synthesize** Which opinion do you think made the strongest argument? Why? Use details from the text to support your answer.

_____

_____

_____

**3** **Analyze** Which fact made the strongest argument? Why? Use details from the text to support your answer.

_____

_____

_____

**4** **Evaluate** After reading this article, based on all the facts and opinions, do you feel cell phones should be allowed in school? Why or why not? Back up your answer with **credible** reasons.

_____

_____

_____

**Write** Answer the following question in your Reader's Journal.

 **5** **Reflect** What can you learn about cell phones from the opinions in the article?

# 3-3 Vocabulary Building Strategies
## Word Origins and Borrowed Words

The English language changes overtime. It is a patchwork quilt with pieces from all over the world. Many words have **origins** in ancient languages, such as Latin, Greek, and Anglo-Saxon mythology. Others are **borrowed words** that were taken directly from contemporary languages such as Spanish, Chinese, and Bantu.

| Origin | Explanation of Origin | Related English Words/Phrases |
|---|---|---|
| domus (Latin origin) | "house" | domestic (having to do with a house) <br> domesticate (to tame) |
| Hercules (Greek myth) | The Greek hero Hercules was known for his strength and for completing twelve difficult tasks. | Herculean effort (a difficult task requiring great strength) |
| historia (Greek origin) | "an account of events" | history (account of what happened in the past) <br> prehistoric (before history) |
| high horse (Anglo-Saxon culture) | In medieval England, nobles were given tall horses to show their importance. The phrase "get off your high horse" developed from this practice. | Get off your high horse (a superior attitude) |

**Directions** Identify the word that completes each sentence.

**1** Lifting the desk off his cat's tail required _____.

    **A.** high horse    **B.** Herculean effort    **C.** domesticated    **D.** historic effort

**2** Dinosaurs came before man during the _____ era.

    **A.** wholesome    **B.** prehistoric    **C.** historic    **D.** domestic

**3** The dog is a(n) _____ animal related to the gray wolf.

    **A.** appendage    **B.** prehistoric    **C.** historic    **D.** domestic

The English language borrows words directly from languages from all around the world. Look at the chart for some examples.

| Word | Meaning | Language |
|------|---------|----------|
| piano | a type of large musical instrument | Italian |
| déjà vu | the feeling that something has happened before | French |
| hurricane | violent storm that begins in tropical waters | Spanish |
| moccasin | soft leather shoe | Algonquian (Native American) |

## Use Context Clues

Use context clues to unlock the meaning of the following boldfaced foreign words.

**1** Everyone had a wonderful time at the **fiesta.** We played games, ate wonderful food, and listened to live music.

**2** Landing a lead role in the film was a **bonanza** for Veronica, who couldn't even afford to pay rent before her big break.

**3** The creator of the painting was verified. The specialists agreed it was a **bona fide** Pablo Picasso.

## Partner Activity

Work with a partner. Sound out each German word in the first column, then read the clue to its meaning. Guess what the English word is. The English word will sound similar but be spelled differently. Check your answers and the origin of these words by using a dictionary.

| Word in German | Clue | English Version |
|----------------|------|-----------------|
| Feder | bird covering | feather |
| Wasser | basic liquid | |
| Blut | red body liquid | |
| Mutter | female parent | |
| Haar | head fluff | |

# 3-4 Literary Analysis
## Reflective Writing

Reflective writing allows you access into the mind of the author. In addition to describing an experience, reflective writing also shows how that experience affected the author.

## Literary Terms

▶ **Reflective writing** presents the writer's thoughts, feelings, or reflections about an important experience or event.

▶ An **essay** is a short nonfiction work that focuses on a specific subject. In a **reflective essay,** the writer reflects on a subject that is personally meaningful.

The following chart shows how a writer might turn a personal experience into a broader insight. Add your own examples at the bottom.

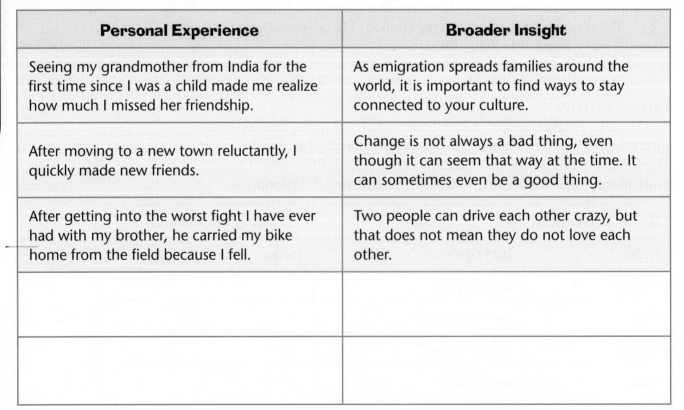

| Personal Experience | Broader Insight |
|---|---|
| Seeing my grandmother from India for the first time since I was a child made me realize how much I missed her friendship. | As emigration spreads families around the world, it is important to find ways to stay connected to your culture. |
| After moving to a new town reluctantly, I quickly made new friends. | Change is not always a bad thing, even though it can seem that way at the time. It can sometimes even be a good thing. |
| After getting into the worst fight I have ever had with my brother, he carried my bike home from the field because I fell. | Two people can drive each other crazy, but that does not mean they do not love each other. |
|  |  |
|  |  |

**while reading your anchor book**

**Directions** Read the example of reflective writing. As you read, underline details that reveal the author's personal experience and broader insights about his topic. Answer the questions that follow.

**Go Online**

**About the Author**
Visit: PHSchool.com
Web Code: exe-7301

## from *Working Fire: The Making of a Fireman*
### by Zac Unger

Some guys seem to know just what to do the moment they see their first fire. They know which tools to grab, which flames to aim for. They know, without having to be told, where the limits of safety lie. But I'm not like that. I still go blank at every fire when I first step off the rig and size up the scene. I still have that moment in which I've got no idea in the world what it is I'm supposed to be doing.

The difference now is that those moments are getting shorter. And even when I'm in the middle of one, I no longer have the fear that the moment will never end. Now when the lieutenant yells at me to "pull a big line," I'm already doing it. My body's quicker than my mind. My hands know what to do: Get water, go to work, stop the fire.

I wonder if maybe nobody is a natural, whether it's all a matter of how convincingly we each learn to play the role. This isn't like tightening a nut as it floats past on an assembly line. Fire is still the unruly, temperamental boss, and I've never met a firefighter who isn't humble for at least a little while after a tough job. Maybe anyone who says he's a natural is only a liar instead.

**1  Identify** What insight does the author share, based on his personal experience? What is the author's purpose?

_____

_____

**2  Analyze** What does the speaker in this passage reveal about himself through his actions and language? How does the reader get a better understanding of who the speaker is?

_____

_____

_____

_____

while reading your anchor book

## Author's Style/Voice

Would you write a thank-you note to your grandmother in the same style of writing you use when you text message your friends? You probably wouldn't because like most writers, you match your writing style to your audience and purpose.

## Literary Terms

**Style** is an author's typical way of writing. Style is not so much *what* a writer says, but *how* he or she says it. This is also called an author's **voice**. An author's style is shaped by many elements, including those in the chart below.

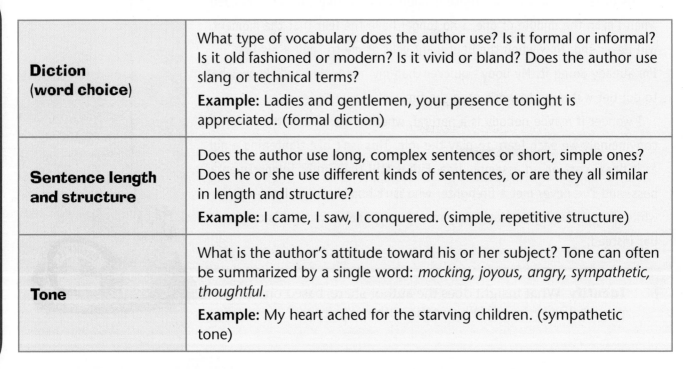

| Diction (word choice) | What type of vocabulary does the author use? Is it formal or informal? Is it old fashioned or modern? Is it vivid or bland? Does the author use slang or technical terms?<br>**Example:** Ladies and gentlemen, your presence tonight is appreciated. (formal diction) |
|---|---|
| Sentence length and structure | Does the author use long, complex sentences or short, simple ones? Does he or she use different kinds of sentences, or are they all similar in length and structure?<br>**Example:** I came, I saw, I conquered. (simple, repetitive structure) |
| Tone | What is the author's attitude toward his or her subject? Tone can often be summarized by a single word: *mocking, joyous, angry, sympathetic, thoughtful.*<br>**Example:** My heart ached for the starving children. (sympathetic tone) |

**Directions** The example below shows an original, formal sentence revised to be less formal. Rewrite the second original sentence using your own style.

**Original**   We cordially request your presence at our humble affair.

**Revised**   Why don't you guys stop by our little gathering?

**Original**   It is clear to me that, despite all of your best efforts and intentions, this is not going to work out.

**Revised** _____

_____

**Directions** Read the following passages and answer the questions.

Go Online
**About the Author**
Visit: PHSchool.com
**Web Code: exe-7302**
**exe-7303**

## *from* A Wagner Matinée *by Willa Cather*

I received one morning a letter, written in pale ink on glassy, blue-lined note-paper, and bearing the postmark of a little Nebraska village. This communication, worn and rubbed, looking as if it had been carried for some days in a coat pocket that was none too clean, was from my uncle Howard, and informed me that his wife had been left a small legacy by a bachelor relative, and that it would be necessary for her to go to Boston to attend to the settling of the estate.

*Author's Craft*

These two passages were written more than 50 years apart. Identify two ways that Kauffman's style reflects a later time period.

## *from* Cyber Chitchat *by Cindy Kauffman*

One day last week, I stood and watched my thirteen-year-old "chat" with some friends via e-mail. I thought I'd take the opportunity to monitor the electronic conversation being passed between these preteens—who long ago decided the telephone wasn't good enough for them.

Looking over her shoulder, I very quickly found that I needed a translator to decipher what was being said. Squinting down at the monitor, I asked my daughter, "What kind of atrocious spelling is *that?* And what does it mean?"

Peeved at the interruption, she kept typing and answered, "Wat duz *WAT* mean?"

**1** **Compare and Contrast** Use the following chart to list key elements that contribute to the style in each passage.

| Elements of Style | Cather | Kauffman |
|---|---|---|
| Diction (word choice) | | |
| Sentence length and structure | | |
| Tone | | |

**2** **Examine** In what ways does an author's style affect the tone of each selection?

_____

_____

In "Melting Pot," watch for characteristics that show you Anna Quindlen's style of writing. *Guiding Question:* **What can we learn about life through the author's personal experiences?**

# FROM MELTING POT
## BY ANNA QUINDLEN

**Background** *In "Melting Pot," Anna Quindlen writes about what happens when younger and wealthier outsiders move into certain neighborhoods like hers. Quindlen reflects upon whether the American ideal of the "melting pot"—that place where different kinds of people "melt" together to become one society—really exists.*

## Vocabulary Builder

**Before you read,** *you will discuss the following words. In the Vocabulary Builder box in the margin, use a vocabulary building strategy to make the words your own.*

**fluent      bigots      demolition      wince**

**As you read,** *draw a box around unfamiliar words you could add to your vocabulary. Use context clues to unlock their meaning.*

### Marking the Text

**Reflective Writing and Style**

**As you read,** *underline details that reveal the author's thoughts, feelings, and insights. Also underline details that show her writing style. In the margin, write notes about the details you have chosen.*

### Vocabulary Builder

**fluent**
(flo͞oʹənt) *adj.*

**Meaning**

My children are upstairs in the house next door, having dinner with the Ecuadorian family that lives on the top floor. The father speaks some English, the mother less than that. The two daughters are **fluent** in both their native and their adopted languages, but the youngest child, a son, a close friend of my two boys, speaks almost no Spanish. His parents thought it would be better that way. This doesn't surprise me; it was the way my mother was raised, American among Italians. I always suspected, hearing my grandfather talk about the "No Irish Need Apply" signs outside factories, hearing my mother talk about the neighborhood kids, who called her greaseball, that the American fable of the melting pot was a myth. Here in our neighborhood it exists, but like so many other things, it exists only person-to-person.

The letters in the local weekly tabloid[1] suggest that everybody hates everybody else here, and on a macro[2] level they do. The old-timers are angry because they think the new-moneyed professionals are taking over their town. The professionals are tired of being blamed for the neighborhood's rising rents, particularly since they are the ones paying them. The old immigrants are suspicious of the new ones. The new ones think the old ones are **bigots.** Nevertheless, on a micro[3] level most of us get along. We are friendly with the Ecuadorian family, with the Yugoslavs across the street, and with the Italians next door, mainly by virtue of our children's sidewalk friendships. It took awhile. Eight years ago we were the new people on the block, filling dumpsters with old plaster and lath, . . . (sitting) on the stoop with our **demolition** masks hanging around our necks like goiters.[4] We thought we could feel people staring at us from behind the sheer curtains on their windows. We were right.

My first apartment in New York was in a gritty warehouse district, the kind of place that makes your parents **wince.** A lot of old Italians lived around me, which suited me just fine because I was the granddaughter of old Italians. Their own children and grandchildren had moved to Long Island and New Jersey. All they had was me. All I had was them.

I remember sitting on a corner with a group of half a dozen elderly men, men who had known one another since they were boys sitting together on this same corner, watching a glazier[5] install a great spread of tiny glass panes to make one wall of a restaurant in the ground floor of an old building across the street. The men laid bets on how long the panes, and the restaurant, would last. Two years later two of the men were dead, one had moved in with his married daughter in the suburbs, and the three remaining sat and watched

---

[1]  **tabloid** (tab´loid´) n. small-format newspaper that often sensationalizes the news.

[2]  **macro** (mak´rō) adj. large-scale.

[3]  **micro** (mī´krō) adj. small-scale.

[4]  **goiters** (goit´ərz) n. swellings in the front of the neck caused by an enlarged thyroid gland.

[5]  **glazier** (glā´zhər) n. someone who cuts and fits glass for doors and windows.

## Vocabulary Builder

**bigots**
(big´əts) n.

**Meaning**


**demolition**
(dem´ə lish´on) n.

**Meaning**


**wince**
(wins) v.

**Meaning**

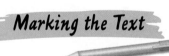

Marking the Text

watched dolefully[6] as people waited each night for a table in the restaurant. "Twenty-two dollars for a piece of veal!" one of them would say, apropos[7] of nothing. But when I ate in the restaurant they never blamed me. "You're not one of them," one of the men explained. "You're one of me." It's an argument familiar to members of almost any embattled race or class: I like you, therefore you aren't like the rest of your kind, whom I hate.

Change comes hard in America, but it comes constantly. The butcher whose old shop is now an antiques store sits day after day outside the pizzeria here like a lost child. The old people across the street cluster together and discuss what kind of money they might be offered if the person who bought their building wants to turn it into condominiums.[8] The greengrocer stocks yellow peppers and fresh rosemary for the gourmands,[9] plum tomatoes and broad-leaf parsley for the older Italians, mangoes for the Indians. He doesn't carry plantains,[10] he says, because you can buy them in the bodega.[11]

---

[6] **dolefully** (dōl′fəl ē) *adv.* sadly; mournfully.

[7] **apropros** (ap′rə pō′ ē) **of nothing** without connection.

[8] **condominiums** (kän′də min′ēəm) *n.* an apartment building or multifamily house in which the apartments are individually owned.

[9] **gourmands** (goor′ mändz) *n.* people who enjoy good or gourmet food.

[10] **plantains** (plan′tinz) *n.* a fruit that is similar to a banana and is popular in tropical regions.

[11] **bodega** (bō dā′gə) *n.* small Latino grocery store.

▼ **Critical Viewing**
How do these pictures reflect the ideas in Quindlen's essay?

Sometimes the baby slips out with the bath water. I wanted to throw confetti the day that a family of rough types who propped their speakers on their station wagon and played heavy metal music at 3:00 A.M. moved out. I stood and smiled as the seedy bar at the corner was transformed into a slick Mexican restaurant. But I liked some of the people who moved out at the same time the rough types did. And I'm not sure I have that much in common with the singles who have made the restaurant their second home.

Yet somehow now we seem to have reached a nice mix. About a third of the people in the neighborhood think of squid as calamari,[12] about a third think of it as sushi,[13] and about a third think of it as bait. Lots of the single people who have moved in during the last year or two are easygoing and good-tempered about all the kids. The old Italians have become philosophical about the new Hispanics, although they still think more of them should know English. The firebrand[14] community organizer with the storefront on the block, the one who is always talking about people like us as though we stole our houses out of the open purse of a ninety-year-old blind widow, is pleasant to my boys.

Drawn in broad strokes, we live in a pressure cooker: oil and water, us and them. But if you come around at exactly the right

---

[12] **calamari** (kä´lə mä´rē) *n.* Italian word for "squid," a type of sea creature.

[13] **sushi** (soo´shē) *n.* Japanese dish that often includes raw fish or seafood.

[14] **firebrand** (fīr´brand´) *n.* (used as adj.) person who stirs up trouble or protest.

time, you'll find members of all these groups gathered around complaining about the condition of the streets, on which everyone can agree. We melt together, then draw apart. I am the granddaughter of immigrants, a young professional—either an interloper[15] or a longtime resident, depending on your concept of time. I am one of them, and one of us.

---

[15] **interloper** (inʹtər lōʹpər) *n.* someone who intrudes on others.

## Vocabulary Builder

**After you read,** *review the words you decided to add to your vocabulary. Write the meaning of words you have learned in context. Look up the other words in a dictionary, glossary, thesaurus, or electronic resource.*

while reading your anchor book

# ANNA QUINDLEN (b.1953)

Anna Quindlen worked as a reporter and editor for the *New York Times* before becoming one of the paper's columnists. "Melting Pot" originally appeared in "Life in the 30s," a popular column that Quindlen created in 1985. In 1992 she won the Pulitzer Prize for commentary for her column "Public and Private."

In 1995 Quindlen left the *Times* to become a novelist. Her bestselling books include the novels *Object Lessons* (1991), *One True Thing* (1994), *Black and Blue* (1998), and *Blessings* (2002), plus several collections of her columns. Quindlen currently writes a column for *Newsweek* magazine.

# Thinking About the Selection

## Melting Pot

**1** **Analyze** What does Quindlen want readers to learn about her neighborhood?

**2** **Draw Conclusions** What insight does Quindlen offer about how different cultures can get along?

**3** **Analyze** How does Quindlen's style help her express her ideas? Does it make her essay more credible?

**4** **Describe** How would you describe Quindlen's tone and diction? How do these style elements affect the way you perceive her message?

**Write** Answer the following questions in your Reader's Journal.

**5** **Interpret** What can we learn about life through the author's personal experiences?

**6** **Analyze** Reflective writing is not the only type of writing that expresses the writer's insights. What important insights are expressed in your Anchor Book? What can you learn from these insights?

while reading your anchor book

# 3-5 Comparing Literary Works
## *Biography and Autobiography*

You've probably heard the phrase "truth is stranger than fiction." It can be just as interesting, too. If you've ever read the story or someone's life—a biography or autobiography— you may know that the twists and turns of people's lives can make for fascinating reading.

while reading your anchor book

## Literary Terms

► In a **biography,** a writer tells the life story of another person. It may tell about all or part of that person's life. Most biographies are written about famous or important people, but they can also be about ordinary people.

► In an **autobiography,** a writer tells his or her own life story. Like a biography, an autobiography may tell about all or part of the subject's life. Autobiographies are always told in the first person.

  • A **memoir** is a type of autobiography. It usually focuses on experiences and events from a specific time in the writer's life, rather than telling about the writer's life story.

  • An **autobiographical narrative** is a shorter essay that focuses on a particular event or episode in the writer's life.

► When you read a biography or an autobiography, it is important to understand the historical and cultural context of the person's life. The **historical and cultural context** of work is the background of events, laws, beliefs, and customs of the particular time and place in which a work is set or in which it was written.

Read this passage aloud.

> Paula stood on the steps of the town hall, handing out flyers announcing her choice for mayor. She was determined to make her voice heard, no matter how hard it would be.

What do we learn about Paula? In the context of the year 1900, Paula's actions are radical and extreme. Women did not have the right to vote in 1900, and Paula's determination shows that she is strongly independent. In the context of today, Paula's actions are not particularly unusual.

**Directions** Read the following excerpt from an autobiographical narrative. Underline details that provide important information about the writer and her mother. Then answer the questions that follow.

**About the Author**
Visit: PHSchool.com
Web Code: exe-7305

## from *"Museum Indians"* by Susan Power

A snake coils in my mother's dresser drawer; it is thick and black, glossy as sequins. My mother cut her hair several years ago, before I was born, but she kept one heavy braid. It is the three-foot snake I lift from its nest and handle as if it were alive.

"Mom, why did you cut your hair?" I ask. I am a little girl lifting a sleek black river into the light that streams through the kitchen window. Mom turns to me.

"It gave me headaches. Now put that away and wash your hands for lunch."

"You won't cut my hair, will you?" I'm sure this is a whine.

"No, just a little trim now and then to even the ends."

I return the dark snake to its nest among my mother's slips, arranging it so that its thin tail hides beneath the wide mouth sheared by scissors. My mother keeps her promise and lets my hair grow long, but I am only half of her; my thin brown braids will reach the middle of my back, and in maturity will look like tiny garden snakes.

**1** **Summarize** What do you learn about the writer and her mother? List at least three details.

_____

_____

_____

**2** **Speculate** Why do you think the writer chose to write about this episode?

_____

_____

**3** **Analyze** Evaluate the details in the selection. Why did the mother cut her hair, and what did she mean by "headaches"?

_____

_____

Read the following two nonfiction stories of people's lives, then compare them. *Guiding Question:* **By reading about the lives of Harriet Tubman and Ji-li Jiang, what can we learn about how real people have struggled for freedom?**

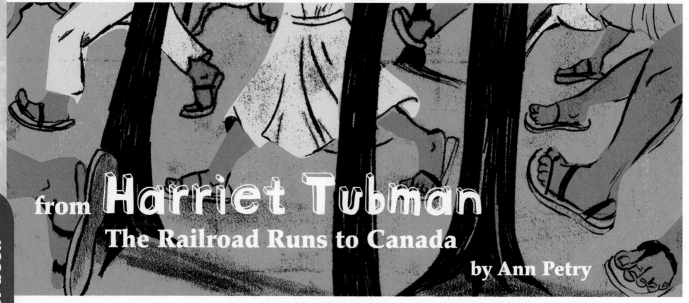

# from Harriet Tubman
## The Railroad Runs to Canada
### by Ann Petry

**Background** *Harriet Tubman was a woman who escaped from slavery in 1849 and became a "conductor" on the Underground Railroad, a network of people who helped slaves escape to freedom. Tubman made nineteen journeys over a ten-year period and rescued more than three hundred slaves. She was called "Moses" because, like Moses in the Bible, she led her people out of slavery.*

## Vocabulary Builder

**Before you read,** *you will discuss the following words. In the Vocabulary Builder box in the margin, use a vocabulary building strategy to make the words your own.*

**succession    incentive    disheveled    dispel**

**As you read,** *draw a box around unfamiliar words you could add to your vocabulary. Use context clues to unlock their meaning.*

### Marking the Text

**Biography and Autobiography**

**As you read,** *underline details that reveal what kind of person Harriet Tubman was. In the margin, explain what you learned from those details.*

Along the Eastern Shore of Maryland, in Dorchester County, in Caroline County, the masters kept hearing whispers about the man named Moses, who was running off slaves. At first they did not believe in his existence. The stories about him were fantastic, unbelievable. Yet they watched for him. They offered rewards for his capture.

They never saw him. Now and then they heard whispered rumors to the effect that he was in the neighborhood. The woods were searched. The roads were watched. There was never anything to indicate his whereabouts. But a few days afterward, a goodly number of slaves would be gone from the plantation. Neither the master nor the overseer had heard or seen anything unusual in the quarter[1]. Sometimes one or the other would vaguely remember having heard a whippoorwill[2] call somewhere in the woods, close by, late at night. Though it was the wrong season for whippoorwills.

Sometimes the masters thought they had heard the cry of a hoot owl, repeated, and would remember having thought that the intervals between the low moaning cry were wrong, that it had been repeated four times in **succession** instead of three. There was never anything more than that to suggest that all was not well in the quarter. Yet when morning came, they invariably discovered that a group of the finest slaves had taken to their heels.

Unfortunately, the discovery was almost always made on a Sunday. Thus a whole day was lost before the machinery of pursuit could be set in motion. The posters offering rewards for the fugitives[3] could not be printed until Monday. The men who made a living hunting for runaway slaves were out of reach, off in the woods with their dogs and their guns, in pursuit of four-footed game, or they were in camp meetings[4] saying their prayers with their wives and families beside them.

Harriet Tubman could have told them that there was far more involved in this matter of running off slaves than signaling the would-be runaways by imitating the call of a whippoorwill, or a hoot owl, far more involved than a matter of waiting for a clear night when the North Star[5] was visible.

In December 1851, when she started out with the band of fugitives that she planned to take to Canada, she had been in the vicinity of the plantation for days, planning the trip, carefully selecting the slaves that she would take with her.

---

[1]  **quarter** *n.* slave quarters, area on a plantation where slaves lived in one-room cabins.

[2]  **whippoorwill** (hwip´ər wil ) *n.* a bird with a distinctive call that sounds like the bird's name.

[3]  **fugitives** (fyoo´ji tivz) *n.* people fleeing from danger. Here the reference is to runaway slaves.

[4]  **camp meetings** religious meetings held outdoors or in a tent.

[5]  **North Star** the North Star helped runaway slaves figure out which direction was north.

She had announced her arrival in the quarter by singing the forbidden spiritual[6]—"Go down, Moses, 'way down to Egypt Land"—singing it softly outside the door of a slave cabin, late at night. The husky voice was beautiful even when it was barely more than a murmur borne on the wind.

Once she had made her presence known, word of her coming spread from cabin to cabin. The slaves whispered to each other, ear to mouth, mouth to ear, "Moses is here." "Moses has come." "Get ready. Moses is back again." The ones who had agreed to go North with her put ashcake and salt herring in an old bandanna, hastily tied it into a bundle, and then waited patiently for the signal that meant it was time to start.

There were eleven in the party, including one of her brothers and his wife. It was the largest group that she had ever conducted, but she was determined that more and more slaves should know what freedom was like.

She had to take them all the way to Canada. The Fugitive Slave Law was no longer a great many incomprehensible words written down on the country's lawbooks. The new law had become a reality. It was Thomas Sims, a boy, picked up on the streets of Boston at night and shipped back to Georgia. It was Jerry and Shadrach, arrested and jailed with no warning.

She had never been in Canada. The route beyond Philadelphia was strange to her. But she could not let the runaways who accompanied her know this. As they walked along she told them stories of her own first flight, she kept painting vivid word pictures of what it would be like to be free.

But there were so many of them this time. She knew moments of doubt when she was half-afraid, and kept looking back over her shoulder, imagining that she heard the sound of pursuit. They would certainly be pursued. Eleven of them. Eleven thousand dollars' worth of flesh and bone and muscle that belonged to Maryland planters. If they were caught, the eleven runaways would be whipped and sold South, but she—she would probably be hanged.

They tried to sleep during the day but they never could wholly relax into sleep. She could tell by the positions they assumed, by their restless movements. And they walked at night. Their progress was slow. It took them three nights of walking to reach the first stop. She had told them about the place where they would stay, promising warmth and good food, holding these things out to them as an **incentive** to keep going.

---

[6] **forbidden spiritual** In 1831, a slave named Nat Turner encouraged an unsuccessful slave rebellion by talking about the biblical story of Exodus, when Moses led the people of Israel out of slavery in Egypt.

## Vocabulary Builder

**incentive**
(in sent´iv) *n.*

**Meaning**

When she knocked on the door of a farmhouse, a place where she and her parties of runaways had always been welcome, always been given shelter and plenty to eat, there was no answer. She knocked again, softly. A voice from within said, "Who is it?" There was fear in the voice.

She knew instantly from the sound of the voice that there was something wrong. She said, "A friend with friends," the password on the Underground Railroad.

The door opened, slowly. The man who stood in the doorway looked at her coldly, looked with unconcealed astonishment and fear at the eleven **disheveled** runaways who were standing near her. Then he shouted, "Too many, too many. It's not safe. My place was searched last week. It's not safe!" and slammed the door in her face.

She turned away from the house, frowning. She had promised her passengers food and rest and warmth, and instead of that, there would be hunger and cold and more walking over the frozen ground: Somehow she would have to instill[7] courage into these eleven people, most of them strangers, would have to feed them on hope and bright dreams of freedom instead of the fried pork and corn bread and milk she had promised them.

They stumbled along behind her, half-dead for sleep, and she urged them on, though she was as tired and as discouraged as

---

[7] **instill** (in stil´) v. introduce or put in gradually.

▲ **Critical Viewing**
How does this image help communicate the mood surrounding this event?

*Marking the Text*

Vocabulary Builder

**disheveled**
(di shev´əld) *adj.*
**Meaning**

Biography and Autobiography **217**

# Literature in Context
## Language Connection

### The Underground Railroad and the Fugitive Slave Act

The Underground Railroad was not a real railroad with tracks and trains. Instead, it was a loosely organized network of people who helped slaves escape to free states in the North or Canada. Runaway slaves were called "passengers," and the people who guided them—like Harriet Tubman—were called "conductors." The homes and businesses where fugitives rested along their escape route were called "stations." The people who hid them were called "stationmasters."

At first, conductors like Tubman led runaway slaves to free states in the North. However, in 1850 Congress passed the Fugitive Slave Act. This law made it legal for slaves who had escaped to free states to be returned to their masters. It also made it a serious crime to help a slave escape and even required citizens to help slave catchers. As a result of this law, Tubman and other conductors on the Underground Railroad began to lead runaways to Canada instead of to the free states.

they were. She had never been in Canada but she kept painting wondrous word pictures of what it would be like. She managed to **dispel** their fear of pursuit, so that they would not become hysterical, panic-stricken. Then she had to bring some of the fear back, so that they would stay awake and keep walking though they drooped with sleep.

Yet during the day, when they lay down deep in a thicket, they never really slept, because if a twig snapped or the wind sighed in the branches of a pine tree, they jumped to their feet, afraid of their own shadows, shivering and shaking. It was very cold, but they dared not make fires because someone would see the smoke and wonder about it.

She kept thinking, eleven of them. Eleven thousand dollars' worth of slaves. And she had taken them all the way to Canada. Sometimes she told them about Thomas Garrett, in Wilmington. She said he was their friend even though he did not know them. He was the friend of all fugitives. He called them God's poor. He was a Quaker and his speech was a little different from that of other people. His clothing was different, too. He wore the wide-brimmed hat that the Quakers wear.

She said that he had thick white hair, soft, almost like a baby's, and the kindest eyes she had ever seen. He was a big man and strong, but he had never used his strength to harm anyone, always to help people. He would give all of them a new pair of shoes. Everybody. He always did. Once they reached his house in Wilmington, they would be safe. He would see to it that they were.

She described the house where he lived, told them about the store where he sold shoes. She said he kept a pail of milk and a

## Vocabulary Builder

**dispel**
(di spel') v.
**Meaning**

### Marking the Text

loaf of bread in the drawer of his desk so that he would have food ready at hand for any of God's poor who should suddenly appear before him, fainting with hunger. There was a hidden room in the store. A whole wall swung open, and behind it was a room where he could hide fugitives. On the wall there were shelves filled with small boxes—boxes of shoes—so that you would never guess that the wall actually opened.

While she talked, she kept watching them. They did not believe her. She could tell by their expressions. They were thinking. New shoes, Thomas Garrett, Quaker, Wilmington—what foolishness was this? Who knew if she told the truth? Where was she taking them anyway?

That night they reached the next stop—a farm that belonged to a German. She made the runaways take shelter behind trees at the edge of the fields before she knocked at the door. She hesitated before she approached the door, thinking, suppose that

he, too, should refuse shelter, suppose—Then she thought, Lord, I'm going to hold steady on to You and You've got to see me through—and knocked softly.

She heard the familiar guttural voice say, "Who's there?"

She answered quickly, "A friend with friends."

He opened the door and greeted her warmly. "How many this time?" he asked.

"Eleven," she said and waited, doubting, wondering.

He said, "Good. Bring them in."

He and his wife fed them in the lamplit kitchen, their faces glowing, as they offered food and more food, urging them to eat, saying there was plenty for everybody, have more milk, have more bread, have more meat.

They spent the night in the warm kitchen. They really slept, all that night and until dusk the next day. When they left, it was with reluctance. They had all been warm and safe and well-fed. It was hard to exchange the security offered by that clean, warm kitchen for the darkness and the cold of a December night.

## Vocabulary Builder

**After you read,** *review the words you decided to add to your vocabulary. Write the meaning of words you have learned in context. Look up the other words in a dictionary, glossary, thesaurus, or electronic resource.*

# Ann Petry (1908–1997)

Born into a middle-class family in Connecticut, Ann Petry was treated unfairly as a child because she was African American—a bitter experience that outraged her. She began her career as a pharmacist and later became a reporter. In 1938, she married and moved to New York City, where she decided to become a writer. Along with her writing, she also founded Negro Women, Inc., served as a recreational director for problem children, was active in the performing arts, and taught business-letter writing for the Harlem NAACP.

Now that you have read an excerpt from *Harriet Tubman: Conductor on the Underground Railroad*, read this excerpt from *Red Scarf Girl: A Memoir of the Cultural Revolution* to compare a biography to an autobiography.

# from RED SCARF GIRL
## A Memoir of the Cultural Revolution

### by Ji-li Jiang

**Background** *In 1966, twelve-year-old Ji-li Jiang was a loyal follower of Chairman Mao and the Chinese Communist Party. When the Cultural Revolution began, she enthusiastically supported Mao's campaign to "Destroy the Four Olds"—old ideas, old culture, old customs, and old habits. But then her family came under attack because they had once been wealthy, and Ji-li's life changed.*

Dad was often kept late at the theater,[1] and sometimes he did not come home until after we were in bed. There were a lot of meetings, he told us. Often I would wake up when I heard him come in, and as I went back to sleep, I heard him and Mom talking in low voices. They must have made their decision about the trunks at one of those late-night conferences, but the first

---

[1] **theater** Ji-li's father is an actor.

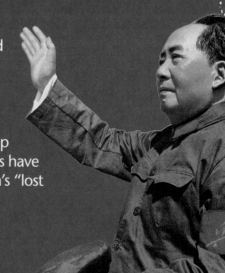
we knew about it was on a Sunday morning when they started carrying the trunks up to the roof.

The four trunks were part of Grandma's dowry.[2] They were a rich red leather, with a pattern stamped in gold. Each trunk had two sets of brass locks on its front and a round brass handle on each end. When they were stacked up on their rack, they made our room shine. Now Dad was going to dye them black so that they would not be considered fourolds.[3]

Four stools were waiting in the middle of the roof, and the first chest was placed upon them. The dark dye was already mixed. Dad set to work.

"Wait a minute," exclaimed Grandma. There was a dark stain about the size of a thumb print on one of the brass handles. She took out her handkerchief and rubbed the handle over and over until it was clean and bright. She looked at the chest with a dreamy expression and gently laid her hand on it. Against the deep red leather her skin seemed even paler.

"It won't look bad after it's painted," Dad said softly.

Grandma seemed to wake up. "Oh, I know," she said. "You go ahead." She went down to the room and did not come back.

"Her mother gave her these trunks when Grandma got married. That's why she's sad," Dad explained.

---

[2] **dowry** (dou´rē) *n.* money or property that a woman's family gives to the man she marries.

[3] **fourolds** *n.* short form of "Four Olds" (see "Background").

## Literature in Context

Link to Social Studies

**The Cultural Revolution** In 1966, Chairman Mao Zedong launched the Cultural Revolution, a political movement and power struggle that lasted for ten years. The Cultural Revolution was Mao's attempt to renew revolutionary passion and "purify" the Communist party of supposedly bad influences. Mao closed China's schools and called for the formation of the Red Guards, an organization of high school and college students that would enforce true Communist values. The Red Guards terrorized their communities. They accused educated people—such as teachers, writers, doctors, and artists—of being enemies of Communism. Families that had once been wealthy, even several generations back, were publicly humiliated and physically attacked. Children were forced to condemn their own parents. Millions of people were sent to the countryside to be "reeducated" by doing hard labor on farms.

The Cultural Revolution caused widespread social and economic chaos. Young people like Ji-li Jiang who grew up during those years have been called China's "lost generation."

I thought of Grandma getting married so long ago, bringing the four beautiful trunks full of gifts her mother had sent from Tianjin[4] to Shanghai.[5] Grandma must have been excited and exhausted, traveling a thousand miles to marry a man she had never met.

Dad started to paint, **wielding** the brush awkwardly.

"Dad, it's too dry. Look how it's streaking."

Dad dipped the brush in the dye again.

"Look out! It's dripping, Dad."

Shouting advice, we ran around the trunks excitedly.

Eventually Dad's painting improved, and the first trunk was finished. But the original color could still be seen through the dye, and he had to put on a second coat. Ji-yun and I grew tired of watching and went back downstairs. Ji-yong stayed to help.

An amazing sight stopped the two of us in the doorway.

"Wow," Ji-yun said.

Glowing silks and satins spilled out of an old trunk. The whole room was alive with color.

Ji-yun grabbed a piece of silk. "Gorgeous! Are these costumes, Mom?"

They were old clothes, long gowns like the ones ancient courtiers and scholars wore in the movies. Many of them were embroidered with golden dragons or phoenixes.[6] Some were printed with magnificent colorful patterns, and some were even crusted with pearls and gold sequins.

"These belonged to our ancestors. Grandma thought they were too nice to throw away, so we kept them in the bottom of this chest." Mom reached in and pulled out a bunch of colorful silk neckties. She threw them all on the floor.

I was worried. "Mom, aren't these all fourolds?"

"That's right. That's why Grandma and I decided to make comforter covers out of them. We can use the ties to make a mop."

"It seems terrible to just cut them all up. Why don't we just give them to the theater or to the Red Guards[7]?" Ji-yun held a gown up in front of her. She was imagining what it would be like to wear it, I knew.

"The theater doesn't need them, and it's too late to turn them in now. The Red Guards would say that we were hiding them and waiting for New China to fall. Besides, even if we did turn them in, the Red Guards would just burn them anyway." Grandma

---

[4] **Tianjin** (tyen´jin´) city in the northeast part of China.

[5] **Shanghai** (shanj´hī´) China's largest city, with a population of about ten million people during the period of the Cultural Revolution.

[6] **phoenixes** (fē´niks´ez) n. a bird in Egyptian mythology that consumed itself by fire and then rose up from the ashes.

[7] **Red Guards** during the Cultural Revolution, an organization of high school and college students who were loyal supporters of Chairman Mao and considered young revolutionary leaders. See "Literature in Context," page 222.

*Marking the Text*

◀ **Good to Know!**
Footnotes provide information that can help you better understand the text. The number in the body of the text lets you know that you can look to the bottom of the page to find more information.

while reading your anchor book

looked at me and shook her head as she picked up her scissors. "I just couldn't bear to sell them," she said sadly. "Even when your father was in college and we needed money." She picked up a lovely gold-patterned robe and said softly, "This was a government official's uniform. I remember my grandfather wearing it."

"It *is* pretty, Grandma," I said, "but it is fourolds. Don't feel bad about it."

The long gowns were so large that the back of one was big enough for half a quilt cover. Mom and Grandma discussed the job while cutting: which parts could be used for covers and which parts for cushions. Ji-yun and I were enchanted by the pearls and gold sequins littering the floor. We pestered Grandma and Mom to let us have them, and finally Mom sighed and yielded.

Ji-yun and I were overjoyed. We sat amid the piles of silks, picking up pearls and putting them in a jar. Little White[8] was happy too. She rolled over and over among the scraps of silk and batted pearls around the floor.

While we played, Mom made two quilt covers out of the gowns, one deep purple and the other a bright gold. Then she made a pair of mops from the ties. We were delighted with them. You could not find anything like our tie mops in the stores.

Dad and Ji-yong finally finished the second coat of dye on the trunks. The gold stamping still **obstinately** showed through the layers, but the deep red had become a dark burgundy. The

---

[8] **Little White** the family cat.

▲ **Critical Viewing**
Why did the Red Guard think that destroying valuable items, such as this fabric, would benefit society?

*Marking the Text*

_____
_____
_____
_____
_____

Vocabulary Builder

**obstinately**
(äb´stə nət´lē) *adv.*

**Meaning**

room seemed dressed up with the glowing new quilts and the repainted trunks. I felt good. We had really done what Chairman Mao asked, breaking with the old and establishing the new.

"You did a nice job on the trunks," Grandma said. "I don't think the Red Guards will notice them."

Ji-yun looked up from the bed where she was lying with her face in the silky new cover. "Are the Red Guards going to come and search our house?" Everyone stood still. I stopped playing with the pearls. Even Little White stopped rolling around the floor.

"It's possible," Mom said slowly, "but you don't have to be afraid. You are just children, and a search would have nothing to do with you."

The new decor lost all its brightness. The pearls I had been playing with lost their **luster,** and I put them down.

\*     \*     \*     \*

*As the Cultural Revolution continues, life gets worse and worse for Ji-li and her family because of their "class status." Her grandfather had been a landlord, considered the worst crime in Communist China. Her grandmother, his widow, is now officially classified as a "landlord's wife" and publicly humiliated. Ji-li's father also comes under suspicion. Eventually he is taken into custody and tortured so that he will confess his supposed counterrevolutionary crimes.*

*Ji-li is surprised when she is chosen to participate in her school's prestigious Class Education Exhibition, intended to expose the evils of the "class enemies" of the Cultural Revolution. She discovers that she is considered an "educable child"—a young person who can overcome her family background. Ji-li throws herself into preparations for the exhibit—but then she is forced to make a terrible choice.*

\*     \*     \*     \*

During Math class a few days later, Teacher Hou from the Revolutionary Committee popped his head into my classroom. He barely glanced at Teacher Li before saying curtly, "Jiang Ji-li,[9] come to our office right away. Someone wants to talk to you."

I stood up nervously, wondering what it could be. I felt my classmates' piercing eyes as I mechanically left the classroom. Teacher Hou walked ahead of me without seeming to notice my presence. I followed silently.

I tried not to panic. Maybe it was not bad. Maybe it was about the exhibition. Maybe Chairman Jin wanted me to help the others with their presentations. At the end of the long, dark hallway Teacher Hou silently motioned me into the office and then walked away.

---

[9] **Jiang Ji-li** In China people are usually called by their last names first, so Ji-li is called "Jiang Ji-li" by her teachers and classmates.

**Vocabulary Builder**

**luster**
(lus´tər) *n.*

**Meaning**

I wiped my hands on my trousers and slowly opened the door. The thin-faced foreman from Dad's theater was right in front of me.

My face must have shown my dismay.

"Sit down, sit down. Don't be afraid." Chairman Jin pointed to the empty chair. "These comrades from your father's work unit are just here to have a study session[10] with you. It's nothing to worry about."

I sat down dumbly.

I had thought about their coming to my home but never imagined this. They were going to expose my family in front of my teachers and classmates. I would have no pride left. I would never be an educable child again.

Thin-Face sat opposite me, with a woman I had never seen before. Teacher Zhang was there too, his eyes encouraging me.

Thin-Face came straight to the point. "Your father's problems are very serious." His cold eyes nailed me to my seat. "You may have read the article in the *Workers' Revolt*[11] that exposed your family's filthy past." I slumped down in my chair without taking my eyes off his face. "In addition to coming from a landlord family, your father committed some serious mistakes during the Antirightist Movement[12] several years ago, but he still obstinately refuses to confess." His cold manner became a little more animated. "Of course we won't tolerate this. We have decided to make an example of him. We are going to have a struggle meeting of the entire theater system to criticize him and force him to confess." He suddenly pounded the table with his fist. The cups on the table rattled.

I tore my eyes away from him and stared at a cup instead.

"As I told you before, you are your own person. If you want to make a clean break with your black family[13], then you can be an educable child and we will welcome you to our revolutionary ranks." He gave Chairman Jin a look, and Chairman Jin chimed in, "That's right, we welcome you."

"Jiang Ji -li has always done well at school. In addition to doing very well in her studies, she participates in educational reform," Teacher Zhang added.

"That's very good. We knew that you had more sense than to follow your father," Thin-Face said with a brief, frozen smile. "Now you can show your revolutionary determination." He

---

[10] **study session** a "reeducation" meeting intended to change someone's thinking or behavior.

[11] **Workers' Revolt** a newspaper published during the Cultural Revolution.

[12] **Antirightist Movement** a movement against people who criticized the Communist Party.

[13] **black family** During the Cultural Revolution, the color red symbolized Communism, and the color black symbolized everything opposed to Communism.

paused. "We want you to testify against your father at the struggle meeting."

I closed my eyes. I saw Dad standing on a stage, his head bowed, his name written in large black letters, and then crossed out in red ink, on a sign hanging from his neck. I saw myself standing in the middle of the stage, facing thousands of people, **condemning** Dad for his crimes, raising my fist to lead the chant, "Down with Jiang Xi-reng." I saw Dad looking at me hopelessly, tears on his face.

"I . . . I . . ." I looked at Teacher Zhang for help. He looked away.

The woman from the theater spoke. "It's really not such a hard thing to do. The key is your class stance.[14] The daughter of our former Party Secretary resolved to make a clean break with her mother. When she went onstage to condemn her mother, she actually slapped her face. Of course, we don't mean that you have to slap your father's face. The point is that as long as you have the correct class stance, it will be easy to testify." Her voice grated on my ears.

"There is something you can do to prove you are truly Chairman Mao's child." Thin-Face spoke again. "I am sure you can tell us some things your father said and did that show his landlord and rightist mentality." I stared at the table, but I could feel his eyes boring into me. "What can you tell us?"

---

14 **class stance** attitude or point of view about issues relating to class status.

▲ **Did You Know?**

During the Cultural Revolution, public humiliations took place frequently as punishment for not following the rules of the Party.

*Marking the Text*

Vocabulary Builder

**condemning**
(kən dem´i[ng]) *v.*

**Meaning**

Biography and Autobiography **227**

"But I don't know anything," I whispered. "I don't know—"

"I am sure you can remember something if you think about it," Thin-Face said. "A man like him could not hide his true beliefs from a child as smart as you. He must have made comments critical of Chairman Mao and the Cultural Revolution. I am sure you are loyal to Chairman Mao and the Communist Party. Tell us!"

"But my father never said anything against Chairman Mao," I protested weakly. "I would tell you if he did." My voice grew stronger with conviction. "He never said anything against the Party."

"Now, you have to choose between two roads." Thin-Face looked straight into my eyes. "You can break with your family and follow Chairman Mao, or you can follow your father and become an enemy of the people." His voice grew more severe. "In that case we would have many more study sessions, with your brother and sister too, and the Red Guard Committee and the school leaders. Think about it. We will come back to talk to you again."

Thin Face and the woman left, saying they would be back to get my statement. Without knowing how I got there, I found myself in a narrow passageway between the school building and the school-yard wall. The gray concrete walls closed around me, and a slow drizzle dampened my cheeks. I could not go back to the classroom, and I could not go home. I felt like a small animal that had fallen into a trap, alone and helpless, and sure that the hunter was coming.

## Vocabulary Builder

**After you read,** *review the words you decided to add to your vocabulary. Write the meaning of words you have learned in context. Look up the other words in a dictionary, glossary, thesaurus, or electronic resource.*

# JI-LI JIANG (b. 1954)

**Ji-Li Jiang** was born in Shanghai, China in 1954. As a young girl, she witnessed the Cultural Revolution, an event that left a lasting impression on her. As a young adult, Ms. Jiang taught science in Shanghai, but she moved to the United States in 1984. Her first book, *Red Scarf Girl,* which focuses on the Cultural Revolution, was published in 1992. It has been read widely by people of all ages. Ji-Li Jiang now lives in the San Francisco Bay area and is active in promoting cultural exchange between China and western countries.

# Thinking About the Selections

## Harriet Tubman: The Railroad Runs to Canada *and* Red Scarf Girl: A Memoir of the Cultural Revolution

**Go Online**

**About the Author**
Visit: PHSchool.com
Web Code: exe-7306
        exe-7307

**1** **Compare and Contrast** Describe the historical context of each selection—the culture and historical period and events that are the writer's focus.

_____

_____

**2** **Infer** Why does Tubman feel that she cannot let the runaways know that she is unfamiliar with the new route they are traveling on? Do you agree with her decision? Why or why not?

_____

_____

_____

**3** **Analyze** What difficult decision is Ji-li forced to make? How does she feel when she is forced to make this choice?

_____

_____

_____

**4** **Compare and Contrast** These two selections describe different cultures. What is each author's perspective on the people and events in her narrative?

_____

_____

_____

_____

**Write** Answer the following questions in your Reader's Journal.

**5** **Apply** By reading about the lives of Harriet Tubman and Ji-li Jiang, what can we learn about how real people have struggled for freedom?

**6** **Analyze** Discuss a character in your Anchor Book that struggles in some way. What can you learn from the character's struggles?

Biography and Autobiography  **229**

while reading your anchor book

# 3-6 Language Coach
## Grammar and Spelling

## Sentence Functions

Sentences are classified into four categories based on their function. The endmark, or punctuation at the end of a sentence, depends on what type of sentence it is.

Go Online

**Learn More**
Visit: PHSchool.com
Web Code: exp-7301

| Category | Function | Endmark | Example |
|---|---|---|---|
| **declarative** | to make statements | . | Our dog chased a chipmunk. |
| **interrogative** | to ask questions | ? | What time is it? |
| **imperative** | to give commands | . or ! | Put your books away. Do not touch that stove! |
| **exclamatory** | to call out or exclaim | ! | What a fantastic idea! |

**Directions** Write a description of your funniest memory. Include dialogue in your description that includes each of the four sentence types above.

_____

_____

_____

_____

_____

_____

_____

_____

_____

_____

_____

**Author's Craft**

The simple change of a period to an exclamation mark can alter a sentence's meaning more than you might expect. Turn to the excerpt from "Melting Pot," on page 206. Change two declarative sentences to exclamatory sentences. How do their meanings change?

# Avoiding Sentence Fragments and Run-On Sentences

**Learn More**
Visit: PHSchool.com
Web Code: exp-7302

A **sentence fragment** is a group of words that does not express a complete thought. To correct a sentence fragment, create a sentence that contains both a subject and a verb, and that communicates a complete thought.

| Sentence Fragment | Reason | Corrected Sentence |
|---|---|---|
| Ran to the store. | This fragment contains no subject, and does not express a complete thought. | I ran to the store. (*I* is the subject and *ran* is the verb) |

A **run-on sentence** contains two or more complete thoughts that aren't appropriately linked or separated. To correct a run-on sentence, make sure that it contains appropriately used conjunctions and punctuation. **Semicolons (;)** connect two independent clauses that are closely related ideas.

| Run-on Sentence | Reason | Corrected Sentence |
|---|---|---|
| Sarah met her father at the beach they went fishing. | There is no punctuation or conjunction to separate the two complete thoughts. | Sarah met her father at the beach. They went fishing. OR Sarah met her father at the beach, and they went fishing. OR Sarah met her father at the beach; they went fishing. |

**Directions** Rewrite the following paragraph, correcting any sentence fragments and run-on sentences.

Joaquin and Ellie decided to form a band. Ellie played drums Joaquin played keyboards and sang. Ellie's younger brother, David, who plays guitar. Offered to play with them. Ellie had mixed feelings about being in the same band as David. Even though he was talented. However, when David played his guitar. Joaquin was mesmerized, Ellie changed her mind. Now the trio performs at least once a week.

# 3-7 Writer's Workshop
## Narration: Autobiographical Narrative

Have you ever had an event in your life that you wanted to tell? Such stories are called **autobiographical narratives**. Follow the steps outlined in this workshop to write your own autobiographical narrative about an important event in your life.

To be effective, your autobiographical narrative should include the following elements.

▶ A clear sequence of events involving you, the writer

▶ A pace that effectively builds the action

▶ Specific details and quotations that help readers vividly imagine movement, gestures, and expressions

▶ Error-free writing, including correct use of complete sentences

**Purpose** To write an autobiographical narrative about an important event in your life

**Audience** You, your teacher, and your classmates

## Prewriting—Plan It Out

To choose an event to narrate, use one of the following two steps.

**Freewrite.** Write for five minutes about whatever comes to mind about one meaningful incident, such as: *funny times, sad times,* or *lessons I have learned.* Review what you have written and circle any ideas that could make a good topic.

**List ideas.** In the following chart, write specific events and the importance of each. Use the sample chart as a guide. Choose the event that will be most interesting for readers.

| Event | Importance |
|---|---|
| shoveled after snowstorm | spent quality time with my father |
| sang in talent show | overcame fear of performing in front of audience |

| Event | |
|---|---|
| | |
| | |
| | |

**Narrow your topic.** Now it's time to choose a specific topic. Some events should seem more significant than others, and will make better topics for your paper. Choose one topic and think about its impact. Jot down notes to further explore how the event affected your life.

**Gather details.** On a separate sheet of paper, jot down specific details of your event in an **idea web** like the one below. Write your event in the center and important details in the boxes around it.

## Drafting—Get It on Paper

Using your idea web as an outline, write your draft. Think about varied ways of beginning your narrative, such as starting in the middle of the action, or beginning with dialogue. At any point in your writing process, return to previous stages to add new ideas. Write in the first-person point of view, using an engaging voice and style. Keep your purpose and audience in mind while drafting.

**Incorporate dialogue into your writing to help build interest.**
Quotations are generally accompanied by expressions such as *she said* or *he asked*. The following rules describe how to punctuate quotations with expressions that come before, after, or in the middle of the quotation.

▶ Place a comma after an introductory expression, and then write the quotation as a full sentence.

   **Example:** Ellie yelled, "Watch out for the hill!"

▶ Place a comma or punctuation mark inside the closing quotation mark, and then write the concluding expression.

   **Example:** "I can do it," I replied.

▶ Place a comma and a quotation mark at the end of the first part of a quotation, a comma after an interrupting expression, and a new set of quotation marks for the rest of the quotation.

   **Example:** "Well," I thought to myself, "it's now or never."

**Student Model: Using Dialogue to Elaborate**

As we came around the corner of the bike path, I started picking up speed. By the time I realized what was happening, it was too late. "The hill," Erika yelled, "Your brakes! Use your brakes!"

This dialogue builds interest and excitement.

## Revising—Make It Better

**Revise your overall structure.** Check the logic of your ideas and rearrange paragraphs and words for consistency. Create interesting sentences by varying the structure.

***Peer Review*** Ask for a partner's response to your autobiographical narrative. Revise to achieve the reaction you had intended.

**Directions** Read this student autobiographical narrative as a model.

**Student Model: Writing**

Go **O**nline

**Student Model**
Visit: PHSchool.com
Web Code: exr-7301

*Alexander Baker, Palos Verdes, CA*
### Bicycle Braking Blues

Crash! Once again, I found myself flying off my bike and toward the grass. At age eight, crashes were an everyday occurrence, and I reminded myself that it was better to practice braking here by the lawn than to risk another episode like "The Club Hill Clobbering."

It all started when I arrived at my grandparents' house in Galesburg to spend the summer. I made many friends in their neighborhood, but they spent most of their time riding bikes, and I didn't have one. Then, my step-grandmother gave me the almost new, metallic green bike that her grandson had outgrown. I was overjoyed to have a bike. . . . I learned to ride it well enough—what I didn't learn was how to use the brakes. . . .

One day my babysitter took me for lunch at the club grill. She rode my grandfather's golf cart while I rode my bike. When we had to climb the big hill leading up to the club, I walked my bike alongside the cart. After lunch, I mounted my bike while Erika drove Grandpa's golf cart. As we headed toward home, neither of us gave a thought to . . . the HILL.

As we came around the corner of the bike path, I started picking up speed. By the time I realized what was happening, it was too late. "The hill!" I yelled to Erika. "Your brakes! Use your brakes!" she shouted. . . . "Well," I thought to myself, "it's now or never." I steered my speeding bike toward the grass alongside the path and jumped off sideways. I leapt off and BAM! The world turned upside down and inside out. The next sound I heard was the grumbling of a golf cart engine. It sounded annoyed about the jumble of parts in its path. The next thing I saw was

With this hint, the writer clearly connects his introduction to the central conflict of his story.

Adding this detail helps move the story along. It shows why the bike is so important to the writer.

The writer narrates events in clear sequence.

Using this precise noun helps vividly convey the scene to readers.

Erika's face. She was so scared that her face was stiff and pale. I stood up to show Erika that I was fine. The only damage I sustained was some dirt on my jeans, and the bike survived without too many scratches too. Also, my pride was hurt. How can you ride a bike if you can never go down hill? So every day, Erika took me to the hill and we'd go a little further up. That way, I learned to brake on a hill, little by little, rather than getting clobbered again!

> Details like *stiff* and *pale* help readers vividly imagine the character's expression.

## Editing—Be Your Own Language Coach

Before you hand in your autobiographical narrative, review it independently for language convention errors.

## Publishing—Share It!

Consider the following idea to share your writing.

**Make a poster.** Arrange photos, artwork, or small souvenirs, along with a clean copy of your narrative, on poster board to display in class.

## Reflecting On Your Writing

**Rubric for Self-Assessment** Assess your essay. For each question, circle a rating.

| CRITERIA | RATING SCALE |
|---|---|
| **IDEAS** Is your paper filled with rich details? | NOT VERY      VERY <br> 1   2   3   4   5 |
| **ORGANIZATION** How logical and consistent is your narrative structure? | 1   2   3   4   5 |
| **VOICE** How well do you draw the reader in with your voice and style? | 1   2   3   4   5 |
| **WORD CHOICE** How appropriate is the language for your audience? | 1   2   3   4   5 |
| **SENTENCE FLUENCY** How varied is your sentence structure? | 1   2   3   4   5 |
| **CONVENTIONS** How well did you avoid sentence fragments, run-on sentences, and other grammatical errors? | 1   2   3   4   5 |

## Reading Skills: Fact and Opinion

**Directions** Read the following passage. Then answer the questions.

> I think that every kid should have a dog. Everyone knows that dogs are a person's best friend. Because I had a dog, I learned many important values. I had to take my dog, Dom, out all the time to walk him. Taking him out for a walk at night was always fun. I also had to remember to feed him every day so he would not go hungry. Besides teaching lessons about life, dogs are much more fun to have around than a cat.

**1** This passage is primarily _____.

　A. incredible

　B. objective

　C. subjective

　D. fact

**2** Which of the following is a fact from the passage?

　F. "I also had to remember to feed him"

　G. "Dogs are much more fun to have around than a cat"

　H. "every kid should have a dog"

　J. "Taking him out for a walk at night was always fun."

**3** "Everyone knows that dogs are a person's best friend." This statement is a(n) _____.

　A. recollection

　B. exclamation

　C. fact

　D. opinion

**4** Which would be a good source to investigate the popularity of the opinions in this passage?

　F. Cat Owners Magazine

　G. personal interviews with dog owners

　H. newspaper articles

　J. online encyclopedia

**5** The primary difference between facts and opinions is that _____.

　A. facts can't be proven

　B. facts can't be investigated

　C. opinions can be proven

　D. facts can be proven

**6** Which of the following is true of opinions?

　F. Two people can have two different opinions.

　G. They are as credible as facts.

　H. No two opinions are the same.

　J. They never contain the phrase *I think*.

# Literary Analysis: Elements of Nonfiction

Read the following passage. Then answer the questions.

I was a champion swimmer at Camp Minnow Lake. My buddies and I would race at all the swim meets, challenging each other as to who was the fastest. It was a very happy chapter in my life. Then, one summer, as I was preparing to make the move from my home town to camp, I discovered that my parents would not be able to afford the fee to send me that year. I was devastated, and didn't know what to do. Then, someone mentioned the local nursery was looking for some part-time help. I applied and was accepted. I spent most of the summer outdoors, enjoying the plants and trees. Before long, I had enough money saved up to go to camp—not that summer but the following one. My buddies and I had a wonderful reunion, and I felt great knowing that I would be with them again for the summer.

**7** This is primarily a reflective essay because it _____.

   **A.** describes how to do a particular task

   **B.** shows the cause and effect of events

   **C.** provides insight into a particular event in the author's life

   **D.** shows the order in which a series of events takes place

**8** This selection could also be considered an example of _____.

   **F.** autobiography

   **G.** biography

   **H.** tone

   **J.** figurative language

**9** What broader insight might the reader gain from the author's personal experience?

   **A.** Camp is expensive.

   **B.** Don't give up on your dreams.

   **C.** Nursery workers make a lot of money.

   **D.** Swimming is a great way to make friends.

**10** A writer's style is _____.

   **F.** why he or she wrote about something

   **G.** when he or she wrote about something

   **H.** what he or she wrote about

   **J.** how he or she wrote about something

## Timed Writing: Narration

**Directions** Think of an experience from your past that helped you gain insight to a broader meaning in life. Write two or three paragraphs on the event. Think about your word choice, tone, topic, and figurative language when writing. **(20 minutes)**

# 3-8 Reading Skills
## Identifying Main Idea and Supporting Details

In learning new reading skills, you will use special academic vocabulary. Knowing the right words will help you demonstrate your understanding.

### Academic Vocabulary

| Word | Meaning | Example Sentence |
|---|---|---|
| **imply** *v.*<br>*Related word:*<br>implied, implication | to indicate or suggest without stating exactly | The teacher *implied* that our behavior with the substitute was unacceptable. |
| **specify** *v.*<br>*Related words:*<br>specified, specification | to mention or state definitely | Please *specify* the flavor of ice cream you would like. |
| **indicate** *v.*<br>*Related words:*<br>indicated, indication | to show or point out | The guide will *indicate* the magnificent rock formations in Arches National Park. |

The **main idea** in a passage is the major topic of what you read or write. It is strengthened by **supporting details**. Authors can state the main idea anywhere in the passage, but they often place it in an introductory paragraph. They might also restate it in the concluding sentence of a passage. Look at the following graphic.

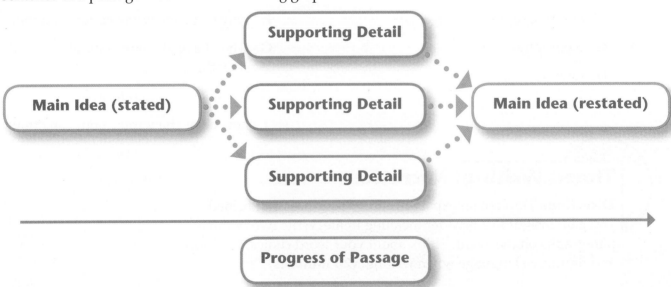

*Sidebar (left margin):* while reading your anchor book

**Directions** Read the following article, underlining details that support the main idea. Then answer the questions.

**NEW ZEALAND and AUSTRALIA** are so far from other continents that many of their animals and plants are found nowhere else on Earth. Only in New Zealand can you find kiwis and yellow-eyed penguins. Eighty-four percent of the plants in New Zealand's forests grow nowhere else. Australia has many unusual creatures, such as the kangaroo and the koala. These marsupials carry their young in a body pouch. Marsupials are found elsewhere in the world. The opossum of North America, for instance, is a marsupial. But in Australia, almost all mammals are marsupials. This is not true anywhere else on Earth.

■ Australia
☐ New Zeland

**1** **Identify** Complete the following organizer by filling in the main idea and supporting details.

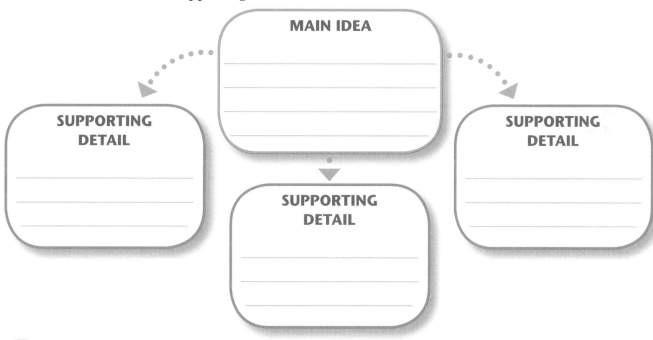

MAIN IDEA

SUPPORTING DETAIL

SUPPORTING DETAIL

SUPPORTING DETAIL

**2** **Explain** Why does the author give examples that show or reveal that Australia and New Zealand have many unique plants and animals?

_____

_____

_____

Identifying Main Idea and Supporting Details **239**

# Implied Main Idea

Sometimes the main idea is **specified**—stated directly—in a topic sentence. However, in some passages the main idea is not stated but **implied** instead. This requires you to identify supporting details that indicate the main idea.

Think of this process as putting together a puzzle whose image remains unclear until all of the pieces are put together.

Read this excerpt from a student essay and answer the questions.

Every time you enter your kitchen, you have the option of making your favorite foods or trying something new. When you prepare your own food, you learn what is in your favorite foods and how to make them. I can guarantee you'll enjoy cooking once you get started—and you'll enjoy eating more, too.

    As you read a recipe, you decide whether to follow it exactly or if you want to change it. Perhaps you don't have all the ingredients and want to use what you have, or maybe you feel creative and think your changes will make the food taste better.

*—Charlie Sage, Roanoke Rapids, NC*

**1** **Identify** Read through the excerpt again and identify three supporting details.

_____

_____

_____

**2** **Analyze** Using the details you identified, write the main idea of the essay.

_____

_____

**3** **Assess** What is a supporting detail you could add to the essay that would support the main idea?

_____

_____

**4** **Evaluate** How does the concluding sentence reinforce the topic sentence?

_____

_____

As you read this excerpt from a social studies textbook, track the main idea and supporting details. *Guiding Question:* How can the details in this passage help you learn about the Dust Bowl?

# The Black Blizzards

During most of the 1930s, the Great Plains region was devastated by drought and high winds. Howling across the Great Plains, these winds whipped up the soil of the over-farmed land and created blizzards of dust. These "black blizzards" were so thick and blinding that daylight seemed more like dusk. Year after year passed without rain, the winds continued to blow, and the dust swirled endlessly. During this terrible period the region came to be called the Dust Bowl.

But the cause of the dust blizzards wasn't just drought and wind. In a strange way patriotism was partly to blame. During World War I, the U.S. government encouraged farmers to support the war effort by planting more wheat. Farmers were eager to do their part to help feed the soldiers overseas. As farmers increased their production, their own profits increased. Following the invention of the farm tractor, farmers plowed up thousands of acres of grassland and planted wheat. Wheat production skyrocketed, but nature soon turned success into disaster.

When the drought began, farmers didn't realize that by plowing up the grasslands, they had destroyed the land's natural protection against soil erosion. The deep roots of the prairie grasses, which had always held the soil in place, were now gone. As the drought continued, one powerful windstorm after another blew across the prairie. Crops dried up and blew away. The dry topsoil rose in towering clouds and rolled across the land, blotting out the sun.

**What conclusions can you draw from the map of the region affected by the Black Blizzards?**

The dust storms made life miserable for the families of the Great Plains. Drifts of dust blanketed fences, porches, and farm equipment. Even people's homes offered little protection against the thick dust. Inside the houses everything was coated with layers of dirt.

Nothing grew for years. Eventually most of the rich topsoil blew away. As the years passed, all the moisture in the ground evaporated, leaving even the deep roots of trees in powdery dust. Trees and animals died, and unproductive farms left families in poverty and despair.

The Great Plains became a desolate place as thousands of people fled to California to escape the dust and look for work. Most found only low-paying agricultural jobs. But there were those who refused to leave. For these farmers, a reprieve was on its way. A federal program encouraged farmers to utilize new methods that would protect the precious topsoil from eroding. But revitalizing the soil took time, and the farmers still needed rain. It wasn't until the fall of 1939 that the farmers began to experience the rain they had been so desperate for. After that, rain began to come regularly again. Rain meant more to the farmers than it ever had before. It meant a future.

▲ A 97-million-acre section of the Great Plains was devastated by the Black Blizzards. Livestock starved and died, clouds of topsoil turned the sky to black, and farmers lost their farms. More than 650,000,000 tons of topsoil were lost, making this one of the largest ecological catastrophes in American history.

# Thinking About the Selection
## The Black Blizzards

**1** **Analyze** What is the main idea of "The Black Blizzards"? Indicate whether the main idea is stated or implied.

_____

_____

_____

**2** **Analyze** In the following chart, write six details that support the passage's main idea.

| Details | |
|---|---|
|  |  |
|  |  |
|  |  |

**3** **Distinguish** Specify why the following statement would not be an appropriate main idea for the passage. "After 1939, rain fell regularly over the Midwest, giving newfound hope to the farmers who remained in the area."

_____

_____

**Write** Answer the following questions in your Reader's Journal.

**4** **Reflect** How can the details in this passage help you learn about the Dust Bowl?

**5** **Identify** What is the main idea of your Anchor Book? Is it stated or implied? What details from the text support your answer?

**Ready for a Free-Choice Book?** _Your teacher may ask you if you would like to choose another book to read on your own. Select a book that fits your interest and that you'll enjoy. As you read, think about how your new book compares with your Anchor Book._

# 3-9 Literary Analysis
## *Expository Writing*

When you want to learn something new, such as how the pyramids were built or who invented the computer, how do you go about getting the information? One good strategy is to read **expository writing**—writing that explains or informs the reader about a particular topic.

In expository writing, the author's purpose is to explain—to give information, describe a process, or discuss an idea. The author does not provide opinions. Examples of expository writing are newspaper and magazine articles, encyclopedia entries, history books, and biographies.

## Literary Terms

Here are four common ways information is organized in expository writing.

| Type of Organization | Example | Signal Words or Transitions |
|---|---|---|
| **Cause-and-effect** explains why or how something happened. | an article about how the invention of the electric lightbulb allowed people to light their houses at night | because of, consequently, therefore |
| **Chronological** arranges events by proper order in time. | a history of electricity from its discovery to its many uses today | first, next, last, later, afterward, when, finally |
| **Compare-and-contrast** shows how two or more subjects are the same and different. | an article that compares a standard lightbulb to an energy-saving lightbulb | similarly, like, differently, however, in contrast to, but |
| **Problem-and-solution** identifies an issue and then provides a resolution. | an essay about the pollution produced by power plants, suggesting using more energy-saving devices to reduce pollution | if/then, the problem is, the question is, one possible solution |

**Directions** Read the following passage. Underline words and phrases that provide details about how information is arranged. Then, answer the questions that follow.

### from "A Growing Remembrance: Art Takes Root Near Ground Zero"

*by Margaret G. Zackowitz*

For nearly a century, the big sycamore in the yard of St. Paul's Chapel provided leafy shade—a welcome thing in the canyons of lower Manhattan. On September 11, 2001, the tree died providing protection. Uprooted during the collapse of the World Trade Center towers across the street, the sycamore fell in such a way that St. Paul's—where George Washington worshipped on his inauguration day in 1789—was shielded from the tide of the buildings' debris. Not even a window was broken in the chapel, which went on to serve for eight months as a relief ministry for ground zero's recovery workers.

Now, in a way, the tree will live on. Last year artist Steve Tobin, a specialist in monumental bronzes of natural forms, took the sycamore's remains back to his Pennsylvania studio for casting. On September 10, 2005, those preserved remains were returned to St. Paul's, and Tobin's 18-foot-high, 23-foot-wide bronze sculpture of the stump and roots were permanently placed in the yard of St. Paul's parent church, Trinity, a few blocks away at Wall Street and Broadway. Donated by the artist, the work, titled "The Trinity Root," is meant as a tribute to the city and to the resilience of the people who live there.

**1** **Analyze** What are two methods of organization the author uses? How do you know?

_____

_____

_____

**2** **Apply** What is the author's purpose for writing this passage?

_____

_____

_____

Look for the organizational structure and author's purpose in this piece of expository writing. *Guiding Question:* **How does learning about the history of baseball help you learn about social injustice as well?**

# THE SHUTOUT

## by Patricia C. McKissack and Frederick McKissack, Jr.

**Background** *In the earliest days of baseball, African American and white players played side by side. Eventually, however, baseball became segregated, or separated, into teams of "blacks" and "whites."*

▲ **Good to Know!**
In 1936, the Newark Dodgers team was purchased by Abe and Effa Manley, who merged the team with the Brooklyn Eagles.

### Vocabulary Builder

**Before you read,** *you will discuss the following words. In the Vocabulary Builder box in the margin, use a vocabulary building strategy to make the words your own.*

**anecdotes    evolved    diverse    irrational**

**As you read,** *draw a box around unfamiliar words you could add to your vocabulary. Use context clues to unlock their meaning.*

*Marking the Text*

**Expository Writing**

**As you read,** *underline important details about the segregation of baseball. In the margin take notes on your details and identify the organizational methods used.*

The history of baseball is difficult to trace because it is embroidered with wonderful **anecdotes** that are fun but not necessarily supported by fact. There are a lot of myths that persist about baseball—the games, the players, the owners, and the fans—in spite of contemporary research that disproves most of them. For example, the story that West Point cadet Abner

**Vocabulary Builder**

**anecdotes**
(an'ik dōt's) *n.*

**Meaning**

Doubleday "invented" baseball in 1839 while at Cooperstown, New York, continues to be widely accepted, even though, according to his diaries, Doubleday never visited Cooperstown. A number of records and documents show that people were playing stick-and-ball games long before the 1839 date.

Albigence Waldo, a surgeon with George Washington's troops at Valley Forge, wrote in his diary that soldiers were "batting balls and running bases" in their free time. Samuel Hopkins Adams (1871–1958), an American historical novelist, stated that his grandfather "played baseball on Mr. Mumford's pasture" in the 1820s.

Although baseball is a uniquely American sport, it was not invented by a single person. Probably the game **evolved** from a variety of stick-and-ball games that were played in Europe, Asia, Africa, and the Americas for centuries and brought to the colonies by the most **diverse** group of people ever to populate a continent. More specifically, some historians believe baseball is an outgrowth of its first cousin, rounders, an English game. Robin Carver wrote in his Book of Sports (1834) that "an American version of rounders called goal ball was rivaling cricket in popularity."

It is generally accepted that by 1845, baseball, as it is recognized today, was becoming popular, especially in New York. In that year a group of baseball enthusiasts organized the New York Knickerbocker Club. They tried to standardize the game by establishing guidelines for "proper play."

The Knickerbockers' rules set the playing field—a diamond-shaped infield with four bases (first, second, third, and home) placed ninety feet apart. At that time, the pitching distance was forty-five feet from home base and the "pitch" was thrown under-handed. The three-strikes-out rule, the three-out inning, and the ways in which a player could be called out were also specified. However, the nine-man team and nine-inning game were not established until later. Over the years, the Knickerbockers' basic rules of play haven't changed much.

In 1857–1858, the newly organized National Association of Base Ball Players was formed, and baseball became a business. Twenty-five clubs—mostly from eastern states—formed the Association for the purpose of setting rules and guidelines for club and team competition. The Association defined a professional player as a person who "played for money, place or emolument (profit)." The Association also authorized an admission fee for one of the first "all-star" games between Brooklyn and New York. Fifteen hundred people paid fifty cents to see that game. Baseball was on its way to becoming the nation's number-one sport.

## Vocabulary Builder

**evolved**
(ē vôlv′d) v.

**Meaning**

**diverse**
(di vurs′) adj.

**Meaning**

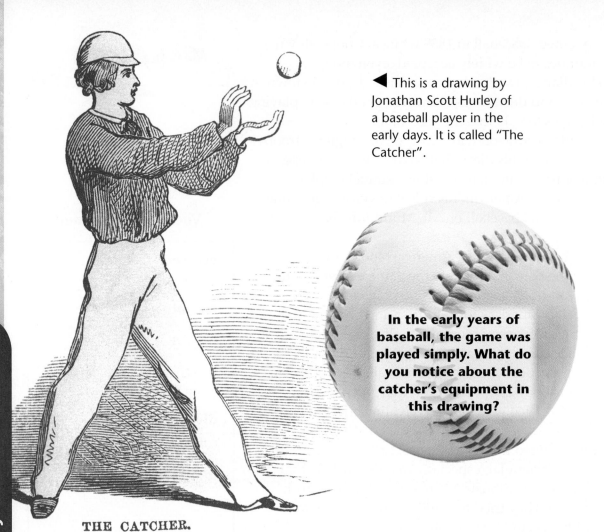

◀ This is a drawing by Jonathan Scott Hurley of a baseball player in the early days. It is called "The Catcher".

In the early years of baseball, the game was played simply. What do you notice about the catcher's equipment in this drawing?

THE CATCHER.

By 1860, the same year South Carolina seceded[1] from the Union, there were about sixty teams in the Association. For obvious reasons none of them were from the South. Baseball's development was slow during the Civil War years, but teams continued to compete, and military records show that, sometimes between battles, Union soldiers chose up teams and played baseball games. It was during this time that records began mentioning African American players. One war journalist noted that black players were "sought after as teammates because of their skill as ball handlers."

Information about the role of African Americans in the early stages of baseball development is slight. Several West African cultures[2] had stick-and-ball and running games, so at least some blacks were familiar with the concept of baseball. Baseball, however, was not a popular southern sport, never equal to boxing, wrestling, footracing, or horse racing among the privileged landowners.

*Marking the Text*

---

[1] **seceded** (si sēd'ed) *v.* withdrew from an alliance or an association.

[2] **West African cultures** *n.* The cultures from which many African Americans originated.

◀ **Good to Know!**
Roberto Clemente, far left, played with the Pittsburgh Pirates for eighteen seasons. Hank Aaron, left, played with the Milwaukee Braves, Atlanta Braves, and the Milwaukee Brewers for a total of twenty-three years.

**Marking the Text**

Slave owners preferred these individual sports because they could enter their slaves in competitions, watch the event from a safe distance, pocket the winnings, and personally never raise a sweat. There are documents to show that slave masters made a great deal of money from the athletic skills of their slaves.

Free blacks, on the other hand, played on and against integrated teams in large eastern cities and in small midwestern hamlets. It is believed that some of the emancipated[3] slaves and runaways who served in the Union Army learned how to play baseball from northern blacks and whites who had been playing together for years.

After the Civil War, returning soldiers helped to inspire a new interest in baseball all over the country. Teams sprung up in northern and midwestern cities, and naturally African Americans were interested in joining some of these clubs. But the National Association of Base Ball Players had other ideas. They voted in December 1867 not to admit any team for membership that "may be composed of one or more colored persons." Their reasoning was as **irrational** as the racism that shaped it: "If colored clubs were admitted," the Association stated, "there would be in all probability some division of feeling whereas, by excluding them no injury could result to anyone . . . and [we wish] to keep out of the convention the discussion of any subjects having a political bearing as this [admission of blacks on the Association teams] undoubtedly would."

So, from the start, organized baseball tried to limit or exclude African American participation. In the early days a few black ballplayers managed to play on integrated minor league teams. A few even made it to the majors, but by the turn of the century, black players were shut out of the major leagues until after World

**Vocabulary Builder**

**irrational**
(i rash′ə nəl) *adj.*

**Meaning**

---

[3] **emancipated** (ē man′sə pāt′ed) *adj.* free from bondage.

# JACKIE ROBINSON (1919-1972)

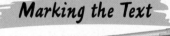

Jackie Robinson changed the face of sports, and possibly the nation. The grandson of a slave, and son of a sharecropper, Robinson played with the Kansas City Monarchs in the Negro National League, a segregated baseball organization that was founded in 1920. Blacks had been banned in white leagues, but in 1946, Robinson was drafted by the Brooklyn Dodgers and became the first African American to play in the major leagues. As his talent overshadowed prejudice, he thrilled the fans, aggressively stealing bases and getting hit after hit. He was Rookie of the Year in 1947, and MVP in 1949. With his help, the Dodgers won six National League pennants and one World Series, and he was elected to the Hall of Fame in 1962. Robinson didn't stop when he retired in 1957. He became a businessman and then an agent for social change. He once told a sports journalist, "We ask for nothing special. We ask only to be permitted to live as you live, and as our nation's Constitution provides."

War II. That doesn't mean African Americans didn't play the game. They did.

Black people organized their own teams, formed leagues, and competed for championships. The history of the old "Negro Leagues" and the players who barnstormed on black diamonds is one of baseball's most interesting chapters, but the story is a researcher's nightmare. Black baseball was outside the mainstream of the major leagues, so team and player records weren't well kept, and for the most part, the white press ignored black clubs or portrayed them as clowns. And for a long time the Baseball Hall of Fame didn't recognize any of the Negro League players. Because of the lack of documentation, many people thought the Negro Leagues' stories were nothing more than myths and yarns, but that is not the case. The history of the Negro Leagues is a patchwork of human drama and comedy, filled with legendary heroes, infamous owners, triple-headers, low pay, and long bus rides home—not unlike the majors.

## Marking the Text

## Vocabulary Builder

**After you read,** *review the words you decided to add to your vocabulary. Write the meaning of words you have learned in context. Look up the other words in a dictionary, glossary, thesaurus, or electronic resource.*

*while reading your anchor book*

# Thinking About the Selection

## The Shutout

**1** **Summarize** Complete the timeline to show some important events in baseball's history.

### Timeline of Baseball in the United States

| 1845 | 1857–1858 | 1860 | 1867 | after World War II (1945) |
|------|-----------|------|------|---------------------------|
|      |           |      |      |                           |

**2** **Identify** What is the authors' main purpose for writing this essay?

_____

_____

**3** **Analyze** What is the main organizational structure the authors used in this essay? Do the authors use another organizational structure as well? Explain.

_____

_____

_____

**4** **Speculate** How would the impact of the article change if it were written using a different organizational structure?

_____

_____

**Write** Answer the following questions in your Reader's Journal.

**5** **Explain** How does learning about the history of baseball help you to learn about social injustice as well?

**6** **Identify** How is most of the information in your Anchor Book organized? Support your answer with details from the text.

while reading your anchor book

# 3-10 Literary Analysis
## Persuasive Writing

Every day you are the target of **persuasion.** Advertisements try to persuade you to buy a product or visit a store. Friends and family might try to persuade you to do something with them or help with a chore. Recognizing these attempts at persuasion can help you decide for yourself how you will respond.

## Literary Terms

▶ **Persuasion** is writing or speech that tries to get people to think or act in a certain way. Persuasion is used in editorials, speeches, and advertisements.

▶ A writer's **position** is his or her opinion about a topic. Persuasive writing is intended to get the reader to agree with this position.

Writers use a variety of persuasive appeals and techniques.

### Persuasive Techniques

| Logical appeals | Emotional appeals | Ethical appeals |
|---|---|---|
| appeal to the reader's sense of logic | appeal to the reader's emotions, such as fear | appeal to the reader's sense of right and wrong |
| present a well-reasoned argument based on facts and evidence | use words with strong emotional associations, or connotations | use words with strong moral or ethical associations |
| "One way to end childhood hunger would be to use federal funds to expand the school breakfast program." | "If we don't act now to solve this terrible problem, our precious children will be in grave danger." | "It is disgraceful that the richest nation in the world allows children to go to bed hungry every night." |

▶ **Propaganda** is a form of persuasion that attempts to influence people into accepting a position without thinking about it too clearly. When someone tries to get you to buy a certain bicycle because it will "make you cool," this is a kind of propaganda.

Here are some common propaganda techniques. You may recognize some of them from advertising in newspapers, periodicals, or online texts.

| Bandwagon effect | trying to get you to do something or buy something just because everyone else does |
|---|---|
| Glittering generalities | statements that sound good and are hard to argue with—but don't really mean anything. For example, a politician running for office might say, "We need to improve our school system!" This is a safe statement that is not likely to be disagreed with; however, it provides no real information on how to improve the school system. |
| Testimonials | using celebrities or experts to make a product or an idea seem worthwhile or believable |

**Directions** Read the following passage. Underline details that show the writer is trying to persuade readers to accept his position. Then answer the questions that follow.

Go Online

**About the Author**
Visit: PHSchool.com
Web Code: exe-7309

*from* **Protect the Rights of Immigrants**

*by Rocío Sáenz*

Immigrant and low-wage workers living in Massachusetts are doubly challenged: They live in one of the most expensive places in the nation at a time when the national political climate both exploits immigrant workers and punishes them for seeking the American dream.

Yet immigrant workers are an important part of the workforce. As the state increasingly relies on them, so should they depend on the elected leadership to look after their rights and interests. Immigrants and low-wage workers, like everyone, need good jobs with living wages and affordable health care.

**1**   **Identify** What type of persuasive technique(s) is/are used?

**2**   **Analyze** Cite one fact the writer uses to support his opinion.

**3**   **Evaluate** Do you think the writer made a strong case for his position? Why or why not?

**4**   **Apply** In small groups, go over various forms of media and identify the persuasive techniques that are used. Analyze how the article repeats or varies words or phrases to emphasize certain ideas or information. Share your findings with the class.

while reading your anchor book

Read the following speech aloud and imagine that you are trying to persuade an audience. As you read, work to read with a rhythm, flow, and meter that sounds like everyday speech.
*Guiding Question:* **How persuasive is Jordan's argument about the best way to learn tolerance?**

# ALL TOGETHER NOW
## by Barbara Jordan

**Background** *During the Civil Rights Movement of the 1950s and 1960s, Congress passed laws to extend equal rights to all Americans. In "All Together Now," Barbara Jordan expresses support for these important laws in this speech, but also stresses that people must work together to improve race relations.*

## Vocabulary Builder

**Before you read,** *you will discuss the following words. In the Vocabulary Builder box in the margin, use a vocabulary building strategy to make the words your own.*

**legislation    tolerant    fundamental    optimist**

**As you read,** *draw a box around unfamiliar words you could add to your vocabulary. Use context clues to unlock their meaning.*

When I look at race relations today I can see that some positive changes have come about. But much remains to be done, and the answer does not lie in more **legislation.** We have the legislation we need; we have the laws. Frankly, I don't believe that the task of bringing us all together can be accomplished by government. What we need now is soul force—the efforts of people working on a small scale to build a truly **tolerant,** harmonious society. And parents can do a great deal to create that tolerant society.

### Marking the Text

**Persuasive Writing**

**As you read,** *underline details that reveal the author's position. In the margin, make notes about the techniques the author uses to persuade the reader to accept her position.*

### Vocabulary Builder

**legislation**
(lej′is lā′shən) *n.*

**Meaning**


**tolerant**
(täl′ər ənt) *adj.*

**Meaning**

We all know that race relations in America have had a very rocky history. Think about the 1960s when Dr. Martin Luther King, Jr. was in his heyday and there were marches and protests against segregation[1] and discrimination.[2] The movement culminated[3] in 1963 with the March on Washington.

Following that event, race relations reached an all-time peak. President Lyndon B. Johnson pushed through the Civil Rights Act of 1964, which remains the **fundamental** piece of civil rights legislation in this century. The Voting Rights Act of 1965 ensured that everyone in our country could vote. At last, black people and white people seemed ready to live together in peace.

But that is not what happened. By the 1990s the good feelings had diminished. Today the nation seems to be suffering from compassion fatigue, and issues such as race relations and civil rights have never regained momentum.

Those issues, however, remain crucial. As our society becomes more diverse, people of all races and backgrounds will have to learn to live together. If we don't think this is important, all we have to do is look at the situation in Bosnia[4] today.

How do we create a harmonious society out of so many kinds of people? The key is tolerance—the one value that is indispensable in creating community.

If we are concerned about community, if it is important to us that people not feel excluded, then we have to do something. Each of us can decide to have one friend of a different race or background in our mix of friends. If we do this, we'll be working together to push things forward.

One thing is clear to me: We, as human beings, must be willing to accept people who are different from ourselves. I must be willing to accept people who don't look as I do and don't talk as I do. It is crucial that I am open to their feelings, their inner reality.

---

[1] **segregation** (seg′rə gā′shən) *n.* the practice of forcing racial groups to live apart from each other.

[2] **discrimination** (di skrim′i na′shən) *n.* unfair treatment based on race, religion, or some other category; prejudice.

[3] **culminated** (kul′mə nā′təd) *v.* reached its highest point.

[4] **Bosnia** (bäz′nē ə) *n.* country located on the Balkan Peninsula in Europe that was the site of a bloody civil war between different ethnic and religious groups during the 1990s.

Vocabulary Builder

**fundamental**
(fun′də ment′l) *adj.*

**Meaning**

▼ **Critical Viewing**
How does this image communicate Dr. Martin Luther King, Jr.'s message of peace and unity?

What can parents do? We can put our faith in young people as a positive force. I have yet to find a racist baby. Babies come into the world as blank as slates and, with their beautiful innocence, see others not as different but as enjoyable companions. Children learn ideas and attitudes from the adults who nurture them. I absolutely believe that children do not adopt prejudices unless they absorb them from their parents or teachers.

The best way to get this country faithful to the American dream of tolerance and equality is to start small. Parents can actively encourage their children to be in the company of people who are of other racial and ethnic backgrounds. If a child thinks, "Well, that person's color is not the same as mine, but she must be okay because she likes to play with the same things I like to play with," that child will grow up with a broader view of humanity.

I'm an incurable **optimist.** For the rest of the time that I have left on this planet I want to bring people together. You might think of this as a labor of love. Now, I know that love means different things to different people. But what I mean is this: I care about you because you are a fellow human being and I find it okay in my mind, in my heart, to simply say to you, I love you. And maybe that would encourage you to love me in return.

It is possible for all of us to work on this—at home, in our schools, at our jobs. It is possible to work on human relationships in every area of our lives.

while reading your anchor book

## Vocabulary Builder

**optimist**
(äp′tə mist) *n.*

**Meaning**

*Marking the Text*

## Vocabulary Builder

**After you read,** *review the words you decided to add to your vocabulary. Write the meaning of words you have learned in context. Look up the other words in a dictionary, glossary, thesaurus, or electronic resource.*

# Barbara Jordan (1936-1996)

Barbara Jordan inherited her talent at public speaking from her father and grandfather, who were both ministers. As a high school student in Houston, Texas, Jordan participated in debates and won public speaking competitions.

After receiving a law degree from Boston University, Jordan was elected to the Texas Senate in 1966. In 1972 she became the first African American woman from the South to be elected to the U. S. House of Representatives, where she served until 1979. During the 1976 Democratic National Convention, Jordan became the first African American to deliver the keynote speech at a major party's political convention. After leaving the House of Representatives, she became a professor of national policy at the University of Texas, and in 1994 she was awarded the Presidential Medal of Honor.

# Thinking About the Selection

## All Together Now

**Go Online**

**About the Author**
Visit: PHSchool.com
Web Code: exe-7310

**1** **Analyze** What opinion is Jordan trying to persuade readers to accept?

_____

_____

**2** **Categorize** Is Jordan's essay primarily a logical appeal, an emotional appeal, an ethical appeal, or a combination of these? Use details from the essay to support your answer.

_____

_____

_____

**3** **Evaluate** If you had just listened to Barbara Jordan deliver this essay as a speech, what questions would you ask her about her position? Is there bias, stereotypes, unclear or conflicting information given the writer's background or qualifications? Would you challenge her ideas or agree with them? Why?

_____

_____

**4** **Compare** Make some connections between the persuasive techniques of this selection and those used in the previous passage, "Protect the Rights of Immigrants."

_____

_____

**Write** Answer the following questions in your Reader's Journal.

**5** **Analyze** How persuasive is Jordan's argument about the best way to learn tolerance? Support your opinion with evidence from the essay.

**6** **Evaluate** Find a persuasive passage in your Anchor Book. What persuasive techniques does the author use? Are they effective? Explain your response.

# 3-11 Listening and Speaking Workshop
*Delivering a Persuasive Speech*

What do a television commercial and a political candidate have in common? They both attempt to persuade their audience to think or behave in a certain way. Delivering a persuasive speech can help you do the same.

while reading your anchor book

## Your Task

▶ Select a topic and a position, or point of view, about the topic. Consider who your audience is and select a point of view with which they will identify.

▶ Gather ideas and information that support your position.

▶ Deliver a formal or informal speech to persuade your audience to think or behave in a certain way.

## Organize Your Presentation

**1** **Choose your topic.** The following chart lists topics that people might disagree about. Write your position, or opinion, on each topic. Then, select one you will enjoy speaking about.

| Topic | Position |
|---|---|
| food choices in the cafeteria | |
| year-round school year | |
| students paying for their team sporting equipment | |
| school uniforms/dress codes | |

**2** **Gather information.** Research definitions, facts, quotations, and ideas, and identify personal experiences that will make your speech persuasive. Be careful to present ideas and information in an ethical way. Avoid misrepresenting someone by slander (misrepresentation in speech) or libel (misrepresentation in print).

# 3 Prepare your presentation.

▶ Arrange ideas you plan to present on index cards.

▶ Include only details and reasons that support your position. As needed, incorporate and define the specialized vocabulary for your topic into your speech.

▶ One of the best ways to persuade people is to inform and entertain them. Write an exciting introduction to capture your audience's attention.

▶ Anticipate your audience's concerns. Think about the logical, ethical, or emotional appeals you can make to persuade your audience.

# 4 Practice your presentation. Ask your friends, relatives, or teacher to act as your initial audience. Consider their feedback. Clarify your sentences, strengthen your arguments, and revise your speech.

# 5 Deliver your presentation. Consider these key elements.

▶ Use your individual style to convince your audience by choosing specific, vivid language and appropriate tone, volume, and pacing.

▶ Avoid reading your cards word for word. Use gestures, eye contact, and body language to emphasize your key points.

**Directions** For each assessment question, circle a rating.

## SPEAK: Rubric for Oral Interpretation

| CRITERIA | RATING SCALE | | | | |
|---|---|---|---|---|---|
| | NOT VERY | | | | VERY |
| CONTENT Was your topic interesting and your viewpoint clear? | 1 | 2 | 3 | 4 | 5 |
| ORGANIZATION How clear and logical was your speech? | 1 | 2 | 3 | 4 | 5 |
| DELIVERY How well did you make eye contact and control pacing, pronunciation, tone, and volume? | 1 | 2 | 3 | 4 | 5 |

## LISTEN: Rubric for Audience Self-Assessment

| CRITERIA | RATING SCALE | | | | |
|---|---|---|---|---|---|
| | NOT VERY | | | | VERY |
| ACTIVE LISTENING How well did you pay attention to and understand the message of each speaker? | 1 | 2 | 3 | 4 | 5 |

Be prepared to summarize or paraphrase the speaker's presentation and to provide constructive feedback.

## Simple and Compound Sentences

A **simple sentence** is a single **independent clause**—a group of words that has a subject and a verb and can stand by itself as a complete thought. See below for a simple sentence diagram. More model diagram sentences and exercises are online.

**Example** <u>Jasmine</u> | <u>slept</u>

A **compound sentence** is made up of two or more independent clauses linked by a comma and a coordinating conjunction such as *and, but,* or *or.*

Rewriting two independent clauses as one compound sentence helps create varied sentence structure. The chart below shows how two independent clauses can be formed into one compound sentence.

| | |
|---|---|
| **Two independent clauses** | The catcher dropped the ball. The runner stole second base. |
| **Compound sentence** | The catcher dropped the ball, and the runner stole second base. |

A semicolon can replace the comma and coordinating conjunction in a compound sentence if the second independent clause explains the first independent clause.

**Directions** Rewrite the following independent clauses to form one compound sentence.

**1** I gave my dog his food. He wagged his tail.

**2** Feeding animals at the zoo can be fun. You should only give them the food that is provided.

**3** The judges tasted the contestants' desserts. They named the chocolate cake the winner.

## Go Online

**Learn More**
Visit: PHSchool.com
Web Code: exp-7303

### Author's Craft

You might think that sophisticated writing always uses long, complicated sentences, but good writers know that simple sentences can sometimes be the most powerful. An unexpectedly short and simple sentence stands out. Good writers use these sentences to highlight profound or intense ideas. Turn to "The Black Blizzards" on page 241 and find two examples of this technique.

# Complex Sentences

A **complex sentence** contains one independent clause (simple sentence) and at least one subordinate clause (phrase that has a subject and a verb but cannot stand alone in a sentence.)

> **Independent clause/simple sentence** I kicked the soccer ball.
>
> **Subordinate clause** before the whistle blew
>
> **Complex sentence** I kicked the soccer ball before the whistle blew.

A **compound-complex sentence** contains two complex sentences or one simple sentence and one complex sentence.

> **Simple sentence** I kicked the soccer ball.
>
> **Compound sentence** I kicked the soccer ball, and Chiara hit it into the net.
>
> **Compound-complex sentence** I kicked the soccer ball, and Chiara hit it into the net before the goalie could react.

A compound sentence can also replace the coordinating conjunction with a semicolon as shown in the example below.

**Example** I kicked the soccer ball; Chiara hit it into the net.

**Directions** Read the following paragraph. Rewrite the paragraph to include at least one simple sentence, one compound sentence, and one complex sentence.

> In Hawaii, surfing is known as the "sport of kings." However, both Hawaiian chiefs and commoners participated in this pastime. The royalty surfed on some beaches. The common people surfed on others. Today, people from all walks of life enjoy surfing the same beaches. Much has changed about surfing from ancient to modern times. One thing has not changed, though. People still love to surf!

**Go Online**

**Learn More**
Visit: PHSchool.com
Web Code: exp-7304

**Author's Craft**

Sometimes complex sentences have so many parts that they are difficult to understand. It helps to know that most of the time, the main idea will be in the independent clause. The subordinate clauses add extra information to modify the main idea. Turn to "The Shutout" on page 246. Find three complex sentences and underline their independent clauses. Do they contain the main ideas? Where might you find the main ideas in compound-complex sentences?

# 3-13 Writer's Workshop
## *Persuasion: Persuasive Essay*

Do you want to change the way people think about a certain issue? A **persuasive essay** is a work in which a writer presents an argument for or against a particular position. Follow the steps outlined in this workshop to write a persuasive essay that identifies a problem in your school or community and suggests a possible solution.

**What to Include** Your essay should include the following elements.

► Your position on an issue that has more than one solution

► Strong evidence to support your position

► A response to possible opposing arguments

► Organized language that appeals to reason and emotion

► Error-free writing, including correct use of complex and compound-complex sentences

**Purpose** To write a persuasive essay that influences readers to share your point of view about an issue in your school or community

**Audience** You, your teacher, and your classmates

## Prewriting—Plan It Out

Follow the steps below to select a topic and plan your arguments.

**Choose your topic and point of view.** Brainstorm ideas. On a sheet of paper, list issues in your school or community that you feel need to be changed. Select an issue or problem about which you have strong feelings and have a possible resolution. See the box to the right for ideas.

**Identify a controlling idea.** Suppose your topic is "violence in the media." For your essay, you might focus only on violence in television shows.

**Gather detailed evidence.** Compile facts, statistics, and personal anecdotes (short accounts of things that have happened) to develop your supporting arguments. You might choose to survey students and create a graph sharing their opinions. Think about arguments readers might have against your point of view. Be sure to gather information you can use to respond to these arguments, which will be your counterarguments. List both in the following chart.

### Problems/Issues

- cafeteria food
- water pollution
- new city pool
- school computer use
- lack of recycling
- school uniforms
- a new club I want added to my school

| Arguments | Counterarguments |
|---|---|
| | |

# Drafting—Get It on Paper

The following steps will help make your essay convincing.

**Develop a thesis statement.** A thesis statement is a sentence that sums up your argument or main idea. Your first paragraph should catch readers' interest and include your thesis.

**Organize your arguments.** Identify your strongest arguments, excluding any unrelated information. Identify responses you can use to address counterarguments. Consider organizing your information as shown in the pyramid.

**Choose your words carefully.** Use connotations, the emotional association of words, figurative language (such as hyperbole), repetition, parallelism, and precise, lively words that stir the readers' emotions. Work to set a unique tone that appeals to your readers' sense of reason, and influences their reactions.

Introduction and thesis

- First set of arguments
- Supporting details

- Concerns and counterarguments
- Statements proving opposition is weak or incorrect

- Strongest argument
- Supporting details

Conclusion

| **Vague, dull** | a *good* candidate |
| **Precise, lively** | a *trustworthy* or *intelligent* candidate |

# Revising—Make It Better

**Revise your overall structure.** To check the organization of your essay, highlight each main point. Then use these tips.

- ▶ If readers need to know one main point to understand a different one, make sure the main points are in the right order.

- ▶ If two main points are similar, consider combining them into one paragraph.

**Revise your content.** The words that you choose when trying to persuade an audience are essential to the success of your mission. Be aware of any technical language you can use to be as authoritative as possible in your essay. If there is specific jargon relating to your topic, use of it will strengthen your work. Delete information and arguments that do not fit your purpose. All evidence should be cited correctly in your essay.

◀ **Good to Know!**
**Jargon** is specialized vocabulary belonging to the same work, profession, or topic.

**Include persuasive techniques.** In an appeal to authority or celebrity endorsements, a writer can use an important event or person to lend credibility to an argument. Alternatively, a writer can ask a rhetorical question, one to which no answer is required, to imply that the answer is obvious. Or, writers pose and answer their own questions as a way of presenting themselves as an authority. Writers also use irony to describe an opponents' perspectives.

*Peer Review* Read your draft to a classmate. Ask if your arguments are clear and convincing. Make revisions based on feedback.

**Student Model: Writing**

**Go Online**

**Student Model**
Visit: PHSchool.com
Web Code: exr-7302

*Amanda Wintenburg, Daytona Beach, FL*
## Decide the Future

To you, voting may seem like just a waste of time, just a mere piece of paper with boxes on it that you have to go through to mark which person you want for that particular job. But to me, it's something more, much more . . . it's your chance to decide the future. Everyone who is eligible should take advantage of the right to vote.

I'm not the only one who thinks voting should be a top priority for people. For years, companies and organizations have supplied numerous reminders and reasons to explain when and why you vote. You've seen the commercials; they've all told us about it. Although there is no financial profit in convincing people to vote, money is being spent to make sure it happens. That should tell you something.

Eenie, meenie, miney mo, . . . maybe you don't want to vote because you feel as if you don't know enough about the candidates to make an informed decision. However, newspapers, television broadcasts, performance records—all these fact-based sources of information are available to the interested voter who wants to make a responsible choice. Find out what the candidates have been doing and what they plan to do. Make your decision based on information.

In many countries, voting is not an option. In countries with kings and queens, leaders are born into their positions. In other countries, the leaders take control rather than being voted into a leadership role. Often leaders who are not elected can be corrupt or tyrannical, because the people can't remove them from power. We are citizens of a free country in which we have the right to vote. Whether or not the system works perfectly, it is better than a system with no voting. Vote because you can. Remind yourself that not everyone is as lucky.

If you don't vote, you have less control over your own life. Voting is your chance to make your voice heard. It's your chance to decide the future.

In the opening paragraph, the writer points out the two "sides" to the voting issue. She follows with her thesis statement.

This evidence supports the idea that voting matters.

Here, the writer identifies and addresses readers' concerns and counterarguments.

The writer reminds readers that not everyone has the right to vote. She uses language that appeals to both reason and emotion.

# Editing—Be Your Own Language Coach

Check your writing for clarity and for grammar, spelling, or punctuation errors. Pay attention to your use of verb tenses; commas, and semicolons in simple, complex and compound–complex sentences, semicolons, and colons introducing lists.

# Publishing—Share It!

Consider one of the following ideas to share your writing.

**Stage a public debate.** Prepare posters announcing the event, and send out invitations to members of your community who may attend.

**Submit your essay to a newspaper.** Many local newspapers will publish well-written persuasive compositions, particularly on the editorial page. Submit your composition and see what happens.

# Reflecting On Your Writing

**Explain** What did you learn about the form of the persuasive essay by writing one?

**Rubric for Self-Assessment** Assess your essay. For each question, circle a rating.

| CRITERIA | RATING SCALE |
|---|---|
| **IDEAS** Does your essay include strong arguments and evidence that supports them? | NOT VERY         VERY<br>1   2   3   4   5 |
| **ORGANIZATION** How clear and logical is your essay's structure? | 1   2   3   4   5 |
| **VOICE** Is your writing lively and engaging? | 1   2   3   4   5 |
| **WORD CHOICE** How well do you use persuasive techniques? | 1   2   3   4   5 |
| **SENTENCE FLUENCY** How varied is your sentence structure? | 1   2   3   4   5 |
| **CONVENTIONS** How correct is your grammar, especially your use of complex and compound-complex sentences? | 1   2   3   4   5 |

## 3-14 Discussing Your Anchor Book
### Literature Circles

**Author's Perspective** In this Literature Circle, your group members will start with an open discussion and then you will explore the perspective of the author of your Anchor Book.

## PART 1: Open Discussion

In your Literature Circle, discuss your Anchor Book following the discussion guidelines outlined in Unit 1. Remember to share your ideas, opinions, and questions from your Reader's Journal.

If you run out of ideas to share, discuss how the main character changes and copes with the central conflict, and how you and your group members might resolve the conflict differently.

## PART 2: Discuss—Author's Perspective

Now, you are going to analyze the author's perspective of your Anchor Book.

Authors' experiences, background, age, gender, and beliefs are factors that shape their understanding of the world, and influence what they choose to address in their writing. This unique point of view is the **author's perspective.**

In your Literature Circle create questions that you would ask the author. These should be questions that are not answered in your Anchor Book.

> ▶ Think of questions that will lead the author to elaborate on how the author's perspective, including opinions, emotions, background, and experiences, influenced his or her writing process.

> ▶ Ask questions that begin with *what, where, when, why,* and *how.* These are called **open-ended questions**. When you ask these types of questions, your subject will likely provide you with interesting and meaningful information.

> ▶ What do you know about the author's background, experience, or beliefs that might affect his or her perspective?

> **Instead of** *Did you like writing about space travel?*

> **Ask** *Why did you choose to write about space travel?*

Now that you have your questions, talk about how the author might answer them. What conclusions can you draw about the author's perspective? There aren't any real right answers here—the "interview" is imaginary. Record your conclusions below.

| Conclusions About the Author's Perspective |
| --- |
|  |

In your Literature Circle, identify factors that might change the author's perspective. Two factors have already been done for you. Together, create two more questions, and answer them by discussing how the author's perspective would change.

| Factors of the Author's Perspective | How might the Anchor Book be different? |
| --- | --- |
| the author was the opposite gender |  |
| born a century earlier |  |
|  |  |
|  |  |

With your group, develop an outline that highlights the important issues you discussed. Record your outline in your Reader's Journal.

## Anchor Book Projects

Now that you have finished reading your Anchor Book, it is time to get creative! Complete one of the following projects.

### Act Out a Scene  A

Lights, camera, action! It's time to bring the events of your Anchor Book to life. In this project, you will form groups and prepare a scene from your Anchor Book to present to your classmates.

1. Choose an event that you read about in your Anchor Book that your group would like to present to the class.

2. Assign roles to each member of your group. Not all members must speak, but each must participate in presenting your chosen event.

3. Organize your scene, using entertaining and informative dialogue as well as appropriate gestures, eye contact, and body language. Think about simple costumes or props that you could use to convey the time period and setting.

4. Practice until your group is able to perform the scene from memory. When your group is comfortable, present your scene to your class.

Your presentation should include the following elements.

▶ A scene taken from your Anchor Book

▶ Costumes or props related to the time period

▶ Appropriate gestures, eye contact, body language, and word choice

### Design a Set  B

As you read a novel, you can picture the setting in your mind because the writer has described it in detail. In plays, the setting is meant to be seen. The stage, backdrops, furniture, and props make up the set. The set should give the audience an idea of the time and place of the action.

1. Choose an important scene from your Anchor Book. Reread it and visualize what the set should look like. Jot down notes about where and when the scene takes place.

2. Design a set for this scene. Draw or use a computer to create a visual of the set.

3. Read the scene. Then present your set to the class. Describe your set and why you chose to design it the way you did.

Your set should include the following elements.

▶ Identifiable and familiar objects from your scene

▶ Visual clues that tell the viewer when and where the scene takes place

## Write a Biography

To understand an author's perspective, it helps to know something about his or her background, experiences, and beliefs. For this Anchor Book project, you will write a biography of the author.

1. Locate information about the author by referencing print and Internet sources. For instance, where did the author spend his or her childhood? Which experiences from the author's life may have contributed to his or her writing? Why did the author decide to become a writer?

2. Make a list of the information and think about how you can use it in writing the biography.

3. Write a brief biography, incorporating the material you've found during your research.

4. List the sources you cited for your biography at the end of your work.

Your biography should include the following elements.

▶ A summary of the author's background, experiences, and beliefs

▶ Information from print and Internet sources

▶ A list of the sources that you cited in your biography

## Free-Choice Book Reflection

You have completed your free-choice book. Before you take your test, read the following instructions to write a brief reflection of your book.

My free-choice book is _____.

The author is _____.

**1** Would you recommend this book to a friend? Yes _____ No _____

Why or why not?

_____

_____

**Write and Discuss** Answer the following question in your Reader's Journal. Then, discuss your answer with a partner.

**2** **Compare and Contrast** *What should we learn?* Compare and contrast the lessons you learned in your Anchor Book with those in your free-choice book. Which lessons were more important to you? Why? To extend the discussion, consider what important things we should all learn from different subject areas, such as math, science, and social studies.

after reading your anchor book

Answer the questions below to check your understanding of this unit's skills.

## Reading Skills: Fact and Opinion

Read this selection. Then answer the questions that follow.

> Last weekend we had the greatest barbeque celebration ever. The food was delicious and there was tons of it—it was the best! We also set up the backyard for games of wiffle-ball, touch football, and horseshoes. The weather was eighty degrees and sunny. Before the party was over, some of us snuck inside and filled up a bunch of water balloons and ended the party with a splash!

**1** Which of the following is a fact?

    **A.** "we had the greatest barbeque celebration ever"

    **B.** "The food was delicious"

    **C.** "it was the best"

    **D.** "The weather was eighty degrees and sunny."

**2** Which word from the first sentence is a clue that the sentence is an opinion?

    **F.** celebration

    **G.** weekend

    **H.** greatest

    **J.** barbeque

## Reading Skills: Main Idea and Supporting Details

Read this selection. Then answer the questions that follow.

> The history of baseball is complicated. Historians have an easier time with basketball. The origins of this game are well known. Unlike baseball or football, basketball is just a version of an earlier sport. The modern game was invented, and we know who invented it—a man named James Naismith.

**3** The main idea of this passage is _____.

    **A.** the history of baseball is complicated

    **B.** basketball is a version of an earlier sport

    **C.** the origins of basketball are well known

    **D.** basketball and baseball are different in many ways

**4** Which of the following best strengthens this passage's main idea?

    **F.** We know who invented it—a man named James Naismith.

    **G.** The history of baseball is complicated.

    **H.** The origins of basketball are well known.

    **J.** Basketball and baseball are different in many ways.

**5** The main idea of an article or essay is often included in the _____ .

A. introductory paragraph

B. second paragraph

C. supporting details

D. bibliography

**6** When the main idea of a passage is not stated directly, it is _____ .

F. specified in the text

G. indicated by supporting details

H. subjective

J. cause-and-effect

## Literary Analysis: Elements of Nonfiction

Choose the best answer for the following questions.

**7** The author's **diction** refers to _____ .

A. the author's attitude towards a subject

B. word choice

C. the sound or manner of expression an author uses

D. the author's style

**8** **Reflective writing** is writing that _____ .

F. explains steps in a process

G. persuades an audience

H. reflects issues about the world

J. shows the author's thoughts and feelings

Read this selection and answer the questions that follow.

As your class president, I will do everything in my power to get us longer lunches. I will do my best to represent all of your opinions throughout the year. Just listen to former class president Tommy O'Hara, who called me "the best person to carry on the torch for eighth grade."

**9** This selection is an example of _____ .

A. persuasive writing

B. expository writing

C. biographical writing

D. reflective writing

**10** **Propaganda** is _____ .

F. an appeal to the reader's sense of logic

G. the author's diction

H. using celebrities to make something seem worthwhile

J. persuading people to accept positions without thinking about them very much

**11** Which of the following techniques are used in this selection?

A. ethical appeals

B. testimonials

C. glittering generalities

D. bandwagon effect

**12** Which of these is the best organizational pattern for **autobiography**?

F. cause-and-effect

G. chronological

H. compare-and-contrast

J. problem-and-solution

**13** In **expository writing,** the words *first, next, last, later, afterward, when,* or *finally* introduce which type of organization?

A. problem-and-solution

B. cause-and-effect

C. compare-and-contrast

D. chronological

**14** A **nonfiction narrative** is a biography if _____ .

F. it has glittering generalities

G. an author is telling the life story of another person

H. the author tells his or her own life story

J. the author tells about his or her involvement in a historical event

**15** **Cause-and-effect** organization _____ .

A. organizes events by the order in which they occur

B. shows how two things are the same and different

C. shows how one event leads to another

D. shows a problem and provides a solution

**16** **Tone** is _____ .

F. the author's attitude towards his or her subject

G. the way a reader feels when reading a text

H. the life story of an author

J. the vocabulary the author uses in his or her writing

**17** *If/then* are signal words for what type of **expository writing**?

A. cause-and-effect

B. problem-and-solution

C. compare-and-contrast

D. chronological

**18** What is the difference between fiction and **nonfiction narrative**?

F. Only fiction narrative can contain a conflict.

G. Only nonfiction narrative can have characters.

H. Fiction narrative tells a story while nonfiction narrative does not.

J. Nonfiction narrative focuses on true events.

## Language Coach: Vocabulary

Choose the best answer.

**19** A word's **origin** is _____ .

A. the meaning of the word

B. the older word from which the word is derived

C. the number of syllables in the word

D. the beginning of the word

**20** One good way to learn the meaning of a word that is borrowed from another language is to _____ .

F. use context clues

G. use a thesaurus

H. learn the language

J. make a guess

**21** Another word for an outdoor market with stalls and shops is a _____ .

    **A.** safari

    **B.** plaza

    **C.** bazaar

    **D.** marketplace

**22** The word *nomination* is derived from a word meaning _____ .

    **F.** win

    **G.** place

    **H.** nation

    **J.** name

**23** Which of the following words is derived from a word meaning "house"?

    **A.** noun

    **B.** history

    **C.** domestic

    **D.** judgment

**24** The word "appendix" comes from a word meaning _____ .

    **F.** feeling

    **G.** attach

    **H.** body part

    **J.** book

## Language Coach: Grammar

Choose the best answer.

**25** Which of the following is a **compound sentence**?

    **A.** I ran down the street, screaming.

    **B.** Having written down the directions, we knew we wouldn't get lost.

    **C.** We forgot to fill up the gas tank, so the car ran out of gas.

    **D.** I put on my glasses and looked at the book.

**26** A sentence is **compound** when _____ .

    **F.** two clauses are joined by a conjunction

    **G.** two independent clauses are joined

    **H.** it has an independent clause and a subordinate clause

    **J.** it has two subordinate clauses

**27** Which of the following sentences is a **simple sentence**?

    **A.** I went to the store before I came home.

    **B.** We sang in the rain.

    **C.** Although we were sick, we still went to school.

    **D.** I looked up and down the street, but I did not see anything.

**28** Which of the following is an **independent clause**?

    **F.** I ran the marathon

    **G.** of the following suggestions

    **H.** with a big eerie grin

    **J.** trying not to look scared

# What is the best way to *communicate*?

**4** Genre focus:
## ose and Poetry

### nchor Book
e many good books that
ork well to support both
Question and the genre
this unit. In this unit you
one of these books as
chor Book. Your teacher
duce the book you will
ng.

### Free-Choice Reading
Later in this unit you will be
given the opportunity to choose
another book to read. This is
called your free-choice book.

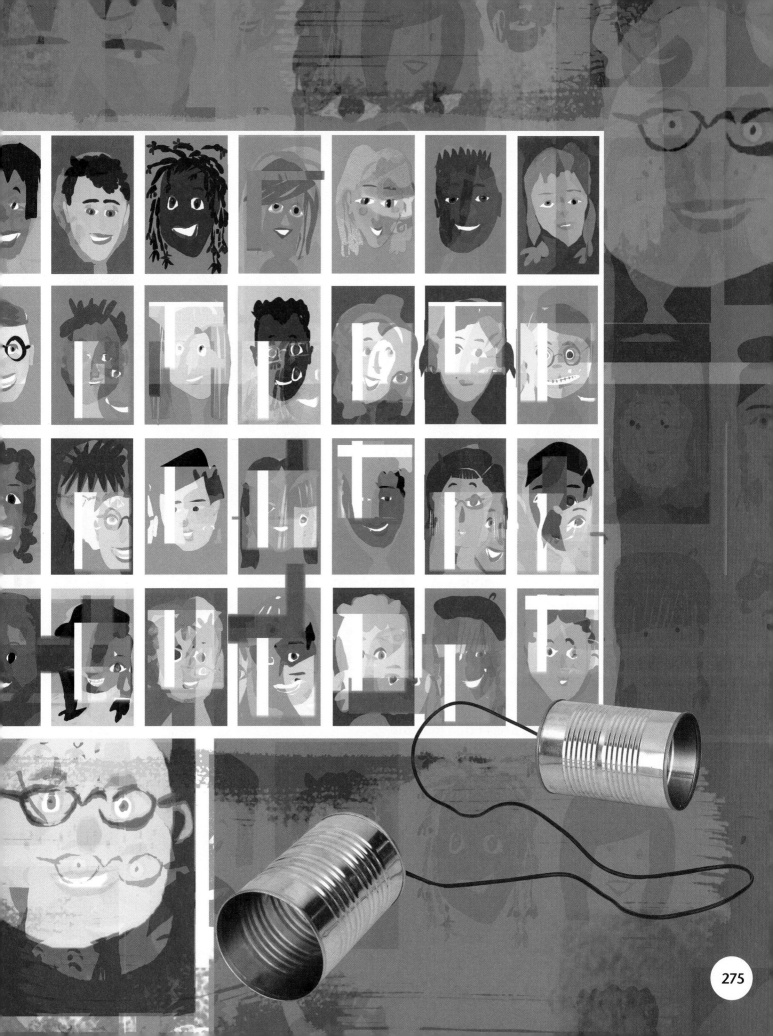

# Thinking About What You Already Know

Did you know that figurative language, descriptive language, and sound devices can be found in both poetry and prose? Learning how authors incorporate these devices will help you to better understand an author's message.

## Partner Activity

With a partner, take turns reading each of the following excerpts aloud. As you read, mark the text for descriptive language that reveals the narrator's thoughts about the character Eric (in the poem) and the nursing home (in the prose piece).

**Poetry**

### from *Describe Somebody* by Jacqueline Woodson

Eric is tall and a little bit mean.

Lamont's just regular.

Angel's kinda chubby. He's got light brown hair.

Sometimes we all hang out,

play a little ball or something. Angel's real good

at science stuff. Once he made a volcano

for science fair and the stuff that came out of it

looked like real lava. Lamont can

draw superheroes real good. Eric—nobody

at school really knows this but

he can sing. Once, Miss Edna took me

to a different church than the one

we usually go to on Sunday.

I was surprised to see Eric up there

with a choir robe on. He gave me a mean look

like I'd better not

say nothing about him and his dark green robe with

gold around the neck.

**Prose**

### from "An Hour With Abuelo" *by Judith Ortiz Cofer*

I get depressed the minute I walk into the place. They line up the old people in wheelchairs in the hallway as if they were about to be raced to the finish line by orderlies who don't even look at them when they push them here and there. I walk fast to room 10, Abuelo's "suite." He is sitting up in his bed writing with a pencil in one of those old-fashioned black hardback notebooks. It has the outline of the island of Puerto Rico on it. I slide into the hard vinyl chair by his bed. He sort of smiles and the lines on his face get deeper, but he doesn't say anything. Since I'm supposed to talk to him, I say, "What are you doing, Abuelo, writing the story of your life?"

How does each excerpt use descriptive language to communicate the narrator's attitude toward the topic?

| "Describe Somebody" | "An Hour With Abuelo" |
| --- | --- |
| | |

What other descriptive language could you add to each excerpt to show the narrator's attitude toward the topic? On your own, write one line for the poem and one sentence for the prose excerpt.

| "Describe Somebody" | "An Hour With Abuelo" |
| --- | --- |
| | |

Good writers use many different tools. Compare your descriptive language with that of your classmates. As you read prose, don't forget to look for examples of descriptive language, figurative language, and other elements you may have thought of as only being used in poetry.

# *What is the best way to communicate?*

How do you speak to your friends? Is it different from the way you speak to your teacher? The way we communicate depends upon our audience.

In the first part of this activity, you and a partner will explore different ways to communicate with different people. Read the following scenarios. In the space provided, describe how each method of communication impacts the situation.

### Scenario #1

The mayor of your city comes to your school, and you tell her that you think more trees should be planted in the city parks.

You say, "Hey, you're the mayor. You should plant more trees in the parks cuz it makes it look cool."

Is this the best way to communicate? Why or why not? Come up with one alternative way to express the thought.

_____

_____

_____

### Scenario #2

You are asking your teacher if you may have an extra day to complete your project, because you forgot to take your book home the night before.

You say, "Mrs. Harrigan, I forgot to take my book home last night. I know it's my fault, but I'd really appreciate an extra day to turn in my paper. Would it be all right if I turned it in tomorrow?"

Is this the best way to communicate? Why or why not? Come up with one alternative way to express the thought.

_____

_____

_____

_____

**Scenario #3**

You won two free passes to your favorite amusement park and are inviting your good friend.

You say, "I won these two passes to Roller Coaster Land, but it's no big deal, it'll probably rain that day. I don't know, if you want to go that's fine."

Is this the best way to communicate? Why or why not? Come up with one alternative way to express the invitation.

Act out each of the following scenarios with a partner, taking turns as the speaker and the listener.

**Keep in mind:**

► Tone of voice—Will your voice be soft or loud, excited or sad?

► Body language and facial expressions—What you say without words helps to reinforce your message.

► Word choice—Choose words that are appropriate to use, whether casual or formal.

| Scenario |
|---|
| You are in the principal's office and have been accused of setting off a stink bomb. You are innocent. How do you communicate this? |
| You have been rewarded with a fun summer vacation for getting good grades. You are allowed to bring one friend. How would you talk to your friend? |
| You want a bike but know that you have to earn money to buy it. Persuading your parents to let you work odd jobs after school will be tough because you have to study. How do you discuss this with them? |

**Explain** Why do you think the way a person communicates changes when the scenario changes?

As you read your Anchor Book and related readings, pay attention to the way in which the author conveys the book's message. How do word choice and tone affect the way the author communicates?

**Getting Ready for Your Anchor Book**

*You will start reading your Anchor Book soon. The next few pages in this book give you some background information plus a reading skill.*

# Introduction to

# Prose and Poetry

Have you ever read a poem that reads like a story, or a story that uses poetic language? What makes one a poem and the other prose? Prose and poetry are different forms of writing that can contain some of the same elements.

**Prose** is a form of written language that is not poetry, drama, or song. It is the kind of writing that sounds the most like everyday speech.

**Poetry** is a type of writing in which every word is meaningful, and it is meant to cause an emotional reaction in the reader.

Though different, poetry and prose share the following elements.

- ▶ **Figurative language** is imaginative language that describes one thing by comparing it to another. It does not mean exactly what it says. It is the symbolic associations we have.

  **Example** After studying for hours, I finally hit a brick wall. (This means that the speaker could not go on, not that he literally hit a wall.)

- ▶ **Imagery** is descriptive language that appeals to one or more of the five senses—sight, hearing, touch, taste, or smell. Imagery is also known as **sensory language.**

Prose and poetry contain literal descriptions and definitions, as well as the symbolic associations we make with the subject being written about.

Look at the graphic organizer below. The outside ovals contain literal descriptions of a coyote while the outside rectangles contain symbolic associations we make with a coyote.

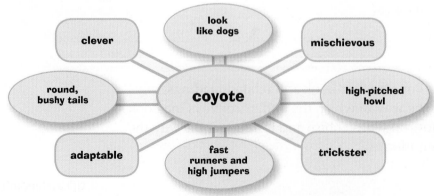

**before reading your anchor book**

**Partner Activity** With your partner, fill in your own descriptions of and associations with snakes in the graphic organizer below.

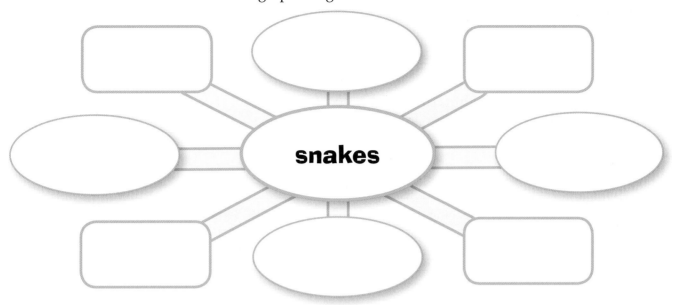

## The Difference Between Prose and Poetry

One of the main differences between prose and poetry is how words and thoughts are arranged on the page. Prose is organized into sentences and paragraphs. Poetry is organized into **lines** and sometimes groups of lines called **stanzas.**

Now, you and your partner will choose: prose or poetry? Using details from your graphic organizer, one of you will create a short piece of prose and one of you will create a poem. After you have written your piece in the space below, compare how you both used the same details in different genres.

**On Your Own** Look for a newspaper article with descriptive details. Rearrange the most powerful details as a poem.

How did this task make you read the newspaper article differently?

As you read prose, think about how the writer might be using figurative language, imagery, and other literary elements we frequently associate only with poetry.

# 4-2 Reading Skills
## *Paraphrasing*

In learning new reading skills, you will use special academic vocabulary. Knowing the right words will help you demonstrate your understanding.

### Academic Vocabulary

| Word | Meaning | Example Sentence |
|---|---|---|
| **emphasize** *v.*<br>*Related words:*<br>emphasizing, emphasis | to give special attention; stress | My English teacher *emphasizes* the importance of good grammar. |
| **identify** *v.*<br>*Related words:*<br>identified, identifying | to recognize or point out | The book report *identifies* the book's most important points. |
| **restate** *v.*<br>*Related words:*<br>restated, restatement | to say something again or in a new way | The speechwriter *restated* the senator's ideas so that everyone could understand them. |

Have you ever found yourself reading a paragraph over and over again because you can't remember what you just read? One way to help you understand is to **paraphrase.** When you paraphrase, you **restate** something in your own words.

### How to Paraphrase

**Step 1** → Reread the selection to make sure you understand the author's meaning and the text.

**Step 2** → **Identify** any unfamiliar words and find their meaning. Replace them with words you know.

**Step 3** → Use your own words to **restate** the information more simply. **Emphasize** the key ideas or events.

**Step 4** → Read your work to be sure it makes sense. Make sure that you do not leave out any important details.

**Directions** Read the following selection. Then answer the questions.

To the east, the sky was washed with a pale, pink light. The trees stood out starkly against the sky as if inked in black, the last leaves fluttering bravely in the cold wind. Antoine got out of his car and looked out at the bleak scene, hands jammed into the pockets of his jacket. It would snow soon, he thought. He intended to be gone before the snowfall, but first he had something to do. Turning on his heel, he strode toward the Tidewater Restaurant. That was where his brother Nick was always to be found this time of morning.

Reaching the restaurant, Antoine pushed open the door and stepped inside. The place was full of people eating an early breakfast, and every single one of them stopped what they were doing to look at him.

Nick's back was to Antoine. As the place went quiet, he turned slowly and squinted his eyes. "Well, well," Nick drawled. "Look who's back in town."

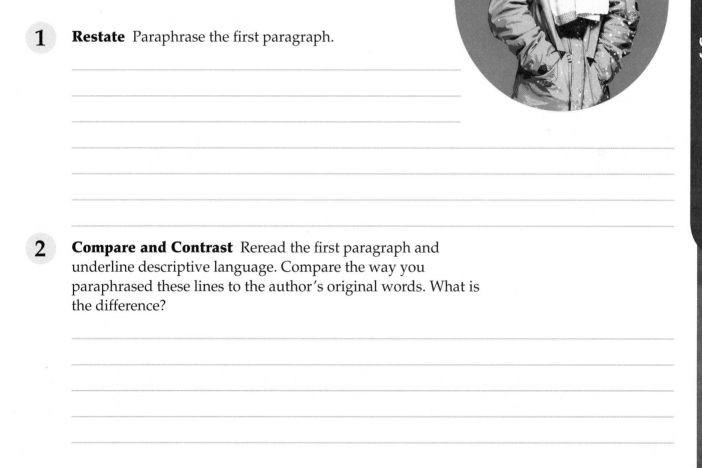

**1** **Restate** Paraphrase the first paragraph.

_____

_____

_____

_____

_____

_____

**2** **Compare and Contrast** Reread the first paragraph and underline descriptive language. Compare the way you paraphrased these lines to the author's original words. What is the difference?

_____

_____

_____

_____

_____

Paraphrasing **283**

Now that you have learned about paraphrasing, practice what you have learned with this technical article. As you read, note important details on a separate sheet of paper. You will use the details to paraphrase the article. *Guiding Question:* **How can paraphrasing help you to communicate your understanding of a text?**

# GLASS

Link to **Science**

The secret of glass's versatility lies in its interior structure. Although it is rigid—and thus like a solid—the atoms are arranged in a random, disordered fashion—characteristic of a liquid. In the melting process, the atoms in the raw materials are disturbed from their normal position in the molecular structure; before they can find their way back to crystalline arrangements, the glass cools.

This looseness in molecular structure gives the material what engineers call tremendous "formability" and capacity for dissolving. "You can cast a huge mirror or draw out glass as a fiber," said Dr. Prindle, a retired Corning technology expert. "And you can dissolve almost anything in it, and in great quantities. The ability to accommodate allows technicians to tailor glass to the need.

"To make a brilliant, sparkling glass, add lead oxide or barium oxide to the basic sand-soda-lime mixture; for a heat-resistant glass, throw in boric oxide; for green sunglasses, add chromium and copper."

Scientists continue to experiment with new mixtures. Corning manufactures 750 different glasses and glass-related products, keeps hundreds of thousands of glass formulas on record, and each week evaluates hundreds more. There, men and women sit in small rooms facing large computers and electron microscopes and other exotic instruments, all probing the elusive atoms.

"We can now understand glass better," said Michael Teter, a research fellow in engineering at Corning. "What has always been missing is a full knowledge of what goes on at the molecular level. Less than one in ten projects involving new uses for glass succeeds. Now at least we have a chance of knowing why things go wrong."

Mike Davies is a London architect, a member of Richard Rogers Partnership, designers of the new Lloyd's of London building. In that edifice Davies and his colleagues had opportunities to test their imaginations with applications of special glasses. The core of the building is a glass atrium, whose 16-story façade is fashioned of 14,350 square yards of glass. Into that glass were rolled thousands of prisms, to forge diamonds out of the sunlight and add sparkle to that towering house of indemnities.

But Mike Davies sees even more dramatic buildings, using molecular chemistry. "Glass is the great building material of the future, the 'dynamic skin,'" he said. "Think of glass that has been treated to react to electric currents going through it, glass that will change from clear to opaque at the push of a button. That gives you instant curtains. Think of how the tall buildings in New York could perform a symphony of colors as the glass in them is made to change colors instantly."

Glass as instant curtains is available now, but the cost is exorbitant. As for the glass changing colors instantly, that may come—but engineers are not yet prepared to transform, say, the John Hancock Tower in Boston into a pillar of green for St. Patrick's Day.

Companies do offer a range of windows designed to conserve energy. There are reflective coatings and other elements in glass to control the amount of sunlight and heat coming into a room. Mike Davies' vision may indeed be on the way to fulfillment.

# Thinking About the Selection
## Glass

**1**    **Analyze**   What is the main purpose of the article?

_____

_____

**2**    **Apply**   Paraphrase the following paragraphs.

Paragraphs 1 and 2

_____

_____

_____

_____

_____

Paragraphs 4 and 5

_____

_____

_____

_____

_____

Paragraphs 7 and 8

_____

_____

_____

_____

_____

Paragraph 9

_____

_____

_____

_____

**Write**   Answer the following question in your Reader's Journal.

 **3**    **Generalize**   How can paraphrasing help you to communicate your understanding of a text?

# 4-3 Vocabulary Building Strategies
## Denotation, Connotation, and Idioms

Sometimes a word or phrase can mean more than what meets the eye. The way it is defined in a dictionary—the **denotation**—is just part of the story. A word can have a **connotation**, a negative or positive association that the word suggests. Phrases such as **idioms** can also have meanings that go beyond their literal definitions.

The following chart contains some words and their denotations. It also contains some of the words' synonyms that have either positive or negative connotations.

| Word | Denotation | Negative Connotation | Positive Connotation |
|------|-----------|----------------------|----------------------|
| inexpensive | low in cost | cheap | economical |
| inquiring | eager to investigate | nosy | curious |
| sportsperson | person trained in sports | jock | athlete |

**Directions** Create a list of sports team names. Then choose one team name, and complete the graphic organizer below.

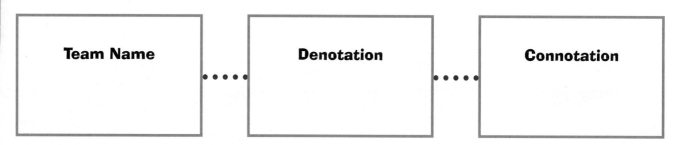

**Directions** Write the words, their denotation, and their connotations on the lines below. Use a dictionary if needed.

An **idiom** is an expression used in a particular language or region that often comes from a figure of speech. It cannot be taken literally. If you read or hear an idiom, you can often use context clues to discover its meaning. Here are a few examples.

| Idiom | Meaning |
|---|---|
| *sitting duck* | easy target |
| *milk him for all he's worth* | to take advantage of |
| *a piece of cake* | simple |
| *in a heartbeat* | quickly |

**Interpret**  For each sentence, underline the idiom and write its meaning.

**1**  Kayla was too tired to talk; she was at the end of her rope.

**2**  Having polished off dinner, he began to clear the table.

**3**  When his practical joke backfired in front of everyone, Jamal knew he had egg on his face.

**4**  Realizing that he was getting an opportunity to perform on national TV, the performer decided to seize the moment.

**Apply**  Read the idiom cards that follow. The expressions are italicized, and the meaning is below each idiom. Count off around the room by sixes. You are responsible for using the idiom that matches your number. When your number is called, be ready to use your idiom in a sentence.

**Idiom Card 1**

*Get up on the wrong side of the bed*

To be in a bad mood

**Idiom Card 2**

*Foam at the mouth*

To display anger

**Idiom Card 3**

*Go the extra mile*

To go beyond what is expected

**Idiom Card 4**

*Wash your hands of it*

To deny responsibility for something

**Idiom Card 5**

*It's neither here nor there*

It's not important to the matter at hand

**Idiom Card 6**

*Pull the wool over her eyes*

To deceive someone

**Ready? Start Reading Your Anchor Book**  *It's time to get started. As you learn from this work text, your teacher will also give you reading assignments from your Anchor Book.*

# 4-4 Literary Analysis
## *Imagery*

Have you ever read or heard a description of a meal that made your mouth water? Sometimes writers use **imagery** that is so vivid, you can almost see, hear, taste, smell, or touch what they are describing.

## Literary Terms

► **Imagery** is language that appeals to one or more of the five senses—sight, sound, touch, taste, or smell. Imagery is also called **sensory language.** Writers use it to describe something so clearly that readers can **visualize** it, or picture it in their minds.

► Writers also use imagery to convey a **mood,** or overall feeling. As you read prose or poetry, think about how the images make you feel, as well as what they describe.

**Directions** Look at the chart below. Write your own example of sight, hearing, touch, taste, and smell.

| Sense | Example | My Image |
|---|---|---|
| Sight | The sky darkened to indigo blue as the sun slipped behind the hills. | |
| Hearing | The cat was howling at the back door to come in. | |
| Touch | The warm, gooey mud squished between my toes. | |
| Taste | I bit into the peach, and its sweet juice squirted into my mouth. | |
| Smell | The delicious aroma of fresh popcorn filled the apartment. | |

**Directions** Read the poem and underline words and phrases that appeal to the senses. In the margin, note which sense the image appeals to.

**Go Online**

**About the Author**
Visit: PHSchool.com
Web Code: exe-7401

### Petals
#### by Pat Mora

have calloused her hands,
brightly colored crepe paper: turquoise,
yellow, magenta, which she shapes
into large blooms for bargain-hunting tourists
5 who see her flowers, her puppets, her baskets,
but not her—small, gray-haired woman
wearing a white apron, who hides behind
blossoms in her stall at the market,
who sits and remembers collecting wildflowers
10 as a girl, climbing rocky Mexican hills
to fill a straw hat with soft blooms
which she'd stroke gently, over and over again
with her smooth fingertips.

**1** **Identify** Use the chart to list examples of images in the poem that appeal to the senses of sight and touch.

| Sense | Image |
|-------|-------|
| Sight | |
| Touch | |

**2** **Analyze** How does the poet use this imagery to make a point about the woman's life?

_____

_____

_____

_____

while reading your anchor book

Imagery **289**

# Understanding Tone

Your tone of voice shows your attitude. Try saying "I'm hungry" in a whiney voice. Now say it in a tone that shows excitement that it's lunchtime. Writers also convey a tone—but we have to "hear" it through their words, not their voices.

while reading your anchor book

## Literary Terms

▶ The **tone** of a work is the writer's or speaker's attitude toward the subject or characters. Tone can often be described by a single adjective, such as *playful, serious, gentle, bitter,* or *loving.*

▶ To "hear" the tone of a work, pay attention to the writer's word choice, or **diction.** Look for words with strong **connotations,** or emotional associations.

| Example | Tone |
|---|---|
| The meal, a heap of unidentifiable objects, lay on the plate. The stink of the food did not help identify what it was. | disgust |

**Directions** Read the poem aloud with a partner, and then answer the question.

**Go Online**

**About the Author**
Visit: PHSchool.com
Web Code: exe-7402

### Thursday
*by Edna St. Vincent Millay*

And if I loved you Wednesday,
　　Well, what is that to you?
I do not love you Thursday—
　　So much is true.

5　And why you come complaining
　　Is more than I can see.
I loved you Wednesday,—yes—but what
　　Is that to me?

**Analyze** What is the speaker's tone? Which words or phrases tell you that?

_____

_____

In the following poems, the poets use vivid imagery and set a clear tone. To better understand each poem's meaning, read it more than once. *Guiding Question:* **How does the imagery in the poems help communicate the tone?**

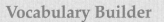

## by E.E. Cummings

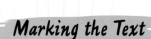

**Background** *When E.E. Cummings (1894–1962) first published his poetry in the early 1920s, it was criticized for its unusual punctuation, lack of capitalization, and odd word spacing. Today, Cummings is one of America's most popular poets, and his poetry is admired for its inventive imagery and style.*

### Vocabulary Builder

**Before you read,** *you will discuss the following words. In the Vocabulary Builder box in the margin, use a vocabulary building strategy to make the words your own.*

**diluted****collision****prospect****sluggish**

**As you read,** *draw a box around unfamiliar words you could add to your vocabulary. Use context clues to unlock their meaning.*

### Marking the Text

**Imagery and Tone**

**As you read,** *underline words and phrases that appeal to one or more of the senses. Circle details that convey a tone. Identify what the tone is in the margin.*

in Just-
spring      when the world is mud-
luscious, the little
lame balloonman

5  whistles      far      and wee

and eddieandbill come
running from marbles and
piracies and it's
spring

10    when the world is puddle-wonderful

      the queer
      old balloonman whistles
      far       and       wee
      and bettyandisbel come dancing

15    from hop-scotch and jump-rope and

      it's
      spring
        and

              the

20              goat-footed

      balloonMan         whistles

      far

      and

      wee

◀ **Discuss with a Partner**
In this poem, E. E.
Cummings capitalizes
two words. Why do you
think the poet wishes to
emphasize these words?
How do capitalization and
unusual word position
help convey the writer's
meaning?

# A CHILD'S PAINTING

## by Cathy Song

**Background** *Cathy Song, a poet from Hawaii, uses descriptive language in her poetry inspired by the colorful Hawaiian landscape.*

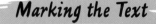

*Marking the Text*

What crossed his mind
when he added this?
A glimpse of sky of blue
so pale
5   it seems **diluted** with vinegar,
the blue wash of an Easter egg.

Where blue runs into black,
a **collision** occurs,
a feathery explosion,
10   the inky spray of a jellyfish.

It all seems so casual
as if his mind were on something else,
the **prospect** of soup and crackers,
a walk to feed the pigeons in the park.
15   Perhaps he was only killing time
the way another
child might de-wing a fly

### Vocabulary Builder

**diluted**
(di loōt′ed) *adj.*

**Meaning**


**collision**
(kə lizh′ən) *n.*

**Meaning**


**prospect**
(präs′pekt′) *n.*

**Meaning**

Imagery and Tone   **293**

or hold a shard[1] of glass
to feel the sun's needle in the eye.

20  In one corner,
what was done without a brush,
a gray smear,
a midnight comet,
a breathless fingerprint
25  trails off the paper
onto an imaginary table
as if the child had wanted
to leave some crumbs:
*This is where I went.*
30  And changed his mind.
For look at this circle of pink.
It blooms in the center like a mouth
calling back the colors—
Did something frighten him?—
35  all the colors of a private alphabet.

---

[1] **shard** (shärd) *n.* a broken piece; sliver.

# Who Burns for the Perfection of Paper

by Martín Espada

**Marking the Text**

**Background** *Martín Espada is a poet of Puerto Rican descent. Many of his poems are based on autobiographical events—his real-life experiences. Here, he remembers the time he spent as a teenager working in a paper printing plant.*

At sixteen, I worked after high school hours
at a printing plant
that manufactured legal pads:
Yellow paper
5   stacked seven feet high
and leaning
as I slipped cardboard
between the pages,
then brushed the red glue
10  up and down the stack.
No gloves: fingertips required
for the perfection of paper.
smoothing the exact rectangle.

**Sluggish** by 9 PM, the hands
would slide along suddenly sharp paper,

## Vocabulary Builder

**sluggish**
(slug′ish) *adj.*

**Meaning**

Imagery and Tone   **295**

15  and gather slits thinner than the crevices[2]

of the skin, hidden.

Then the glue would sting,

hands oozing

till both palms burned

20  at the punchclock[3].

Ten years later, in law school,

I knew that every legal pad

was glued with the sting of hidden cuts,

that every open lawbook

25  was a pair of hands

upturned and burning.

---

[2]  **crevices** (krev′is ez) *n.* narrow cracks or openings.

[3]  **punchclock** (punch′kläk) *n.* a machine that records when workers arrive and leave work. The worker inserts a card that is punched with a time.

## Vocabulary Builder

**After you read,** *review the words you decided to add to your vocabulary. Write the meaning of words you have learned in context. Look up the other words in a dictionary, glossary, thesaurus, or electronic resource.*

# Thinking About the Selections

## in Just-, A Child's Painting, *and* Who Burns for the Perfection of Paper

Go Online
About the Author
Visit: PHSchool.com
Web Code: exe-7403
7404
7405

**1** **Analyze** Give examples from "in Just-" of images that appeal to the senses. What tone do the invented words "mud-luscious" and "puddle-wonderful" convey?

_____

_____

_____

**2** **Interpret** Many of the images in "A Child's Painting" are figures of speech that make imaginative comparisons. How do these comparisons help you visualize the painting?

_____

_____

_____

**3** **Analyze** In "Who Burns for the Perfection of Paper," what images appeal to the sense of touch?

_____

_____

_____

**4** **Compare and Contrast** How are the tones of "A Child's Painting" and "Who Burns for the Perfection of Paper" similar? How are they different?

_____

_____

_____

_____

**Write** Answer the following questions in your Reader's Journal.

**5** How does the imagery in the poems help communicate the tone?

**6** Select a passage from your Anchor Book in which the author uses sensory language. What senses does the passage appeal to? How does the author's use of sensory language communicate the tone of the text?

while reading your anchor book

Imagery and Tone **297**

Now that you have read some poetry, read a piece of prose. As you read the following story, notice that imagery and tone are also important elements in prose. *Guiding Question:* **Do tone and imagery work differently in prose than in poetry?**

# The Trout

## by Sean O'Faolain

**Background** *Sean O'Faolain (1900–1991) was born in Cork, Ireland. In this story, he wrote about a young girl who finds a trout in a well and feels a connection to it. Notice how O'Faolain used Irish dialect to capture the sound of his characters' speech.*

### Vocabulary Builder

**Before you read,** *you will discuss the following words. In the Vocabulary Builder box in the margin, use a vocabulary building strategy to make the words your own.*

**squabbled   incredulous   resolutely   radiant**

**As you read,** *draw a box around unfamiliar words you could add to your vocabulary. Use context clues to unlock their meaning.*

### Marking the Text

**Imagery and Tone**

**As you read,** *underline imagery. Circle details that reveal the tone. In the margin, note which sense the image appeals to or the tone conveyed.*

One of the first places Julia always ran to when they arrived in G——— [4] was The Dark Walk. It is a laurel walk, very old, almost gone wild; a lofty midnight tunnel of smooth, sinewy[5] branches. Underfoot the tough brown leaves are never dry enough to crackle: there is always a suggestion of damp and cool trickle.

---

[4] **G———** style used by fiction writers to suggest that they do not want to provide the full name of a place or person.

[5] **sinewy** (sin'yoo ē) *adj.* tough and stringy.

She raced right into it. For the first few yards she always had the memory of the sun behind her, then she felt the dusk closing swiftly down on her so that she screamed with pleasure and raced on to reach the light at the far end; and it was always just a little too long in coming so that she emerged gasping, clasping her hands, laughing, drinking in the sun. When she was filled with the heat and glare she would turn and consider the ordeal again.

This year she had the extra joy of showing it to her small brother, and of terrifying him as well as herself. And for him the fear lasted longer because his legs were so short and she had gone out at the far end while he was still screaming and racing.

When they had done this many times, they came back to the house to tell everybody that they had done it. He boasted. She mocked. They **squabbled.**

"Cry baby!"

"You were afraid yourself, so there!"

"I won't take you anymore."

"You're a big pig."

"I hate you."

Tears were threatening, so somebody said, "Did you see the well?" She opened her eyes at that and held up her long lovely neck suspiciously and decided to be **incredulous.** She was twelve and at that age little girls are beginning to suspect most stories: they have already found out too many, from Santa Claus to the stork. How could there be a well! In The Dark Walk? That she had visited year after year? Haughtily[6] she said, "Nonsense."

---

[6] **haughtily** (hôt'il ē) *adv.* acting superior; scornfully.

## Vocabulary Builder

**squabbled**
(skwäb'əld) *v.*

**Meaning**

**incredulous**
(in krej'oo ləs) *adj.*

**Meaning**

◀ **Critical Viewing**
How does this artwork contribute to the mood of the story?

Imagery and Tone  **299**

But she went back, pretending to be going somewhere else, and she found a hole scooped in the rock at the side of the walk, choked with damp leaves, so shrouded by ferns that she uncovered it only after much searching. At the back of this little cavern there was about a quart of water. In the water she suddenly perceived a panting trout. She rushed for Stephen and dragged him to see, and they were both so excited that they were no longer afraid of the darkness as they hunched down and peered in at the fish panting in his tiny prison, his silver stomach going up and down like an engine.

Nobody knew how the trout got there. Even old Martin in the kitchen garden laughed and refused to believe that it was there, or pretended not to believe, until she forced him to come down and see. Kneeling and pushing back his tattered old cap he peered in.

"Be cripes[7], you're right. How the divil[8] . . . did that fella get there?"

She stared at him suspiciously.

"You knew?" she accused; but he said, "The divil a' know," and reached down to lift it out. Convinced, she hauled him back. If she had found it, then it was her trout.

Her mother suggested that a bird had carried the spawn[9]. Her father thought that in the winter a small streamlet might have carried it down there as a baby, and it had been safe until the summer came and the water began to dry up. She said, "I see," and went back to look again and consider the matter in private. Her brother remained behind, wanting to hear the whole story of the trout, not really interested in the actual trout but much interested in the story which his mummy began to make up for him on the lines of, "So one day Daddy Trout and Mammy Trout . . ." When he retailed[10] it to her she said, "Pooh."

It troubled her that the trout was always in the same position; he had no room to turn; all the time the silver belly went up and down; otherwise he was motionless. She wondered what he ate, and in between visits to Joey Pony and the boat, and a bath to get cool, she thought of his hunger. She brought him down bits of dough; once she brought him a worm. He ignored the food. He just went on panting. Hunched over him she thought how all the winter, while she was at school, he had been in there. All the winter, in The Dark Walk, all day, all night, floating around alone. She drew the leaf of her hat down around her ears and chin and stared. She was still thinking of it as she lay in bed.

---

[7] **cripes** (krīps) *interj.* word used to express annoyance or anger.

[8] **divil** (dīv'əl) *n.* dialect word for "devil."

[9] **spawn** (spôn) *n.* fish eggs.

[10] **retailed** (rē'tāld) *v.* told or repeated.

while reading your anchor book

It was late June, the longest days of the year. The sun had sat still for a week, burning up the world. Although it was after ten o'clock it was still bright and still hot. She lay on her back under a single sheet, with her long legs spread, trying to keep cool. She could see the D of the moon through the fir tree—they slept on the ground floor. Before they went to bed her mummy had told Stephen the story of the trout again, and she, in her bed, had **resolutely** presented her back to them and read her book. But she had kept one ear cocked.

"And so, in the end, this naughty fish who would not stay at home got bigger and bigger and bigger, and the water got smaller and smaller . . ."

Passionately she had whirled and cried, "Mummy, don't make it a horrible old moral story!" Her mummy had brought in a fairy godmother then, who sent lots of rain, and filled the well, and a stream poured out and the trout floated away down to the river below. Staring at the moon she knew that there are no such things as fairy godmothers and that the trout, down in The Dark Walk, was panting like an engine. She heard somebody unwind a fishing reel. Would the *beasts* fish him out!

She sat up. Stephen was a hot lump of sleep, lazy thing. The Dark Walk would be full of little scraps of moon. She leaped up and looked out the window, and somehow it was not so lightsome now that she saw the dim mountains far away and the black firs against the breathing land and heard a dog say *bark-bark*. Quietly she lifted the ewer[11] of water and climbed out the window and scuttled along the cool but cruel gravel down to the

Vocabulary Builder

**resolutely**
(rez′ə lo͞ot′lē) *adv.*

**Meaning**

---

[11] **ewer** (yo͞o′ər) *n.* pitcher.

maw[12] of the tunnel. Her pajamas were very short so that when she splashed water it wet her ankles. She peered into the tunnel. Something alive rustled inside there. She raced in, and up and down she raced, and flurried, and cried aloud, "Oh, gosh, I can't find it," and then at last she did. Kneeling down in the damp she put her hand into the slimy hole. When the body lashed they were both mad with fright. But she gripped him and shoved him into the ewer and raced, with her teeth ground, out to the other end of the tunnel and down the steep paths to the river's edge.

All the time she could feel him lashing his tail against the side of the ewer. She was afraid he would jump right out. The gravel cut into her soles until she came to the cool ooze of the river's bank where the moon mice on the water crept into her feet. She poured out, watching until he plopped. For a second he was visible in the water. She hoped he was not dizzy. Then all she saw was the glimmer of the moon in the silent flowing river, the dark firs, the dim mountains, and the **radiant** pointed face laughing down at her out of the empty sky.

She scuttled[13] up the hill, in the window, plonked down the ewer, and flew through the air like a bird into bed. The dog said *bark-bark.* She heard the fishing reel whirring. She hugged herself and giggled. Like a river of joy her holiday spread before her.

In the morning Stephen rushed to her, shouting that "he" was gone, and asking "where" and "how." Lifting her nose in the air, she said superciliously[14], "Fairy godmother, I suppose?" and strolled away patting the palms of her hands.

---

[12] **maw** (mô) *n.* mouth; opening.

[13] **scuttled** (skut'ld) *v.* ran quickly with short steps.

[14] **superciliously** (soo'pər sil'ē əs lē) *adv.* scornfully.

## Vocabulary Builder

**radiant**
(rā'dē ənt) *adj.*

**Meaning**

## Vocabulary Builder

**After you read,** *review the words you decided to add to your vocabulary. Write the meaning of words you have learned in context. Look up the other words in a dictionary, glossary, thesaurus, or electronic resource.*

while reading your anchor book

# Thinking About the Selection
## The Trout

Go Online

**About the Author**
Visit: PHSchool.com
Web Code: exe-7406

**1** **Analyze** Go back over the images you underlined in the story and the notes you wrote in the margin. Which senses does the writer appeal to in these images? Use the chart below to provide one vivid example of each type of image.

| Sense | Image |
|---|---|
| Sight | |
| Touch | |
| Hearing | |

**2** **Interpret** Reread the first two paragraphs. How does the imagery in these two paragraphs help set the mood of the story?

_____

_____

_____

**3** **Analyze** How would you describe the writer's tone? Specifically, what is his attitude toward Julia? What is his attitude toward her mother?

_____

_____

_____

**Write** Answer the following questions in your Reader's Journal.

**4** **Evaluate** Do tone and imagery work differently in prose than in poetry? Explain.

**5** **Analyze** Choose a poem with vivid imagery and compare it to a descriptive prose passage in your Anchor Book. Do the authors use imagery in the same or different ways? What is the tone of each piece?

Imagery and Tone   303

*while reading your anchor book*

# 4-5 Comparing Literary Works
## *Figurative Language*

Think of a time when you said something like, "She is as slow as a snail." You didn't mean it literally. You were using figurative language.

## Literary Terms

**Figurative language** is imaginative language that is not supposed to be taken literally. It describes something in a fresh, vivid way. The many types of figurative language are known as **figures of speech.**

| Figure of Speech | Description | Example | My Example |
|---|---|---|---|
| Simile | uses *like* or *as* to compare two seemingly different things | *Fame is like a bee.* | |
| Metaphor | describes one thing as if it were another, without using *like* or *as* | *Fame is a bee.* | |
| Personification | gives human qualities to something nonhuman | *Fame smiled at me.* | |
| Hyperbole | exaggerates speech for emphasis | *He is so proud he could burst.* | |

An **analogy** makes a connection between two or more things that are similar in some ways, but are otherwise unlike. Both metaphors and similes are types of analogies.

An **idiom** is a figurative expression that is a part of popular speech.

**Directions**  Look back at the poem in the previous lesson, "A Child's Painting." Identify two idioms in the poem. What do they add to the poem's meaning?

_____

_____

_____

_____

_____

_____

**Directions** As you read the following poem, imagine looking up at the sky, down into a greenhouse, and all around.

Read the poem three times. First focus on the poem's literal meaning. The second time, identify examples of figurative language and underline them. The third time, try to interpret the poet's message. Then answer the questions.

**Go Online**
**About the Author**
Visit: PHSchool.com
Web Code: exe-7407

## Child on Top of a Greenhouse
### by Theodore Roethke

The wind billowing[1] out the seat of my britches[2],
My feet crackling splinters of glass and dried putty,
The half-grown chrysanthemums staring up like accusers,
Up through the streaked glass, flashing with sunlight,
5 A few white clouds all rushing eastward,
A line of elms plunging and tossing like horses,
And everyone, everyone pointing up and shouting!

---
[1] **billowing** (bil′ ¯o i[ng]) v. filling with air.  [2] **britches** (brich′ iz) n. pants.

**1** **Analyze** Imagery and figurative language are often used together. Go back to the poem and circle one example of imagery. What kind of mood does the imagery create?

**2** **Compare** Notice the figure of speech in line 3. What two different types of figurative language does it combine? What does it compare, and how does it reveal the speaker's feelings?

**3** **Analyze** Explain the simile in line 6. How does it help you visualize the trees? How does it help you better understand the poem?

**Partner Activity** Work with a partner and replace one simile and one metaphor from the poem with your own invented ones.

*while reading your anchor book*

Now that you've been introduced to different types of figurative language, read the following poems aloud and compare their use of figurative language. Read in a way that sounds like natural speech.
*Guiding Question:* **How effectively does each poet use figurative language to communicate ideas and emotions?**

## Vocabulary Builder

**Before you read,** *you will discuss the following word. In the Vocabulary Builder box in the margin, use a vocabulary building strategy to make the word your own.*

### haunches

**As you read,** *draw a box around unfamiliar words you could add to your vocabulary. Use context clues to unlock their meaning.*

## Marking the Text

### Figurative Language

**As you read,** *underline examples of figurative language. In the margin, identify the type of figure of speech and tell what two things are being compared.*

# Fame Is a Bee

by Emily Dickinson

Fame is a bee.

It has a song—

It has a sting—

Ah, too, it has a wing.

# Fog

by Carl Sandburg

## Vocabulary Builder

**haunches**
(hôn′ chez) *n.*

**Meaning**

The fog comes
on little cat feet.

It sits looking
over the harbor and city
5  on silent **haunches**
and then moves on.

**Background** *This poem is a dramatic monologue, a type of poem in which a speaker directly addresses another person. Read the poem aloud with a rhythm, flow, and meter that sounds like everyday speech. As you read the poem, think about what message the speaker is trying to communicate to her son.*

# Mother to Son

by Langston Hughes

Well, son, I'll tell you:
Life for me ain't been no crystal stair.
It's had tacks in it,
And splinters,
5   And boards torn up,
And places with no carpet on the floor—
Bare.
But all the time
I'se been a-climbin' on,
10  And reachin' landin's,
And turnin' corners,
And sometimes goin' in the dark
Where there ain't been no light.
So boy, don't you turn back.
15  Don't you set down on the steps
'Cause you finds it's kinder hard.
Don't you fall now—
For I'se still goin', honey,
I'se still climbin',
20  And life for me ain't been no crystal stair.

▲ **Critical Viewing**
How does this image contribute to the poem's mood and meaning?

*Marking the Text*

## Vocabulary Builder

**After you read,** *review the words you decided to add to your vocabulary. Write the meaning of words you have learned in context. Look up the other words in a dictionary, glossary, thesaurus, or electronic resource.*

# Literature in Context
## The Harlem Renaissance

During the 1920s, the New York City neighborhood of Harlem became the center of a cultural movement known as the Harlem Renaissance, which means "rebirth." This remarkable period explored all aspects of African American life and celebrated its culture. Langston Hughes was one of the movement's leaders. Other important members included the writer Zora Neale Hurston, the musician Duke Ellington, the artist Aaron Douglas, and the photographer James Van Der Zee.

Center: Blues singer Bessie Smith
Right: Writer Zora Neale Hurston

# Langston Hughes (1902–1967)

Born in Joplin, Missouri, Langston Hughes began writing poetry in high school and wrote his first great poem, "The Negro Speaks of Rivers", during his senior year. His first book of poetry, *The Weary Blues* (1926), made him famous. Hughes became a leading figure in the Harlem Renaissance. In his poetry, Hughes expressed pride in his African American heritage and frustration with racial oppression. Though best known for his powerful poetry, Hughes also wrote fiction, drama, an autobiography, and screenplays. Today he is considered one of the most important American poets of the twentieth century.

# Thinking About the Selections

## Fame Is a Bee, Fog, *and* Mother to Son

**Go Online**

**About the Author**
Visit: PHSchool.com
Web Code: exe-7408
7409
7410

**1** **Analyze** In "Fame Is a Bee," what aspects of fame does Dickinson explore in this metaphor? What are fame's "song", "sting", and "wing"?

_____

_____

_____

_____

**2** **Analyze** Which type of figure of speech does Sandburg use in "Fog"? Explain the comparison.

_____

_____

_____

**3** **Interpret** In "Mother to Son," which type of figure of speech is the line "Life for me ain't been no crystal stair"? How can you tell?

_____

_____

_____

_____

**4** **Synthesize** Reread "Mother to Son". What qualities does the mother demonstrate through her words and actions? Why does she need these qualities?

_____

_____

_____

_____

**Write** Answer the following questions in your Reader's Journal.

**5** **Compare and Contrast** How effectively does each poet use figurative language to communicate ideas and emotions?

**6** **Discuss** Choose a poem or passage in your Anchor Book that includes vivid figurative language. Identify the type or types of figures of speech, and explain what the writer is comparing. Then discuss how this figurative language adds to the meaning and mood of the poem or passage.

while reading your anchor book

## Coordinating Conjunctions

Too many short sentences can lead to choppy writing. **Conjunctions** are words that help combine these short sentences to create a smoother writing style.

A **coordinating conjunction** connects words or groups of words that are similar. They are *and, for, or, yet, but, nor,* and *so.*

**Go Online**

**Learn More**
Visit: PHSchool.com
Web Code: exp-7401

> **Original** He sat down. He read a book.
> **Combined** He sat down and read a book.

**Directions** Rewrite the sentences to make one sentence. Use the appropriate conjunction to combine the sentences.

**1** He left after the game. He went to the grocery store.

_____

**2** On the weekends, Caroline could sew. She could knit. She could paint.

_____

_____

**3** It was a bumpy ride. The plane landed safely.

_____

**Directions** Find the choppy sentences in this paragraph. Rewrite the paragraph, adding conjunctions to make it better.

> Spring is a beautiful season of the year. It comes after winter. It comes before summer. Flowers everywhere bloom in brilliant reds, purples, blues, and yellows. I see birds flying through the air. I see insects flying too. The sun feels tingly on my skin. It makes me feel energetic. Spring is my favorite season.

_____

_____

_____

_____

# Subordinating Conjunctions

A **subordinating conjunction** is used to introduce a dependent clause—a phrase that has a noun and a verb but cannot stand by itself as a complete sentence. It is only part of a sentence. Some subordinating conjunctions are *after, until, since, while, although, even if,* and *because*.

**Incomplete sentence** After we finish our chores (The subordinating conjunction "After" introduces the dependent clause "we finish our chores".)

**Complete sentence** After we finish our chores, we are going to the movies.

**Directions** Combine the pair of sentences using the subordinating conjunction in parentheses. Write the new sentence.

**1** She couldn't choose between the two meals on the menu. Her dad decided for her. (since)

_____

_____

**2** You think baseball is fun. I don't. (although)

_____

**3** Joanna cannot go to the concert. She must finish her homework. (until)

_____

_____

**4** Both pies were equally delicious. The judge couldn't decide which baker should receive the blue ribbon. (because)

_____

_____

**Directions** Write a sentence using the assigned subordinating conjunction.

**5** Since _____

**6** Until _____

**7** Because _____

**8** While _____

**Go Online**

**Learn More**
Visit: PHSchool.com
Web Code: exp-7402

**Author's Craft**

Conjunctions are important in prose, but are they also important in poetry? Turn to the poem "Mother to Son" on page 307. Cross out all of the coordinating and subordinating conjunctions. Read your revised poem to a partner then listen as your partner reads it to you. Does it still make sense? Is one type of conjunction more important than the other?

## Correlative Conjunctions

Go Online

**Learn More**
Visit: PHSchool.com
Web Code: exp-7403

A **correlative conjunction** is a pair of words that is used to connect two parts of a sentence. The second word of the pair is always a coordinating conjunction.

| Correlative Conjunctions | | |
|---|---|---|
| both . . . and | neither . . . nor | whether . . . or |
| either . . . or | not only . . . but also | |

**Example**  Both my sister and I love to ski.

**Directions**  Combine each pair of sentences with a correlative conjunction. Write the new sentence.

**1**  It is fun to learn about my family history. It is interesting too.

_____

**2**  Angela may go to the matinee. She may go to the evening showing.

_____

**3**  Henry must decide if he wants to study science. He must also decide if he wants to study engineering.

_____

**4**  The fire ruined the restaurant. The fire ruined the store next to the restaurant too.

_____

**Partner Activity**  Work with a partner. Write the correlative conjunctions from the box above on index cards or slips of paper. Shuffle the pile and randomly choose one card or slip of paper. Write a sentence with the set of correlative conjunctions. Repeat the exercise until you've gone through them all. Check your partner's work.

both . . . and

whether . . . or

_____

_____

_____

_____

# Interjections

An **interjection** is a part of speech that expresses a feeling or an emotion, such as pain, excitement, fear, or confusion. Some common interjections are *wow, oh, aw, darn, ouch, gee, uh, tsk, huh, whew, well, oops, hey, boy, ugh, yuck, yikes,* and *hmm.* An interjection may be set off with a comma or an exclamation mark.

**Examples**  Ouch! The bee stung me.
Wow, those fireworks are amazing!

Use interjections to make your writing more lively and descriptive. However, make sure not to use too many interjections or your writing will seem too busy. Interjections can be used in dialogue to capture the speaker's tone and emotions.

**Directions**  Read the paragraph. Add interjections to the dialogue to make it more lively. Use commas and exclamation marks where appropriate.

Jessica and I had been hiking on the mountain trail for more than two hours. I was exhausted. "Can we stop for a few minutes? My feet are killing me!" I panted. "Fine, but only for five minutes. We have to reach the top before the sun goes down," said Jessica, impatiently. After the short five-minute break, we continued up the trail. When we finally reached the top, we saw a breathtaking view. "Aren't you glad we hiked up the mountain?" asked Jessica. "Yes, I am," I answered. "This is the most beautiful sight I have ever seen."

**Learn More**
Visit: PHSchool.com
Web Code: exp-7404

**Author's Craft**

Most authors don't use many interjections. Scan "The Trout" on page 298. Find a section where the author could have used interjections, but chose not to. Rewrite it, adding interjections. Read the original text and your revised text to a partner, and listen to your partner's text. Does adding interjections strengthen the story? Why do you think the author chose not to use them?

# 4-7 Writer's Workshop
## Response to Literature: Literary Review

When you evaluate an author's work, you discuss what you like and do not like about it. This can help you understand why the writing creates a particular response in you. Follow the steps in this workshop to write a review of a story or poem.

To be effective, your review should include the following elements.

**Purpose** To write a review of a selection you have read in this unit

**Audience** You, your teacher, and your classmates

- ▶ A clear focus on a feature of the selection
- ▶ A summary of important features of the work
- ▶ A judgment about the value of the work
- ▶ Evidence that defends your ideas
- ▶ Error-free writing, including correct use of conjunctions and interjections

## Prewriting—Plan It Out

To plan your review, use the following steps.

**Choose your topic.** Browse this worktext and choose a selection to review. Choose a selection that you understood well and have a strong feeling about.

**Take a position.** Ask yourself the questions to the right about the selection and take a position. Choose one aspect of the story to focus on, such as the imagery, characters, or theme.

**Gather details.** To give your readers a feeling for the story, poem, or informational text, and to support your judgments or interpretations, compile evidence that reinforces your position. Complete the chart on the following page to help you gather and organize your ideas.

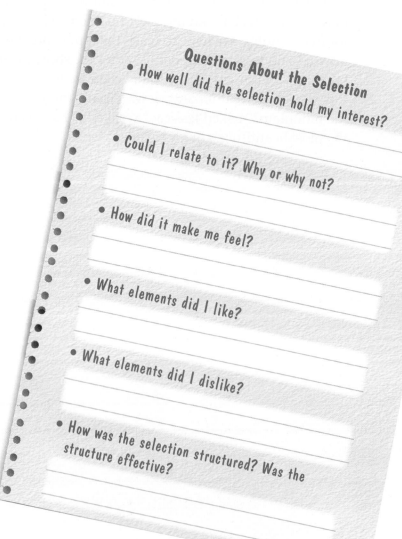

### Questions About the Selection
- How well did the selection hold my interest?

- Could I relate to it? Why or why not?

- How did it make me feel?

- What elements did I like?

- What elements did I dislike?

- How was the selection structured? Was the structure effective?

| 1. My Response | 2. What Caused It | 3. My Focus |
|---|---|---|
| What is my main response to the selection?<br><br>**Example:** *The suspense and characters in King's short story made it thoroughly enjoyable.*<br><br>**My Response:** | What features of the selection caused my reaction? Use examples to back up your answers.<br><br>**Example:** *King's descriptions of the setting lead me to anticipate that something bad would happen.*<br><br>**What Caused It:** | What conclusion can I draw about the selection's features?<br><br>**Example:** *The best way to engage an audience is to create strong characters and suspense.*<br><br>**My Focus:** |

## Drafting—Get It on Paper

Using your notes, create your draft. Use specific language to create a strong, engaging voice. Include the following elements in your introduction, body, and conclusion.

**Introduction** In the first paragraph, state your position clearly, and give an idea of what the selection is about.

**Body** Provide evidence for your position. Use details from the story or poem, such as specific scenes, characters, or images, and give more reasons to support your opinions.

**Conclusion** Restate your position and sum up your reasons for your opinions.

## Revising—Make It Better

Review your draft to find places to support your position. Organize your paragraphs around your strongest idea. Begin the first sentence of each paragraph with an engaging idea, such as, "This author is a master of suspense."

▶ Circle your strongest point. Consider moving this point to the end of your review.

▶ If you move your strongest point to the end, revise all the paragraphs to build to your concluding point.

***Peer Review*** Ask for a partner's response to your review. Revise based on the feedback. Then, explain the importance of the revisions you chose to make.

**Directions** Read this student response to literature as a model for your own.

**Student Model: Writing**

Go Online
**Student Model**
Visit: PHSchool.com
Web Code: exr-7401

*Tyler Blair, Somerset, NY*

## *The Lesson of "Rikki-tikki-tavi"*

The short story "Rikki-tikki-tavi" is a well-known story written by Rudyard Kipling. . . . The message of the story is that although you may be small, you can still overcome major enemies. This story is enjoyable because it can teach you helpful morals while keeping you entertained at the same time.

The beginning of this story is heavy-hearted and dramatic. A small boy named Teddy thinks that the mongoose is dead following a bout with its first enemy—a flood that swept him away from his burrow. The mood of the story changes when the boy realizes that the mongoose is still alive, but weak. He decides to keep it, and takes care of it much like a pet, feeding it and naming it Rikki-tikki-tavi.

When Rikki-tikki goes outside into the little boy's garden to explore his surroundings, he comes upon a bird, which he confronts. The story switches back to a gloomy mood when the mongoose discovers that Nag, a cobra, ate one of the bird's eggs. When Rikki-tikki hears this, Nag comes out of the tall grass behind him.

This is when the story gets scary because Rikki faces another enemy. Nag quickly spreads his hood to intimidate the small mongoose. Then, Nagaina, Nag's wife, pulls a surprise attack on Rikki-tikki and nearly eats him. Because Rikki-tikki is young and dodges the cobra's blow from behind, he gains plenty of confidence. Readers wonder whether the mongoose will stay safe.

As the story progresses, Rikki mets Karait, another snake and this builds excitement and tension. This snake isn't after the mongoose, although he is after the family. When Teddy runs out to pet Rikki-tikki, the snake strikes at the boy, but Rikki-tikki

The writer focuses on the message, or theme, of the story.

The writer supports his ideas about the story by giving examples.

The writer summarizes the most important plot events in the order in which they occur.

lunges at the snake and paralyzes it by biting it before it can bite Teddy. . . .

This story is exciting and thought provoking. It ends, leaving me and other readers to think about its real meaning. Most people can relate to a time when they have faced a challenge in their life, but have felt that they were unable to overcome it. However, when they kept trying and put their minds to it, they eventually ended with success, as Rikki-tikki did.

> The writer explains what message readers can take away from the story.

## Editing—Be Your Own Language Coach

Examine your review for language convention errors. Pay attention to your use of conjunctions, interjections, and tone.

## Publishing—Share It!

Consider the following idea to share your writing.

**Present your review.** Use poster board or software to turn your review into a presentation. Deliver it in front of your classmates and invite them to respond with their opinions.

## Reflecting On Your Writing

**Rubric for Self-Assessment** Assess your essay. For each question, circle a rating.

| CRITERIA | RATING SCALE |
|---|---|
| | NOT VERY           VERY |
| **IDEAS** Is your paper clear and focused, with rich details? | 1  2  3  4  5 |
| **ORGANIZATION** How well do you employ a clear and logical organization? | 1  2  3  4  5 |
| **VOICE** Is your writing lively and engaging, drawing the reader in? | 1  2  3  4  5 |
| **WORD CHOICE** How appropriate is the language for your audience? | 1  2  3  4  5 |
| **SENTENCE FLUENCY** How varied is your sentence structure? | 1  2  3  4  5 |
| **CONVENTIONS** How correct is your grammar, especially your use of conjunctions and interjections? | 1  2  3  4  5 |

### Literature Circles

**Think-Aloud** After you discuss your Anchor Book with members of your Literature Circle, you will learn how to participate in a new type of discussion called a **Think-Aloud.**

## PART 1: Open Discussion

Begin your open discussion sharing your thoughts, opinions, and questions about your Anchor Book. If you run out of ideas to share, try the following conversation starter.

Write one word that relates to the Anchor Book on a piece of scrap paper and throw it into the center of your Literature Circle. Pick a paper from the pile. If you choose your own paper, return it to the pile and choose another. Take turns reading each member's word and discussing how it relates to your Anchor Book.

## PART 2: Discuss—Think-Aloud

In this Literature Circle, you will read an important passage from your Anchor Book aloud to your Literature Circle members. Each member will refer to specific parts of the passage and explain how they interpreted those parts. This strategy is called a **Think-Aloud.**

**How to participate in a Think-Aloud**

► Think aloud about the connections you make to other parts of your Anchor Book, to your own life, to another text, or to something you know about the world.

  • "When I heard/read [identify part of the passage], it made me think of…"

  • "When I heard/read [identify part of the passage], the words created an image in my head of…"

► Think aloud about any questions you have.

  • "I was wondering what the passage means when it says [identify part of the passage]."

  • "Why does the author use these words [identify part of the passage] to describe…?"

  • "I was confused when I heard/read [identify part of the passage], but then I thought about…"

  • "If I could talk to the main character, I would ask…"

## How did the discussion go?

Record the page numbers of the important passages and summarize your passage's Think-Aloud responses in the table.

| Passage appears on page(s) | Think-Aloud Summary |
|---|---|
| | |
| | |
| | |

**Active Listening**  A good discussion happens when all Literature Circle members demonstrate active listening. Many key elements of active listening are things you *do*, not say. Make eye contact, nod, take turns, disagree politely, and always be respectful. Use the idea bubbles below to identify ways in which you and your group members demonstrated active listening in today's discussion. Then, brainstorm additional ways you can do so in future Literature Circles. Add additional idea bubbles as needed.

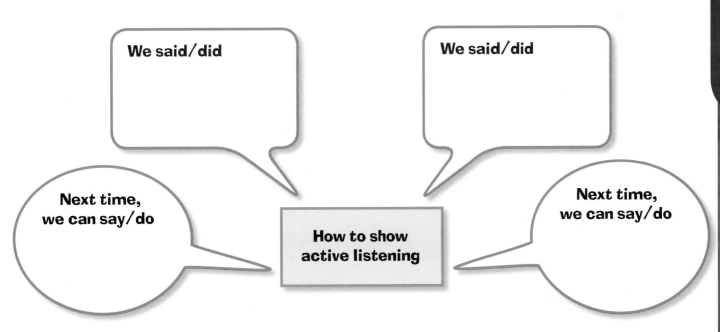

## Reading Skill: Paraphrasing

Read the passage. Then answer the questions.

> Jordan felt uneasy standing before the massive ivy-covered gate. Normally he liked cemeteries, especially at night, when the soft flapping of owl wings broke the silence. He liked the chirping of crickets, a symphony of the dark, filling the air in what he wanted to think was a celebration of his arrival.
>
> But tonight he didn't feel comfortable. His uneasiness wasn't because of what his classmates always said about him behind his back: *Jordan is a weirdo! Jordan thinks he's a vampire!*
>
> No, he felt uncomfortable because there were two new additions to the cemetery gate, two stone statues, each one guarding a side. They weren't ordinary statues—not the sorrowful angels gazing over headstones. They were gargoyles, mythical beasts, and their wings were unfurled, like parachutes for the dead. And the gargoyles were glaring right at him. They didn't like the living.

**1** Which statement best paraphrases the first two sentences?

   **A.** The gate to the cemetery was covered with ivy.

   **B.** Jordan was nervous as he stood at the cemetery entrance.

   **C.** Jordan didn't know why he was uneasy.

   **D.** Jordan loved to visit cemeteries.

**2** Which statement is an example of **simile?**

   **F.** Jordan felt uneasy.

   **G.** Their wings were unfurled like parachutes.

   **H.** Jordan is a weirdo.

   **J.** They were gargoyles.

**3** What is one good reason to paraphrase?

   **A.** To help understand a passage.

   **B.** To memorize a passage.

   **C.** To know what will happen next.

   **D.** To relate a passage to your own life.

**4** Which sentence might be a good paraphrase of "their wings were unfurled, like parachutes for the dead"?

   **F.** The gargoyles were dead.

   **G.** Jordan didn't like the look of the gargoyles.

   **H.** The gargoyles' wings were spread wide open.

   **J.** The gargoyles use parachutes to fly.

# Literary Analysis: Elements of Prose and Poetry

Read the passage. Then answer the questions that follow.

Mia found the annual family picnic exhausting. She loved the cluster of tall pines and the cheerful chirps of larks, wrens, and the occasional bullfrog. She looked forward to the feel of the wooden dock on the soles of her bare feet. These things were actually calming—it was the people who made Mia so tired.

Take, for example, her uncle Frank. Built like a grizzly bear, he'd always been one of Mia's favorites. But when he spoke in his booming voice, you had to watch out for flying objects—his hands, to be exact. His wild arm gestures made Mia want to take a nap. Then, there was Aunt Angie. Mercifully, her speech was quite ordinary. It was her clothes that shouted—bright striped blouses and paisley-patterned pants that reflected the sun straight into your eyes.

**5** Which sentence from the passage uses **sensory language?**

    **A.** These things were actually calming—it was the people who made Mia so tired.

    **B.** She looked forward to the feel of the wooden dock on the soles of her bare feet.

    **C.** Mercifully, her speech was quite ordinary.

    **D.** Take, for example, her uncle Frank.

**6** Which **connotation** of the word *quiet* would BEST create a mysterious **tone?**

    **F.** peaceful

    **G.** hushed

    **H.** calm

    **J.** silent

**7** Which phrase or sentence from the passage helps create a light, humorous **tone?**

    **A.** Mia found the annual family picnic exhausting.

    **B.** watch out for flying objects—his hands, to be exact.

    **C.** These things were actually calming.

    **D.** Then, there was Aunt Angie.

**8** Which phrase uses **imagery** that appeals to the senses of sight and sound?

    **F.** Built like a grizzly bear

    **G.** His wild arm gestures

    **H.** the cluster of tall pines and the cheerful chirps

    **J.** speech was quite ordinary

## Timed Writing: Narration

**Directions** Identify sensory images and tone in a favorite book or story. Next, write details from your story that appeal to the senses. Then, write the tone the author conveys and at least three details from the story that help convey this tone. **(20 minutes)**

# 4-9 Reading Skills
## Drawing Conclusions

In learning new reading skills, you will use special academic vocabulary. Knowing the right words will help you demonstrate your understanding.

## Academic Vocabulary

| Word | Meaning | Example Sentence |
|---|---|---|
| **detect** *v.* <br> *Related words:* <br> detected; detecting | to notice or discover something | Mai-Lin can easily *detect* errors in grammar. |
| **illustrate** *v.* <br> *Related words:* <br> illustration; illustrating | to make clear or give examples | Kevin chose two examples to *illustrate* his point. |
| **refer** *v.* <br> *Related words:* <br> referred; reference | to consult a source for information; mention a source for information | Ariel had to *refer* to the encyclopedia to complete her history assignment. |

**Drawing conclusions** means arriving at an overall judgment or idea by pulling together several details.

Read the passage below. Then, see how the student completed the graphic organizer in order to draw a conclusion.

> Max dieted and was careful about the foods he ate. He exercised every day for an hour. By January, he was pleased that he saw results.

**Which details are included and emphasized?**
Detail: Max dieted.          Detail: Max exercised every day.

**Ask questions about the details.**
What were the results?

**Use prior knowledge.**
Diet and exercise can help a person lose weight.

**Draw a conclusion.**
The results were that Max lost weight.

while reading your anchor book

By drawing conclusions, you can **detect** meanings that are not directly stated in the text. Always **refer** to the text for important details the author uses to **illustrate** his or her points.

**Directions** Read the passage, underlining details that help you draw conclusions about the Klondike gold rush.

The year was 1896. Seldom in American history have economic conditions been as bad as they were then. The Depression of the 1890s pushed people to seek new ways to make money. An American named George Washington Carmack was crouching down at the bank of an ice-cold creek, sifting sand. Suddenly he let out a loud yell that shattered the silence. He and two of his friends immediately began to dance out there in the middle of nowhere. Carmack later described their dance as an Irish jig, a Scottish hornpipe, a hula, and a fox trot all in one.

Their lives had made a turn for the better. Suddenly, instant wealth seemed within reach. Carmack's news spread to many settlers in the American territories, and a new era was born—the Klondike gold rush.

**Which details are included and emphasized?**

Detail: _____

Detail: _____

**Ask questions about the details.**

_____
_____

**Use prior knowledge.**

_____
_____
_____

**Draw a conclusion.**

_____
_____

Look at the details in the following article and draw conclusions based on those details. *Guiding Question:* **What ideas is the author trying to communicate about Chico Mendes?**

# Chico Mendes and the Amazon Rain Forest

Many environmental activists encounter resistance and personal hardship in their fight to protect the world's endangered ecosystems. In his fight, Chico Mendes lost his life.

▲ A cut and burned section of trees on federal land known as "terra do meio," or "the land in between," referring to its location between two major rivers, in Brazil's Amazonian state of Para.

Mendes was born into a family of rubber tappers living and working in Brazil's Amazon rain forest. Rubber tappers cut slits in the bark of rubber trees and collect the latex sap that oozes out. Tapping trees does not kill or injure trees.

In the 1970s, the Brazilian government started opening the rain forest to development. Developers use vast fires in their "slash-and-burn" clearing method that release huge quantities of carbon dioxide, eliminating the plant life that consumes this heat-trapping gas. Deforestation contributes to the greenhouse effect threatening to alter Earth's climate through global warming.

Realizing that the rain forest was in danger, Mendes created a rural workers' union. Mendes used nonviolence to block deforestation. Whenever work crews threatened the land, Mendes called together rubber tappers to form a human barrier. These peaceful blockades are estimated to have saved 3 million acres of rain forest.

Mendes wanted large sections of the rain forest set aside only for harvesting renewable resources, such as rubber. He also helped persuade the Inter-American Development Bank to stop a highway extension through the rain forest. As a result of Mendes's efforts—and the international fame and support he was beginning to receive—the Brazilian government finally designated five million acres of rain forest for permanent preservation.

Mendes's successful efforts earned him the hatred of developers. Five times Mendes survived attempts on his life and was assigned police guards to protect him. However in 1988, he was struck down by a shotgun blast. Today his union colleagues carry on his work.

Shortly before he was murdered, Mendes wrote in a letter to a friend: "I wish no flowers after I die, for I know they would be taken from the forest."

# Thinking About the Selection

## Chico Mendes and the Amazon Rain Forest

**1** **Draw Conclusions** Draw a conclusion and complete the diagram.

> **Which details are included and emphasized?**
>
> Detail: _____
>
> Detail: _____
>
> Detail: _____

> **Ask questions about the details.**
>
> _____
>
> _____
>
> _____

> **Use prior knowledge.**
>
> _____
>
> _____
>
> _____
>
> _____

> **Draw a conclusion.**
>
> _____
>
> _____

**Write** Answer the following questions in your Reader's Journal.

 **2** **Infer** What ideas is the author trying to communicate about Chico Mendes?

 **3** **Draw Conclusions** What questions do you think the author wants you to answer about your Anchor Book? What conclusions does the author want you to draw about life?

 **Ready for a Free-Choice Book?** *Your teacher may ask you if you would like to choose another book to read on your own. Select a book that fits your interest and that you'll enjoy. As you read, think about how your new book compares with your Anchor Book.*

# 4-10 Literary Analysis
## *Sound Devices, Rhythm, and Meter*

The music and lyrics you listen to are a form of poetry. Poets, like musicians, pay attention to the way their poems sound. The sound of poetry affects its mood, or overall feeling.

## Literary Terms

Writers use **sound devices** to create musical effects through language.

| Sound Device | Meaning | Example |
|---|---|---|
| **Repetition** | repeating a sound, word, phrase, sentence, or group of lines | *down, down, down, into the sea* |
| **Alliteration** | the repetition of consonant sounds at the beginning of words | *while I nodded, nearly napping* |
| **Consonance** | the repetition of consonant sounds at the end of words | *tick tock* |
| **Assonance** | the repetition of vowel sounds in words | *black cat* |
| **Onomatopoeia** | the use of a word that sounds like what it means | *bang, boom, swoosh, slurp, crack, howl, hiss* |
| **Rhyme** | the repetition of sounds at the end of words | *fair and share* |
| **End Rhyme** | rhyme that occurs at the end of lines of poetry | *as I was walking down the street grumbling about my aching feet* |
| **Internal Rhyme** | rhyme that occurs within a line of poetry | *falling leaves whirl and twirl* |

Here are some other important poetic devices.

▶ A **rhyme scheme** is a regular pattern of end rhymes. Each rhyming sound is given a different letter. For example, a **stanza,** or group of lines, might have the rhyme scheme *abab*. This means that lines 1 and 3 rhyme, and lines 2 and 4 rhyme.

▶ Both poetry and prose have a **rhythm**—a pattern of beats. It can follow a regular pattern, or it can be loose and conversational. A poem's rhythm should suit its meaning.

- When the rhythm of a poem has a regular pattern, it is called **meter.** Poems with a regular meter have a specific pattern of strong (stressed) and weak (unstressed) beats.

- To identify the meter of a poem, you **scan** it to find the pattern of strong and weak beats in each line. Mark each stressed syllable with a slanted line (/) called an **accent.** Mark each unstressed syllable with a horseshoe symbol (⌣).

⌣ / ⌣ / ⌣ / ⌣
the it sy bit sy spi der

**Directions**  Now it's time to make some noise! Read the poem below aloud as a class and clap to the beat of the poem. Read it a second time and scan the poem by marking it with accents and horseshoe symbols.

*Summer* by *Walter Dean Myers*

1  I like hot days, hot days

   Sweat is what you got days

   Bugs buzzin from cousin to cousin

   Juices dripping

5  Running and ripping

   Catch the one you love days

   Birds peeping

   Old men sleeping

   Lazy days, daisies lay

10 Beaming and dreaming

   Of hot days, hot days,

   Sweat is what you got days

**Go Online**

**About the Author**
Visit: PHSchool.com
Web Code: exe-7411

**Identify**  Write examples of the poem's sound devices and describe its rhythm in the chart below.

| Assonance | |
|---|---|
| Consonance | |
| End rhyme | |
| Internal rhyme | |
| Rhythm | |

Read the following poems aloud. Listen for how sound devices create a musical quality. *Guiding Question:* **How do sound devices help communicate ideas and express the mood in each poem?**

## Vocabulary Builder

**Before you read,** *you will discuss the following words. In the Vocabulary Builder box in the margin, use a vocabulary building strategy to make the words your own.*

### dispersed          murmurs

**As you read,** *draw a box around unfamiliar words you could add to your vocabulary. Use context clues to unlock their meaning.*

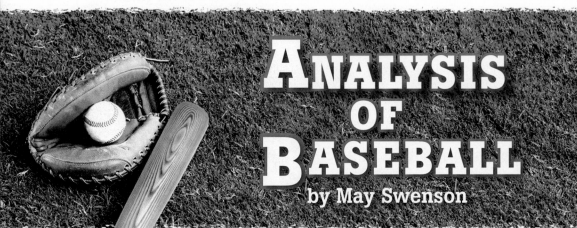

# ANALYSIS OF BASEBALL
### by May Swenson

It's about
the ball,
the bat,
and the mitt.
Ball hits
bat, or it
hits mitt.
Bat doesn't
hit ball, bat
meets it.
Ball bounces
off bat, flies
air, or thuds
ground (dud)
or it
fits mitt.
Bat waits

> ## Marking the Text
>
> **Sound Devices, Rhythm, and Meter**
>
> **As you read,** *underline sound devices. In the margin, write notes identifying the sound device you have underlined.*

*while reading your anchor book*

for ball
to mate.
Ball hates
to take bat's
bait. Ball
flirts, bat's
late, don't
keep the date.
Ball goes in
(thwack) to mitt,
and goes out
(thwack) back
to mitt.

Ball fits
mitt, but
not all
the time.
Sometimes
ball gets hit
(pow) when bat
meets it,
and sails
to a place
where mitt
has to quit
in disgrace.
That's about
the bases
loaded,
about 40,000
fans exploded.

It's about
the ball,
the bat,
the mitt,
the bases
and the fans.
It's done
on a diamond,
and for fun.
It's about
home, and it's
about run.

Sound Devices, Rhythm, and Meter   **329**

Now that you've read a fun poem aloud, try reading this thoughful poem about nature aloud.

# Wind and Water and Stone
by Octavio Paz

The water hollowed the stone,
the wind **dispersed** the water,
the stone stopped the wind.
Water and wind and stone.

The wind sculpted the stone,
the stone is a cup of water,
the water runs off and is wind.
Stone and wind and water.

The wind sings in its turnings,
the water **murmurs** as it goes,
the motionless stone is quiet.
Wind and water and stone.

One is the other, and is neither:
among their empty names
they pass and disappear,
water and stone and wind.

**Vocabulary Builder**

**dispersed**
(di spʉrs'd) v.
**Meaning**

**murmurs**
(mʉr' mərz) v.
**Meaning**

# Octavio Paz (1914-1998)

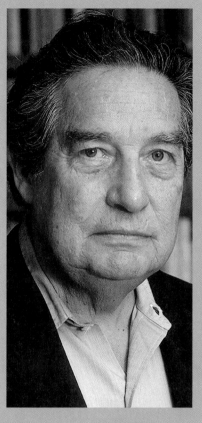

Octavio Paz (ôk tä'vyō päs) was born in Mexico City to a family with Spanish and Mexican roots. Both his father and grandfather were writers, and both were active in progressive politics. As a teenager, Paz founded a literary magazine and published his first book of poetry. As a young man, he became a diplomat and was sent to France, where he became involved in the French literary scene. In 1962, Paz was appointed Mexico's ambassador to India. However, he resigned this post in 1968 to protest his government's brutality against student demonstrators during the Olympics, which were held in Mexico.

Paz continued to write and edit throughout his long life, publishing many collections of poetry, as well as essays and literary criticism. In 1990, he won the Nobel Prize in Literature.

# I've Had This Shirt

by Michael Rosen

I've had this shirt
that's covered in dirt
for years and years and years.

It used to be red
but I wore it in bed
and it went gray
cos I wore it all day
for years and years and years.

The arms fell off
in the Monday wash
and you can see my vest
through the holes in the chest
for years and years and years.

As my shirt falls apart
I'll keep the bits
in a biscuit tin
on the mantelpiece
for years and years and years.

## Vocabulary Builder

**After you read,** *review the words you decided to add to your vocabulary. Write the meaning of words you have learned in context. Look up the other words in a dictionary, glossary, thesaurus, or electronic resource.*

# Thinking About the Selections

## Analysis of Baseball, Wind and Water and Stone, *and* I've Had This Shirt

**Go Online**

**About the Author**
Visit: PHSchool.com
Web Code: exe-7412
7413
7414

**1**    **Identify** Use the chart to list a few examples of sound devices in the following poems.

| Sound Device | Analysis of Baseball | Wind and Water and Stone |
|---|---|---|
| Repetition | | |
| Alliteration | | |
| Onomatopoeia | | |

**2**    **Compare and Contrast** How is the rhyme in "Analysis of Baseball" different from the rhyme in "I've Had This Shirt"?

 

**3**    **Compare and Contrast** How is the rhythm of "I've Had This Shirt" different from the rhythm of the other two poems? What sound devices create the rhythm in the other two poems?

 

**Write** Answer the following questions in your Reader's Journal.

 **4**    **Interpret** How do sound devices help communicate ideas and express the mood in each poem?

 **5**    **Compare and Contrast** Compare and contrast the sound devices from a poem or prose passage in your Anchor Book with the sound devices from a poem in this lesson. Are they similar or different? Support your answer with details from the texts.

while reading your anchor book

Sound devices give poetry a musical quality. As you will discover in this story, they can also play a key role in prose. *Guiding Question:* **How does the writer use sound devices to communicate her characters' thoughts and feelings?**

# The Wounded Wolf

## BY JEAN CRAIGHEAD GEORGE

**Background** *Jean Craighead George based her story on a real-life event that a wolf expert told her about while she was observing wolves in Alaska's Denali National Park.*

### Vocabulary Builder

**Before you read,** *you will discuss the following words. In the Vocabulary Builder box in the margin, use a vocabulary building strategy to make the words your own.*

**massive   penetrates   procession   barren**

**As you read,** *draw a box around unfamiliar words you could add to your vocabulary. Use context clues to unlock their meaning.*

**Marking the Text**

**Sound Devices, Rhythm, and Meter**

**As you read,** *underline examples of onomatopoeia and other sound devices. In the margin, make notes on how these sound devices function in the story.*

A wounded wolf climbs Toklat Ridge, a **massive** spine of rock and ice. As he limps, dawn strikes the ridge and lights it up with sparks and stars. Roko, the wounded wolf, blinks in the ice fire, then stops to rest and watch his pack run the thawing Arctic valley.

They plunge and turn. They fight the mighty caribou[1] that struck young Roko with his hoof and wounded him. He jumped between the beast and Kiglo, leader of the Toklat pack. Young

**Vocabulary Builder**

**massive**
(mas'iv) *adj.*

**Meaning**

---
[1] **caribou** (kar'ə boo) *n.* a type of large North American reindeer.

Roko spun and fell. Hooves, paws, and teeth roared over him. And then his pack and the beast were gone.

Gravely injured, Roko pulls himself toward the shelter rock. Weakness overcomes him. He stops. He and his pack are thin and hungry. This is the season of starvation. The winter's harvest has been taken. The produce of spring has not begun.

Young Roko glances down the valley. He droops his head and stiffens his tail to signal to his pack that he is badly hurt. Winds wail. A frigid blast picks up long shawls of snow and drapes them between young Roko and his pack. And so his message is not read.

A raven scouting Toklat Ridge sees Roko's signal. "Kong, kong, kong," he bells—death is coming to the ridge; there will be flesh and bone for all. His voice rolls out across the valley. It **penetrates** the rocky cracks where the Toklat ravens rest. One by one they hear and spread their wings. They beat their way to Toklat Ridge. They alight upon the snow and walk behind the wounded wolf.

"Kong," they toll with keen excitement, for the raven clan is hungry, too. "Kong, kong"—there will be flesh and bone for all.

Roko snarls and hurries toward the shelter rock. A cloud of snow envelops him. He limps in blinding whiteness now.

A ghostly presence flits around.

"Hahahahahahaha," the white fox states—death is coming to the Ridge. Roko smells the fox tagging at his heels.

The cloud whirls off. Two golden eyes look up at Roko. The snowy owl has heard the ravens and joined the deathwatch.

Roko limps along. The ravens walk. The white fox leaps. The snowy owl flies and hops along the rim of Toklat Ridge. Roko stops. Below the ledge out on the flats the musk-ox herd is circling. They form a ring and all face out, a fort of heads and horns and fur that sweeps down to their hooves. Their circle means to Roko that an enemy is present. He squints and smells the wind. It carries scents of thawing ice, broken grass—and earth. The grizzly bear is up! He has awakened from his winter's sleep. A craving need for flesh will drive him.

Roko sees the shelter rock. He strains to reach it. He stumbles. The ravens move in closer. The white fox boldly walks beside him. "Hahaha," he yaps. The snowy owl flies ahead, alights, and waits.

The grizzly hears the eager fox and rises on his flat hind feet. He twists his powerful neck and head. His great paws dangle at his chest. He sees the animal **procession** and hears the ravens' knell[2] of death. Dropping to all fours, he joins the march up Toklat Ridge.

Roko stops; his breath comes hard. A raven alights upon his back and picks the open wound. Roko snaps. The raven flies

---

2 **knell** (nel) *n.* the sound of a bell ringing.

**Marking the Text**

**Vocabulary Builder**

**penetrates**
(pen'i trāts) *v.*
**Meaning**

**procession**
(prō sesh'ən) *n.*
**Meaning**

while reading your anchor book

335

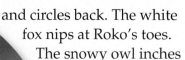
and circles back. The white fox nips at Roko's toes. The snowy owl inches closer. The grizzly bear, still dulled by sleep, stumbles onto Toklat Ridge.

Only yards from the shelter rock, Roko falls.

Instantly the ravens mob him. They scream and peck and stab at his eyes. The white fox leaps upon his wound. The snowy owl sits and waits.

Young Roko struggles to his feet. He bites the ravens. Snaps the fox. And lunges at the stoic[3] owl. He turns and warns the grizzly bear. Then he bursts into a run and falls against the shelter rock. The wounded wolf wedges down between the rock and **barren** ground. Now protected on three sides, he turns and faces all his foes[4].

The ravens step a few feet closer. The fox slides toward him on his belly. The snowy owl blinks and waits, and on the ridge rim roars the hungry grizzly bear.

Roko growls.

The sun comes up. Far across the Toklat Valley, Roko hears his pack's "hunt's end" song. The music wails and sobs, wilder than the bleating wind. The hunt song ends. Next comes the roll call. Each member of the Toklat pack barks to say that he is home and well.

"Kiglo here," Roko hears his leader bark. There is a pause. It is young Roko's turn. He cannot lift his head to answer. The pack is silent. The leader starts the count once more. "Kiglo here."—A pause. Roko cannot answer.

The wounded wolf whimpers softly. A mindful raven hears. "Kong, kong, kong," he tolls—this is the end. His booming sounds across the valley. The wolf pack hears the raven's message that something is dying. They know it is Roko, who has not answered roll call.

The hours pass. The wind slams snow on Toklat Ridge. Massive clouds blot out the sun. In their gloom Roko sees the deathwatch move in closer. Suddenly he hears the musk-oxen thundering into their circle. The ice cracks as the

---

³ **stoic** (stō′ik) *adj.* not seeming to feel pain; tough.

⁴ **foes** (fōz) *n.* enemies.

## Vocabulary Builder

**barren**
(bar′ən) *adj.*

**Meaning**

# Literature in Context
## Wolves in the Wild

Jean Craighead George has written several books and stories about wolves, including her Newbery Medal–winning novel *Julie of the Wolves.* She learned about wolves by studying them in their natural habitat in Alaska and by working with scientists at the Naval Arctic Research Lab near Barrow. These scientists even taught George how to "talk" to a female wolf by using a language of sounds, actions, and body language.

Wolves make good characters in fiction because they have many behavioral traits in common with people. For example, though wolves struggle for survival in the wild, they are devoted parents and loyal to members of their pack. Here are some more facts about wolves.

- The wolves in this story are arctic wolves, a type of gray wolf.
- Wolves usually live in packs that consist of adult parents and their children from the past two or three years. Sometimes other wolves join the pack.
- The parent wolves, known as the alpha wolves, are the leaders of the pack. All the other pack members must follow their rules.
- The size of the pack varies, but an arctic wolf pack may have more than 30 members. The pack's territory ranges from 300 to 1,000 square miles.

grizzly leaves. The ravens burst into the air. The white fox runs. The snowy owl flaps to the top of the shelter rock. And Kiglo rounds the knoll[5].

In his mouth he carries meat. He drops it close to Roko's head and wags his tail excitedly. Roko licks Kiglo's chin to honor him. Then Kiglo puts his mouth around Roko's nose. This gesture says "I am your leader." And by mouthing Roko, he binds him and all the wolves together.

The wounded wolf wags his tail. Kiglo trots away.

Already Roko's wound feels better. He gulps the food and feels his strength return. He shatters bone, flesh, and gristle and shakes the scraps out on the snow. The hungry ravens swoop upon them. The white fox snatches up a bone. The snowy owl gulps down flesh and fur. And Roko wags his tail and watches.

For days Kiglo brings young Roko food. He gnashes[6], gorges[7], and shatters bits upon the snow.

*Marking the Text*

---

[5] **knoll** (nōl) *n.* small hill.

[6] **gnashes** (nash' ez) *v.* bites by grinding teeth.

[7] **gorges** (gôrg' ez) *n.* eats hungrily.

A purple sandpiper winging north sees ravens, owl and fox. And he drops in upon the feast. The long-tailed jaeger gull flies down and joins the crowd on Toklat Ridge. Roko wags his tail.

One dawn he moves his wounded leg. He stretches it and pulls himself into the sunlight. He walks—he romps. He runs in circles. He leaps and plays with chunks of ice. Suddenly he stops. The "hunt's end" song rings out. Next comes the roll call.

"Kiglo here."

"Roko here," he barks out strongly.

The pack is silent.

"Kiglo here," the leader repeats.

"Roko here."

Across the distance comes the sound of whoop and yips and barks and howls. They fill the dawn with celebration. And Roko prances down the Ridge.

## Vocabulary Builder

**After you read,** *review the words you decided to add to your vocabulary. Write the meaning of words you have learned in context. Look up the other words in a dictionary, glossary, thesaurus, or electronic resource.*

while reading your anchor book

# Thinking About the Selection
## The Wounded Wolf

**Go Online**
**About the Author**
Visit: PHSchool.com
Web Code: exe-7415

**1** **Identify** Use the chart to list examples of sound devices in the story.

| Onomatopoeia | |
|---|---|
| Repetition | |

**2** **Evaluate** Which sound device do you think is more important, onomatopoeia or repetition? What function does it serve in the story?

_____

_____

_____

**3** **Analyze** Describe the story's rhythm. What elements create that rhythm? How does the rhythm help convey the story's meaning or mood?

_____

_____

_____

**4** **Compare and Contrast** Compare and contrast the use of sound devices and rhythm in the story with one of the poems in this lesson.

_____

_____

_____

_____

**Write** Answer the following questions in your Reader's Journal.

 **5** **Analyze** How does the writer use sound devices to communicate the characters' thoughts and feelings?

 **6** **Analyze** Choose a poem or prose passage in your Anchor Book that includes sound devices. How do these sound devices affect the meaning or mood of the selection?

while reading your anchor book

# 4-11 Literary Analysis
## *Symbolism*

You probably already know a lot about symbolism. For example, what does a rose represent to you? What about a dove? You have most likely seen these objects used to symbolize love or peace. When an object is used to stand for an idea, it is called symbolism.

▶ A **symbol** is an object, a person, an animal, or a place that represents something beyond its literal meaning.

▶ **Symbolism,** or the use of symbols, can involve a certain object, setting, or image. For example, in a poem or story, a forest might represent uncertainty.

▶ An **allusion** is a reference to a well-known person, place, thing, event, or literary work. Like a symbol, an allusion means something more than itself.

Both symbols and allusions allow writers to express complex ideas without spelling them out.

| Traditional Symbol | Meaning |
|---|---|
| heart | love |
| Uncle Sam | the United States |
| four-leaf clover | luck |

| Allusion | Meaning |
|---|---|
| Romeo | romantic boy or man, from Shakespeare's *Romeo and Juliet* |
| Scrooge | stingy person, from Charles Dickens' *A Christmas Carol* |
| Waterloo | a place where a person meets failure, from Napoleon's battle at Waterloo |

Allusions help the reader make a connection between the text and what they already know. In order for an allusion to work, however, the reader must be aware of the allusion and must be familiar with what it alludes—refers—to.

**Directions** Write your interpretations of these sentences and state whether they are symbols or allusions.

**1** The two groups were tired of fighting; they held out the olive branch.

_____

_____

**2** He was a natural Babe Ruth and led the team to the championship with his home runs.

_____

_____

**Work with a partner.** Come up with your own sentences using allusion or symbolism.

Then, read the poem and answer the questions.

## Epigram
### by Langston Hughes
Oh, God of dust and rainbows, help us see
That without dust the rainbow would not be.

◀ **Good to Know!**
An epigram is a short poem with a clever twist.

**3** **Analyze** Does the word _dust_ have positive or negative connotations or associations? Why?

_____

_____

**4** **Analyze** Does the word _rainbows_ have positive or negative connotations? Why?

_____

_____

**5** **Interpret** What do you think dust and rainbows symbolize in this poem? What idea is the poet using these symbols to express?

_____

_____

_____

_____

In the following poem, notice how ordinary things take on symbolic meaning. *Guiding Question:* **How does Frost use symbolism to communicate the theme of his poem?**

# Stopping by Woods on a Snowy Evening
## by Robert Frost

### Vocabulary Builder

**Before you read,** *you will discuss the following words. In the Vocabulary Builder box in the margin, use a vocabulary building strategy to make the words your own.*

harness          downy

**As you read,** *draw a box around unfamiliar words you could add to your vocabulary. Use context clues to unlock their meaning.*

### Marking the Text

**Symbolism**

**As you read,** *write notes in the margin about what you think the speaker is saying on a literal level. Underline words or phrases that suggest a deeper meaning. Write notes in the margin about what these things might symbolize.*

Whose woods these are I think I know.
His house is in the village, though;
He will not see me stopping here
To watch his woods fill up with snow.
5   My little horse must think it queer
To stop without a farmhouse near
Between the woods and frozen lake
The darkest evening of the year.
He gives his **harness** bells a shake
10   To ask if there is some mistake.
The only other sound's the sweep
Of easy wind and **downy** flake.
The woods are lovely, dark, and deep,
But I have promises to keep,
15   And miles to go before I sleep.
And miles to go before I sleep.

### Vocabulary Builder

**After you read,** *review the words you decided to add to your vocabulary. Write the meaning of words you have learned in context. Look up the other words in a dictionary, glossary, thesaurus, or electronic resource.*

### Vocabulary Builder

**harness**
(här′nis) *n.*

**Meaning**


**downy**
(dou′nē) *adj.*

**Meaning**

# Thinking About the Selection
## Stopping by Woods on a Snowy Evening

Go Online
**About the Author**
Visit: PHSchool.com
Web Code: exe-7416

**1** **Analyze** Why does the speaker stop in the woods? Why does he assume that his horse will be confused by his decision to stop?

_____

_____

_____

**2** **Interpret** What are the only two sounds the speaker hears? In what way might these two sounds represent conflicting ideas or desires for the speaker?

_____

_____

_____

_____

**3** **Analyze** In the last stanza, what symbolic meaning do you see in the phrases "promises to keep" and "miles to go"?

_____

_____

_____

_____

**4** **Interpret** On a literal level, the speaker is saying that he can't stay in the woods because he has a long trip ahead of him before he can go to sleep. What symbolic meaning do you think sleep might have? What do you think the "lovely, dark, and deep" woods represent?

_____

_____

_____

**Write** Answer the following questions in your Reader's Journal.

 **5** **Analyze** How does Frost use symbolism to communicate the theme of his poem?

 **6** **Analyze** Find a poem or passage in your Anchor Book that includes a symbol—something that seems to mean more than its literal meaning. What clues suggest that the writer is using symbolism? How does this symbol relate to the theme of the work?

Symbolism **343**

# 4-12 Literary Analysis
## Forms of Poetry

What do we mean by the form of a poem? Is it the way it looks on the page? The type of story it tells? Its use of rhyme and meter? How many lines it contains? If you answered "yes" to some or all of these questions, you are right.

## Literary Terms

There are three main types of poetry.

| |
|---|
| **Narrative poetry** tells a story, using elements such as plot, characters, and setting. |
| **Lyric poetry** has a musical quality and expresses the feelings of a single speaker. |
| **Dramatic poetry** presents a dramatic situation and the speech of a character. |

Within each of these broad categories, there are many specific forms of poetry. Here are some examples.

▸ An **epic poem** is a long narrative poem that tells about a larger-than-life hero.

▸ A **ballad** is a songlike narrative poem that often deals with adventure and romance. Most ballads use rhyme, meter, four-line stanzas, and a **refrain**—a repeated line or group of lines.

▸ An **ode** is a long, formal lyric poem. Odes often honor people, events, and nature.

▸ **Free verse** is poetry that does not use a regular meter. Instead, the poet uses any rhythm and line length that suits the poem's meaning.

▸ A **haiku** is a Japanese verse form that consists of seventeen syllables arranged into three unrhymed lines. The first and third lines have five syllables, and the second line has seven syllables. A haiku tries to capture a "snapshot" of nature.

▸ A **limerick** is a humorous five-line poem with a specific meter and rhyme scheme: *aabba*.

**Directions** The following poem is a **concrete poem.** It has a shape that looks like its subject. Read the poem. Then, answer the questions.

Go Online

**About the Author**
Visit: PHSchool.com
Web Code: exe-7417

## The Sidewalk Racer or On the Skateboard

*by Lillian Morrison*

Skimming
an asphalt sea
I swerve, I curve, I
sway; I speed to whirring
sound an inch above the
ground; I'm the sailor
and the sail, I'm the
driver and the wheel
I'm the one and only
single engine
human auto
mobile.

**1** **Evalute** Which image most effectively conveys the sense of being on a skateboard? Why?

_____

_____

_____

**2** **Analyze** How does the shape of the poem affect its meaning or impact on the reader? Would the poem be as effective if it were not written in the form of a concrete poem? Explain.

_____

_____

_____

_____

**3** **Interpret** Read the poem again and focus on the sound devices. What sound devices are being used in this poem and how do they contribute to the imagery and mood?

_____

_____

_____

while reading your anchor book

As you read the following poems, notice the characteristics of each poetic form. *Guiding Question:* **How does the form of each poem affect the way the poet communicates ideas and emotions?**

## Vocabulary Builder

**Before you read,** *you will discuss the following words. In the Vocabulary Builder box in the margin, use a vocabulary building strategy to make the words your own.*

**coveted**      **tomb**      **lava**

**As you read,** *draw a box around unfamiliar words you could add to your vocabulary. Use context clues to unlock their meaning.*

*Marking the Text*

**Forms of Poetry**

**As you read** *each poem, identify elements, such as rhyme, rhythm, tone, and subject, that help you identify the form of each poem. In the margin, write whether you think each form is effective.*

# Annabel Lee
## by Edgar Allan Poe

**Background** *Edgar Allan Poe (1809–1849) achieved lasting fame during his short life. He also suffered terrible personal tragedy. His mother died when he was only two years old. He lost his young wife, Virginia, to tuberculosis. Poe finished "Annabel Lee," which tells a tale of tragic love, about a year after her death.*

It was many and many a year ago,
     In a kingdom by the sea.
That a maiden there lived whom you may know
     By the name of Annabel Lee;—
And this maiden she lived with no other thought
     Than to love and be loved by me.

She was a child and I was a child,
     In this kingdom by the sea.
But we loved with a love that was more than love—
     I and my Annabel Lee—
With a love that the wingèd seraphs[1] of Heaven
     **Coveted** her and me.

---
[1] **wingèd seraphs** (wi[ng] id′ ser′əfs) *n.* angels.

## Vocabulary Builder

**coveted**
(kuv′it ed) *v.*

**Meaning**

*while reading your anchor book*

And this was the reason that, long ago,
    In this kingdom by the sea,
A wind blew out of a cloud by night
    Chilling my Annabel Lee;
So that her highborn kinsmen[2] came
    And bore her away from me,
To shut her up in a sepulcher[3]
    In this kingdom by the sea.

The angels, not half so happy in Heaven,
    Went envying her and me:—
Yes! that was the reason (as all men know,
    In this kingdom by the sea)
That the wind came out of a cloud, chilling
    And killing my Annabel Lee.

But our love it was stronger by far than the love
    Of those who were older than we—
    Of many far wiser than we—
And neither the angels in Heaven above
    Nor the demons down under the sea,
Can ever dissever[4] my soul from the soul
    Of the beautiful Annabel Lee:—

For the moon never beams without bringing
    me dreams
Of the beautiful Annabel Lee;
And the stars never rise but I see the bright eyes
    Of the beautiful Annabel Lee;
And so, all the nighttide, I lie down by the side
Of my darling, my darling, my life and my bride,
    In her sepulcher there by the sea—
    In her **tomb** by the side of the sea.

### Vocabulary Builder

**tomb**
(tōōm) *n.*

**Meaning**

---

[2] **kinsmen** (kinz′mən) *n.* relatives.

[3] **sepulcher** (sep′əl kər) *n.* vault or chamber for burial; tomb.

[4] **dissever** (di sev′ər) *v.* separate; divide.

Now let's read a poem in free verse.

# Describe Somebody
## by Jacqueline Woodson

*Marking the Text*

**Background** *"Describe Somebody" is told from the point of view of Lonnie Collins Motion, who lives with his foster mother in Brooklyn, New York. As Lonnie works on his teacher's assignment to describe somebody, he offers insight into his classmates.*

Today in class Ms. Marcus said
*Take out your poetry notebooks and describe somebody.*
*Think carefully,* Ms. Marcus said.
*You're gonna read it to the class.*
I wrote, Ms. Marcus is tall and a little bit skinny.
Then I put my pen in my mouth and stared down
at the words.
Then I crossed them out and wrote
Ms. Marcus's hair is long and brown.
Shiny.
When she smiles it makes you feel all good inside.
I stopped writing and looked around the room.
Angel was staring out the window.
Eric and Lamont were having a pen fight.
They don't care about poetry.
*Stupid words,* Eric says.
*Lots and lots of stupid words.*
Eric is tall and a little bit mean.
Lamont's just regular.
Angel's kinda chubby. He's got light brown hair.
Sometimes we all hang out,
play a little ball or something. Angel's real good
at science stuff. Once he made a volcano
for science fair and the stuff that came out of it
looked like real **lava.** Lamont can
draw superheroes real good. Eric—nobody
at school really knows this but
he can sing. Once, Miss Edna took me
to a different church than the one
we usually go to on Sunday.
I was surprised to see Eric up there

## Vocabulary Builder

**lava**
(lä′və) *n.*

**Meaning**

with a choir robe on. He gave me a mean look
like I'd better not
say nothing about him and his dark green robe with
gold around the neck.
After the preacher preached
Eric sang a song with nobody else in the choir singing.
Miss Edna started dabbing at her eyes
whispering *Yes, Lord.*
Eric's voice was like something
that didn't seem like it should belong
to Eric.
Seemed like it should be coming out of an angel.

Now I gotta write a whole new poem
'cause Eric would be real mad if I told the class
about his angel voice.

Here are three poems in haiku form. Notice the number of lines and syllables in each one.

# HAIKU
## by Yosa Buson

O foolish ducklings,
you know my old green pond is
watched by a weasel!

———

After the moon sets,
slow through the forest, shadows
drift and disappear.

# HAIKU
## by Matsuo Bashō

An old silent pond . . .
A frog jumps into the pond,
splash! Silence again.

## Vocabulary Builder

**After you read,** *review the words you decided to add to your vocabulary. Write the meaning of words you have learned in context. Look up the other words in a dictionary, glossary, thesaurus, or electronic resource.*

*while reading your anchor book*

# Thinking About the Selections

## Annabel Lee, Describe Somebody, *and* Two haiku

Go Online

**About the Author**
Visit: PHSchool.com
Web Code: exe-7418
7419  7420  7421

**1**  **Identify** Complete the following chart. Identify the topic and the characteristics of the form of each poem.

| Annabel Lee | Describe Somebody | Two haiku |
|---|---|---|
|  |  |  |
|  |  |  |
|  |  |  |
|  |  |  |

**2**  **Compare** Which poems tell a story? How does the presence or absence of rhyme affect the mood and tone of the narrative poems?

_____

_____

_____

**3**  **Evaluate** How does the form of the haiku contribute to the feeling that the poems create?

_____

_____

**4**  **Analyze** Could the poem "Annabel Lee" by Edgar Allan Poe be classified as a ballad? Why or why not? Could it be described as an epic poem? Why or why not?

_____

_____

_____

**Write** Answer the following questions in your Reader's Journal.

**5**  **Evaluate** How does the form of each poem affect the way the poet communicates ideas and emotions?

**6**  **Apply** Select a powerful passage or poem from your Anchor Book. If it is prose, rewrite it as a poem. Choose the most descriptive phrases, rearrange the words, break sentences into lines and paragraphs into stanzas. If it is a poem, rewrite it as prose.

# 4-13 Listening and Speaking Workshop
## *Reading Poetry Aloud*

Poetry comes to life when you read it aloud. A poem's rhyme, rhythm, sound devices, and overall feeling come across even more strongly with a good reading. Hearing a poem read aloud can also help you understand its meaning. In this group activity, you and your group members will each select poems that share a common theme, and then read the poems aloud to help convey the theme.

while reading your anchor book

## Your Task

▶ Each member of your group will select a poem that reflects a common theme.

▶ Analyze each poem together and unlock its meaning.

▶ Create a visual for your poem. Your visual should be large enough to display to the class.

▶ Read your poem aloud to the class.

## Organize and Practice Your Presentation

**1** **Choose a theme.** Work with your group to choose a common poetic theme, such as love, nature, or hard times. Then find three or four poems addressing it, from sources approved by your teacher.

| Theme | Poems |
|---|---|
| Nature as a place for reflection | "Stopping by Woods on a Snowy Evening" <br> Two haiku |

**2** **Read and discuss the poem.**

▶ Have each group member read a poem aloud for practice.

▶ Discuss how each poem relates to the theme.

▶ Note any cultural or historic differences among the poems.

▶ Discuss how these differences affect the poems' meanings.

**3** **Identify elements in the poem.** Look for tone, symbolism, and form as clues to the poems' central meanings. With your group, decide on and present one interpretation of each poem.

**4** **Create a visual.** Create a visual to illustrate each poem's theme and to support your presentation.

**5** **Plan your delivery.** Your voices and actions should convey each poem's content, mood, and meaning. Consider your tone, volume, pacing, and pitch. Emphasize words using gestures.

**6** **Rehearse your presentation.** Practice speaking clearly. Review the following rubric to make sure you are meeting all the guidelines.

## SPEAK: Rubric for Oral Interpretation

| CRITERIA | RATING SCALE |
|---|---|
| | NOT VERY        VERY |
| CONTENT How well did the group convey each poem's ideas? Were the poems' elements clear? | 1   2   3   4   5 |
| ORGANIZATION Did group members have a good sense of when and how to read their poems? | 1   2   3   4   5 |
| DELIVERY How well did the group use tone, volume, pacing, and pitch to express meaning? | 1   2   3   4   5 |
| COOPERATION How well did the group work together? | 1   2   3   4   5 |

## LISTEN: Rubric for Audience Self-Assessment

| CRITERIA | RATING SCALE |
|---|---|
| | NOT VERY        VERY |
| ACTIVE LISTENING How well did you focus your attention on the speakers? | 1   2   3   4   5 |
| ACTIVE LISTENING How well did you demonstrate active listening with appropriate silence, responses, and body language? | 1   2   3   4   5 |

Be prepared to discuss the theme and cultural or historical significance of each poem in addition to the group's delivery.

## Prepositions and Prepositional Phrases

A **preposition** is a word that links words to other phrases in a sentence. In the sentence *Kunthary's water spilled onto the table*, the preposition *onto* links *water* to *table*. A **prepositional phrase** begins with a preposition and ends with a noun or pronoun. In the previous example, *onto the table* is a prepositional phrase.

**Go Online**

**Learn More**
Visit: PHSchool.com
Web Code: exp-7405

Look at the following list of prepositions. Notice that a preposition can consist of more than one word.

| | | | | |
|---|---|---|---|---|
| aboard | about | above | according to | across |
| after | against | along | among | around |
| at | before | behind | below | beneath |
| beside | down | between | beyond | but |
| by | in | during | except | for |
| from | into | like | inside | with |
| instead of | on | onto | near | of |
| off | over | past | out | through |
| outside | until | to | since | under |
| throughout | underneath | up | toward | within |

Prepositional phrases make writing more descriptive and specific.

**Directions** Write a sentence using each prepositional phrase.

**1** before the play _____

_____

**2** along the shadowy street _____

_____

**Directions** Write two sentences containing prepositional phrases.

**3** _____

_____

**4** _____

_____

*Author's Craft*

Reread the poem "Annabel Lee" on page 346. Choose a stanza and highlight all of the prepositional phrases. How many details do they provide? How important are they to the poem?

# Infinitives

An **infinitive** is a verb form that acts as a noun, an adjective, or an adverb. An infinitive is the word *to* plus the verb, such as *to hear, to think*, or *to feel*.

**Example**   Soccer is the game *to play.* (infinitive as an adjective modifying the noun *game*)

An **infinitive phrase** is an infinitive plus its own modifiers or complements.

**Example**   Soccer is the game *to play in the spring.* (phrase modifying the noun *game*)

A **split infinitive** occurs when a word or phrase, usually an adverb or adverbial phrase, is placed between the word *to* and the verb form. To make your writing stronger and clearer, you should usually avoid using split infinitives.

**Incorrect:**   Soccer is the game *to competitively play in the spring.* (adverb splitting the word *to* and the verb *play*)

**Correct:**   Soccer is the game *to play competitively in the spring.*

**Directions**   Read the following sentences and underline the infinitives. Then, identify whether they are an infinitive (I), an infinitive phrase (IP), or an error of split infinitive (SI) on the line at the end of each sentence.

**1**   To run marathons is my favorite pastime. _____

**2**   There is nothing more rewarding than to eagerly run down a nature trail in the warm weather. _____

**3**   My friend Vlad wants us to run in the marathon this year. _____

**4**   If we really want to succeed, we must find time to study. _____

**Directions**   In the space below, write a short poem about a hobby or activity that you enjoy. Use infinitives and infinitive phrases.

_____

_____

_____

_____

_____

_____

Go **O**nline

**Learn More**
Visit: PHSchool.com
Web Code: exp-7406

*Author's Craft*

Why do poets use infinitives? Reread "Stopping by Woods on a Snowy Evening" on page 342. Rewrite lines that contain infinitives without using infinitives. Read the reworded poem to a partner. Then listen to your partner's reworded poem. How does the poem change without infinitives? Which version is more effective?

# 4-15 Writer's Workshop
## Exposition: Writing for Assessment

You take essay tests and standardized writing tests that evaluate your writing skills. **Writing for assessment** often depends on specific instructions and limited time or space in which to write. Use these steps to write an essay in response to the following prompt. *Compare and contrast how various poems address the same theme.*

To be effective, your essay should include these elements.

- ► A position that addresses the writing prompt
- ► Clear, concise writing
- ► Evidence supporting the main points, drawn from your reading or class discussion
- ► Consistent organization
- ► Error-free grammar, including proper use of prepositional phrases and infinitives

**Purpose** To write an essay in response to the provided prompt

**Audience** You, your teacher, and your classmates

## Prewriting—Plan It Out

Use the following steps to help you choose your theme. Spend about one-quarter of your time prewriting.

**Choose your theme.** Look back at the poetry you have read in this unit. Arrange the poems by theme in the chart below. Choose the theme you like best and two poems with that theme. An example has been provided for you.

| Theme | Poem |
|---|---|
| Nature provides an opportunity for reflection. | "Stopping by Woods on a Snowy Evening" |
|  |  |
|  |  |
|  |  |
|  |  |
|  |  |

**Analyze the prompt.** Circle key words to identify what the question asks. This chart shows what common verbs ask you to do.

| Key Word | Writing Direction |
|---|---|
| Analyze | Examine how parts contribute to the whole. |
| Compare/Contrast | Explain similarities and differences. |
| Discuss | Support a generalization with facts and examples. |
| Explain | Clarify by providing reasons, causes, and effects. |

**Gather details.** Use the following **Venn diagram** to compile details that show similarities and differences between how the poems address the same theme. In the two outside sections, list how the theme is treated differently. In the center overlapping area, list how the theme is treated similarly. Add more ovals as needed.

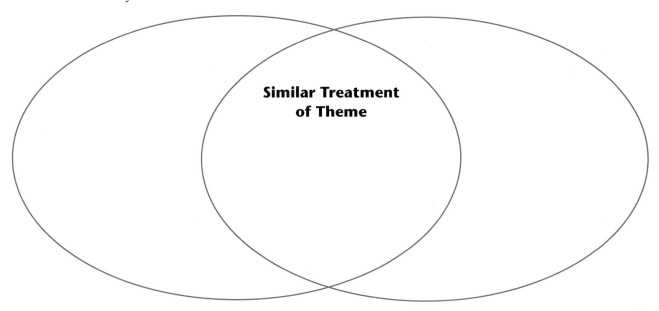

Similar Treatment of Theme

# Drafting—Get It on Paper

Using your Venn diagram, write your draft. You should spend about half your time drafting. Use these steps as a guide.

**Shape your writing.** Write a sentence that states your thesis, or main idea. Each paragraph should relate to this sentence. Consider creating an outline. Either discuss all the similarities first and then the differences, or address one topic at a time. Plan to conclude with a detailed summary linked to the purpose of the composition.

**Provide elaboration.** Add supporting details, such as facts, examples, or descriptive language, that convey mood and tone. List details and examples within a sentence and from paragraph to paragraph.

# Revising—Make It Better

Now revise your draft for better clarity and precision. You should spend about one-quarter of your time revising and editing.

**Revise your structure.** Identify the main idea in each paragraph. Also, check your details and word choice. Consider replacing sentences with ones that offer more effective support.

*Peer Review* Ask for a partner's response to your writing for assessment. Based on the feedback, create a plan to revise your essay.

**Directions** Read this student writing for assessment as a model for your own.

**Student Model: Writing**

**Go Online**
Student Model
Visit: PHSchool.com
Web Code: exr-7402

*Miguel Guzman, Galveston, TX*

**Writing Prompt: Compare and contrast how various poems address the same theme.**

Langston Hughes was an African American poet whose writing focuses on important subjects such as racial equality and achieving your dreams. In the poems "A Dream Deferred" and "The Dream Keeper," Hughes explores the theme of the importance of dreams. Both poems contain similarities and differences.

> In the introduction, the writer clearly identifies the focus.

Both poems have warnings for the reader. In "A Dream Deferred" the reader is cautioned not to postpone one's dreams. The dream may disappear, cause aggravation, anger, or become a burden. The poem is a list of similes that are all negative consequences of postponing one's dreams. In "The Dream Keeper" there is a warning not to let dreams fall into the wrongs hands. The "too-rough fingers of the world" might not provide the support needed for dreams to come true. "The Dream Keeper" offers to protect our dreams from the disrespectful ways of the world.

> The writer uses examples to show how they are similar.

There are differences between the two poems. "A Dream Deferred" focuses on the negative outcome of delaying one's dreams. In "The Dream Keeper," the focus is on protecting one's dreams from the world. The world is filled with obstacles, and our dreams need to be kept safe. This poem carries the message that dreams are important and should be protected so they can grow.

> The writer gives examples from both poems to show how they differ.

Both poems focus on how special and necessary dreams are. Both poems warn the reader to do what it takes to achieve a dream. These poems provide the reader with a view of what can happen if dreams are not cared for. The difference between the two poems is "A Dream Deferred" focuses on the dangers of postponing your dreams, whereas "The Dream Keeper" warns readers that their dreams must be protected from the harsh world. In writing two poems on the same theme, Langston Hughes clearly felt that people needed to be reminded that dreams are not just distractions from our regular lives, but are essential to helping us grow and be the people we want to be.

> The writer concludes with a statement of why the theme of both poems is important.

## Editing—Be Your Own Language Coach

Review your draft for language convention errors. Pay attention to sentence structure, use of prepositional phrases, and infinitives.

## Publishing—Share It!

Consider the following idea to share your writing.

**Prepare for future exams.** Keep a notebook of past tests, and review the strategies you used to plan and organize for this assignment.

## Reflecting On Your Writing

**Rubric for Self-Assessment** Assess your essay. For each question, circle a rating.

| CRITERIA | RATING SCALE | | | | |
|---|---|---|---|---|---|
| | NOT VERY | | | | VERY |
| **IDEAS** Is your essay clear and focused, with rich details? | 1 | 2 | 3 | 4 | 5 |
| **ORGANIZATION** How well do you employ a clear and logical organization? | 1 | 2 | 3 | 4 | 5 |
| **VOICE** Is your writing lively and engaging, drawing the reader in? | 1 | 2 | 3 | 4 | 5 |
| **WORD CHOICE** How appropriate is the language for your audience? | 1 | 2 | 3 | 4 | 5 |
| **SENTENCE FLUENCY** How varied is your sentence structure? | 1 | 2 | 3 | 4 | 5 |
| **CONVENTIONS** How correct is your grammar, especially your use of prepositional phrases and infinitives? | 1 | 2 | 3 | 4 | 5 |

## Anchor Book Projects

Now that you have finished reading your Anchor Book, it is time to get creative! Complete one of the following projects.

### From Me to You                                                                                    A

Sometimes a poem is addressed to a particular person. This person might not be directly named, but there are usually clues in the poem, such as "you" or "your," which show that the poem is written to someone.

1. Choose a character from your Anchor Book whom you think is important. Write a poem to the character, using either free verse or rhyme and meter.

2. Use figurative language (such as idioms, metaphors, and similes) and sound devices (such as alliteration and onomatopoeia). Think about the rhythm and tone of your poem. What attitude will you convey as the speaker—anger, tenderness, or some other emotion?

3. Read your poem aloud to a partner. See if your partner can identify and explain poetic devices, including the literal and figurative meanings of words. Can they "hear" the emotions and rhythm you are trying to convey? Revise your poem based on feedback.

Your project should include the following elements.

▶ Figurative language and sound devices

▶ A strong address to the character with a clear tone and message

▶ A poetry workshop discussing poetic devices and how they contribute to the meaning and tone of the poem

### Create a Visual Interpretation                                                                    B

If you close your eyes after reading literature, what do you "see" in your mind? If you put what you saw on paper, how would it look?

1. Choose a selection from your Anchor Book. Think about a strong image or emotion the author is trying to convey, such as joy or fear.

2. Decide how you want to represent this image or emotion visually. Your artwork may be representational or abstract. You may use paint, photography, collage, video, or illustration software.

3. Write a brief statement explaining your visual interpretation.

Your visual interpretation should include the following elements.

▶ An image or emotion from the selection expressed visually

▶ A brief statement explaining the ideas behind your artwork

# E-mail an Author

C

Have you ever read a poem or passage and wanted to let the writer know what you thought about it? If you had the opportunity, what would you say? Most authors have Web sites where you can e-mail them questions and comments about their books.

1. Find a selection in your Anchor Book that you loved, strongly disliked, or that confused you in some way. Jot down your questions, concerns, or comments.

2. Use your notes to write a friendly e-mail to the author. If you loved the selection, tell the author why. If you disagreed with its message, explain your objection. If something confused you, ask a question.

3. Be sure to use a respectful tone and proper formatting. Include a subject line, a greeting, the title of the selection, and a closing. You may also choose to tell the author your age and grade level.

4. Swap your e-mail with a partner. Read and suggest revisions for your partner's e-mail.

Your letter should include the following elements.
▶ Specific questions, concerns, or comments about the selection
▶ Sincere, courteous language

## Free-Choice Book Reflection

You have completed your free-choice book. Before you take your test, read the following instructions to write a brief reflection on your book.

My free-choice book is _____ .

The author is _____ .

**1** Would you recommend this book to a friend? Yes _____ No _____

Why or why not?

_____

_____

**Write and Discuss** Answer the following question in your Reader's Journal. Then, discuss your answer with a partner.

**2** **Compare and Contrast** Great literature asks us to consider recurring thematic questions, such as, *What is the best way to communicate?* Select a poem or passage from your Anchor Book and one from your free-choice book that communicates a similar idea. Which writer communicates this idea more effectively? Why? To extend the discussion, consider how a journalist, a scientist, an artist, an athlete, or a musician might answer the question.

Answer the questions below to check your understanding of this unit's skills.

## Reading Skill: Paraphrasing

Read this passage. Then, answer the questions that follow.

> Jack's mom had a new project: keeping her family healthy. Despite his fears, Jack actually grew to like these "healthy habits." Mom made a delicious vegetable medley. And, the new juice drinks made Jack forget about his usual cola. But now, Mom was insisting that he and his brother exercise more.
>
> Jack was *not* an athlete. So, he researched the Internet and discovered that he did not need to play a sport to stay fit. Instead, he could walk to school instead of getting a ride. He could bike around the neighborhood or swim at the Y. Jack smiled—he was warming up to this new health kick.

**1** Which statement best **paraphrases** the first sentence?

    **A.** Jack's mom wanted her family to be healthy.

    **B.** Jack's mom had a new project.

    **C.** Jack liked his mom's project.

    **D.** Jack liked his mom's vegetable medley.

**2** Which statement best paraphrases the second paragraph?

    **F.** Jack was *not* an athlete.

    **G.** Rather than play a sport, Jack discovered other ways to stay fit.

    **H.** Jack will stay fit by biking and swimming.

    **J.** Jack's mom wanted him to stay healthy.

## Reading Skills: Drawing Conclusions

Read this passage. Then, answer the questions that follow.

> It was the first day of school, and Dan couldn't wait to get to history class. He'd been assigned to Mr. Potter, whom his sister Gina had last year. Mr. Potter's reputation was legendary. His lectures included jokes. His projects combined fun with learning. And each year, he took his students on four field trips. "Luck of the draw, old buddy," Dan told his friend Rick as they rounded the corner. "I know," Rick said with a sigh. "Well, I guess it's this way to Ms. Cleary's history class." With a weary wave, Rick trudged down the hallway.

**3** Based on passage details, what **conclusion** can you draw?

　A. Mr. Potter is an easy grader.

　B. Dan's favorite subject is history.

　C. Rick is disappointed he was assigned to Ms. Cleary.

　D. Gina got good grades in history last year.

**4** What phrase from the story helps you draw this conclusion?

　F. each year

　G. whom his sister Gina had

　H. first day of school

　J. With a weary wave

## Literary Analysis: Elements of Prose and Poetry

Read this poem and answer the questions that follow.

**5** **Imagery** is language that _____ .

　A. supports an opinion

　B　tells a story

　C. appeals to the senses

　D. uses difficult vocabulary

**6** To understand the **tone** of a literary work, pay attention to _____ .

　F. the writer's word choices

　G. the plot twists and turns

　H. the characters' actions

　J. the writer's opinions

Choose the best answer for the following questions.

---

**Suds and Song**

1　Such a bore, said Ned, this chore, this washing up
　this scrubbing pots and pans and casseroles caked
　with the crud of sixty suppers.
　So high the pile, the suds they steam and sing.

5　Ned hears a ring and spies a swallow
　swooping, singing. Soon, Ned joins the tune
　their notes collide, this bird, this boy.
　When music fills the sky, one frying pan remains.
　I'll get those stains, Ned thinks, then winks,

10　and pours into the sink a squeeze of
　lemon-scented detergent.

---

**7** Which words from the poem represent an example of **alliteration?**

　A. chore/bore

　B. high/pile

　C. thinks/winks

　D. casseroles/caked

**8** In which line does the poet use **assonance** to create sounds?

　F. So high the pile

　G. spies a swallow swooping

　H. When music fills the sky

　J. pours into the sink a squeeze

**9** Which sound device does the author use in lines 8 and 9?

A. end rhyme

B. internal rhyme

C. repetition

D. onomatopoeia

**10** In which phrase does the poet use **consonance** to create sounds?

F. When music fills the sky

G. their notes collide

H. Soon, Ned joins the tune

J. I'll get those stains, Ned thinks

## Language Skills: Vocabulary

Choose the best answer.

**11** Which synonym for the word *dark* has a **connotation** that creates a mysterious feeling?

A. unlit

B. shadowy

C. brunette

D. joyless

**12** What is the **denotation** of the word *tyrant* in the following sentence?

The tyrant ruled over his subjects as if they were slaves.

F. an angry, rambling speech

G. an oppressive leader

H. a royal family member

J. a democratic governor

**13** Which synonym for *home* has a **negative connotation?**

A. dwelling

B. mansion

C. slum

D. apartment

**14** Complete the following sentence with a word that has a **positive connotation.**

Although the test was _____, Ellen thought she did quite well.

F. back-breaking

G. challenging

H. laborious

J. troublesome

## Language Skills: Grammar

Choose the best answer.

**15** The earth was frozen, _____ Jean could not plant the seeds.

A. so

B. yet

C. but

D. for

**16** Nick raked leaves _____ his father called him for lunch.

F. because

G. until

H. since

J. while

**17** Which sentence contains a **prepositional phrase?**

    **A.** Mike found his homework just in time.

    **B.** Bob studied vocabulary before the test.

    **C.** Judy finished the project and went to sleep.

    **D.** Tom missed the lesson yet aced the exam.

**18** Complete the sentence with an **infinitive phrase.**

    Music is something _____ during work.

    **F.** I enjoy

    **G.** we enjoyed

    **H.** she enjoys

    **J.** to enjoy

**19** Which sentence contains a **split infinitive?**

    **A.** Nadia worked the car wash to help raise money.

    **B.** Our teacher decided to seriously scrub each windshield.

    **C.** The sun promised to shine throughout the day.

    **D.** Paolo wanted to dry cars instead of rinse them.

**20** Complete the sentence with the correct **preposition.**

    _____ the game, Beth scored two goals.

    **F.** Before

    **G.** After

    **H.** Inside

    **J.** During

**21** Complete this sentence with the correct **prepositional phrase.**

    _____ , Don spent a month studying in Spain.

    **A.** Saving his allowance

    **B.** Traveling and touring

    **C.** During the summer

    **D.** To learn French

**22** Identify the **preposition** in the following sentence.

    I will go to the party with my friends.

    **F.** will

    **G.** go

    **H.** with

    **J.** my

# Do others *see* us more clearly than we *see* ourselves?

## Unit 5 Genre focus:
# Drama

### Your Anchor Book

There are many good books that would work well to support both the Big Question and the genre focus of this unit. In this unit you will read one of these books as your Anchor Book. Your teacher will introduce the book you will be reading.

### Free-Choice Reading

Later in this unit you will be given the opportunity to choose another book to read. This is called your free-choice book.

# Thinking About What You Already Know

Have you ever had a debate with someone about which was better, the movie or the book? Have you ever had a teacher tell you that if you loved the movie, you should read the book? Many playwrights and screenwriters use popular short stories or novels as inspiration for plays and films. Before you start learning about what drama is, apply what you already know about it to turn an excerpt from a book into notes for your own theater production.

## Partner Activity

You and your partner have been hired to direct a play based on Toni Cade Bambara's story "The War of the Wall." Read the following excerpt and consider what details you would add to a production of this excerpt to make it come alive for an audience.

### from *"The War of the Wall"* by *Toni Cade Bambara*

Me and Lou had no time for courtesies. We were late for school. So we just flat out told the painter lady to quit messing with the wall. It was our wall, and she had no right coming into our neighborhood painting on it. Stirring in the paint bucket and not even looking at us, she mumbled something about Mr. Eubanks, the barber, giving her permission. That had nothing to do with it as far as we were concerned. We've been pitching pennies against the wall since we were little kids. Old folks been dragging their chairs out to sit in the shade of the wall for years. Big kids been playing handball against the wall since so-called integration when the crazies 'cross town poured cement in our pool so we couldn't use it. I'd sprained my neck one time boosting my cousin Lou up to chisel Jimmy Lyons's name into the wall when we found out he was never coming home from the war in Vietnam to take us fishing.

"If you lean close," Lou said, leaning hipshot against her beat-up car, "you'll get a whiff of bubble gum and kids' sweat. And that'll tell you something—that this wall belongs to the kids of Taliaferro Street." I thought Lou sounded very convincing. But the painter lady paid us no mind. She just snapped the brim of her straw hat and hauled her bucket up the ladder.

## The Actor

Pick one of the following roles (the narrator, Lou, or the painter lady) and explain to the actor how he or she should look and move to communicate what is happening in the excerpt.

_____

_____

_____

_____

## The Set Designer

What props are necessary to convey the story accurately? What type of props and backdrop will communicate the mood of the scene? Explain to the set designer what you want for your production.

_____

_____

_____

_____

# Class Discussion

Now, have a class discussion. Compare your answers with those of your classmates. How are they different? How are they the same?

_____

_____

_____

_____

As you read the drama selections in this unit, remember to think about the text as something that is interpreted by those who stage it. Interpretation always happens when we read, but with a play we are sometimes more aware of how different readers can interpret the same text differently.

## 5-1 Understanding the Big Question

### Do others see us more clearly than we see ourselves?

Different people can "see," or perceive, the world in different ways. What is the difference between how you see yourself and how others see you?

You know that two people can have very different understandings of the same event or person. Eyewitness accounts are rarely identical. They vary because individuals perceive the world differently.

**Think About It** Often, we have a different view of ourselves than others have of us. On your own, answer the following questions.

**1** What does it feel like when someone doesn't see you for who you really are?

_____

_____

_____

_____

**2** Why do you think that people sometimes see you differently from the way you see yourself?

_____

_____

_____

_____

**3** Do you think other people really see you for who you are? Why or why not?

_____

_____

_____

_____

Reading is an experience that makes you aware of the different ways people see the world and how much the way we see things affects how we think and behave. When you read, you remain yourself, but you also see another individual's view of the world, such as that of the author or of a character in the book.

before reading your anchor book

**Partner Activity**  With a partner, choose a character who feels others do not understand him or her.

Character _____

From _____ By_____

▶ In the graphic organizer "Character's Perception of Self," list adjectives, such as *honest* or *impulsive*, that you think the character would use to describe himself or herself.

▶ In the graphic organizer "Others' Perceptions of the Character," list adjectives that you, the reader, or another character would use to describe the character.

| **Character's Perception of Self** | **Others' Perceptions of the Character** |

**4**  Just like people in real life, characters react to others' perceptions of them. Frequently, they react in ways that affect the plot. How does the character you chose show that he or she is responding to other characters' perceptions of him or her?

_____

_____

_____

_____

 As you read your Anchor Book and the related readings, you may encounter characters who see themselves differently from the way another character, or even the reader, sees them. How does that affect the characters' behaviors and the plot?

**Getting Ready for Your Anchor Book**

*You will start reading your Anchor Book soon. The next few pages in this book give you some background information plus a reading skill.*

# Introduction to
# Drama

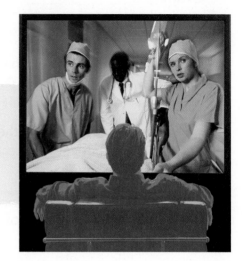

When you turn on the television to watch your favorite program, you might not realize that the origins of television are in **drama,** stories written to be performed by actors and watched by an audience.

The word *drama* comes from the Greek word for "action." Read the graphic organizer below to see how drama is unique from other literary genres.

```
                        DRAMA

   consists of two kinds of writing      can be presented in two ways

┌──────────────┐  ┌──────────────────┐  ┌──────────────┐  ┌──────────────────┐
│ the dialogue │  │ the stage        │  │ as           │  │ as               │
│ that the     │  │ directions that  │  │ literature,  │  │ performance,     │
│ characters   │  │ tell the actors  │  │ the text of  │  │ the production   │
│ speak        │  │ how to move      │  │ the play     │  │ of the play in a │
│              │  │ and speak, and   │  │ itself       │  │ theater          │
│              │  │ describe the sets│  │              │  │                  │
│              │  │ and props        │  │              │  │                  │
└──────────────┘  └──────────────────┘  └──────────────┘  └──────────────────┘
```

A **play** is a form of storytelling in which actors make the characters come alive through speech and action. Even though an actor may perform the same play many times, the actor's performance is different each time. An actor's performance is influenced by the audience.

To be part of an audience watching a play is an experience far different from reading the play alone. When we watch a play, the response of the audience around us affects our own responses. We laugh louder when an audience is laughing with us.

before reading your anchor book

In this unit you will have the opportunity to experience drama both as text and as performance. Think about how seeing and hearing the play performed affects your understanding of the text.

## Types of Drama

In general, there are two types of drama, which are determined by the outcome of the story. The origin of these two types can be traced back to the ancient Greeks.

▶ A **tragedy** shows the downfall or death of the **tragic hero,** or main character. In ancient Greek drama, the hero was an outstanding person brought down by a **tragic flaw,** a mistaken action or defect in character. In modern tragedy, the hero can be an ordinary person destroyed by an evil in society.

▶ A **comedy** usually shows a conflict between a young hero and an older authority. Typical comedies involve confusion, jokes, and a happy ending. While tragedy emphasizes human greatness, comedy stresses human weaknesses.

The author of a play is called a **playwright.** Playwrights, like other writers, frequently find inspiration for their writing in current events.

**Connect** Find two newspaper or magazine articles—one that describes a tragedy and one that describes a comedy. You may choose to write a play using the details of the article as inspiration.

**Reflect** What is an example of a real-life "drama," and how is it similar to a dramatic work?

# 5-2 **Reading Skills**
## *Setting a Purpose*

In learning new reading skills, you will use special academic vocabulary. Knowing the right words will help you demonstrate your understanding.

## Academic Vocabulary

| Word | Meaning | Example Sentence |
|------|---------|------------------|
| **critique** *v.*<br>*Related word:* critiquing | to review or discuss critically | My peer group is *critiquing* my story today. |
| **acquire** *v.*<br>*Related words:* acquiring; acquisition | to obtain; to gain through one's own efforts or actions | Cheryl *acquired* knowledge about repairing cars by helping an auto mechanic. |
| **skim** *v.*<br>*Related words:* skimming; skimmed | to read quickly, noting only the important information | Krista *skimmed* the newspaper article to identify the main points. |

**Setting a purpose** for reading is a strategy you can use to decide what you want to get out of a text.

## How to Set a Purpose for Reading

### Before You Read

* Notice the form of writing, such as a bulleted list, essay, or advertisement.

* Preview the title, headings, illustrations, captions, charts, graphs, maps, key words, photos, introduction, and conclusion. **Skim** and scan the pages for information, such as text organization, that helps you identify what sort of reading you will be doing.

* Look at the style of the text by noticing sentence length, vocabulary level, and the tone of the writing. Use this preview to decide whether you feel the text will be challenging to you.

* If there are questions at the end of the reading, skip to the end and review the questions before you read.

* Think about what you already know about the topic and then ask yourself, *What else do I want to know?*

## While You Read

* Adjust your reading rate to suit the style of text and your purpose. If your purpose is entertainment, you will read more quickly and with less attention to detail than if your purpose is to **acquire** information.
* Look for answers to the questions you already have. Ask new questions as you learn more.
* If necessary, read more slowly or use a dictionary and other resources to understand difficult words and concepts.

## After You Read

* Evaluate how the form and text features help to communicate the meaning.
* **Critique** what you have read. Remember your purpose for reading and ask yourself whether it was fulfilled.

**Apply** Set a purpose for reading the following text. Follow each set of steps before you read, while you read, and after you read the selection. Then answer the questions.

# Don't Forget to VOTE!

Tuesday is the day to cast your vote for class president, vice-president, secretary, and treasurer. You've seen the signs and heard the speeches.

### The Candidates

**President:** Jerry Sampras and Suzy Long

**Vice President:** Megan Mack and Tiffany Ramos

**Secretary:** Jamal Christian and Michael Benedetto

### How to Vote

Cast your ballot during lunch at the cafeteria. All you have to do is fill out your ballot and sign your name to the registry.

▲ **Good to Know!**
The staff at Smithsonian's National Museum of American History made this flag out of campaign buttons from the 1970s.

**Assess** What was your purpose for reading this selection? What text elements helped you set your purpose?

**Directions** Preview the selection on the following page. Before you begin reading it, complete the graphic organizer below. This will help you set a purpose for reading.

## Before You Read

### Preview
What do the title, headings, images, and graphics tell you about the reading?

### Preview
What do the questions tell you to focus on?

### Know
What do you already know about this topic?

### Want to Know
What do you want to know about this topic?

### Set a Purpose
What is your purpose for reading this selection?

# THE HUMAN EYE

The next time you look at a flower or another person's face, consider how amazing the human eye is. It lets us see details as small as the period at the end of this sentence. It lets us see objects a hundred yards away. And it lets us see all the colors of the rainbow.

Our vision requires the eye and brain to work together. But without two special kinds of cells in the retina, we would be unable to see.

## THE IMPORTANCE OF RODS AND CONES

When light enters the eye, it passes through the cornea, pupil, and lens before reaching the retina. The retina contains two types of light-sensing cells, rods and cones. The **rods** are extremely sensitive to light, allowing us to see in dim light and at night. But the rod cells are blind to color. This is why if you go outside on a moonlit night, you can see shapes but no colors.

It is the **cones** that give us color vision. The cones operate in bright light. They help us to see accurately and in color. Each cone cell has one of three kinds of pigments for sensing color: blue-sensitive, red-sensitive, and green-sensitive. The human eye can detect almost any color made up of one or more of these pigments.

Within your eyes, the rods and the cones make an uneven pattern. But the center of your eye, which you use to see fine details, contains only cones.

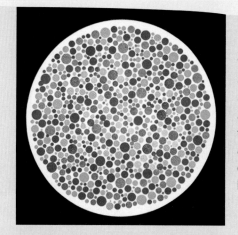

This test uses different colored dots arranged in the shape of a number to check for color blindness.

## WHY CAN'T SOME PEOPLE SEE CERTAIN COLORS?

By now you can probably figure out why some people are color blind. The most common type is red-green color blindness. It is inherited and affects about 8 percent of men and boys. In a person with red-green color blindness, the cones that detect red and green are missing or defective.

Other types of color blindness can be caused by injuries to the eye. There is no known cure for either type of color blindness.

▼ **Diagram of the Human Eye**

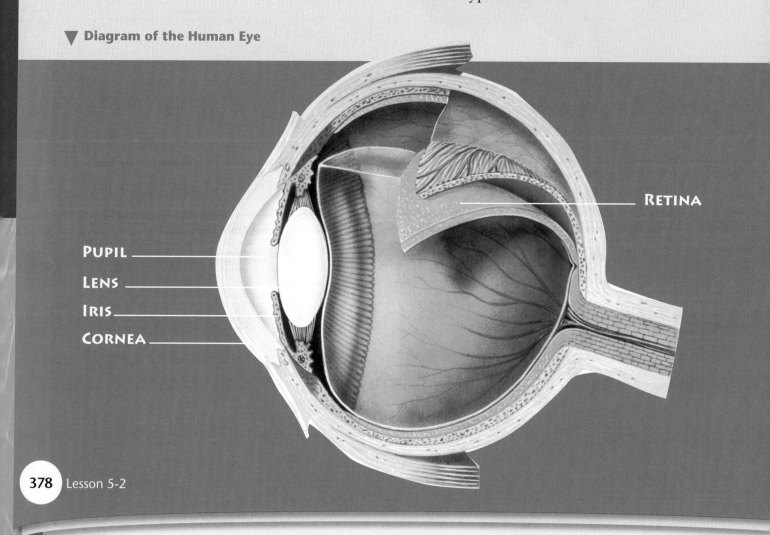

RETINA

PUPIL

LENS

IRIS

CORNEA

# Thinking About the Selection
## The Human Eye

**1**  **Identify**  Now that you have read the selection, consider what new information you gathered after you set a purpose for reading.

> **Learn**
> What did you learn about this topic?

**2**  **Explain**  Why can't some people see certain colors?

**3**  **Explain**  Does the article's structure, captions, and graphics clearly state the purpose and main idea of the article? Explain.

**4**  **Critique**  Did the textbook excerpt fulfill the purpose you set for reading? Why or why not?

**5**  **Synthesize**  You just practiced setting a purpose with a textbook selection. How could using this skill help you to better understand your reading for school assignments?

**Write**  Answer the following question in your Reader's Journal.

**6**  **Generalize**  What can other people see about you by using their eyes? What can't they see?

# 5-3 Vocabulary Building Strategies
## Synonyms, Antonyms, and Homonyms

When you encounter a word you do not know, the meaning might be found right there in the text. The word's meaning may be provided through the use of context clues such as definition, example, restatement, or contrast. Two important kinds of context clues are **synonyms** (restatement) and **antonyms** (contrast). Some words look the same but have different meanings, which can be figured out by the context in which they are used. These words are called **homonyms.**

A **synonym** is a word that has the same or almost the same meaning as another word.

> **Example**   **Sedentary** individuals—people who are <u>inactive</u>—often have poor health.

An **antonym** is a word that has the opposite meaning of another word.

> **Example**   Unlike her <u>quiet</u> parents, Jasmine is **loquacious.**

**Directions**  Skim this unit or your Anchor Book for a word whose meaning you do not know. Then complete the chart below.

- ▸ See if there are any context clues in the surrounding text to help you identify the word's meaning. If not, use a dictionary to identify the word's meaning.

- ▸ Identify at least two synonyms and antonyms for the word. Use a thesaurus to help you.

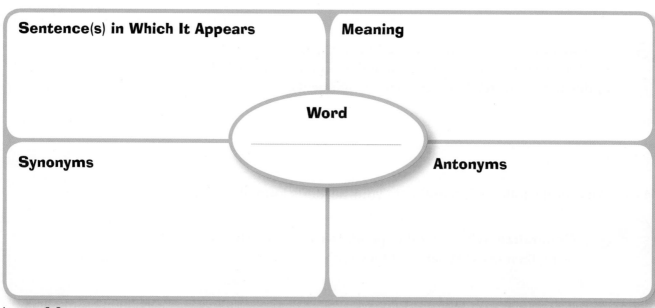

**Sentence(s) in Which It Appears**

**Meaning**

**Word**
_____

**Synonyms**

**Antonyms**

A **homonym** is a word that has the same pronunciation as another word but has a different meaning. It may have the same spelling as the other word. You can use the context of the word to identify its meaning.

> **Example** I decided to <u>hide</u> his birthday present in the closet. Here, *hide* means to stash away or keep secret.
>
> As the bear ran through the thorn bushes, his <u>hide</u> became tangled. Here, *hide* means the thick skin of an animal.

A **homophone** is a type of homonym. It has the same pronunciation as another word, but it has a different spelling and a different meaning.

> **Example** *Tail* refers to the end part of something. A *tale* is a type of story. They are pronounced the same, but their spellings and meanings are different.

**Directions** Write two sentences with different meanings for the homonym. Use a dictionary if you need help.

**just**

Sentence 1:

_____

_____

Sentence 2:

_____

_____

**Analogies** Synonyms, antonyms, and homonyms are all word relationships that help you understand the meaning of words. Another word relationship is an analogy. In an **analogy**, two things are compared because they share a similarity or because they are opposites. The chart below shows relationships common to analogy construction.

| Relationship | Example |
|---|---|
| purpose | chair: sit |
| cause/effect | sun: burn |

Understanding the relationship between two words leads to a higher level of comprehension.

# 5-4 Literary Analysis
## Dialogue and Stage Directions

Everything a playwright writes must appear onstage—either through **dialogue** or **stage directions.**

## Literary Terms

**Dialogue** is what the characters say. Playwrights use dialogue to reveal the personalities of their characters. Dialogue also helps to develop the conflict and advance the plot.

**Stage directions** are notes in the script that tell how the play is to be performed. Stage directions are usually written in italics and enclosed in brackets or parentheses. Stage directions usually describe where and when a scene takes place, how the characters should say their lines, and how the characters should move onstage.

Stage directions can also describe the sets, costumes, props, lighting, and sound effects. They might even explain what a character is feeling.

**Characterization in drama** works the same way as characterization in prose. The author creates static characters, who do not change during the play, and dynamic characters who do. The author shows readers through the characters' thoughts, words, and speech patterns. Other forms of dramatic characterization information include the narrator's description and the thoughts, words, and actions of other characters.

The following snippet from a play includes both dialogue and stage directions.

[*Scene: A warm, sunny day at the neighborhood pool. It is late in the afternoon. PETE is lying out on a lounge chair.*]

[*DANNY enters, dripping wet*]

Stage Directions

**PETE:** What happened to you?

Dialogue

**DANNY:** [*angrily*] Max. I'm gonna get him.

**PETE:** [*smiling*] Guess you shouldn't stand so close to the pool.

*while reading your anchor book*

**Directions** Read the passage. Underline the dialogue and stage directions that provide important information about the characters and plot. Then answer the questions.

[*MIKA is crouched, staring at something poking out of the ground. Her brow is furrowed as if she is in deep thought. She holds a small chisel in her left hand and a large brush in her right.*]

**MIKA:** [*quavering*] James?

[*JAMES does not hear MIKA. He is ten feet away, kneeling on a pile of dirt, rock, and other debris. He is purposefully hammering at a clump of milky white rock. MIKA stands up and cautiously steps toward JAMES.*]

**MIKA:** [*urgently*] James.

**JAMES:** [*continues to hammer*] Yeah?

**MIKA:** James, you need to see this. Now.

[*JAMES turns to look up at MIKA, who has turned pale. JAMES rises.*]

**JAMES:** Mika, are you okay?

[*MIKA doesn't answer, but motions for JAMES to follow her to where she had been digging. There, protruding from the ground, is a large red crystal. It appears to be glowing.*]

**JAMES:** What is that?

**MIKA:** [*softly*] Touch it.

[*JAMES looks at MIKA, uncertain of her command. He bends down and reaches for the crystal. As his fingertips brush the crystal's polished edge, his entire body jerks, as if shocked.*]

**JAMES:** [*in disbelief*] Do you think it is the—

**MIKA:** It is. We need to get it out of here. Now. Before they get it first.

**1** **Classify** What types of information do the stage directions provide?

_____

_____

_____

**2** **Analyze** What do the dialogue and stage directions reveal about James? What do they reveal about Mika?

_____

_____

_____

_____

# Staging

Drama is made up of more than just words on a page. Many other elements go into producing a play—the way characters move, what they wear, the lights, and scenery. These elements of **staging** all help bring a play to life.

## Literary Terms

▶ **Staging** is the process of putting on a play. Some details of staging are included in the stage directions. However, the director and the production designers take what the playwright has described and bring it to life with their own ideas.

▶ **Sets** are the scenery, backdrops, and furniture that create the setting. A production may have different sets for different scenes. For example, some scenes might take place in a character's living room, while others take place on a city street.

▶ **Props** are things like dishes, telephones, and books that the actors use onstage during the performance.

Stage directions use certain terms to describe the stage. Look at the following diagram.

**AUDIENCE**

| Downstage Left | Downstage Center | Downstage Right |
|---|---|---|
| Stage Left | Center Stage | Stage Right |
| Upstage Left | Upstage Center | Upstage Right |

**Directions** The following passage is the beginning of a play based on *A Christmas Carol* by Charles Dickens. Read the passage and underline details that help you imagine the staging. Then, complete the activity that follows.

## from *A Christmas Carol: Scrooge and Marley*
### *by Israel Horovitz*
*based on the story* **A Christmas Carol** *by Charles Dickens*

**Go Online**

**About the Author**
Visit: PHSchool.com
Web Code: exe-7501

### Scene 1

*[Ghostly music in auditorium. A single spotlight on JACOB MARLEY D.C. He is ancient; awful, dead-eyed. He speaks straight out to auditorium.]*

**MARLEY.** *[Cackle-voiced]* My name is Jacob Marley and I am dead. *[He laughs.]* Oh, no, there's no doubt that I am dead. The register of my burial was signed by the clergyman, the clerk, the undertaker . . . and by my chief mourner . . . Ebenezer Scrooge . . . *[Pause; remembers]* I am dead as a doornail.

*[A spotlight fades up, Stage Right, on SCROOGE, in his countinghouse[1], counting. Lettering on the window behind SCROOGE reads: "SCROOGE AND MARLEY, LTD." The spotlight is tight on SCROOGE'S head and shoulders. We shall not yet see into the offices and setting. Ghostly music continues, under. MARLEY looks across at SCROOGE; pitifully. . . .]*

[1] **countinghouse** (kount´ i[ng] hous´) *n.* older term for an office carrying on accounting or financial business.

**Directions** Use the chart to record the playwright's staging information. Then, add your own staging ideas to bring the action to life.

|  | **Playwright's Staging** | **My Staging Ideas** |
|---|---|---|
| Sets |  |  |
| Props |  |  |
| Costumes |  |  |
| Lighting |  |  |
| Music |  |  |
| Sound Effects |  |  |
| Visual Effects |  |  |

while reading your anchor book

Read the following text with a partner. Choose the role of Rudy or Alex. Silently read the stage directions. Read your role aloud with a rhythm, flow, and meter that sounds like everyday speech.

*Guiding Question:* **How does Rudy see himself, and how does he want other people to see him?**

from

# Novio Boy

by Gary Soto

**Background** *Gary Soto's mingling of English and Spanish captures his characters' Mexican American dialect. The title of the play is a mixture of Spanish and English. "Novio" is Spanish for "sweetheart."*

## Vocabulary Builder

**Before you read,** *you will discuss the following words. In the Vocabulary Builder box in the margin, use a vocabulary building strategy to make the words your own.*

**philosophizing   sarcastically   dilemma**

**As you read,** *draw a box around unfamiliar words you could add to your vocabulary. Use context clues to unlock their meaning.*

*(For translations of the other Spanish words and phrases in the play, see "Literature in Context.")*

### SCENE ONE

*The scene begins in a backyard where two boys, both Mexican American, are* **philosophizing** *about girls. They are sloppy-looking, with holes in the knees of their pants. Stage right, two girls are*

---

**Marking the Text**

**Dialogue, Stage Directions, and Staging**

**As you read,** *underline dialogue that gives information about the characters and how they feel. Circle important stage directions, and make notes in the margin about your staging ideas.*

Vocabulary Builder

**philosophizing**
(fi läs´ ə fiz´ ing) *v.*

**Meaning**

*silhouetted on a couch in a living room. The room is dim. Lights come up on RUDY and ALEX. RUDY paces back and forth and ALEX tries to keep up with him. RUDY throws himself down on a lawn chair. ALEX keeps pacing for a moment and then, noticing that his friend has sat down, joins him.*

**RUDY:** What am I gonna talk about? She's older than me and good-looking.

**ALEX:** Just level with her. Tell her you're sorry you look like you do.

**RUDY:** Sorry? You mean I should be sorry that I look like Tom Cruise? *(pause)* You're cold, homes[2]. You're no help at all.

**ALEX:** *(giggling)* Just joking, Rudy. Listen, man, you got to start simple. Break the ice. Ask her . . . what her favorite color is or something.

**RUDY:** Color?

**ALEX:** Yeah, color. Like, red or white.

**RUDY:** You mean, like, blue or yellow?

**ALEX:** Lavender!

**RUDY:** Purple!

**ALEX:** Forest green!

**RUDY:** Chevy chrome!

**ALEX:** That's it, man.

---

[2] **homes** *n.* close friend from the neighborhood (short for "homeboy").

*(RUDY gets up and starts to pace. ALEX gets up, too.)*

**RUDY:** *(incredulous)* Colors?

**ALEX:** Colors. I picked up this little *secreto* from Mama Rosa on the Spanish station.

**RUDY:** Mama Rosa! You get your advice from her?

**ALEX:** She's for real. She's an expert about love and things. She says you got to get your *boca* rattling. One thing leads to the next, you know.

**RUDY:** No, I don't know.

**ALEX:** Listen, man. Sometimes I'm talking about nothing and the next thing I know people are listening. Like I'm the president or something.

**RUDY:** You're not the president.

**ALEX:** I know that. What I'm saying is that you got to just talk stuff—anything!

*(Pause. RUDY reflects.)*

**RUDY:** I just start talking?

**ALEX:** That's right.

**RUDY:** Just . . . say things?

**ALEX:** Colors, start with colors. Just ask, "Patricia, what's your favorite color?"

**RUDY:** She won't think I'm weird?

**ALEX:** No. She'll know immediately you're trying to start something, so she'll play along. She'll say something like "Green" or "Pink."

**RUDY:** And I'll tell her that my favorite color is dark blue.

**ALEX:** There you go, homes. *(pause)* So guess mine.

**RUDY:** Your what?

**ALEX:** My favorite color!

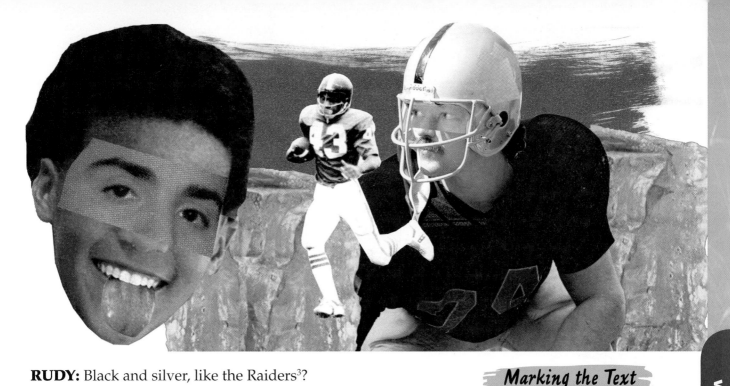

**RUDY:** Black and silver, like the Raiders[3]?

**ALEX:** Nope.

**RUDY:** Blue and gold, like the Chargers[4]?

**ALEX:** Nah. It's red, like my tongue.

*(ALEX wiggles tongue at RUDY.)*

**RUDY:** *(punching ALEX)* That's *asco!*

**ALEX:** *(chuckling)* Don't worry, homes. Just be cool.

**RUDY:** Cool.

**ALEX:** Like an iceberg.

*(The boys pace around the stage. They stop.)*

**RUDY:** Man, I can't believe I'm going out with a girl in the eleventh grade. And yesterday, guess what I was doing.

**ALEX:** Helping your dad pour cement at a job site?

*(RUDY shakes his head.)*

**ALEX:** Lifting weights?

**RUDY:** You won't laugh if I tell you?

Marking the Text

---

[3] **Raiders** (rād´ ərz) *n.* a professional football team in Oakland, California.

[4] **Chargers** (chär´ jərz) *n.* a professional football team in San Diego, California.

**ALEX:** Laugh at my best friend?

**RUDY:** *(hesitates; long pause)* I was playing soldiers with my cousin Isaac. Man, it was fun. One soldier was beating up another one, and a girl doll was kicking back watching the *pleitos*.

*(ALEX laughs.)*

**RUDY:** I got another problem. I told Patricia I was taking her to grub at Steaks, Steaks, y Más Steaks[5].

**ALEX:** You told her you were taking her there? What's wrong with you, homes? Those hamburgers cost twice as much as John's Café. And you got to tip, too.

*(RUDY reflects on his error.)*

**ALEX:** You got enough money?

**RUDY:** How much do you think I'll need?

**ALEX:** At least fifteen bones.

**RUDY:** Fifteen dollars!

*(RUDY shakes his head and shrugs his shoulders. ALEX starts to go through his pockets.)*

**ALEX:** *(teasing)* Here, this should help.

---

[5] **Steaks, Steaks, y Más Steaks** "Steaks, Steaks, and More Steaks."

*(RUDY takes ALEX's quarter and looks at it.)*

**RUDY:** *(sarcastically)* You're cool, Alex. This quarter might get me a piece of gum.

*(They sit and reflect on the **dilemma.**)*

**ALEX:** *(perks up)* Let me give you some advice. You got to talk intelligent, like you know something.

**RUDY:** Like I know something?

**ALEX:** Remember, she's two years ahead of you and in eleventh grade. You got to be **suave**[6], kind of like—*pues*, like me. *(hooks a thumb at himself)*

**RUDY:** Help me then, Alex.

**ALEX:** *(thinking about it)* It so happens I got this love letter from Sylvia Hernandez. Remember her?

**RUDY:** No.

**ALEX:** Yeah, you do. She threw up huevos con weenies[7] in fifth grade. *(imitates someone vomiting)* It was all over the classroom and down the hall. It was like that old movie *The Blob* after she was all done.

**RUDY:** *(reflecting)* Yeah, I remember that girl now. She got some on my shoes. *(pause)* So what did the letter say?

**ALEX:** *(reaches into his pocket)* Got it right here.

*(ALEX sniffs the letter for perfume, and RUDY sniffs it as well. ALEX starts to read letter.)*

**ALEX:** "Alex, I think you have the coolest eyes. And the cutest nose."

**RUDY:** You got a fat *huango* nose.

**ALEX:** Hey, dude, you want me to help you or not?

**RUDY:** I take that back. You got a real cute nose. *(pulls up his own nose into the shape of a pig's snout)*

**ALEX:** That's better. *(continues reading)* "I really care about you a lot, Alex. I really don't know how to say this, but here goes. I

**Vocabulary Builder**

**sarcastically**
(sär kas´ tik lē) *adv.*
**Meaning**

**dilemma**
(di lem´ə) *n.*
**Meaning**

while reading your anchor book

---
[6] **suave** (swä vā) *adj.* confident and charming.

[7] **huevos con weenies** (wā vös kön wē´ nēz) *n.* eggs with hot dogs.

think that you like me but don't want to tell me because of what your friends might say. Forget them. They don't have to live your life. You do! Last year I fell totally in love with this guy Kendall—"

**RUDY:** What kind of name is Kendall?

*(ALEX gives RUDY a look.)*

**ALEX:** *(continues reading)* "At first Kendall was nice to me. Then he started being mean to me and talking behind my back. It hurt me when he told this girl from Selma that I was stuck-up. I guess it was to get me to stop liking him. But I didn't stop liking him for a long time. Now I like you, Alex. I dream about—"

**RUDY:** Man, she knows how to talk.

**ALEX:** *¡Cállate!* You're interrupting the flow of my love letter. *(pause)* Here's a good part. "Alex, you're nicer than Kendall. You're cute, too. All the boys from Roosevelt are cute, but you're the cutest. Please don't be like Kendall. I will shower you with kisses forever and ever."

**RUDY:** *(takes the letter and examines it)* Sounds like poetry. No, like *mi abuelita's telenovelas.*

**ALEX:** This letter should be the floor plan for your love life. You got to lay it on thick. Be romantic, *ese.* Suave.

**RUDY:** *(reflecting)* Suave. *(pulls out a small notepad)* I better write some of this stuff down so I don't forget: "Be romantic." "Lay it on thick."

**ALEX:** I went on a date once.

**RUDY:** You're lying.

**ALEX:** No, I did. *(pause)* It wasn't exactly a date. Me and this girl went to the playground.

**RUDY:** Get serious.

**ALEX:** Yeah, I picked her up on my bike and . . . don't laugh.

**RUDY:** Why would I laugh at my best friend?

**ALEX:** I can see it. You're gonna laugh!

**RUDY:** No, I promise.

Marking the Text

*(RUDY and ALEX trade glances.)*

**ALEX:** She had to pedal the bike because I didn't have enough leg strength. It's hard with two people!

*(RUDY chokes, muffling his laugh.)*

**ALEX:** *(continuing)* It was a lot of fun. We spent a couple hours on the monkey bars. Then we played tetherball, and then a game of chess. Yeah, it was going pretty good—until Frankie Torres came by and started teasing me.

**RUDY:** Frankie did that?

**ALEX:** Yeah. Because I was all dressed up. *(laughs)* I had on this pink shirt, and a bow tie, and buckets of my dad's cologne.

**RUDY:** Dressed up at the playground?

**ALEX:** Yeah, plus . . .

**RUDY:** What?

*(ALEX kicks at the ground, embarrassed.)*

**RUDY:** Hey, I'm your *carnal*.

**Marking the Text**

Dialogue, Stage Directions, and Staging  **393**

# Literature in Context

Throughout the play, the author uses Spanish words and phrases to reflect the flavor of life for his Mexican American characters.

- **secreto** (sā krāt´ō) *n.* secret.
- **boca** (bō´ kə) *n.* mouth.
- **asco** (ä´ skō) *adj.* sickening, nauseated feeling.
- **pleitos** (plā´ ē tōs) *n.* fighting.
- **pues** (pwās) *interj.* well, uh.
- **huango** (yoō än´ go) *adj.* stretched out.
- **¡Cállate!** (kay ə tā) *interj.* Be quiet, shut up!
- **mi abuelita's telenovelas** (mē äb wā´ lē täs tā´ lā nô vā´ läs) my grandmother's television soap operas
- **ese** (ā´ sā) *n.* guy.
- **carnal** (kär näl´) *n.* close friend.

**ALEX:** She was getting a drink of water, so I was holding her purse.

**RUDY:** And that's when Frankie saw you.

**ALEX:** *(nodding his head)* He called me a girl because I had her purse on my shoulder. *(Pause. ALEX stands up.)* That was my first date. Age nine.

*(RUDY shakes his head sympathetically. He takes the letter from ALEX and reads it silently. Lights fade.)*

## Marking the Text

_____

_____

_____

_____

_____

## Vocabulary Builder

**After you read,** *review the words you decided to add to your vocabulary. Write the meaning of words you have learned in context. Look up the other words in a dictionary, glossary, thesaurus, or electronic resource.*

# Thinking About the Selection
## *from* Novio Boy

Go Online

**About the Author**
Visit: PHSchool.com
Web Code: exe-7502

**1** **Recall** In this scene, what does Rudy want Alex to do?

_____

_____

**2** **Analyze** How do the dialogue and stage directions reveal Rudy's feelings about his date? List specific details.

_____

_____

_____

_____

**3** **Analyze** How do the dialogue and stage directions reveal Alex's personality and his attitude toward Rudy?

_____

_____

_____

_____

**4** **Evaluate** Both this play and the poem "Describe Somebody" in Lesson 4-12 address the theme of identity. How do the two literary genres use the unique elements of their forms to address the same theme?

_____

_____

_____

_____

**5** **Apply** If you were directing this scene, what would you direct the actors to do onstage in addition to what the stage directions mention? What props would you use?

_____

_____

**Write** Answer the following questions in your Reader's Journal.

**6** **Infer** How does Rudy see himself, and how does he want other people to see him? Use details from the text to support your answer.

**7** **Analyze** Think of a character in your Anchor Book who, like Rudy, is worried about something. How does the writer use dialogue and stage directions to reveal this character's emotions?

Dialogue, Stage Directions, and Staging **395**

while reading your anchor book

# 5-5 Language Coach
## *Grammar and Spelling*

## Formal and Informal Language

Would you speak to your friends during lunchtime in the same way that you would during a class presentation? The situation you are in determines whether you should use formal or informal language.

**Go Online**

**Learn More**
Visit: PHSchool.com
Web Code: exp-7501

**Formal language** is used when you want to discuss something in a serious way. **Informal language** is used when you are speaking or writing casually. When deciding to use formal or informal language, consider your audience and subject. Here are examples of how to spot formal and informal language and when to use it.

| Formal Language | Informal Language |
|---|---|
| **How to Spot It**<br>▸ Proper grammar<br>▸ Polite, impersonal tone<br>▸ No contractions<br><br>**When to Use It**<br>▸ Complaint letter to a business<br>▸ History paper<br>▸ Job application<br><br>**Example**<br>Please consider me for the position of server at Goodman's Ice Cream Parlor. I am a hard worker and a team player. | **How to Spot It**<br>▸ Use of slang or idioms<br>▸ Personal, emotional tone<br>▸ Contractions<br><br>**When to Use It**<br>▸ E-mail to a friend<br>▸ Short story<br>▸ Diary entry<br><br>**Example**<br>How's it going? I'll see you at the movie theater after school. I heard this movie is awesome! See you then! |

**Directions** Revise the informal language in the formal speech below.

### Jonathan Spagnoletti's Speech for Class President

Hey, what's up? My name's Jon and I'm running for eighth grade class prez. I feel I'm like totally qualified to run our student council because my communication and leadership skills are slammin'. You should totally vote for me. Later.

_____

_____

_____

**Author's Craft**

Writers choose a specific writing style to serve a purpose. Scan "The Human Eye" on page 377. Choose a paragraph and rewrite it twice, first in more formal language, then in less formal language. Which style better matches the author's purpose? Why?

# Spelling High-Frequency Words

As your vocabulary grows, you will notice certain words appear more frequently than others in your reading and writing. These are known as **high-frequency words.** Since high-frequency words are so common, it is especially important to learn how to spell them correctly.

Go Online

**Learn More**
Visit: PHSchool.com
Web Code: exp-7502

| High-Frequency Word List | | |
|---|---|---|
| temperature | license | furniture |
| groceries | transportation | equipment |
| continue | environment | vegetable |
| structure | instrument | muscles |
| quarter | conversation | immediately |
| potato/potatoes | community | experience |
| recommend | principal | |

**Author's Craft**

Many words are not spelled phonetically—the way they are pronounced. Scan "Novio Boy" on page 386. Find five words that are not spelled phonetically. Rewrite each word, spelling it phonetically. Exchange words with a partner. See if you can correct your partner's misspelled words.

## Tips for Remembering High-Frequency Words

▶ Create a list of words that are difficult to spell. Review the list regularly and add new words as needed.

▶ Look up the correct spelling of a word in the dictionary if you are unsure of how to spell it.

▶ Pay attention to the pronunciation of words that are spelled differently than they sound. For example, *through* is not spelled the way it sounds. Add these tricky words to your list.

**Directions** Underline the misspelled words in each sentence. Rewrite them correctly on the line provided.

**1** Taking public transpertasion helps the envirement.

_____

**2** When Mom goes to the store and buys grosseries, she usually buys potatos and other vegtables.

_____

**3** The principle asked me to continu our conversasion in her office.

_____

**4** The day I turned seventeen, I imediately went to get my driver's lisense.

_____

# 5-6 Writer's Workshop
## Research: Interview Report

People hold a wealth of knowledge. Asking people questions about certain subjects can reveal informative, if not surprising, responses. An **interview** is an information-gathering technique in which you ask someone questions and record his or her responses. Follow the steps outlined in this workshop to write your own interview report.

Your interview report should include the following elements.

▶ An introduction to your subject that creates context

▶ Thought-provoking questions

▶ Important points provided by the subject

▶ Accurate recording of the subject's answers

▶ A clear organizational method

▶ Error-free grammar, including correct use of formal and informal language.

**Purpose** To write an interview report

**Audience** You, your teacher, and your classmates

## Prewriting—Plan It Out

To choose your topic, use the following strategy.

**Choose your topic.** Think of people you have a personal interest in, or who have interesting stories to tell. List them in a two-column chart. Review your list and choose the person whom you want to interview.

| Interesting People | What Makes Them Interesting |
| --- | --- |
|  |  |

**Compose questions.** Think about the specific topic you want to cover. What do you want to know? What do you think others want to learn from your interview? Think of interesting questions that would prompt your interview subject to answer with more than a *yes* or a *no*. For example, instead of asking "Do you like your job?" ask "What do you like about your job?" Write each question on the front of a note card. Arrange your questions in an order that will allow the interview to move smoothly.

What inspired you to become a musician?

house full of music, guitars, drums, melodies, mom's voice

**Conduct the interview.** Ask questions slowly and record notes on the back of each note card. Go in the direction the interview takes you. When you are finished, immediately fill in any missing information.

## Drafting—Get It on Paper

Using your note cards, write your draft. The following step will help make your report organized and engaging.

**Shape your writing.** Write an outline to organize your report. Think about using a question-and-answer format, but begin by writing an introduction to your subject that will engage the reader. Then, order your questions based on their importance. For instance, if you are planning to interview an actor, you might organize your questions into three groups—personal motivation, education, and favorite films. Use a title that fits the topic of your report.

To determine which information should be included, ask yourself these questions and write down your answers.

*I. Introduction*
*II. First question*
   *A. Answer*
*III. Second question*
   *A. Answer*
*IV. Third question*
   *A. Answer*

| | |
|---|---|
| What part of the interview was the most insightful? | |
| Which questions received the best answers? | |
| Was anything surprising? | |

## Revising—Make It Better

Now that you have a draft, revise your report to make it more precise and focused. Review your draft and locate questions or responses that can be shortened. Think of ways to remove unnecessary words, phrases, or sentences without changing the meaning. As the interviewer, use formal language when asking questions. However, if your interview subject responds with informal language, do not revise it. Include it in your report as is.

**Student Model: Revising for Precision**

| | |
|---|---|
| , The Long Black Veil,<br>One band seems destined for national stardom. ~~They are The Long Black Veil.~~ | The writer combined two sentences into one in order to remove unnecessary words. |

*Peer Review* Ask for a partner's response to your interview report. Revise to achieve the reaction you had intended.

**Student Model: Writing**

*Baxter Nunn, Madison, Wisconsin*

Over the last couple of years, the local music scene has produced a number of great bands. Such acts include Star Bodies, Suburban Relapse, and Silent Judgment. One band, The Long Black Veil, seems destined for national stardom. The lead singer and songwriter is Robi Point.

> In his opening paragraph, the writer introduces his subject in an interesting way.

**What inspired you to become a musician?**

I grew up in a home that was filled with the sounds of guitars, drums, and melodies. [My mom] had a great voice . . . I would hear her singing throughout the house.

> Brackets help clarify the subject of the sentences.

**The local music scene is buzzing right now. How would you describe it?**

It's like over-inflating a tire. The more air you add, the greater chances that it'll explode. There are so many bands making great music. I'm glad to be a part of it.

> This quotation provides insight into the subject's personality.

**Your band recently released a new album. How is it being received?**

People seem to like it. We haven't gotten any complaints.

**Where do you get inspiration when you begin writing a song?**

From everyday life, emotions, and memories. When I'm walking down the street and something catches my eye, usually I'll keep it in mind. If it stays with me, I'll write a song about it. The most important thing is to allow life into my music.

> In his final question, the writer asks a thought provoking question.

**Where do you see the Madison music scene in 10 years?**

The vibe in this city is strong. As long as people support local musicians, we'll make good music.

# Editing—Be Your Own Language Coach

Before you hand in your interview report, review it for language convention errors. Pay attention to your use of formal and informal language.

# Publishing—Share It!

When you publish a work, you produce it for a specific audience. Consider one of the following ideas to share your writing.

**Submit it to your town newspaper.** Ask your town newspaper to publish your report. If possible, include a photograph of your subject.

**Present it to your subject.** Give your subject a clean copy of your report once it has been returned from your teacher. Make any necessary changes before you present it to your subject.

**1** **Reflecting On Your Writing** Respond to the following questions on a separate sheet of paper and hand it in with your final draft. What new insights did you gain about writing an interview report? What did you do well? What do you need to work on? Set a goal you can meet in your next workshop.

**2** **Rubric for Self-Assessment** Assess your report. For each question, circle a rating.

| CRITERIA | RATING SCALE |
|---|---|
| IDEAS Does your report reflect a clear understanding of your subject? | NOT VERY 1 2 3 4 5 VERY |
| ORGANIZATION How well do you use a clear and logical organization? | 1 2 3 4 5 |
| VOICE Is your writing lively and engaging, drawing the reader in? | 1 2 3 4 5 |
| WORD CHOICE How appropriate is the language for your audience? | 1 2 3 4 5 |
| SENTENCE FLUENCY How varied is your sentence structure? | 1 2 3 4 5 |
| CONVENTIONS How correct is your grammar, especially your use of formal and informal language? | 1 2 3 4 5 |

# 5-7 Discussing Your Anchor Book
## *Literature Circles*

**Asking Questions** After you meet with members of your Literature Circle for an open discussion, you will learn how to expand upon others' ideas by asking good questions.

## PART 1: Open Discussion

Gather into your Literature Circles and begin your open discussion. Share your comments, thoughts, and ideas about your Anchor Book with other members of your group. Refer to your Reader's Journal or talk about the book's themes if you need conversation starters.

## PART 2: Discuss—Asking Questions

When you want to know more about something, **asking questions** is a good strategy to use. Asking good questions can help you become a better reader and an active participant in discussions.

> ### Questions of Personal Importance
>
> **Question stems:** How can I learn from…? How does…remind me of…?
>
> *My Question:*

> ### Questions That Connect to Real Life
>
> **Question stems:** How is [an event or character in the book] like [an event or character in real life]?
>
> *My Question:*

> ### Questions About Elements of the Text
>
> **Question stems:** What caused…? Why is…important?
>
> *My Question:*

Now, return to your Literature Circle to discuss your questions and the possible answers.

**1** Each member should share all of his or her questions with the group.

**2** Determine which questions for each member are the strongest. Record them in the "Original Questions" box below.

**3** As a group, discuss the answers to these questions. Record your answers in the space provided.

**4** Ask another question based on something that was in the answer. Record the question in the "Follow-Up Questions" box. You may think of more than one follow-up question for each answer.

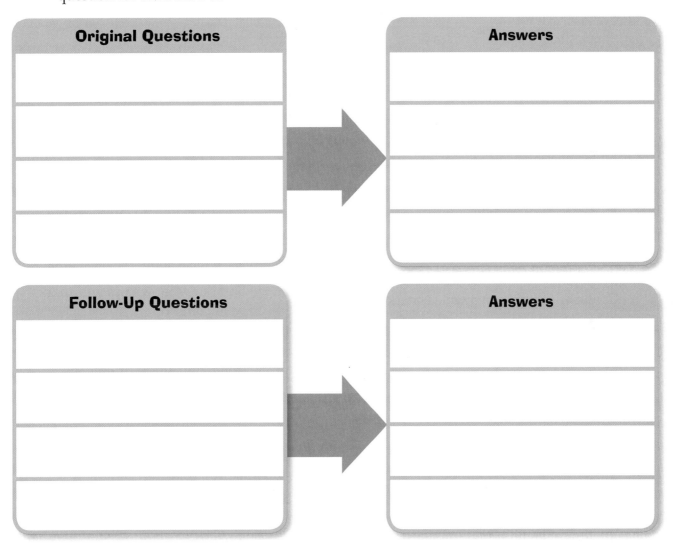

| Original Questions | Answers |
| --- | --- |
| | |

| Follow-Up Questions | Answers |
| --- | --- |
| | |

Which of your original questions resulted in the most follow-up questions? Why do you think that was?

_____

Answer the questions below to check your understanding of this unit's skills.

## Reading Skills: Setting a Purpose

**Directions** Read the passage. Then answer the questions.

---

When is a whale not a whale? When it's a whale shark. The largest of all sharks, it is also the biggest fish in the sea. A whale shark is flat and wide, with white and yellow specks on dark gray skin. What many people find most amazing, however, is how—and how much—it eats. First, it gulps huge mouthfuls of seawater, which it flushes out through its gills. Then organs, which are equipped with thousands of tiny gill rakers or bristles, capture prey such as plankton, little fish, and even small squid. Often, a whale shark rises up and down vertically, taking in and flushing out water. In this way, it can filter about 400,000 gallons of water per hour.

---

**1** This passage is mainly about _____.

   **A.** how a whale shark eats

   **B.** the size of a whale shark

   **C.** the appearance of a whale shark

   **D.** how a whale shark swims

**2** Which sentence BEST helps you set a **purpose for reading?**

   **F.** ". . . it is also the biggest fish in the sea."

   **G.** "First, it gulps huge mouthfuls of water. . . ."

   **H.** "When is a whale not a whale?"

   **J.** "Often, a whale shark rises up and down vertically. . . ."

**3** What is the most likely **purpose for reading** this passage?

   **A.** to learn facts about whale sharks

   **B.** to find out what whales and sharks have in common

   **C.** to enjoy reading about the biggest fish

   **D.** to become inspired by amazing shark tales

**4** After determining the topic of this passage, what else could help you set a **purpose for reading?**

   **F.** Skim for inspiring examples.

   **G.** Look for humorous details.

   **H.** Decide which parts will be most entertaining.

   **J.** Think about what you want to know.

# Literary Analysis: Elements of Drama

Read the following passage. Then answer the questions.

(Scene opens outside high school. STUDENTS are milling about. JOE enters stage by running up center aisle.)

**JOE:** (breathlessly, to SUSAN) Sorry! My mom couldn't give me a ride! Did you bring the flyers?

**SUSAN:** Marco has them. (Looks at watch.) But he's late, too.

**JOE:** What are we going to do? If we don't post them this morning, people won't know about the meeting.

**SUSAN:** Tell me about it. The School Committee is meeting tomorrow. We have to get students to show support for Mr. Franklin—they just can't replace the best teacher in the whole school!

**GABY:** (waving) Susan! Joe! I heard there's a sub for Mr. Franklin today.

**JOE:** (dropping his backpack) What? Why? I wonder what that means.

**SUSAN:** (exasperated) What I'm wondering is, where is Marco?

**1** What can readers tell from the **stage directions**?

A. Marco has the flyers.

B. Joe is out of breath.

C. The School Committee meets tonight.

D. Mr. Franklin may lose his job.

**2** What does the **dialogue** reveal about Mr. Franklin?

F. He is running late.

G. He has the flyers.

H. He might be replaced.

J. He is on the School Committee.

**3** What do the **stage directions** suggest about Susan?

A. She is anxious and worried.

B. She is used to giving orders.

C. She is critical of others.

D. She is an easygoing person.

**4** How does Marco's tardiness help to create a mood of **suspense?**

F. Readers think he is rude.

G. Readers wonder why he's absent.

H. Readers think he missed his ride.

J. Readers think he overslept.

## Timed Writing: Response to Literature

**Directions** Read a brief scene from a play. Describe what the scene reveals about one of the main characters. Identify examples of stage directions and dialogue that reveal this information. **(20 minutes)**

# 5-8 Reading Skills
## Cause and Effect

In learning new reading skills, you will use special academic vocabulary. Knowing the right words will help you demonstrate your understanding.

### Academic Vocabulary

| Word | Meaning | Example Sentence |
|------|---------|------------------|
| **affect** *v.*<br>*Related words:*<br>affected, affecting | to influence | The argument between the two main characters *affected* the outcome of the plot. |
| **effect** *n.*<br>*Related word:*<br>effective | result or outcome | The snowstorm's *effect* was felt for days afterward. |
| **enable** *v.*<br>*Related words:*<br>enabled, enabling | to allow or facilitate | The money raised by our club *enabled* us to buy a new computer. |

A **cause** is an event, action, or situation that produces a result. That result is called an **effect.** Identifying causes and effects can help you see the relationship between situations or events.

Sometimes the **cause-and-effect** relationship in a piece of writing is clear.

> **Example**  Each time the river floods, it deposits silt on the land downstream.
> **Cause:**  The river floods.
> **Effect:**  It deposits silt on the land downstream.

Other times, the cause-and-effect relationship is not as clear. When this happens, reread the passage to look for connections among words and sentences, asking yourself questions as you read. This will **enable** you to determine how causes can **affect** a situation.

## How to Identify a Cause-and-Effect Relationship

The following chart lists questions and clue words to help you identify causes and effects.

| Questions to Ask | Words to Look For | | |
|---|---|---|---|
| What happened?<br>What will happen as a result of this?<br>Why did this happen? | because<br>therefore<br>due to | since<br>as a result of<br>for this reason | so |

**Directions** As you read the following passage, look for cause-and-effect relationships. Then answer the questions.

## A Plentiful Harvest

"Let me tell you," said Grandmother, "how our people came to plant corns, beans, and squash." Because we loved Grandmother's tales, we all settled back to listen.

"One day," she continued, "an early frost came to the land. Many of the crops died. My great-great grandfather and his wife were very worried. How would they feed their children that winter?

"So, Great-great Grandfather traveled into the forest, asking the animals and the plants for help. After a time, he grew tired and fell asleep. He dreamed that a basket of seeds was set before him. A voice told him that if he planted these seeds, his family would not starve.

"When he awoke, he found a basket of seeds—corn, beans, and squash seeds. The weather had grown warmer again as well. He thanked the forest and hurried home. There was just enough time to plant and harvest the corn, beans, and squash.

"Great-great Grandfather and his family ate well that winter. And at each meal, they remembered to thank the forest for its help. As a result, they were never again hungry."

**1** **Cause and Effect** Why did Great-great Grandfather travel into the forest to ask for help? What was the result?

_____

_____

**2** **Identify** What clue words help you identify cause-and-effect relationships in the story?

_____

_____

Look for the cause-and-effect relationship that shows how plants can affect their environment through chemical signals.
*Guiding Question:* **In what way does understanding the effects of plant chemicals enable you to see plants in a new way?**

 Link to Science

# Plants on the Warpath
## The Roots of Combat
*by* **Joel Achenbach**

At some point in the 1970s, people started talking to houseplants. They figured plants would grow better if made the recipients of verbal nourishment and a little extra $CO_2$. There was an even bigger presumption: Plants were gentle, peace-loving, tolerant organisms. (Hippies, obviously.)

But now we know the sordid truth: Some plants are stone-cold killers.

Consider the spotted knapweed, accursed invader of the American West. The dogma among ecologists is that invasive alien species thrive because they're free of the diseases, insects, and other enemies that keep them in check on their native turf.

Knapweed, however, has a secret weapon: Its roots secrete a chemical that kills other plants. This is known as allelopathy, and it's tough to prove because soil is such a dense stew of microbes, mites, nematodes, and all sorts of chemicals. How do you tweeze a toxin from the mix and know where it came from and what it's doing?

Colorado State University scientists recently managed to identify knapweed's killer chemical. They grew the plant in a sterile liquid, then examined the compounds its roots released into the liquid. When one chemical, catechin, was applied to the roots of other plants, it triggered the production of free radicals, which passed from the roots upward, activating a wave of cell death. In essence, a tiny amount of catechin induced other plants to commit suicide.

◄ spotted knapweed

"People think plants are innocuous. We're showing that plants can be as mean as any animal," says Jorge Vivanco, leader of the team.

Plants may also use chemicals to "communicate" with one another. In the case of knapweed, the message is simple: "You die now." (Vivanco's group calls this "negative communication." To say the least.) But sometimes the message, delivered to fellow members of the species, is something along the lines of "mites attacking; shore up your defenses."

For example, when lima bean plants are attacked by spider mites, they call out the cavalry, emitting a chemical distress signal that attracts carnivorous mites that eat the spider mites. The signal inspires nearby uninfested lima bean plants to do the same thing.

◄ lima bean

Because we humans are so biased toward visual and auditory signals, and don't tend to sniff everything and lick random objects, we don't realize how much the world around us is shot through with chemical warnings.

Plants don't make that mistake. When something crosses them, they take action. So the next time you take a stroll in a garden, maybe you should be looking over your shoulder.

# Thinking About the Selection

## Plants on the Warpath—The Roots of Combat

**1**    **Recall** When spider mites attack a lima bean plant, how does the plant protect itself?

_____

_____

_____

**2**    **Cause and Effect** Complete the chart to show the effects of the chemical secreted by the knapweed.

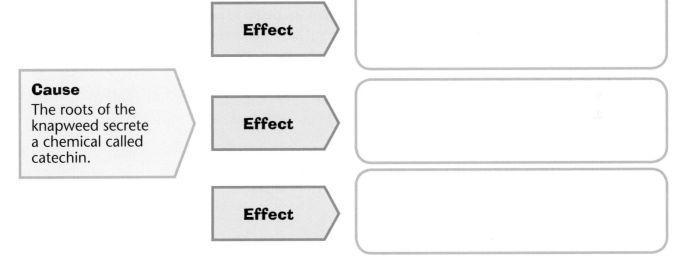

**Cause**
The roots of the knapweed secrete a chemical called catechin.

**Effect**

**Effect**

**Effect**

**Write** Answer the following questions in your Reader's Journal.

 **3**    **Evaluate** In what way does understanding the effects of plant chemicals enable you to see plants in a new way?

 **4**    **Write and Discuss** The problems in your Anchor Book are the causes for the actions of your characters. Identify a problem in your Anchor Book and list at least two possible realistic solutions to the problem. Which solution would be the best for all characters? What would happen in the book if this solution was the actual outcome? Discuss your ideas with your Literature Circle.

 **Ready for a Free-Choice Book?** _Your teacher may ask if you would like to choose another book to read on your own. Select a book that fits your interest and that you'll enjoy. As you read, think about how your new book compares with your Anchor Book._

# 5-9 Literary Analysis
## Character Motivation

Why do you do the things you do? Not only might you ask this about yourself and the people around you, but you can also ask it about the characters you read about in literature.

while reading your anchor book

## Literary Terms

**Character motivation** is the reason or reasons for a character's actions. Character motivation may be external, internal, or both.

- ▶ **Internal motivation** comes from a person's emotions like fear or anger. Example: *Tony was frustrated that his baseball team lost, so he argued with his teammates.*

- ▶ **External motivation** comes from outside situations that a person faces. Example: *When Carla's mother explained that good grades could get her a scholarship, Carla started working harder in school.*

A character's motivation might be a combination of internal and external causes. The writer might state a character's motivation directly, but more often the reader has to figure it out from clues.

Revealing (or hinting at) a character's motivation is an important aspect of **characterization.** If a character changes the way the character is portrayed—this is called **dynamite characterization.** If a character stays the same, the characterization is **static.**

**Directions** Try identifying a character's motivations and the actions they cause by filling in the empty boxes in the chart.

| Action | Motivation |
|---|---|
| Brianna brushed past her best friend and stormed out of the cafeteria. | Brianna was angry because her friend told a secret she swore she wouldn't tell. |
| Scott quit the swim team. | |
| | Lucy's father lost his job. |
| | Josh was thrilled that he got an A on his history exam. |

**Go Online**
**About the Author**
Visit: PHSchool.com
Web Code: exe-7503

## from *The Secret Adversary* by *Agatha Christie*

It was 2 p.m. on the afternoon of May 7, 1915. The *Lusitania* had been struck by two torpedoes in succession and was sinking rapidly, while the boats were being launched with all possible speed . . . One girl stood alone, slightly apart from the rest. She was quite young, not more than eighteen. She did not seem afraid, and her grave, steadfast eyes looked straight ahead.

"I beg your pardon."

A man's voice beside her made her start and turn. She had noticed the speaker more than once amongst the first-class passengers. There had been a hint of mystery about him which had appealed to her imagination. . .

"Yes?" Her grave eyes met his inquiringly.

He stood looking at her with a kind of desperate irresolution.

"It must be!" he muttered to himself. "Yes—it is the only way." Then aloud he said abruptly: "You are an American?"

"Yes."

"A patriotic one?"

The girl flushed.

"I guess you've no right to ask such a thing! Of course I am!"

"Don't be offended. You wouldn't be if you knew how much there was at stake. But I've got to trust some one . . . I'm carrying papers—vitally important papers. They may make all the difference to the Allies in the war. You understand? These papers have *got* to be saved! They've more chance with you than with me. Will you take them?"

The girl held out her hand.

"Wait—I must warn you. There may be a risk—if I've been followed. I don't think I have, but one never knows. If so, there will be danger. Have you the nerve to go through with it?"

The girl smiled.

"I'll go through with it all right. And I'm real proud to be chosen! What am I to do with them afterwards?"

"Watch the newspapers! I'll advertise in the personal column of the Times, beginning 'Shipmate.' At the end of three days if there's nothing—well, you'll know I'm down and out. Then take the packet to the American Embassy, and deliver it into the Ambassador's own hands. Is that clear?"

"Quite clear."

"Then be ready—I'm going to say good-bye." He took her hand in his. "Good-bye. Good luck to you," he said in a louder tone.

Her hand closed on the oilskin packet that had lain in his palm.

**1**    **Analyze**   How does the girl's attitude toward the man change after she learns of the papers?

_____

_____

**2**    **Interpret**   Are the man's motivations internal, external, or both? Explain your interpretation.

_____

_____

_____

_____

**3**    **Interpret**   What motivates the girl to accept the papers?

_____

_____

**4**    **Respond**   Imagine you are in the same position as the girl in the story. What would motivate you to either accept or not accept the papers from the man? Explain your answer.

_____

_____

_____

Sometimes the cultural context of a literary work helps explain a character's motivation. *Guiding Question:* **Why does the narrator think that an umbrella will make other people see her in a different way—and why does she change her mind?**

# The White umbrella

## By Gish Jen

**Background** *The narrator and her sister Mona were born in the United States, but they are torn between their parents' Chinese heritage and the life they are leading in the U.S.*

## Vocabulary Builder

**Before you read,** *you will discuss the following words. In the Vocabulary Builder box in the margin, use a vocabulary building strategy to make the words your own.*

> **audible    discreet    credibility    revelation**

**As you read,** *draw a box around unfamiliar words you could add to your vocabulary. Use context clues to unlock their meaning.*

### Marking the Text

**Character Motivation**

**As you read,** *underline details that provide clues about the narrator's motivation. In the margin, write notes about what you think these clues reveal.*

When I was twelve, my mother went to work without telling me or my little sister.

"Not that we need the second income." The lilt of her accent drifted from the kitchen up to the top of the stairs, where Mona and I were listening.

"No," said my father, in a barely **audible** voice. "Not like the Lee family."

The Lees were the only other Chinese family in town. I remembered how sorry my parents had felt for Mrs. Lee when she started waitressing downtown the year before; and so when

## Vocabulary Builder

**audible**
(ô′də bəl) *adj.*

**Meaning**

Character Motivation   **413**

my mother began coming home late, I didn't say anything, and tried to keep Mona from saying anything either.

"But why shouldn't I?" she argued. "Lots of people's mothers work."

"Those are American people." I said.

"So what do you think we are? I can do the pledge of allegiance with my eyes closed."

Nevertheless, she tried to be **discreet;** and if my mother wasn't home by 5:30, we would start cooking by ourselves, to make sure dinner would be on time. Mona would wash the vegetables and put on the rice; I would chop.

For weeks we wondered what kind of work she was doing. I imagined that she was selling perfume, or testing dessert recipes for the local newspaper. Or maybe she was working for the florist. Now that she had learned to drive, she might be delivering boxes of roses to people.

"I don't think so," said Mona as we walked to our piano lesson after school. "She would've hit something by now."

A gust of wind littered the street with leaves.

"Maybe we better hurry up," she went on, looking at the sky. "It's going to pour."

"But we're too early." Her lesson didn't begin until 4:00, mine until 4:30, so we usually tried to walk as slowly as we could. "And anyway, those aren't the kind of clouds that rain. Those are cumulus clouds[1]."

We arrived out of breath and wet.

"Oh, you poor, poor dears," said old Miss Crosman. "Why don't you call me the next time it's like this out? If your mother won't drive you, I can come pick you up."

"No, that's okay," I answered. Mona wrung her hair out on Miss Crosman's rug. "We just couldn't get the roof of our car to

---
[1] **cumulus** (kyoo′ myə ləs) **clouds** *n.* white, puffy clouds that usually indicate fair weather.

**Vocabulary Builder**

**discreet**
(di skrēt′) *adj.*

**Meaning**

close, is all. We took it to the beach last summer and got sand in the mechanism." I pronounced this last word carefully, as if the **credibility** of my lie depended on its middle syllable. "It's never been the same." I thought for a second. "It's a convertible."

"Well then make yourselves at home." She exchanged looks with Eugenie Roberts, whose lesson we were interrupting. Eugenie smiled good-naturedly. "The towels are in the closet across from the bathroom."

Huddling at the end of Miss Crosman's nine-foot leatherette couch, Mona and I watched Eugenie play. She was a grade ahead of me and, according to school rumor, had a boyfriend in high school. I believed it. . . . She had auburn hair, blue eyes, and, I noted with a particular pang, a pure white folding umbrella.

"I can't see," whispered Mona.

"So clean your glasses."

"My glasses are clean. You're in the way."

I looked at her. "They look dirty to me."

"That's because your glasses are dirty."

Eugenie came bouncing to the end of her piece.

"Oh! Just stupendous[2]!" Miss Crosman hugged her, then looked up as Eugenie's mother walked in. "Stupendous!" she said again. "Oh! Mrs. Roberts! Your daughter has a gift, a real gift. It's an honor to teach her."

Mrs. Roberts, radiant with pride, swept her daughter out of the room as if she were royalty, born to the piano bench. Watching the way Eugenie carried herself, I sat up, and concentrated so hard on sucking in my stomach that I did not realize until the Robertses were gone that Eugenie had left her umbrella. As Mona began to play, I jumped up and ran to the window, meaning to call to them—only to see their brake lights flash then fade at the stop sign at the corner. As if to allow them passage, the rain had let up; a quivering sun lit their way.

The umbrella glowed like a scepter[3] on the blue carpet while Mona, slumping over the keyboard, managed to eke out[4] a fair rendition[5] of a catfight. At the end of the piece, Miss Crosman asked her to stand up.

"Stay right there," she said, then came back a minute later with a towel to cover the bench. "You must be cold," she continued. "Shall I call your mother and have her bring over some dry clothes?"

"No," answered Mona. "She won't come because she . . ."

"She's too busy," I broke in from the back of the room.

**Vocabulary Builder**

**credibility**
(kred′ ə bil′ ə tē) *n.*

**Meaning**

---

[2] **stupendous** (stoo′ pen′dəs) *adj.* outstanding; marvelous.

[3] **scepter** (sep′ tər) *n.* a rod covered with ornaments, held by rulers as a symbol of royalty.

[4] **eke** (ēk) **out** *v.* barely manage.

[5] **rendition** (ren dish′ ən) *n.* performance; interpretation.

"I see." Miss Crosman sighed and shook her head a little. "Your glasses are filthy, honey," she said to Mona. "Shall I clean them for you?"

Sisterly embarrassment seized me. Why hadn't Mona wiped her lenses when I told her to? As she resumed abuse of the piano, I stared at the umbrella. I wanted to open it, twirl it around by its slender silver handle; I wanted to dangle it from my wrist on the way to school the way the other girls did. I wondered what Miss Crosman would say if I offered to bring it to Eugenie at school tomorrow. She would be impressed with my consideration for others; Eugenie would be pleased to have it back; and I would have possession of the umbrella for an entire night. I looked at it again, toying with the idea of asking for one for Christmas. I knew, however, how my mother would react.

"Things," she would say. "What's the matter with a raincoat? All you want is things, just like an American."

Sitting down for my lesson, I was careful to keep the towel under me and sit up straight.

"I'll bet you can't see a thing either," said Miss Crosman, reaching for my glasses. "And you can relax, you poor dear." She touched my chest, in an area where she never would have touched Eugenie Roberts. "This isn't a boot camp[6]."

When Miss Crosman finally allowed me to start playing I played extra well, as well as I possibly could. See, I told her with my fingers. You don't have to feel sorry for me.

"That was wonderful," said Miss Crosman. "Oh! Just wonderful."

An entire constellation rose in my heart.

"And guess what," I announced proudly. "I have a surprise for you."

Then I played a second piece for her, a much more difficult one that she had not assigned.

"Oh! That was stupendous," she said without hugging me. "Stupendous! You are a genius, young lady. If your mother had started you younger, you'd be playing like Eugenie Roberts by now!"

I looked at the keyboard, wishing that I had still a third, even more difficult piece to play for her. I wanted to tell her that I was the school spelling bee champion, that I wasn't ticklish, that I could do karate.

"My mother is a concert pianist," I said.

She looked at me for a long moment, then finally, without saying anything, hugged me. I didn't say anything about bringing the umbrella to Eugenie at school.

---

[6] **boot camp** *n.* place where soldiers receive basic training under strict discipline.

The steps were dry when Mona and I sat down to wait for my mother.

"Do you want to wait inside?" Miss Crosman looked anxiously at the sky.

"No," I said. "Our mother will be here any minute."

"In a while," said Mona.

"Any minute," I said again, even though my mother had been at least twenty minutes late every week since she started working.

According to the church clock across the street we had been waiting twenty-five minutes when Miss Crosman came out again.

"Shall I give you ladies a ride home?"

"No," I said. "Our mother is coming any minute."

"Shall I at least give her a call and remind her you're here? Maybe she forgot about you?"

"I don't think she forgot," said Mona.

"Shall I give her a call anyway? Just to be safe?"

"I bet she already left," I said. "How could she forget about us?"

Miss Crosman went in to call.

"There's no answer," she said, coming back out.

"See, she's on her way," I said.

"Are you sure you wouldn't like to come in?"

"No," said Mona.

▶ **Critical Viewing**
According to this image, what internal conflict might the narrator be having?

417

"Yes," I said. I pointed to my sister. "She meant yes too. She meant no, she wouldn't like to go in."

Miss Crosman looked at her watch. "It's 5:30 now, ladies. My pot roast will be coming out in fifteen minutes. Maybe you'd like to come in and have some then?"

"My mother's almost here," I said. "She's on her way."

We watched and watched the street. I tried to imagine what my mother was doing; I tried to imagine her writing messages in the sky, even though I knew she was afraid of planes. I watched as the branches of Miss Crosman's big willow tree started to sway; they had all been trimmed to exactly the same height off the ground, so that they looked beautiful, like hair in the wind.

It started to rain.

"Miss Crosman is coming out again," said Mona.

"Don't let her talk you into going inside," I whispered.

"Why not?"

"Because that would mean Mom isn't really coming any minute."

"But she isn't," said Mona. "She's working."

"Shhh! Miss Crosman is going to hear you."

"She's working! She's working! She's working!"

I put my hand over her mouth, but she licked it, and so I was wiping my hand on my wet dress when the front door opened.

"We're getting even wetter," said Mona right away. "Wetter and wetter."

"Shall we all go in?" Miss Crosman pulled Mona to her feet. "Before you young ladies catch pneumonia? You've been out here an hour already."

"We're freezing." Mona looked up at Miss Crosman. "Do you have any hot chocolate? We're going to catch pneumonia."

"I'm not going in." I said. "My mother's coming any minute."

"Come on," said Mona. "Use your noggin[7]."

"Any minute."

"Come on, Mona," Miss Crosman opened the door. "Shall we get you inside first?"

"See you in the hospital," said Mona as she went in. "See you in the hospital with pneumonia."

I stared out into the empty street. The rain was pricking me all over; I was cold; I wanted to go inside. I wanted to be able to let myself go inside. If Miss Crosman came out again, I decided, I would go in.

She came out with a blanket and the white umbrella.

I could not believe that I was actually holding the umbrella, opening it. It sprang up by itself as if it were alive, as if that were what it wanted to do—as if it belonged in my hands, above my

---

[7] **noggin** (näg' in) *n.* head (slang).

head. I stared up at the network of silver spokes, then spun the umbrella around and around and around. It was so clean and white that it seemed to glow, to illuminate everything around it.

"It's beautiful," I said.

Miss Crosman sat down next to me, on one end of the blanket. I moved the umbrella over so that it covered that too. I could feel the rain on my left shoulder and shivered. She put her arm around me.

"You poor, poor dear."

I knew that I was in store for another bolt of sympathy, and braced myself by staring up into the umbrella.

"You know, I very much wanted to have children when I was younger," she continued.

"You did?"

She stared at me a minute. Her face looked dry and crusty, like day-old frosting.

"I did. But then I never got married."

I twirled the umbrella around again.

"This is the most beautiful umbrella I have ever seen," I said. "Ever, in my whole life."

"Do you have an umbrella?"

"No. But my mother's going to get me one just like this for Christmas."

"Is she? I tell you what. You don't have to wait until Christmas. You can have this one."

"But this one belongs to Eugenie Roberts," I protested. "I have to give it back to her tomorrow in school."

"Who told you it belongs to Eugenie? It's not Eugenie's. It's mine. And now I'm giving it to you, so it's yours."

"It is?"

She hugged me tighter. "That's right. It's all yours."

"It's mine?" I didn't know what to say. "Mine?" Suddenly I was jumping up and down in the rain. "It's beautiful! Oh! It's beautiful!" I laughed.

Miss Crosman laughed too, even though she was getting all wet.

"Thank you, Miss Crosman. Thank you very much. Thanks a zillion. It's beautiful. It's stupendous!"

"You're quite welcome," she said.

"Thank you," I said again, but that didn't seem like enough. Suddenly I knew just what she wanted to hear. "I wish you were my mother."

Right away I felt bad.

"You shouldn't say that," she said, but her face was opening into a huge smile as the lights of my mother's car cautiously turned the corner. I quickly collapsed the umbrella and put it up my skirt, holding onto it from the outside, through the material.

"Mona!" I shouted into the house. "Mona! Hurry up! Mom's here! I told you she was coming!"

Then I ran away from Miss Crosman, down to the curb. Mona came tearing up to my side as my mother neared the house. We both backed up a few feet, so that in case she went onto the curb, she wouldn't run us over.

"But why didn't you go inside with Mona?" my mother asked on the way home. She had taken off her own coat to put over me, and had the heat on high.

"She wasn't using her noggin," said Mona, next to me in the back seat.

"I should call next time," said my mother. "I just don't like to say where I am."

That was when she finally told us that she was working as a check-out clerk in the A&P. She was supposed to be on the day shift, but the other employees were unreliable, and her boss had promised her a promotion if she would stay until the evening shift filled in.

For a moment no one said anything. Even Mona seemed to find the **revelation** disappointing.

"A promotion already!" she said, finally.

I listened to the windshield wipers.

"You're so quiet." My mother looked at me in the rear view mirror. "What's the matter?"

"I wish you would quit," I said after a moment.

She sighed. "The Chinese have a saying: one beam cannot hold the roof up."

"But Eugenie Robert's father supports their family."

She sighed once more. "Eugene Roberts's father is Eugenie Roberts's father," she said.

As we entered the downtown area, Mona started leaning hard against me every time the car turned right, trying to push me over. Remembering what I had said to Miss Crosman, I tried to maneuver the umbrella under my leg so she wouldn't feel it.

"What's under your skirt?" Mona wanted to know as we came to a traffic light. My mother, watching us in the rear view mirror again, rolled slowly to a stop.

"What's the matter?" she asked.

"There's something under her skirt!" said Mona, pulling at me.

"Under her skirt?"

Meanwhile, a man crossing the street started to yell at us.

"Who do you think you are, lady?" he said. "You're blocking the whole crosswalk."

We all froze. Other people walking by stopped to watch.

"Didn't you hear me?" he went on, starting to thump on the hood with his fist. "Don't you speak English?"

My mother began to back up, but the car behind us honked. Luckily, the light turned green right after that. She sighed in relief.

"What were you saying, Mona?" she asked.

We wouldn't have hit the car behind us that hard if he hadn't been moving too, but as it was our car bucked violently, throwing us all first back and then forward.

"Uh oh," said Mona when we stopped. "Another accident."

## Vocabulary Builder

**revelation**
(rev´ə lā´shən) *n.*

**Meaning**

I was relieved to have attention diverted[8] from the umbrella. Then I noticed my mother's head, tilted back onto the seat. Her eyes were closed.

"Mom!" I screamed. "Mom! Wake up!"

She opened her eyes. "Please don't yell," she said. "Enough people are going to yell already."

"I thought you were dead," I said, starting to cry. "I thought you were dead."

She turned around, looking at me intently, then put her hand to my forehead.

"Sick," she confirmed. "Some kind of sick is giving you crazy ideas."

As the man from the car behind us started tapping on the window, I moved the umbrella away from my leg. Then Mona and my mother were getting out of the car. I got out after them; and while everyone else was inspecting the damage we'd done, I threw the umbrella down a sewer.

---

[8] **diverted** (də vərt' əd) *v.* turned in a different direction.

## Vocabulary Builder

**After you read,** *review the words you decided to add to your vocabulary. Write the meaning of words you have learned in context. Look up the other words in a dictionary, glossary, thesaurus, or electronic resource.*

# Gish Jen (b. 1955)

Like the narrator in "The White Umbrella," Gish Jen grew up in the suburbs of New York City, the daughter of Chinese immigrants. For most of her childhood, her family was one of the only Asian American families in town.

Although Jen wrote her first story in the fifth grade, she did not decide to become a writer until after she had attended business school. In her novels and short stories, Jen explores the issue of what it means to be an American in a multicultural nation. You can read more about the Chang family in Jen's novels *Typical American* (1991) and *Mona in the Promised Land* (1996), as well as in her short story collection *Who's Irish?* (1999).

Marking the Text

while reading your anchor book

# Thinking About the Selection
## The White Umbrella

**Go Online**

**About the Author**
Visit: PHSchool.com
Web Code: exe-7504

**1** **Infer** What is the cause of the narrator's mother getting a job? What is the effect?

_____

_____

_____

**2** **Infer** Why does Miss Crosman give the narrator the white umbrella? In other words, what is her motivation?

_____

_____

_____

**3** **Interpret** What is the effect on the narrator when she first sees the white umbrella? What might it symbolize, or represent, to her in terms of her cultural identity?

_____

_____

_____

**4** **Speculate** At the end of the story, the narrator does a surprising thing. Why do you think she throws away the umbrella? Is her motivation external, internal, or both?

_____

_____

_____

**Write** Answer the following questions in your Reader's Journal.

**5** **Deduce** Why does the narrator think that an umbrella will make other people see her in a different way—and why does she change her mind?

**6** **Analyze** Choose a character and an event that he or she is involved in from your Anchor Book. Is the character's response to the event an example of internal or external motivation, or a combination of the two? Use examples from the text to support your answer.

while reading your anchor book

# 5-10 Comparing Literary Works
## *Dramatization*

How does a play get its start? Some plays are completely new works. Others are adapted from novels, short stories, or even nonfiction. To turn an existing work into a play, the playwright takes the scenes, characters, and action and dramatizes them.

## Literary Terms

▶ A **dramatization** is a play that was once a novel, short story, folk tale, biography, or even a magazine article.

▶ To create a dramatization, the playwright needs to think about how to tell the original story using only **dialogue** and **stage directions.** The playwright must consider how sets, costumes, props, lighting, and other elements of **staging** will bring the play to life.

**Directions** Read the following excerpt from "The White Umbrella." Then read the dramatization and answer the question.

while reading your anchor book

| Story |
|---|
| She came out with a blanket and the white umbrella. |
| I could not believe that I was actually holding the umbrella, opening it. It sprang up by itself as if it were alive, as if that were what it wanted to do—as if it belonged in my hands, above my head. I stared up at the network of silver spokes, then spun the umbrella around and around and around. It was so clean and white that it seemed to glow, to illuminate everything around it. |
| "It's beautiful," I said. |
| Miss Crosman sat down next to me, on one end of the blanket. I moved the umbrella over so that it covered that too. I could feel the rain on my left shoulder and shivered. She put her arm around me. |
| "You poor, poor dear." |

| Dramatization |
|---|
| **Scene 4** *In front of Miss Crosman's house. It is a brick Colonial-style house from the 1930s with well-kept shrubs and flowers along a stone walkway leading to the sidewalk.* |
| [*GIRL sits on the front steps. MISS CROSMAN enters, carrying blanket and white umbrella. She hands the umbrella to GIRL and spreads the blanket on a step.*] |
| GIRL: [*Opens the umbrella, spins it, and stares up at it in wonder.*] It's beautiful. |
| [*MISS CROSMAN sits next to GIRL. GIRL shifts umbrella to cover MISS CROSMAN, then shivers. MISS CROSMAN puts an arm around her.*] |
| MISS CROSMAN: You poor, poor dear. |

**1** **Compare and Contrast** What similarities and differences do you see between the dramatization and the story?

_____

_____

_____

_____

**Directions** The following chart lists some things you might need for dramatizing and staging the excerpt from "The White Umbrella." Study the chart and complete the activity that follows.

| Sets and Props | ▸ painted backdrop—brick house with shrubs<br>▸ flowers and walkway—on floor of stage?<br>▸ white umbrella, blanket |
|---|---|
| Costumes | ▸ girl—skirt (late '60s style), glasses, headband?<br>▸ Miss Crosman—plaid skirt, knee-length, cardigan sweater, pearls |
| Sound Effects | ▸ faint sound of classical music coming from inside the house<br>▸ sound of cars whooshing in the distance |
| Lighting and Visual Effects | ▸ blue light to show dusk, gradually getting darker during scene<br>▸ spray girl with water from above?<br>▸ car headlights every few minutes |

**2** **Apply** Use the chart to plan how to dramatize and stage a scene from an Anchor Book you have read. On a separate piece of paper, write the dramatization.

| Source | |
|---|---|
| Sets and Props | |
| Costumes | |
| Sound Effects | |
| Lighting and Visual Effects | |

Read the excerpt from the novel *Dragonwings*. Then compare it to the next selection, a dramatization of the same section of the novel. *Guiding Question:* **How does the dramatization change the way you see the characters in the novel?**

## *from the novel*
# DRAGONWINGS
*by Laurence Yep*

**Background** *In 1903, when Moon Shadow is eight, he leaves China to join his father, Windrider, in San Francisco. Moon Shadow becomes caught up in his father's dream of building and flying an airplane. In this excerpt, it is 1909, and Moon Shadow awakens to find that his uncle and several other men have arrived to help him and his father get their flying machine, Dragonwings, up a hill.*

### Vocabulary Builder

**Before you read,** *you will discuss the following words. In the Vocabulary Builder box in the margin, use a vocabulary building strategy to make the words your own.*

**toiling    coils    abominable    haul**

**As you read,** *draw a box around unfamiliar words you could add to your vocabulary. Use context clues to unlock their meaning.*

I do not know when I fell asleep, but it was already way past sunrise when I woke up. The light crept through the cracks in the walls and under the shutters and seemed to delight especially in dancing on my eyes. Father lay huddled, rolled up in his blanket. He did not move when the knock came at our door. I was still in my clothes because it was cold. I crawled out of the blankets and opened the side door.

*Marking the Text*

**Dramatization**

**As you read,** *underline details that reveal important information about the plot, characters, and setting. In the margin, write notes about how you might use these details in a dramatization of the novel.*

The fog lay low on the hill. Tendrils[1] drifted in through the open doorway. At first I could not see anything but shadows, and then a sudden breeze whipped the fog away from the front of our barn. Hand Clap stood there as if he had appeared by magic. He bowed.

"There you are." He turned and called over his shoulder. "Hey, everybody, they're here."

I heard the clink of harness and the rattle of an old wagon trying to follow the ruts in the road. **Toiling** up the hill out of the fog was Red Rabbit[2], and behind him I saw Uncle on the wagon seat. The rest of the wagon was empty—I suppose to give Red Rabbit less of a load to pull. Behind the wagon came the Company, with **coils** of ropes over their shoulders and baskets of food. I ran down the hill, my feet pounding against the hard, damp earth. I got up on the seat and almost bowled Uncle over[3]. For once Uncle did not worry about his dignity but caught me up and returned my hug.

"Ouch," he said, and pushed me away. He patted himself lightly on his chest. "I'm not as young as I used to be."

Then Hand Clap, Lefty, and White Deer crowded around.

"Am I ever glad you're here," I said. "Poor Father—"

Uncle held up his hands. "We know. That's why we came."

"But how? Why?" I was bursting with a dozen questions all at once.

"Why, to help you get that thing up to the top of the hill," Uncle said. "Why else would we close up our shop and take a boat and climb this **abominable** hill, all on the coldest, wettest day ever known since creation?"

"But you don't believe in flying machines."

"I still don't," Uncle said sternly. "But I still feel as if I owe you something for what was done to you by that man who once was my son[4]. I'll be there to **haul** your machine up the hill, and I'll be there to haul it back down when it doesn't fly." "We were all getting fat anyway," White Deer said, "especially Uncle."

---

[1] **tendrils** (ten drəlz) *n.* long, thin, curling structures, such as hair or shoots from a plant. Here the word is used to describe the way the fog moves.

[2] **Red Rabbit** a horse named after the speedy horse ridden by Kuan Kung, the Chinese god of war.

[3] **bowled . . . over** knocked over.

[4] **man . . . son** Black Dog, who robbed Moon Shadow and his father.

## Vocabulary Builder

**After you read,** *review the words you decided to add to your vocabulary. Write the meaning of words you have learned in context. Look up the other words in a dictionary, glossary, thesaurus, or electronic resource.*

## Vocabulary Builder

**toiling**
(toil i[ng]) *v.*

**Meaning**


**coils**
(koilz) *n.*

**Meaning**


**abominable**
(ə bäm′ə nə bəl) *adj.*

**Meaning**


**haul**
(hôl) *v.*

**Meaning**

Now that you have read an excerpt from the novel *Dragonwings*, read this excerpt from a dramatization of *Dragonwings* to compare a novel to a dramatization.

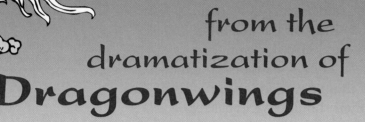

## from the dramatization of **Dragonwings**

### by Laurence Yep

**Background** *Laurence Yep dramatized* Dragonwings *twenty-two years after he published the novel. He transformed the 248-page novel into a one-hour play performed by just five actors. Note that in the stage directions,* L *means stage left,* U *means upstage (the back of the stage),* D *means downstage (the front of the stage), and* C *means the center of the stage.*

### Vocabulary Builder

**Before you read,** *you will discuss the following words. In the Vocabulary Builder box in the margin, use a vocabulary building strategy to make the words your own.*

**extension    contraption    propeller**

**As you read,** *draw a box around unfamiliar words you could add to your vocabulary. Use context clues to unlock their meaning.*

### CAST OF CHARACTERS

**RED RABBIT** a horse that pulls the company's laundry wagon

**MISS WHITLAW** owner of a stable in San Francisco where the narrator and his father live

**WHITE DEER** the third laundry owner

**MOON SHADOW** the narrator of the story

**UNCLE BRIGHT STAR** another laundry owner

**WINDRIDER** Moon Shadow's father

**SCENE 9** *Piedmont, later that day outside the stable.*

MOON SHADOW: September twenty-second, Nineteen-ought-nine[5]. Dear Mother. I have bad news. We are going to lose Dragonwings before

---

[5] **Nineteen-ought-nine** old-fashioned way of saying 1909. *Ought* (ôt) means "nothing" or "zero" (usually spelled *aught*).

father can fly it. Black Dog stole all we have, and the landlord will not give us an **extension** on our rent. So we'll have to move and leave Dragonwings behind. We have asked Miss Whitlaw for help, but her new house has taken up all of her money. And even if Uncle would speak to us, he has probably spent all he has on rebuilding his laundry.

[UNCLE BRIGHT STAR *and* MISS WHITLAW *enter from* L.]

MISS WHITLAW: I could have gotten down from the wagon by myself.

UNCLE BRIGHT STAR: Watch gopher hole.

MISS WHITLAW: I'm younger than you.

MOON SHADOW: Uncle, Miss Whitlaw!

MISS WHITLAW: How are you?

[*Shaking* MOON SHADOW'S *hand.* WINDRIDER *enters from* U. *He now wears a cap.*]

WINDRIDER: Come to laugh, Uncle?

UNCLE BRIGHT STAR: I came to help you fly your **contraption.**

MOON SHADOW: But you don't believe in flying machines.

UNCLE BRIGHT STAR: And I'll haul that thing back down when it doesn't fly. Red Rabbit and me were getting fat anyway. But look at how tall you've grown. And how thin. And ragged. [*Pause.*] But you haven't broken your neck which was more than I ever expected.

MISS WHITLAW: As soon as I told your uncle, we hatched the plot together. You ought to get a chance to fly your aeroplane[6].

UNCLE BRIGHT STAR: Flat purse, strong backs.

WINDRIDER: We need to pull Dragonwings to the very top.

UNCLE BRIGHT STAR: That hill is a very steep hill.

WINDRIDER: It has to be that one. The winds are right.

UNCLE BRIGHT STAR: Ah, well, it's the winds.

WINDRIDER: Take the ropes. [*Pantomimes[7] taking a rope over his shoulder as he faces the audience.*] Got a good grip?

OTHERS: [*Pantomiming taking the ropes.*] Yes, right, etc.

WINDRIDER: Then pull.

[*They strain.* MOON SHADOW *stumbles but gets right up. Stamping his feet to get better footing, he keeps tugging.*]

---

6  **aeroplane** (er'ə plān) *n.* old-fashioned spelling of airplane.

7  **pantomimes** (pan'tə mīm') *v.* acts out silently.

Vocabulary Builder

**extension**
(ek sten' shən) *n.*

**Meaning**

**contraption**
(kən trap'shən) *n.*

**Meaning**

MOON SHADOW: [*Giving up.*] It's no good.

UNCLE BRIGHT STAR: Pull in rhythm. As we did on the railroad[8]. [*In demonstration,* UNCLE BRIGHT STAR *stamps his feet in a slow rhythm to set the beat and the others repeat. The rhythm picks up as they move.*] Ngúng, ngúng. Dew gùng.

OTHERS: Ngúng, ngúng. Dew gùng.

UNCLE BRIGHT STAR: [*Imitating the intonation of the Cantonese[9].*] Púsh, púsh. Wòrk, Wòrk.

OTHERS: Púsh, púsh. Wòrk, Wòrk.

UNCLE BRIGHT STAR: Seen gà. Gee gá.

[*High rising tone on the last syllable.*]

OTHERS: Seen gá. Gee gá.

[*High rising tone on the last syllable.*]

UNCLE BRIGHT STAR: Get rich, Go hóme.

OTHERS: Get rich, Go hóme.

[MOON SHADOW, WINDRIDER, UNCLE BRIGHT STAR *and* MISS WHITLAW *arrive D.*]

MOON SHADOW: [*Panting.*] We made it. Tramp the grass down in front.

[WINDRIDER *stands C as the others stamp the grass. They can't help smiling and laughing a little.*]

WINDRIDER: That's enough.

MOON SHADOW: [*To* MISS WHITLAW.] Take that **propeller.**

[MISS WHITLAW *takes her place before the right propeller with her hands resting on the blade.* MOON SHADOW *takes his place beside the left propeller.* WINDRIDER *faces U, his back to the audience.*]

MISS WHITLAW: Listen to the wind on the wings.

UNCLE BRIGHT STAR: It's alive.

WINDRIDER: All right.

[MOON SHADOW *and* MISS WHITLAW *pull down at the propellers and back away quickly. We hear a motor cough into life. Propellers begin to turn with a roar.*]

UNCLE BRIGHT STAR: [*Slowly turning.*] What's wrong? Is it just going to roll down the hill?

[MISS WHITLAW *crosses her fingers as they all turn to watch the aeroplane.*]

---

[8] **railroad** (rāl′rōd′) *n.* Uncle Bright Star had helped dig tunnels through the mountains for the railroad.

[9] **Cantonese** (kan′tə nēz′) *n.* dialect of Chinese.

# Literature in Context
## The History of Flying Machines

In the late 1400s, the Renaissance artist and inventor Leonardo da Vinci drew up plans for a flying machine. However, it would be hundreds of years before someone built and actually flew one.

The earliest designers of flying machines took their ideas from the flight of birds, constructing planes with wings that would flap. These efforts were unsuccessful. Historians believe that the first successful, manned flight occurred in 1853. It took place in England, in a glider designed by Sir George Cayley. Toward the end of the 1800s, German engineer Otto Lilienthal made perhaps as many as two thousand glider flights before crashing to his death. During the same period, inventors around the world were experimenting with engines. It is the brothers Orville and Wilbur Wright who are given credit for the first successful manned, powered flight. Their historic flight took place on December 17, 1903, in Kitty Hawk, North Carolina. Orville flew a small airplane a distance of one hundred twenty feet in twelve seconds.

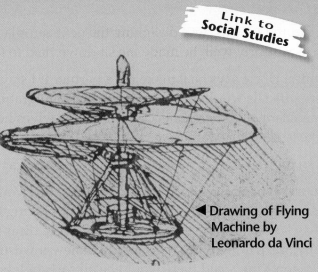

◀ Drawing of Flying Machine by Leonardo da Vinci

MISS WHITLAW: He's up!

[WINDRIDER *starts to do his flight ballet.*]

MOON SHADOW: [*Pointing.*] He's turning.

UNCLE BRIGHT STAR: He's really flying.

MISS WHITLAW: I never thought I'd see the day. A human up in the sky. Off the ground.

[*They turn and tilt their heads back.*]

MISS WHITLAW: Free as an eagle.

UNCLE BRIGHT STAR: [*Correcting her.*] Like a dragon.

MOON SHADOW: Father, you did it. [*Wonderingly.*] You did it.

[*The aeroplane roars loudly overhead.* MOON SHADOW *as an adult steps forward and addresses the audience.*]

MOON SHADOW: I thought he'd fly forever and ever. Up, up to heaven and never come down. But then some of the guy wires[10] broke, and the right wings separated. Dragonwings came crashing to earth. Father had a few broken bones, but it was nothing serious. Only the aeroplane was wrecked. Uncle took him back to the laundry to recover. Father didn't say much, just thought a

*Marking the Text*

---

[10] **guy wires** (gī wīrz) *n.* wires that help to steady the plane's two sets of wings.

lot—I figured he was busy designing the next aeroplane. But when Father was nearly well, he made me sit down next to him.

**WINDRIDER:** Uncle says he'll make me a partner if I stay. So the western officials would have to change my immigration class. I'd be a merchant, and merchants can bring their wives here. Would you like to send for Mother?

**MOON SHADOW:** [*Going to* WINDRIDER] But Dragonwings?

**WINDRIDER:** When I was up in the air, I tried to find you. You were so small. And getting smaller. Just disappearing from sight. [*Handing his cap to* MOON SHADOW.] Like you were disappearing from my life. [*He begins his ballet again.*] I knew it wasn't the time. The Dragon King[11] said there would be all sorts of lessons.

[MOON SHADOW *turns to audience as an adult.*]

**MOON SHADOW:** We always talked about flying again. Only we never did. [*Putting on cap.*] But dreams stay with you, and we never forgot.

[WINDRIDER *takes his final pose. A gong sounds.*]

---

[11] **Dragon King** *n.* In Chinese legends, most dragons are not evil creatures. Earlier in the play (and the novel), Windrider relates a dream sequence in which he was given his name by the Dragon King and learned he had once been a flying dragon.

# Laurence Yep (b. 1948)

Laurence Yep was born in 1948 in San Francisco, California. In high school, he spent many hours working in his parent's grocery store but still found time to write for a science fiction magazine—earning a penny per word. Yep has had a long and prestigious career as an author, producing literature for both young people and adults. *Dragonwings* is one of Yep's many works, which include various forms such as science fiction, realistic fiction, nonfiction, and drama.

## Thinking About the Selections
*from the novel* **Dragonwings** *and*
*from the dramatization of* **Dragonwings**

**Go Online**
**About the Author**
Visit: PHSchool.com
Web Code: exe-7505

**1** **Compare and Contrast** In the novel excerpt, how do Uncle and the others plan to get the flying machine up the hill? In the scene from the play, what helps the audience understand how Dragonwings will be moved to the hilltop?

_____

_____

_____

**2** **Compare and Contrast** How is the dialogue in the dramatization different from the dialogue in the novel? Use examples to support your answer.

_____

_____

_____

_____

**3** **Infer** How does Windrider change as a result of his flight? What motivates him to change?

_____

_____

_____

**4** **Evaluate** Do Windrider's decision and motivation seem believable to you, based on your own experience and observations? Explain.

_____

_____

_____

**Write** Answer the following questions in your Reader's Journal.

 **5** **Interpret** How does the dramatization change the way you see the characters in the novel?

 **6** **Analyze** Does your author divide your Anchor Book into different acts? If so, why does he or she break scenes at certain times?

while reading your anchor book

# 5-11 Listening and Speaking Workshop
*Reading Drama Aloud*

In this activity, you and your group members will create and present a scene from your Anchor Book. Pay special attention to dialogue delivery, stage direction, and setting.

## Your Task

- ▶ Organize, prepare, and rehearse a scene from one of your Anchor Books.

- ▶ Present the final version of your scene to the class.

## Organize Your Presentation

**1** **SELECT A SCENE.**

- ▶ With your group, select a scene from your Anchor Book in which each member of your group will be able to participate.

- ▶ Discuss the overall meaning of the scene, and how your group can express it through gestures, tone, and body language.

**2** **PREPARE YOUR SCENE.**

- ▶ Assign each member of your group a role. Every member must have a speaking part in the scene.

- ▶ Go over your assigned role and think about your character's emotions and the motivations behind his or her actions. See the following chart for examples.

| Character's emotion | Gesture reflecting that emotion |
| --- | --- |
| sadness | crying, pouting, sniffling, moping, moving sluggishly, quiet tone |
| anger | scowling aggressive tone, quick movements, wide-eyed look |
| amusement | laughing, smiling, loud and excited tone |

**3** **GATHER THE PROPS YOU NEED.**

- ▶ Are there essential props you will need—dishes, chairs, or other items? Decide if you want to gather the items or simply pretend you have them when you perform.

*while reading your anchor book*

# 4 REHEARSE YOUR SCENE.

▶ Have each group member go over his or her own lines. Discuss any confusing dialogue until the meaning is clear.

▶ Practice your scene until each member is comfortable with the dialogue and stage directions and reads with a rhythm that sounds like everyday speech.

▶ Adjust your pitch, tone, speed, and volume to best represent the characters in the scene.

# 5 PRESENT YOUR SCENE.

▶ Present the final version. Use props if you can.

## SPEAK: Rubric for Oral Interpretation

Assess your performance. For each question, circle a rating.

| CRITERIA | RATING SCALE |
|---|---|
| | NOT VERY      VERY |
| **CONTENT** How well did the group's presentation reflect the content of the scene? | 1  2  3  4  5 |
| **ORGANIZATION** How organized was the group when presenting the scene? | 1  2  3  4  5 |
| **DELIVERY** How well did the group demonstrate eye contact, pitch, volume, pacing, and tone appropriate to the characters? | 1  2  3  4  5 |
| **COOPERATION** How well did the group work together? | 1  2  3  4  5 |

## LISTEN: Rubric for Audience Self-Assessment

Assess your role as an audience. For each question, circle a rating.

| CRITERIA | RATING SCALE |
|---|---|
| | NOT VERY      VERY |
| **ACTIVE LISTENING** How well did you focus your attention on the performance? | 1  2  3  4  5 |
| **ACTIVE LISTENING** How well did you demonstrate active listening with silence, responses, and body language? | 1  2  3  4  5 |

Be prepared to summarize how the actors' posture, gestures, and facial expressions help you better understand the scene.

# 5-12 Language Coach
## Grammar and Spelling

## Participles

A **participle** is a verb form that is used as an adjective. Participles answer questions such as *What kind? Which one? How?* and *How much?* Using participles can add interest and detail to your writing.

**Go Online**

**Learn More**
Visit: PHSchool.com
Web Code: exp-7503

Present participles are formed from the present tense of a verb and commonly end in *-ing*. Past participles are formed from the past tense and usually end in *-ed*.

| Present Participle | Crying, the baby woke up her parents. [*crying* modifies *baby*] |
|---|---|
| Past Participle | The man, frightened, closed his eyes while watching the scary movie. [*frightened* modifies *man*] |

**Directions** Circle the participles in the following sentences and indicate whether they are present or past participles.

| Sentence | Present or past participle? |
|---|---|
| The laughing children watched the clown. | |
| Rested, the athletes began the second day of events. | |

**Author's Craft**

Reread the dramatization of "Dragonwings" on page 428. Why do you think the playwright used participles in the stage directions?

**Directions** Participles can make your writing more descriptive. Rewrite the following paragraph, inserting a present or past participle for each asterisk (*).

> *, my friends and I head to Washington Square Park after school. Usually, a * musician plays his guitar nearby. * and *, children play hide-and-seek around the monument. *, their parents watch them. An old woman feeds * pigeons bread crumbs. Eventually, we head home, *.

_____

_____

_____

_____

# Participial Phrases

Participles may stand alone as single words, or they may be part of a group of words called a **participial phrase.** Like participles, participial phrases function as adjectives.

Go Online

**Learn More**
Visit: PHSchool.com
Web Code: exp-7504

To add sentence variety to your writing, combine two short sentences using a participial phrase.

| Original | Lucille worked quietly. She finished her project. |
|---|---|
| Combined | Lucille, **working quietly,** finished her project. |

**Directions** Write the participial phrase in each sentence on the line. Circle the word it modifies.

**1** One of the greatest problems affecting humankind is water pollution.

_____

**2** Polluted by waterfront industries, the Cuyahoga River was topped with oil and debris.

_____

**3** In 1969, ignited by a spark, the river's surface caught fire.

_____

**Directions** Write a paragraph about your favorite food. Include at least three participial phrases in your paragraph. Choose the participial phrases from the list below or come up with your own.

| smelling delicious | tasted with a spoon | chewing loudly | sipped through a straw | stirring with a spoon |
|---|---|---|---|---|
| topped with a cherry | filled with crunch | looking like a dream come true | easily made | sniffing the sweet aroma |

_____

_____

_____

_____

Go Online

**Learn More**
Visit: PHSchool.com
Web Code: exp-7505

# Dangling Modifiers

Modifiers improve writing by adding description. However, **dangling modifiers** create confusing sentences. A dangling modifier has no clearly stated subject. To avoid confusion, place the modifier by the noun it is meant to describe or modify.

**Sentence with**       *Running swiftly*, the house was passed.
**Dangling Modifier**

     Here, *running* modifies *house*, rather than some unnamed person.

**Corrected Sentence** *Running swiftly*, the *jogger* passed the house.

     In this sentence, *running* modifies *jogger*.

| Sentence with Dangling Modifier | Explanation |
|---|---|
| *After reading the comic book,* the movie seemed uninteresting. | *After reading the comic book* modifies *movie*. The phrase was probably meant to modify the comic book reader, who isn't mentioned in the sentence. |
| The test remained incomplete, *having not studied the night before.* | *Having not studied the night before* is meant to refer to a student, but the way it's written causes it to modify *test*. |

**Directions** Revise the following passage and eliminate all dangling modifiers. Rewrite the paragraph on the lines provided.

     Tired from walking, the apartment was a welcome sight. After unpacking the groceries, the table was set for dinner. Eager to eat dinner, the oven was turned on. Hungry, dinner was devoured. Waiting to wash the dishes, they piled up in the sink. After finishing homework, our favorite television show was watched. Finally ready for bed, the lights were turned off.

# Spelling Tricky or Difficult Words

The English language contains many words that sound similar but have different meanings and spellings. In addition to using general spelling rules such as *i* before *e* except after *c,* use the following study strategies to help you with your spelling.

**Create and study a list.** Write a list of words that you misspell. Look at each word carefully and notice the arrangement or pattern of letters. Study your list until you can write each word correctly.

**Use a resource.** Write the word and check the spelling and meaning in a dictionary, thesaurus, or online resource.

**Listen to pronunciation.** Listen carefully when others pronounce a word. If it isn't clear, politely ask the speaker to repeat it. Pronounce each syllable yourself.

**Directions** The following list contains commonly confused words. Complete the list with similar sounding words. Some words have more than one answer. Write the ones you know.

| accept their piece right too affect your | except _____ _____ _____ _____ _____ _____ |
|---|---|

**Go Online**

**Learn More**
Visit: PHSchool.com
Web Code: exp-7506

**Author's Craft**

Some words have more than one meaning, but the same spelling. Reread "A Plentiful Harvest" on page 407. Find two words with more than one meaning. If you need assistance, use a dictionary to look up the definitions of the words. What are the words' different meanings? Which meanings did the author use?

**Directions** Each sentence contains a commonly confused word that is used incorrectly. Underline it and write a new sentence, using the word correctly.

**1** The rider brushed the horse's main.

_____

**2** In the passed, knights were supposed to be the bravest in the land.

_____

**3** The bald eagle is a cymbal of strength.

_____

**4** Teresa pulled the rope with all of her mite.

_____

A **cause-and-effect essay** is expository writing that explains why something happens or what happens as a result of something else. Follow the steps in the workshop to write a cause-and-effect essay about a question or issue that interests you.

To be effective, your cause-and-effect essay should include the following elements.

► A well-defined topic and a clear organizational pattern in your writing

► Information gathered from reference materials and resources

► Detailed, factual explanations of events or situations and the relationships among them

► Error-free grammar, including correct use of participles and participial phrases

**Purpose** To write a cause-and-effect essay about a question or issue that interests you

**Audience** You, your teacher, and your classmates

## Prewriting—Plan It Out

Use the following steps to help you choose the topic of your essay.

**Choose your topic.** Brainstorm by writing for five minutes about whatever questions come to mind. Use phrases such as "What causes . . ." or "Why does . . ." to begin each question. Circle any questions that really interest you. Choose a question from your list that you will enjoy learning and writing about.

**Gather details.** Use the following two-column chart to help you gather details. In one column, list the causes involved in your topic. In the other column, list the effects. Use library resources, online references, or interview an expert on the topic.

| Cause(s) | Effect(s) |
|---|---|
|  |  |

# Drafting—Get It on Paper

Before you begin your essay, decide on the best way to organize your details. Think about using a method that will be effective in conveying your ideas to your audience.

- ▶ If you are writing about a single effect with many causes, devote a paragraph to each cause and one paragraph to the effect.

- ▶ If you are writing about a single cause with many effects, devote a paragraph to the cause and a paragraph to each effect.

- ▶ If you are writing about a series of causes and effects, organize your paragraphs in chronological order.

**Write a strong introduction.** Explain the importance of your topic in one or two sentences and identify the main points of your essay.

**Explain causes and effects.** Use specific statistics, dates, names, or places to explain the connection between each relationship. For example, if the cause is a tornado and you are describing its effect on a town, include facts that drive home the tornado's impact.

**Use the SEE Technique.** For each main point that you identify, use the SEE technique to add depth to your essay. Write a sentence. Then, elaborate on the idea. Finally, extend the elaboration.

### Student Model: Using SEE to elaborate and extend

**Statement:** Many people say that cell phones cause a disturbance.

**Elaboration:** You cannot go on a train or be in a mall without constantly hearing people's phones ring and their conversations.

**Extension:** The effect of this is that more people are feeling stressed, and their lives are disrupted by cell phones.

> The writer states the main point, elaborates on it with examples, and extends it by explaining the effect.

# Revising—Make It Better

Make your essay interesting and precise by revising your sentence structure. Look for sentences that can be expanded or combined by using participles or participial phrases at either the beginning or the end.

| We walked along the boardwalk. We saw many types of birds. | Walking along the boardwalk, we saw many types of birds. |
|---|---|

*Peer Review* Ask for a partner's response to your cause-and-effect essay. Revise to achieve the reaction you had intended.

**Directions** Read this student's cause-and-effect essay as a model for your own.

**Student Model: Writing**

*Sarah Langsam, South Orange, NJ*

## The Invention of Cell Phones

Imagine our world today without cell phones. This portable way of communicating is a part of many people's everyday lives. If we did not have cell phones, moms would not be able to call from the store, more kids might have trouble staying in touch, and emergencies would be harder to report.

However, people did, and still do, manage without them. Cell phones weren't invented that long ago. In 1973, Dr. Martin Cooper invented the first portable handset and soon after created the first prototype of a cellular phone. Four years later, cell phones became available to the public and cell phone testing began.

What effect has the invention of cell phones had on the world? With everything in life there are pros and cons. Today, most teenagers own cell phones. This means there is no excuse for not letting a parent or guardian know where you are . . . .

Many people say that cell phones cause a disturbance. You cannot go on a train or shop in a mall without constantly hearing people's phones ring and listening to other people's conversations. The effect of this is that more people are stressed, and their lives are disrupted by cell phones. A teacher in school left her cell phone at school over the weekend. She was in the office on Monday recalling her story angrily, reporting that it was an awful experience and that she could not function without her phone.

Although there are many negative aspects of cell phones, these items have also caused our world to be more secure. If you ask people why they first bought their cell phone, many will mention safety. Cell phones are very effective when people get into car accidents and can call "911" immediately. Parents can always know where their kids are.

The invention of cell phones has changed our lives immensely. There are positive and negative effects. However, despite the nuisance some cell phones present, I believe the safety issues cell phones solve can make us all feel a little more secure.

The writer defines her topic in the first paragraph.

The writer uses facts in explanation.

Here, the writer restates her topic and begins to support it with examples.

The writer gives an example to show that cell phones can be disruptive.

In the conclusion, the writer sums up the effects of cell phones.

# Editing—Be Your Own Language Coach

Before you hand in your cause-and-effect essay, review it for language convention errors and effective organization. Pay attention to your use of participles and participial phrases.

# Publishing—Share It!

When you publish a work, you produce it for a specific audience. Consider one of the following ideas to share your writing.

**Present a diagram.** On a poster board or an overhead slide, create a diagram of the cause-and-effect chain in your essay. Read your essay aloud, pointing to appropriate parts of the diagram as you go.

**Produce a talk show.** With a partner, take turns being a talk show host and a guest expert. Answer questions about your topic. Then, ask questions about your partner's topic.

# Reflecting On Your Writing

**Rubric for Self-Assessment** Assess your essay. For each question, circle a rating.

| CRITERIA | RATING SCALE | | | | |
|---|---|---|---|---|---|
| | NOT VERY | | | | VERY |
| **IDEAS** Is your paper clear and focused, with rich details? | 1 | 2 | 3 | 4 | 5 |
| **ORGANIZATION** How well do you employ a clear and logical organization? | 1 | 2 | 3 | 4 | 5 |
| **VOICE** Is your writing lively and engaging, drawing the reader in? | 1 | 2 | 3 | 4 | 5 |
| **WORD CHOICE** How appropriate is the language for your audience? | 1 | 2 | 3 | 4 | 5 |
| **SENTENCE FLUENCY** How varied is your sentence structure? | 1 | 2 | 3 | 4 | 5 |
| **CONVENTIONS** How correct is your grammar, especially your use of participles and participial phrases? | 1 | 2 | 3 | 4 | 5 |

Now that you have completed reading your Anchor Book, it's time to get creative! Choose one of the following projects.

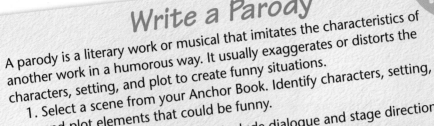

## Write a Parody

**A**

A parody is a literary work or musical that imitates the characteristics of another work in a humorous way. It usually exaggerates or distorts the characters, setting, and plot to create funny situations.

1. Select a scene from your Anchor Book. Identify characters, setting, and plot elements that could be funny.

2. Write your parody as a script. Include dialogue and stage directions.

3. Read your parody to a partner. Ask your partner if any necessary information is missing or unclear.

Your plan should include the following elements.

▶ notes on your scene selection

▶ a focused script with dialogue and stage directions

▶ a revised script that may include your partner's comments

## Rewrite the Ending

**B**

A comedy and a tragedy can both be about serious issues. One major difference between the two types of dramas is that a comedy has a happy ending and a tragedy does not. Decide whether your Anchor Book is a comedy or a tragedy. Then, rewrite the ending to reflect the opposite type of drama.

1. Is your Anchor Book a comedy or tragedy? Briefly describe the conflict and tell if it is presented in a funny way or in a serious way. Tell how the conflict is resolved and which characters are involved.

2. Use your imagination and your notes about the conflict and characters. Rewrite the ending of your Anchor Book so it reflects the opposite type of drama. Be sure to include elements of either a comedy or a tragedy.

Your ending should include the following elements.

▶ A thoughtful analysis of the conflict and the characters.

▶ An imaginative, rewritten ending that reflects your analysis and the drama chosen

▶ Error-free writing

after reading your anchor book

# Be a Film Critic

A film critic is someone who watches films and writes reviews about them for a living.

1. Write a list of questions about your Anchor Book that are important and interesting to you.

2. Watch a film version of your Anchor Book, analyzing the film's characters, plot, and theme.

3. Think about how the film answers any questions you have about your Anchor Book.

4. Write a review, comparing and contrasting your Anchor Book and the film. Did your film accurately present the characters, setting, and plot? Did the film provide an additional insight into or leave out important parts of the book?

Your project should include the following elements.

► A list of questions you have about your Anchor Book

► A review comparing and contrasting the book and its film version

## Free-Choice Book Reflection

You have completed your free-choice book. Before you take your test, read the following instructions to write a brief reflection of your book.

My free-choice book is _____.

The author is _____.

**1** Would you recommend this book to a friend?  Yes _____   No _____

Briefly explain why.

_____

_____

**Write and Discuss**  Answer the following question in your Reader's Journal. Then, discuss your answer with a partner.

**2**  **Compare and Contrast** *Do others really see us more clearly than we see ourselves?* Compare and contrast how your Anchor Book and free-choice book help to answer this question. Use specific details from both books to support your answer.

Answer the questions below to check your understanding of this unit's skills.

## Reading Skills: Setting a Purpose

**Directions** Read this passage. Then answer the questions that follow.

> You can't help but notice Hillary Cole. First of all, she's tall—and not just for a girl. At 6 foot 1, she towers over many of the senior boys at Pelham High. She walks with shoulders thrust back and head held high. And Hillary does not do beige. No muted wardrobe for her—Hillary's fashion color palette includes fuschia, tangerine, and turquoise. Topping her off is a mass of shiny copper curls. No, you can't miss Hillary Cole.

**1** How does the first sentence help set a **purpose for reading?**

   **A.** It tells readers the passage is about a celebrity.

   **B.** It makes readers curious about Hillary Cole.

   **C.** It tells readers the passage will be humorous.

   **D.** It lets readers know that Hillary Cole is a fantasy character.

**2** Which is the most valid **purpose for reading** this passage?

   **F.** to discover facts about a real person

   **G.** to compare and contrast two characters

   **H.** to find out why Hillary Cole inspires others

   **J.** to learn what makes Hillary Cole so interesting

## Reading Skills: Cause and Effect

Read this passage. Then answer the questions that follow.

> Porcupine trotted along the pine-needle path, sniffing the earthy scents of May. Sun winked in and out of the leaves, throwing spots of shadow on the forest floor. His mind on the glorious day, Porcupine suddenly tripped, rolling off the path and into a shallow puddle. "What was that?" he exclaimed, glancing quickly around. He hoped no one had witnessed his clumsiness. "Wait a minute . . ." he said. There, in the middle of the path, sat a small round rock. Shaking off puddle water, he climbed back onto the path—just as the rock began to uncurl. "Hedgehog!" Porcupine knew that Hedgehog only curled into a ball to fool predators. "Quick!" Hedgehog shouted. "We need to hide!"

**3** Why did Porcupine fall and tumble off the path?

   A. He was distracted by the glorious day.

   B. His mind was on predators.

   C. He stepped into a puddle.

   D. He was avoiding pine needles.

**4** Porcupine's fall made him feel _____.

   F. angry at Hedgehog

   G. afraid of predators

   H. fearful of getting lost

   J. embarrassed at his clumsiness

## Literary Analysis: Elements of Drama

Choose the best answer for the following questions.

**5** A **dramatization** is _____.

   A. an emotional event

   B. a scene from a play

   C. a play adapted from another source

   D. a speech by a central character

**6** **Character motivation** is _____.

   F. an introduction to a character's personality

   G. the reason for a character's actions

   H. a description of a character's traits

   J. an unusual action displayed by a character

Read this scene and answer the questions that follow.

> *(Setting is a park. A bench and a tree are nearby. Sound effects: birds chirping, kids calling out to one another, cars honking. CARLA and BOB enter.)*
>
> **CARLA:** I'm not arguing. I just want to discuss it. *(BOB rolls his eyes and sighs.)*
>
> **CARLA:** *(still standing)* Kenny is our little brother. Why did you tell him he stinks at shooting hoops?
>
> **BOB:** *(through clenched teeth)* Because he does. *(He looks offstage suddenly and begins to walk off.)*
>
> **CARLA:** Where are you going? *(She looks offstage as KENNY enters.)*
>
> **BOB:** *(exiting)* Home!

**7** What does the **dialogue** suggest about Carla?

   A. She does not want to sit down.

   B. She likes Kenny better than Bob.

   C. She is concerned about Kenny.

   D. She is in a hurry to get home.

**8** Which **stage direction** tells readers that Bob is angry?

   F. *exiting*

   G. *He looks offstage suddenly*

   H. *through clenched teeth*

   J. *still standing*

**9** What do the **stage directions** and **dialogue** reveal about Carla and Bob?

_____

_____

_____

_____

_____

_____

**10** What **motivates** Bob to leave the park?

A. He is mad at Carla.

B. He sees Kenny coming.

C. He wants to go home.

D. He thinks the park is noisy.

**11** An important aspect of **characterization** is (are) _____.

F. set and props

G. stage directions

H. character motivation

J. dialogue

## Language Skills: Vocabulary

Choose the best answer.

**12** Choose the **synonym** for the underlined word in this sentence.

Jean felt <u>clumsy</u> walking in her mom's high heels.

A. stylish

B. awkward

C. balanced

D. graceful

**13** Choose the **antonym** for the underlined word in this sentence.

Dana would need to be <u>sneaky</u> to ensure the party was a surprise.

F. careful

G. skillful

H. scheming

J. straightforward

**14** What meaning for the **homonym** _might_ is used in this sentence?

Dan marveled at the <u>might</u> of the weight lifter.

A. weakness

B. possibility

C. strength

D. rule

**15** Complete the following sentence with the correct **homophone.**

He used a map to get back on _____.

F. coarse

G. curse

H. course

J. chord

# Language Skills: Spelling

Circle the letter of the word that completes each sentence correctly.

**16** Kim didn't want her knee injury to _____ her performance.

    **A.** afect

    **B.** affect

    **C.** effect

    **D.** efect

**17** I don't think _____ going to like this.

    **F.** you're

    **G.** your

    **H.** yore

    **J.** your'e

**18** Celia and Jon finished _____ project.

    **A.** they're

    **B.** there

    **C.** their

    **D.** thier

**19** Dad never let the toddler out of his _____.

    **F.** site

    **G.** cite

    **H.** sight

    **J.** cight

# Language Skills: Grammar

Choose the best answer.

**20** In which sentence is the **participle** underlined?

    **A.** Writing, Beth <u>didn't</u> notice the bell.

    **B.** <u>Writing</u>, Beth didn't notice the bell.

    **C.** Writing, Beth didn't <u>notice</u> the bell.

    **D.** Writing, Beth didn't notice the <u>bell</u>.

**21** Which sentence contains a **dangling modifier?**

    **F.** Finishing work, dinner was made.

    **G.** After finishing work, Ben made dinner.

    **H.** After work, Ben made dinner.

    **J.** Work was finished, and so was dinner.

**22** Which of the following sentences uses **formal language?**

    **A.** Hey, I apologize for my bad moves at soccer today!

    **B.** I'm totally sorry my game was off at soccer today.

    **C.** I regret that my play during the game today was not sharp.

    **D.** My soccer moves stunk today.

**23** In which of these situations would you most likely use **informal language?**

    **F.** a history paper

    **G.** a speech

    **H.** a letter of complaint

    **J.** a radio commerical

# *Community* or *individual*: which is more important?

## [Uni]t 6 Genre focus:
## [Th]e Research Process

### [A]nchor Book
[…]e many good books that
[…]ork well to support both
[…]Question and the genre
[…]this unit. In this unit you
[…] one of these books as
[…]chor Book. Your teacher
[…]oduce the book you will
[…]ng.

### Free-Choice Reading
Later in this unit you will be
given the opportunity to choose
another book to read. This is
called your free-choice book.

Conducting research is not only a chance for you to become an expert on a topic but also allows you to share your expertise with the world.

## Group Activity

Read aloud the following informational excerpts from "The Black Blizzards" and "Chico Mendes and the Amazon Rain Forest" in a small group. Then, discuss what topics these excerpts could help you research, and answer the following questions.

### from "The Black Blizzards"

During most of the 1930s, the Great Plains region was devastated by drought and high winds. Howling across the Great Plains, these winds whipped up the soil of the over-farmed land and created blizzards of dust. These "black blizzards" were so thick and blinding that daylight seemed more like dusk. Year after year passed without rain, the winds continued to blow, and the dust swirled endlessly. During the terrible period the region came to be called the Dust Bowl.

But the cause of the dust blizzards wasn't just drought and wind. In a strange way patriotism was partly to blame. During World War I, the U.S. government encouraged farmers to support the war effort by planting more wheat. Farmers were eager to do their part to help feed the soldiers overseas. As farmers increased their production, their own profits increased. Following the invention of the farm tractor, farmers plowed up thousands of acres of grassland and planted wheat. Wheat production skyrocketed, but nature soon turned success into disaster.

What topics could "The Black Blizzards" help you research? What keywords are related to each of these topics?

_____

_____

_____

## from "Chico Mendes and the Amazon Rain Forest"

Mendes was born into a family of rubber tappers living and working in Brazil's Amazon rain forest. Rubber tappers cut slits in the bark of rubber trees and collect the latex sap that oozes out. Tapping trees does not kill or injure trees.

In the 1970s, the Brazilian government started opening the rain forest to development. Developers use vast fires in their "slash-and-burn" clearing method that release huge quantities of carbon dioxide, eliminating the plant life that consumes this heat-trapping gas. Deforestation contributes to the greenhouse effect threatening to alter Earth's climate through global warming.

Realizing the rain forest was in danger, Mendes created a rural workers' union. Mendes used nonviolence to block deforestation. Whenever work crews threatened the land, Mendes called together rubber trappers to form a human barrier. These peaceful blockades are estimated to have saved three million acres of rain forest.

Mendes wanted large sections of the rain forest set aside only for harvesting renewable resources, such as rubber. He also helped persuade the Inter-American Development Bank to stop a highway extension through the rain forest. As a result of Mendes's efforts—and the international fame and support he was beginning to receive—the Brazilian government finally designated five million acres of rain forest for permanent preservation.

What topics could "Chico Mendes and the Amazon Rain Forest" help you research? What keywords are related to each of these topics?

_____

_____

Which topic would this excerpt be the best source for? Explain why.

_____

_____

Notice that you used a text feature—the title—to help you identify the main topic in the excerpts. Always review text features when previewing sources for your research to determine if the source will help you with your topic.

## Community or individual: which is more important?

A community is a group of people who have something in common with one another. Your classroom, school, family, neighborhood, or spiritual communities are just a few that you may be a member of. What happens when you and your community have different goals? How can you decide whose goals are more important?

As individuals, we all have free will, which is the ability to make our own decisions. As members of a community, we are also responsible to one another. Every individual's life is a balance between free will and responsibility to the community.

**Directions** On your own, define ways in which you have free will and ways in which you are responsible to a community.

**I show free will by**

**I show that I am responsible to a community by**

before reading your anchor book

**Directions** Read and discuss the following scenario with a partner. Consider the question, *Community or individual: which is more important?*, while answering the questions that follow.

### Scenario

A town wants to build a new highway, which would benefit its economy. One resident protests because the highway would tear up his yard.

### Look at the scenario from both sides.

**Why is the town (community) right?**

**Why is the resident (individual) right?**

**Is there a solution that could make both the individual and the community happy?**

**Why or why not?**

**What is the right thing to do in this situation?**

When answering the question, *Community or individual: which is more important?*, it is helpful to consider from whose point of view you are looking. When reading your Anchor Book, you might encounter a character whose decisions differ from his or her community. Yet, you might agree with the character because you have learned so much about his or her life.

In this unit you will learn about the research process. Consider exploring the idea of community when writing your research project.

 As you read your Anchor Book and related readings, think about the relationship between the individual and the community and how you can determine which, if either, is more important.

 **Getting Ready for Your Anchor Book**

*You will start reading your Anchor Book soon. The next few pages in this book give you some background information plus a reading skill.*

# Introduction to the
# Research Process

In past centuries, explorers sailed around the world to discover new places and peoples. In today's modern world, there exists another type of person in search of new discoveries—the researcher.

## What Is Research?

**Research** is a process of investigation. It affects the way we live by improving and expanding our understanding of the world. Many fields, including business, science, and even art, have researchers investigating topics to understand more about them.

Think of a subject that interests you. What is the subject, and what would you like to learn about it?

_____

Researching a subject requires gathering information about it. Researchers write **research papers** to present the information they have discovered.

# How Do I Begin My Research?

You will write a research report of four to eight pages, depending on your choice of topic and your teacher's expectations. Pick an interesting topic that you will enjoy learning about.

## Steps in the Research Process

The main steps involved in writing a research report are *choosing a topic, researching, drafting, revising,* and *publishing.* Each will be discussed in this unit. Use the following schedule to help you plan your report.

### Choosing a Topic (Lesson 6-4)

Choose a topic and narrow it down so it is not too difficult to research.

Date Due _____     Date Completed _____

### Researching (Lessons 6-5 and 6-6)

Gather information and take notes from primary and secondary sources.

Date Due _____     Date Completed _____

### Drafting (Lesson 6-11)

- Develop a thesis statement.
- Write your first draft.
- Organize your ideas in an outline.
- Cite your sources accurately.

Date Due _____     Date Completed _____

### Revising (Lesson 6-12)

- Clarify your message. Get rid of unnecessary information.
- Seek advice from your teacher or family members on how to improve your paper.

Date Due _____     Date Completed _____

### Publishing (Lesson 6-13)

Present your final draft.

Date Due _____     Date Completed _____

# 6-2 Reading Skills
## Compare and Contrast

In learning new reading skills, you will use special academic vocabulary. Knowing the right words will help you demonstrate your understanding.

### Academic Vocabulary

| Word | Meaning | Example Sentence |
|------|---------|------------------|
| **contrast** *v.*<br>*Related words:*<br>contrasting, contrastable | compare in a way to find differences | The boy's messy hair *contrasts* with his clean clothing. |
| **reveal** *v.*<br>*Related word:*<br>revelation, revealing | make known to others | Jason will not *reveal* the location of his favorite fishing spot. |
| **characteristic** *n.*<br>*Related words:*<br>character, characterize | a feature that describes a person, place, or thing | Cuteness is one *characteristic* that is shared by most puppies. |

From differences between sports to similarities in cars, people make comparisons every day. Thinking about how things are alike and different **reveals** important information about a selection and helps you remember the text.

► A **comparison** tells how two or more people, things, or ideas are alike.

► A **contrast** tells how two or more people, things, or ideas are different.

**Directions** Preview the questions below before reading the selection.

**1** **Contrast** What **characteristics** of hybrid dogs and mutts are different?

_____

_____

**2** **Evaluate** How do the graph and chart help you compare and contrast the two types of mixed breed dogs?

_____

_____

# Which Dog to Choose: Hybrid or Mutt?

What's in a mutt? One never knows for sure. A mutt is a mixed breed dog that is not purebred. Most mixed breed dogs have unknown backgrounds. Through no fault of their own, they often end up in shelters or rescue situations.

Many people would rather have a mixed breed dog, because it has a better chance of being healthy. Purebred dogs often inherit disorders such as blindness, hip problems, and bad knees. About one fourth of all purebred dogs inherit one undesirable disorder.

Now there are other mixed breed dogs that are taking the country by storm. These new dogs are called "hybrids" or "designer dogs." These dogs are no accidents, and their parents are purebreds. These new hybrids include dogs like the puggle (half pug, half beagle), the schnoodle (half schnauzer, half poodle), or the morkie (half Yorkie, half maltese).

The hybrids have been created for consumers who want dogs that are cute, smart, and do not shed. (Dogs that do not shed are good for people with allergies.) Breeders have mixed shed-free and intelligent poodles with popular breeds prone to inherited disorders like Labrador retrievers, cocker spaniels, golden retrievers, schnauzers, and Yorkies. They come with names like labradoodles, cockapoos, goldendoodles, schnoodles, and yorkiepoos.

When choosing a dog, remember that all mixed breeds are not created equal. This chart might help you determine which dog is best for you.

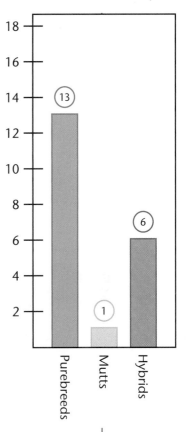

Occurrence of Inherited Disorders in Dogs 2008, Lakeville Township

| Mixed Breed Dogs | |
|---|---|
| **Hybrids** | **Mutts** |
| **Pros** | **Pros** |
| Can be shed-free | Can avoid inherited disorders |
| Can avoid inherited disorders | Low price |
| Parentage is known | Might save the life of an abandoned dog |
| Can be smart | |
| | **Cons** |
| **Cons** | Unknown inherited traits |
| No guarantee on inherited traits | Parentage unknown |
| High price | |

The following selection compares and contrasts two kinds of plays in Japan. *Guiding Question:* **In what ways do the Noh and Kabuki forms of drama appeal to the Japanese community?**

# Kabuki and Noh Plays

*An important part of Japanese culture are two forms of plays called Noh and Kabuki. This article explains the differences between the two.*

◀ **Above left,** A Kabuki performer in Japan, a man playing the role of a woman, is helped with his wig.
▲ **Above,** Women wear traditional attire as they dance during a Noh play in Kyoto, Japan.

Plays are an important form of entertainment in most countries. Two kinds of drama unique to Japan are Noh and Kabuki. Music is used in both types of drama. Originally, men performed both men's and women's parts in Noh and Kabuki plays. These are the only similarities between the two types.

Kabuki costumes are fancy, bright, and heavy. On the other hand, Noh costumes are quite simple. Kabuki stages are huge and elaborate. Noh stages are only 18 feet (5.4 meters) square. The only scenery used on a Noh stage is a background wall with a tree painted on it. The audience must use a lot of imagination.

Noh plays started in the fourteenth century to entertain the upper classes. All parts of a Noh play must follow a certain set of rules. A Noh actor may look as if he is sleepwalking. The action of the play is slow. Certain actions stand for certain things. For example, a few steps forward mean the end of a journey. An important part of a Noh play is the chorus that chants much of the story.

Kabuki plays were developed in the seventeenth century for the common people. Theater was the main amusement of the merchants of that time. The players wear thick makeup and exaggerate their movements and facial expressions to communicate feelings.

Music is important to Kabuki plays. Actors sing, dance, and speak to music in the background. Musicians play such instruments as flutes, drums, and gongs. They also use the *samisen,* a three-stringed instrument shaped somewhat like a banjo. Another common instrument consists of two small blocks of wood that are banged on the floor.

# Thinking About the Selection
## Kabuki and Noh Plays

**1** **Compare and Contrast** Reread the passage to clarify basic facts and ideas. Then complete the Venn diagram with characteristics showing how Noh and Kabuki plays are alike and different.

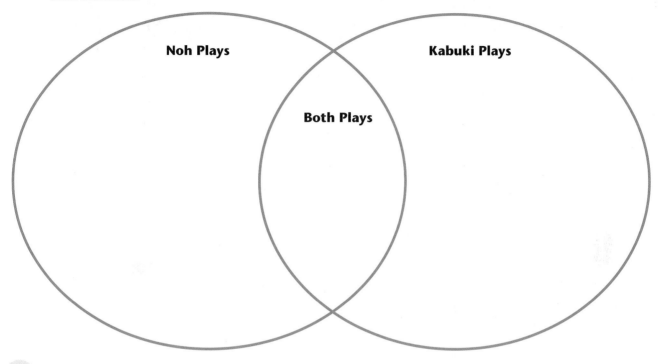

Noh Plays

Kabuki Plays

Both Plays

**2** **Analyze** What text features does the author use to compare and contrast the two play forms?

_____

_____

_____

_____

**3** **Infer** Which type of play is most like the plays you see on stage in the United States? Why?

_____

_____

_____

_____

**Write** Answer the following question in your Reader's Journal.

**4** **Analyze** In what ways do the Noh and Kabuki forms of drama appeal to the Japanese community?

# 6-3 Vocabulary Building Strategies
## Using a Dictionary

before reading your anchor book

You have used a dictionary to look up the meaning of a word, but dictionaries, among other references, aid in understanding more than just a word's meaning.

A word's **etymology** is its history. Etymology traces how a word's form has altered, usually from another language, to its current form. Knowing a word's etymology can help you understand other similar words, which in turn strengthens your vocabulary.

If you need to find a word's part of speech to clarify something you have read or written, use a dictionary.

Read this dictionary entry and answer the questions that follow.

> **sim • i • lar** [sĭm′ə lər] *adj* **1.** Being alike in appearance or nature, although not exactly the same; related. **2.** *Mathematics.* Having equal corresponding angle measures and proportional line segment lengths: *similar triangles.* [French *similaire*, from Latin *similis*, "like," Proto-Indo-European base *sem/som*, "same."]

A word's part of speech comes before the definition.

Definitions are indicated by numbers, the most common definition listed first.

A word's etymology traces its development from one language to another and often identifies its root.

**Directions** First, skim through the pages of this unit and identify three unfamiliar words. Add the words to the tables below. Then, use a dictionary to complete each row as in the student model.

**Student Model**

| word and part of speech | similar *adj.* |
| --- | --- |
| meaning | having characteristics in common |
| etymology | from Latin *similis* |
| related words | similarity, resemble |

| word and part of speech | |
| --- | --- |
| meaning | |
| etymology | |
| related words | |

| word and part of speech | |
|---|---|
| meaning | |
| etymology | |
| related words | |

| word and part of speech | |
|---|---|
| meaning | |
| etymology | |
| related words | |

You can also determine a word's etymology, meaning, and part of speech by using digital resources such as an online dictionary, a Web site on word origins, or a thesaurus.

**Directions** A dictionary is a great resource for information about unfamiliar words, but to make these words your own, you need to work with them. Complete a vocabulary map for one of the three new words.

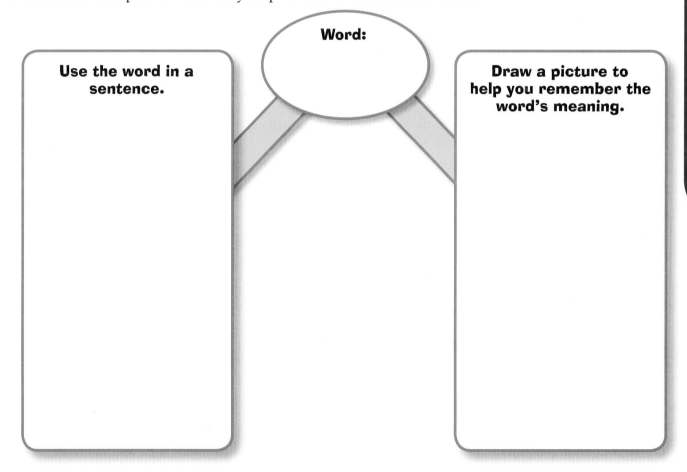

Word:

Use the word in a sentence.

Draw a picture to help you remember the word's meaning.

**Ready? Start Reading Your Anchor Book**

*It's time to get started. As you learn from this work text, your teacher will also give you reading assignments from your Anchor Book.*

# 6-4 The Research Process
## Choosing Your Topic

How do you choose a topic for a research report? Begin by thinking about the things that interest you the most—a famous person, an important scientific discovery, or even an issue you heard about on the news last night.

Use the strategies on this page to help choose a topic for your research report. Even if you already have a general topic area to work from, you can use these strategies to focus your ideas.

## Partner Activity

Interview a partner about his or her personal interests. Encourage your partner to be specific in his or her answers by asking questions like the ones below.

▸ What do you like most about _____?

▸ What have you always wondered about _____?

On a separate piece of paper, write down what your partner says. Then, your partner should interview you and record your answers.

Look over the notes your partner took about you and identify the most interesting topic.

## Free-Write

Free-writing is a strategy to help generate ideas. Give yourself five minutes. In the space below, list all the ideas that come to mind for the topic that is most interesting to you.

Topic _____

Ideas _____

_____

_____

_____

*while reading your anchor book*

# Narrowing Your Topic

Now that you have chosen a topic, you need to make sure it is specific enough to cover in a research report. How do you go about narrowing your focus?

In order to narrow your topic, first identify what you already know about the topic, and what you would like to learn.

| What Do I Already Know? | What Do I Want to Learn? |
| --- | --- |
| | |

Then, ask yourself questions about your topic.

Make sure that your questions are neither too narrow nor too broad.

**Too broad**   Who was Jesse Owens?

**Too narrow**   What year did he win the gold medal?

Use the question stems below to create two questions about your topic.

| Question Stems | |
| --- | --- |
| • How do/does/did… | • What causes/caused… |
| • What procedures or actions… | • What are/were the effects/results of… |
| • What problems… | • How/why did…decide to… |
| • What happens when… | • Who/what influenced…to… |
| • What is/was the role of … in … | • What is/was the relationship between …and… |
| • What is/was the difference between … and… | • How does/did …change… |

**Using a search engine** Use your questions to guide and focus your research. The picture below shows the first page of results of a student's Internet search. The student knew that *whales* was too broad a topic. He decided he wanted to answer the following questions. *How many different types of whales exist? How do they differ from one another?*

These questions helped the student narrow his search by using the keywords *whale* and *type* in a search engine.

**Directions** Study the results of this Internet search, and then answer the questions.

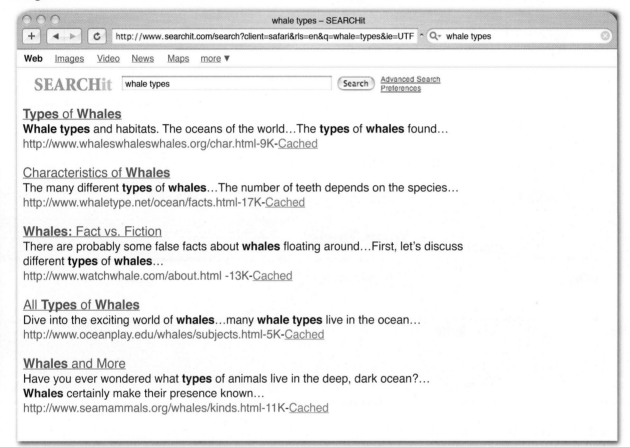

1 **Synthesize** Write two questions the student might ask to narrow the topic even further.

_____

_____

## Research

Now think about your own research report.

2 **Apply** Create a list of keywords for your topic that will help you focus an Internet search.

_____

_____

**Using a library catalog** You can search a library catalog by author, title, keyword, or subject. You can also specify what type of material you want, such as books, periodicals (magazines and newspapers), or DVDs.

The picture below shows the final results page of a student's library catalog search.

▶ First, the student did a keyword search using *whales*, but came up with too many results.

▶ Then, the student added the keyword *types*, but ended up with too few results.

▶ Finally, the student did a subject search on *whales*, searching for books and periodicals.

**Directions** Study this library catalog search page, and then answer the questions.

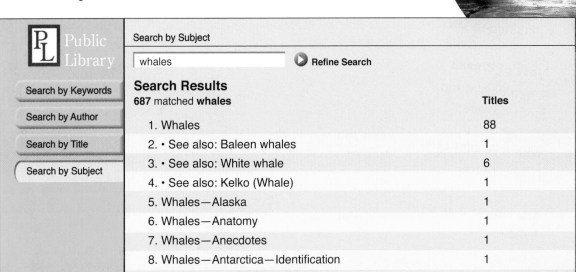

| Search by Subject | | |
|---|---|---|
| whales | ▶ Refine Search | |
| **Search Results** | | |
| **687** matched **whales** | | **Titles** |
| 1. Whales | | 88 |
| 2. • See also: Baleen whales | | 1 |
| 3. • See also: White whale | | 6 |
| 4. • See also: Kelko (Whale) | | 1 |
| 5. Whales—Alaska | | 1 |
| 6. Whales—Anatomy | | 1 |
| 7. Whales—Anecdotes | | 1 |
| 8. Whales—Antarctica—Identification | | 1 |

Search by Keywords
Search by Author
Search by Title
Search by Subject

**3** **Apply** Use the search results to identify a specific topic that is even narrower in focus than "types of whales."

_____

_____

## Research

Now think about your own research report.

**4** **Apply** Search your library catalog for books and periodicals related to your topic. Study the search results to look for ways to narrow your topic. Choose three ideas.

_____

_____

**Using a table of contents and index** Once you have searched the library catalog, analyzed the search results, and found a book on your topic, it's time to take a look at the book itself.

**Directions** This sample table of contents and partial index page come from a student's beginning research on the topic "types of whales." Study the materials. Then answer the questions.

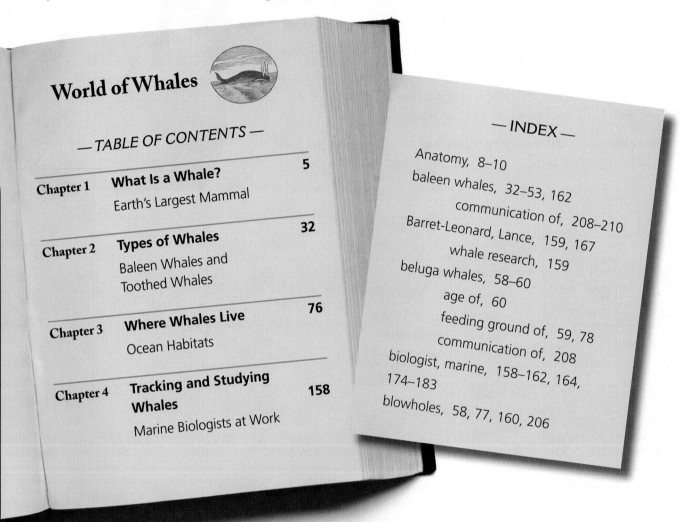

5   **Research** Study the table of contents. Which chapter might have information about the size of the beluga whale?

6   **Research** A student has become curious about how scientists study whales. How could she use the table of contents and index to find information on this topic?

# Thinking About the Research Process
## Choosing and Narrowing Your Topic

**1** **Analyze** The flow chart shows how a student narrowed a broad research topic. Complete the chart to show how this student could use the table of contents and index on the previous page to narrow the topic even further.

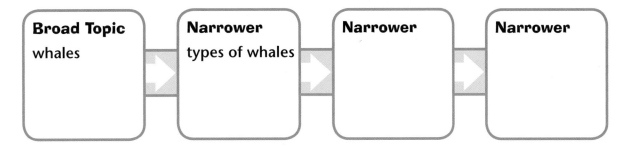

| Broad Topic | Narrower | Narrower | Narrower |
| --- | --- | --- | --- |
| whales | types of whales | | |

## Research

Now think about your own research report.

**2** **Organize** If you were about to do research to narrow your topic, which resource would you use first? Why?

_____

_____

_____

**3** **Synthesize** Use one of the strategies explained on page 464 to choose a broad topic for your research report. What topic did you choose?

_____

**4** **Apply** Narrow your topic by using the three research methods you learned in this lesson. Also, ask yourself two questions about your topic. Write your questions on a separate sheet of paper. Then, use the flow chart to show how you narrowed your topic.

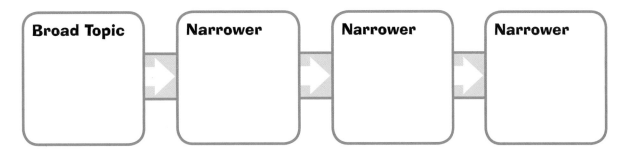

| Broad Topic | Narrower | Narrower | Narrower |
| --- | --- | --- | --- |
| | | | |

# 6-5 The Research Process
## Finding Reliable Sources

You need to figure out the bus schedule. You want to find out how your favorite team did last night. You need to learn more about a great new band you heard. How do you find the information you require? You will probably check a variety of sources, such as newspapers, magazines, and the Internet. These and other sources can also provide the information you need to write a research report.

**Directions** Read the two sources on whales. Then, answer the questions that follow.

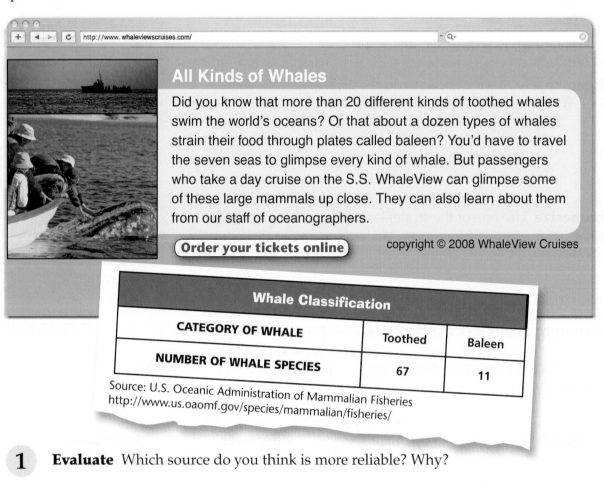

**All Kinds of Whales**

Did you know that more than 20 different kinds of toothed whales swim the world's oceans? Or that about a dozen types of whales strain their food through plates called baleen? You'd have to travel the seven seas to glimpse every kind of whale. But passengers who take a day cruise on the S.S. WhaleView can glimpse some of these large mammals up close. They can also learn about them from our staff of oceanographers.

Order your tickets online

copyright © 2008 WhaleView Cruises

| Whale Classification | | |
|---|---|---|
| CATEGORY OF WHALE | Toothed | Baleen |
| NUMBER OF WHALE SPECIES | 67 | 11 |

Source: U.S. Oceanic Administration of Mammalian Fisheries
http://www.us.oaomf.gov/species/mammalian/fisheries/

**1** **Evaluate** Which source do you think is more reliable? Why?

_____

_____

_____

**2**   What are some characteristics of a reliable source?

_____

_____

_____

## Think You Know a Good Source When You See One?

Use the guidelines below to help you evaluate the credibility, or reliability, of a source.

| Guidelines for Evaluating Sources |
|---|
| Make sure the information is **accurate.** Check the author's background to see if he or she is an expert on the topic. |
| Use more than one source to **verify,** or confirm, facts. If two sources contradict each other, check a third. Be particularly careful about checking Internet sources. |
| Check that the source is **unbiased,** or fair. Avoid sources whose authors might have a special interest in a topic—a reason to support a certain viewpoint. |
| Use information that is **current,** or up-to-date. Check the publication date of your source. For most topics, you want the most recent information available. |
| In addition to being reliable, your sources should apply, or be **relevant,** to your topic. Preview a book's table of contents, index, bibliography, introduction, and conclusion for references to your topic. |

Anyone can create a Web site. How can you tell which ones provide **credible,** or trustworthy, information?

▶ Look for sites whose addresses end with _.edu_ (educational institutions), _.gov_ (government agencies), or _.org_ (nonprofit organizations).

▶ Avoid most sites that end with _.com_ (commerical Web sites). Also avoid personal Web sites. If you are not sure, check the site's home page.

**3**   **Evaluate** Identify a Web site for your project. Think about the point of view, attitude, and opinions. Explain whether it is a reliable source or not.

_____

_____

_____

# Avoiding Plagiarism

Stealing someone's words or ideas, **plagiarism,** is against the law and if it is from a published source, then the theft is a violation of copyright law.

If you present someone else's words, ideas, opinions, or research as your own, then you are guilty of plagiarism. Plagiarism is academic stealing—a serious form of cheating. To avoid plagiarism and copyright infringement, take careful notes and always cite your sources.

► Enclose someone else's exact words in quotation marks so readers do not think those words are your own.

► Even when you paraphrase someone else's words, credit the original source if your wording or ideas are similar.

► Do not copy and paste the information into your notes from Internet sources. You might forget that those are not your own words.

◄ **Good to Know!**
Copyright infringement is the unauthorized reproduction of a copyrighted work.

**Directions** Compare the paragraphs, and then answer the question.

| AUTHOR'S PARAGRAPH | STUDENT'S PARAGRAPH |
|---|---|
| When a dead bowhead whale was examined in Barrow, Alaska, scientists discovered part of a lance embedded in a shoulder blade. Smaller than a pencil, this harpoon-tipped projectile contained distinct markings. These, along with an analysis of other features, indicated that the weapon was probably used around the year 1890 (New Bedford Whaling Museum). | In Barrow, Alaska, scientists examined a dead bowhead whale and found part of a lance embedded in its shoulder blade. This harpoon-tipped lance was smaller than a pencil. When the lance was analyzed, the scientists found distinct markings indicating that it was probably used around the year 1890. |
| **Works cited** **The New Bedford Whaling Museum,** "125-Year-Old New Bedford Bomb Fragment Found Embedded in Alaskan Bowhead Whale," 7 June 2007. <http://www.whalingmuseum.org>. | |

**Explain** Why is the student's paragraph an example of plagiarism? How could the student have avoided this problem?

---

while reading your anchor book

# Note Taking

Note-taking is a great resource not only for research, but also for self-monitoring your comprehension as you read.

## The Note-Taking Process

Following a careful note-taking method will help you credit your sources for the information you use. The steps are modeled below for one of the most common methods to take notes—using **note cards.**

Williams, Richard. <u>Whales</u>          2
New York: Seaport Press, 2001.

Williams, Richard   (p. 78)   Bowhead Traits      2
▸ Bowhead whale belongs to baleen category.
▸ Known as a "slow-moving" whale
▸ Has 350 pairs of baleen plates
▸ Baleen filters plankton and krill through open mouth.
▸ When eating, bowheads swim slowly, eating constantly.

Williams, Richard   (p. 75)   Bowhead Traits      2

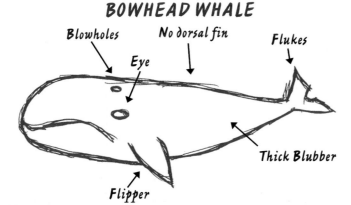

**BOWHEAD WHALE**

Blowholes    No dorsal fin    Flukes

Eye

Thick Blubber

Flipper

If an idea is confusing, check other sources for a clearer explanation.

**Create source cards**
Make one card for each source you use. Assign a number to each source card to help you organize your notes. Record essential information about each source: the title, author, publication date, and place of publication.

**Record each source**
As you take notes, record the source number after your note. Also, include the page number(s) where you found the information in your note.

**Record quotations**
When you copy exact words from a source, put them in quotation marks. Reread your quote and check it against the original text to make sure you recorded it accurately.

**Summarize information**
In your own words, write one main idea and its supporting details on each card.

**Use visual aids**
As you record information, include visuals such as charts, tables, graphs, and maps.

# Note-Taking Methods

Using note cards is just one of several popular methods of note taking. Use whichever method works best for you.

▶ Another way of taking notes is to create an **idea map.** Draw a cluster diagram of one main idea and its supporting details. Be sure to include the source you are taking your information from.

**Delong, Joan (p. 21)**

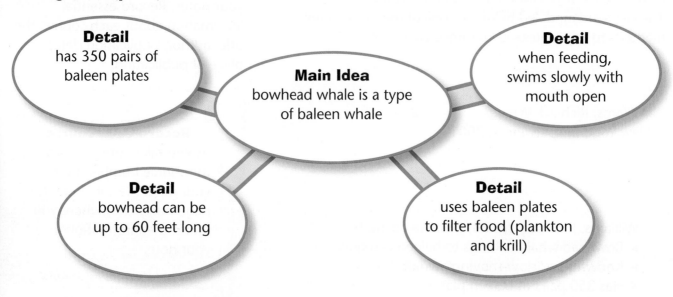

You can combine an idea map with other note-taking methods. For example, you can draw an idea map on an index card.

▶ A third way of taking notes is called the **Cornell method.** When you use this method, you take notes on a sheet of notebook paper divided into three sections.

Use the left column to write questions and key words.

Delong, Joan (p. 21)

**Prompts**
What are some other baleen whales?
What does baleen filter OUT?
Can't visualize it—find photo.

**Notes**
▶ Bowhead whales one of 15 types of baleen whales
▶ 350 pairs of baleen plates include fine, filtering hairs
▶ Eats by filtering plankton and krill through baleen
▶ Up to 60 feet long

Use the right column to take detailed notes on one source.

**Summary**
With its long "straining plates," the bowhead whale illustrates how all baleen whales eat by skimming and straining.

At the bottom, summarize your notes in one or two sentences.

while reading your anchor book

Now that you have learned about note-taking methods, practice taking notes on an article about a scientific discovery. *Guiding Question:* **How can the discovery of clues from the past help us understand our world and our community?**

# Clue from the past

What is the lifespan of a bowhead whale? If you asked a marine biologist this question, the answer would probably be, "Well, that's hard to say." Figuring out the age of a whale has been a mystery that has frustrated scientists—until recently. Now an unexpected clue has reached across time, providing experts with vital new information.

On May 26, 2007, wildlife biologist Craig George was observing a crew of Eskimo whale hunters in Barrow, Alaska, as they cut open a dead 50-ton bowhead whale. Suddenly, he saw them pull a fragment of a small pointed projectile from the layers of bone and blubber. The captain of the whaling crew, Arnold Brower, Sr., gave George the fragment because he knew it was an important scientific discovery. At the time, George had no idea of what he had stumbled upon. Scientists had analyzed weapon fragments before. But pinning down exactly when these projectiles had been fired into the whale was always tricky. Even if the weapon seemed old, experts had no way of telling exactly when it had been manufactured or used. Their luck was about to change.

George sent the fragment to John Bockstoce, a whaling historian at the New Bedford Whaling Museum in New Bedford, Massachusetts. Bockstoce identified the fragment as a piece of a type of exploding lance that had been made in New Bedford in the late 1800s. Bomb lances were a type of weapon used by whalers. Small metal cylinders were filled with explosives and then shot into the whale after the animal had been struck by a harpoon. A time-delay fuse caused the lance to explode inside the whale a

Use a note card to take notes on the first paragraph.

Use the Cornell method to take notes on the next three paragraphs. Use a separate sheet of paper.

▼ **Good to Know!**
This bomb lance fragment, patented in 1879, was removed from the neck of a bowhead whale captured at Barrow, Alaska, in May 2007. The shiny scars are the result of a saw cut.

Finding Reliable Sources, Avoiding Plagiarism, and Note Taking **475**

## Whale of a Tale

The recent discovery of a 19th-century bomb lance in a bowhead whale suggests the species may be able to live well over 100 years. The bowhead was hunted nearly to extinction in its native Arctic and subarctic water for its blubber, oil, and baleen.

Tail marking grows bigger and whiter with age

Layer of blubber up to 2 feet thick

50 to 60 feet

**Bowhead whale,** *balaena mysticentus*

▼ **Below**
A close up of baleen, which the bowhead whale uses to filter its food.

few seconds later. Bockstoce discovered that these fragments came from a lance that had been patented in 1879. The lance was discontinued in 1885, when improvements were made to the design. The news was incredible. The whale had likely been wounded sometime between 1885 and 1895. The whale was probably at least 112 years old.

Scientists can analyze the teeth of toothed whales, such as the orca and the sperm whale, to help them determine a whale's age. But the bowhead whale is a baleen whale. Baleen is a strainer-like device made of keratin, the same material that makes up our fingernails. The bowhead has 350 pairs of baleen plates, which are lined in bristly hair. These filter tiny plankton and krill as the whale feeds by skimming the water with an open mouth.

Because scientists cannot analyze the age of baleen, they have been trying to analyze bowheads by running a chemical analysis of the lenses in their eyes. However, this process is not precise, suggesting only that bowhead whales live between 100 and 150 years, and maybe longer. So finding the lance fragment was a significant development. Its ability to pinpoint the age of the whale is as precise as the aim of the whale hunter so many years ago.

▲ **Good to Know!**
Orcas can have between forty and fifty-six teeth in their mouths—each tooth around three inches long!

Use an idea map to take notes on the last paragraph. Use a separate sheet of paper.

while reading your anchor book

# Thinking About the Research Process
## Clue from the Past

**1** **Compare and Contrast** Which method of note taking did you find the easiest to use? Which was the hardest? Explain your answer.

_____

_____

_____

**2** **Evaluate** Which note-taking method helped you take the most complete notes? Explain your answer.

_____

_____

_____

**3** **Apply** Which method do you think you will use in your own research report? Why?

_____

_____

_____

## Research

Now think about your own research project.

**4** **Apply** Find a reliable source to use for your research report. Take notes on this source, using the methods you have decided will work best. Be sure to cite your source and to avoid plagiarism.

**Write** Answer the following questions in your Reader's Journal.

 **5** **Draw Conclusions** How can the discovery of clues from the past help us understand our world and our community?

 **6** **Connect** Do some research about the author or subject of your Anchor Book. If you were writing a research report on this topic, would your Anchor Book be a good source? Why or why not?

# 6-6 Research Process
## Primary and Secondary Sources

Now that you have learned how to evaluate the reliability and relevance of a source, it's time to learn another way to think about sources. Some are classified as **primary sources,** and others are classified as **secondary sources.**

Both primary and secondary sources can be reliable and relevant sources, but it is important to understand the difference.

▶ A **primary source** is an account of an experience written by a participant or an eyewitness. Here are some examples.

- Diaries and journals
- Letters
- Speeches
- Autobiographies and memoirs

▶ A **secondary source** is an account written by someone who was not a participant or an eyewitness. The writer of a secondary source pulls together ideas from different sources and often relies on primary sources for information. Here are some examples.

- Textbooks
- Encyclopedias
- Biographies
- History books

This chart shows a primary source and a secondary source. The primary source is a letter written by a Civil War soldier. The secondary source describes the letter and explains its significance.

| PRIMARY SOURCE | SECONDARY SOURCE |
|---|---|

Dear Miss Han. M. Cone

... I Have not Room to tell you any thing about our Expedition for it Would take about 20 Sheets of Paper to tell all But Suffice it to say that we Had a pretty Hard time & Sufferd considerable with Sickness & Done But little Damage only in the Destruction of Cotton & Property I Have See a great many large Buildings & Fencing Burned and any Amount of other Property taken ....

Respectfully yours Newton Scott

**N**ewton Robert Scott wrote a letter on April 9, 1863, to his friend Hannah Cone, whom he later married. Scott was a private in Company A of the 36th Infantry, Iowa Volunteers, during the Civil War. The letter described his company's march through Arkansas destroying "Cotton & Property." Scott's letters provide vivid details of the war and its hardships—the violence committed by both sides and the diseases that killed more men than bullets did.

**THE BIG ?**

Read this selection about the life of Dr. Martin Luther King, Jr. Then, compare it to the speech by King that follows.
*Guiding Question:* According to King, how does the American dream address the relationship between the community and the individual?

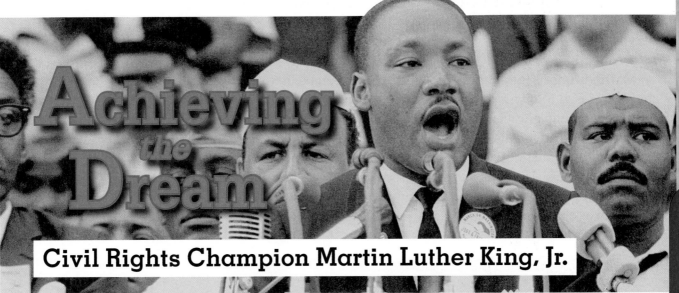

# Achieving the Dream

## Civil Rights Champion Martin Luther King, Jr.

while reading your anchor book

▲ In 1963, Martin Luther King, Jr. delivered his "I Have A Dream" speech in front of the Lincoln Memorial in Washington.

## Vocabulary Builder

**Before you read,** *you will discuss the following words. In the Vocabulary Builder box in the margin, use a vocabulary building strategy to make the words your own.*

prominence    assassinated    exploitation    trite

**As you read,** *draw a box around unfamiliar words you could add to your vocabulary. Use context clues to unlock their meaning.*

Dr. Martin Luther King, Jr., (1929–1968) first gained **prominence** as a civil right leader in 1955, when he led a boycott against the segregated bus system in Montgomery, Alabama. At least 17,000 African Americans took part in this nonviolent demonstration, refusing to ride the buses for more than a year. The boycott ended when the U.S. Supreme Court ruled that segregated buses were unconstitutional.

After the Montgomery Bus Boycott, King continued to lead boycotts, marches, and sit-ins to protest segregation, injustice, and the oppression of African Americans. He became known as the most eloquent and influential leader of the civil rights movement. King continued working to achieve his "dream of a land where men of all races, of all nationalities and of all creeds can live together as brothers," an idea he expressed in a 1961 graduation speech called "The American Dream."

### Marking the Text

#### Primary and Secondary Sources

As you read, *underline details in the biography that show what type of source it is. In the margin, write notes explaining what these details reveal.*

### Vocabulary Builder

**prominence**
(präm'ə nəns) *n.*

**Meaning**

King was arrested 30 times, most famously in April 1963 for protesting racial segregation in Birmingham, Alabama. A few months later, King led the massive March on Washington. More than 200,000 Americans gathered around the Lincoln Memorial and heard King deliver his "I Have a Dream" speech, in which he once again expressed his dream for America. "I have a dream that my four little children will one day live in a nation where they will not be judged by the color of their skin but by the content of their character."

Martin Luther King, Jr., was threatened and even beaten, but he refused to give up on his dream. He also continued to advocate nonviolent resistance as the best way to fight for that dream for all Americans. In 1964, at the age of 35, King was awarded the Nobel Peace Prize. Sadly, just four years later, he was **assassinated** in Memphis, Tennessee. Today we continue to honor King and his fight for civil rights by celebrating his birthday as a national holiday.

## Vocabulary Builder

**assassinated**
(ə sas' ə nā ted') *v.*

**Meaning**

◀ **Critical Viewing**
What does this photo reveal about the struggles Martin Luther King, Jr. faced during the civil rights movement?

Now that you have read a brief biography of Martin Luther King, Jr., read this speech by King to compare a primary and a secondary source.

from

# The American Dream

## by Martin Luther King, Jr.

**Background** *Dr. Martin Luther King, Jr., delivered this speech on June 6, 1961, as a graduation address at Lincoln University in Pennsylvania. King is best known for his "I Have a Dream" speech, delivered two years later, but this speech explores a similar theme. As you read, think about what King is trying to persuade his audience to do or believe.*

America is essentially a dream, a dream as yet unfulfilled. It is a dream of a land where men of all races, of all nationalities and of all creeds[1] can live together as brothers. The substance of the dream is expressed in these sublime words, words lifted to cosmic proportions: "We hold these truths to be self-evident, that all men are created equal, that they are endowed by their Creator with certain unalienable rights, that among these are life, liberty, and pursuit of happiness."[2] This is the dream.

One of the first things we notice in this dream is an amazing universalism. It does not say some men, but it says all men. It does not say all white men, but it says all men, which includes black men. It does not say all Gentiles[3], but it says all men, which includes Jews. It does not say all Protestants, but it says all men, which includes Catholics.

**Marking the Text**

**Primary and Secondary Sources**

As you read, *underline details in the speech that show what type of source it is. In the margin, write notes explaining what these details reveal.*

*while reading your anchor book*

---

[1] **creeds** *n.* systems of belief.

[2] **"We hold these truths . . . pursuit of happiness."** opening words of the Declaration of Independence.

[3] **Gentiles** (jen'tīlz) *n.* people who are not Jewish.

And there is another thing we see in this dream that ultimately distinguishes democracy and our form of government from all of the totalitarian regimes[4] that emerge in history. It says that each individual has certain basic rights that are neither conferred by nor derived from the state. To discover where they came from it is necessary to move back behind the dim mist of eternity, for they are God-given. Very seldom if ever in the history of the world has a sociopolitical document expressed in such profoundly eloquent and unequivocal[5] language the dignity and the worth of human personality. The American dream reminds us that every man is heir to the legacy of worthiness.

Ever since the Founding Fathers of our nation dreamed this noble dream, America has been something of a schizophrenic[6] personality, tragically divided against herself. On the one hand we have proudly professed the principles of democracy, and on the other hand we have sadly practiced the very antithesis[7] of those principles. Indeed slavery and segregation have been strange paradoxes[8] in a nation founded on the principle that all men are created equal. This is what the Swedish sociologist, Gunnar Myrdal, referred to as the American dilemma.

But the shape of the world today does not permit us the luxury of an anemic[9] democracy. The price America must pay for the continued **exploitation** of the Negro and other minority groups is the price of its own destruction. The hour is late; the clock of destiny is ticking out. It is **trite,** but urgently true, that if America is to remain a first-class nation she can no longer have second-class citizens. Now, more than ever before, America is challenged to bring her noble dream into reality, and those who are working to implement[10] the American dream are the true saviors of democracy.

[4] **totalitarian regimes** (tō tal ə târ′ ē ən ri zhēmz) countries in which those in power control every aspect of citizens' lives.

[5] **unequivocal** (un i kwiv′ ə kel) *adj.* clear; plainly understood.

[6] **schizophrenic** (skit sə fren′ ik) *adj.* characterized by a separation between the thought processes and emotions, popularly known as "split personality."

[7] **antithesis** (an tith′ ə sis) *n.* opposite.

[8] **paradoxes** (par′ ə dok′ siz) *n.* things that seem to contradict each other.

[9] **anemic** (ə nē′ mik) *adj.* weak.

[10] **implement** (im′ plə ment′) *v.* to put into effect.

while reading your anchor book

Vocabulary Builder

**exploitation** (eks′ploi tā′shən) *n.*

**Meaning**

**trite** (trīt) *adj.*

**Meaning**

◄ **Good to Know! Footnotes** Often define complex vocabulary, concepts, and allusions that help you better understand what you are reading.

Vocabulary Builder

**After you read,** *review the words you decided to add to your vocabulary. Write the meaning of words you have learned in context. Look up the other words in a dictionary, glossary, thesaurus, or electronic resource.*

# Thinking About the Research Process

## Achieving the Dream *and from* The American Dream

**About the Author**
Visit: PHSchool.com
Web Code: exe-7601

**1**   **Distinguish** Which of the two selections is a primary source? Which is a secondary source? Explain your answer.

_____

_____

_____

**2**   **Analyze** How is "Achieving the Dream" strengthened by the quotations from King's speeches in the second and third paragraphs?

_____

_____

**3**   **Interpret** What is the denotation of "America"? What are some connotations people associate with "America"? (See page 286)

_____

_____

_____

## Research

Now think about your own research project.

**4**   **Classify** Which of your sources are primary, and which are secondary? If all your sources are secondary, find a primary source and explain what new perspective it offers.

_____

_____

**Write** Answer the following questions in your Reader's Journal.

 **5**   **Interpret** According to King, how does the American dream address the relationship between the community and the individual?

 **6**   **Evaluate** Is your Anchor Book a primary or secondary source? Explain how you know.

while reading your anchor book

# 6-7 Analyzing an Informational Text
## Reading a Science Article

Science articles discuss advancements in fields such as biology, chemistry, and physics, and explain how the advancements affect human lives. These articles often use text features such as charts and illustrations to enhance the reader's understanding.

Set a purpose for reading by previewing the questions below, and the text features of the article about DNA fingerprinting on the following page. Read the text, noting how the text features strengthen your grasp of this complex process. Then answer the questions.

**1** **Explain** How does previewing the text features help you understand this article?

_____

_____

_____

**2** **Analyze** What is the author's purpose in writing this article?

_____

_____

_____

**3** **Evaluate** Which of the article's text features best explain the process of DNA fingerprinting? Explain your answer.

_____

_____

_____

**4** **Assess** How could you determine whether the article you read was accurate, credible, and current?

_____

_____

_____

_____

_____

while reading your anchor book

# DNA Fingerprinting

What do you have that no one else has? Unless you have an identical sibling, it's your DNA! Because a person's DNA is unique, it can act like a genetic "fingerprint." This is why scientists can study DNA and find out whose body it came from. Here's how they do it.

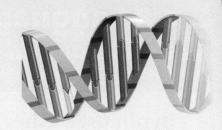

**1** After a sample of DNA is extracted from the body, an enzyme cuts the DNA strand into several smaller pieces.

T T C G | A A T T C G | A A T T C T G | A A T T C T A G | A A T T C G A A

4 bases    6 bases    7 bases    8 bases    8 bases

> Numbered steps break the processes into manageable parts.

DNA is made up of two base strands. This diagram shows an enzyme cutting one base strand of DNA after the G every time it encounters the DNA sequence GAATTC.

> Captions provide additional information that helps explain the text.

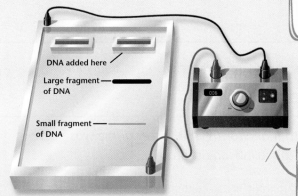

DNA added here

Large fragment of DNA

Small fragment of DNA

**2** The cut-up DNA fragments are loaded into a gel. Scientists use electric current to separate fragments. Larger fragments of DNA move through the gel more slowly than the smaller fragments.

> Diagrams clarify the text by showing ideas visually.

**3** Once the DNA fragments have separated, the gel is stained. The unique banded pattern is a DNA fingerprint.

> Subheadings help you prepare for a passage by introducing the subtopics.

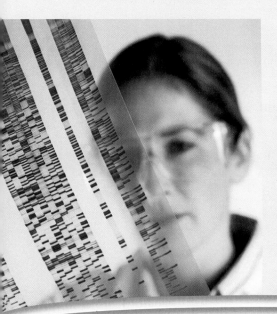

## Analyzing DNA

In one method of DNA analysis, DNA from saliva, blood, bones, teeth, or other fluids or tissues is taken from cells. Special enzymes cut the DNA into small pieces, which are put into a machine that sorts them by size, using an electric current. The DNA is stained and photographed, and a unique banded pattern, similar to a product bar code, is revealed. The pattern can be compared to other samples of DNA to determine a match.

## Hyphens/Dashes/Colons

**Hyphens** (-) are used to connect numbers and closely related words. They strengthen your writing by linking words together and eliminating confusion. Look at the following examples.

**Directions** Look at the following example. Then, write your own example for each rule on the line provided.

| Rule | Example |
| --- | --- |
| connecting compound numbers and fractions used as adjectives | *Helen's grandfather is seventy-three years old.* |
| linking prefixes *all-*, *ex-*, and *self-* to words | *All-powerful; ex-member of the student council* |
| linking a compound modifier to a noun, when the modifier comes before the noun | *The well-groomed Great Dane won the dog show.* |
| breaking a word at the end of a line | *Due to the thunderstorms, the soccer game was post-poned until the following Saturday.* |

**Dashes** (—) are used to emphasize a main idea or show a quick change of thought. Unlike hyphens, dashes look longer and are used between words.

**Example:** Let's invite Hosea—he just moved in next door to me.

**Colons** (:) are used before a list of items that follows an independent clause.

**Example:** The recipe requires the following ingredients: rice, cumin, shrimp, and beans.

**Directions** Revise each sentence, adding dashes or colons.

**1** We went to the party last Friday it was a blast!

_____

**2** She plays four sports soccer, basketball, baseball, and track.

_____

# Capitalization

You know you need to capitalize the first word of a sentence and proper nouns, but there are other instances when capitalization is necessary.

**Go Online**

**Learn More**
Visit: PHSchool.com
Web Code: exp-7602

## Historical Events and Documents

Capitalize significant events in history, such as battles and wars, as well as eras, such as the Renaissance.

| Historical Events and Documents | |
| --- | --- |
| the Industrial Revolution | the Classical Era |
| the War of 1812 | the Constitution |

## Regional Names

Capitalize names of countries, states, state abbreviations, counties, cities, and towns, as well as parks and landmarks.

| Regional Names | Landmarks |
| --- | --- |
| Sarasota, Florida | the North Bridge |
| Duchess County, NY | Arches National Park |

## Lists and Outlines

Capitalize the first word of each item in an outline or a numbered list.

| Numbered List | Outline |
| --- | --- |
| Some uses of capitalization include:<br>1. Historical events and eras<br>2. Regional names<br>3. Numbered lists | I. Island Nations<br>  A. Indonesia<br>    1. Geography<br>    2. Culture<br>  B. Fiji |

**Author's Craft**

With a partner, select a nonfiction passage that you have read in this book. Locate all the capitalized words that do not start a sentence. Discuss with your partner why each word is capitalized. Are there any types of words that are not capitalized, but which you think should be? Why?

**Directions** Rewrite the following text, adding proper capitalization.

**1** How far is orange county from san francisco?

_____

**2**

To do before winter vacation:

1. collect money for fundraiser

2. complete project on civil war

To do before winter vacation:

1. _____

2. _____

A **compare-and-contrast essay** analyzes the similarities and differences between two or more related subjects. Use the steps in this workshop to write your own essay discussing how a selection you have read compares and contrasts with your own personal life, values, beliefs, traditions, or experiences.

To be effective, your essay should include the following elements.

► Discussion of a selection that you can compare and contrast with your experiences

► Details illustrating both similarities and differences

► Clear organization highlighting the points of comparison

► Error-free writing, including correct use of punctuation and capitalization

**Purpose** To write an essay discussing how a selection compares and contrasts with your own life

**Audience** You, your teacher, and your classmates

## Prewriting—Plan It Out

Use the following strategies to help you write your essay.

**Gather details.** Choose a selection that deals with topics you have encountered in your life. Use the following **Venn diagram** to compile details that show similarities and differences between how the selection discusses a topic and your experience.

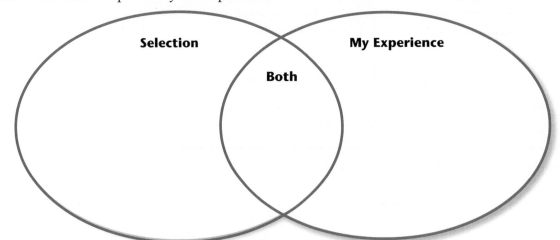

Identify your topic and perspective. Look at the student example. Then, write a topic statement for your own essay.

**Example** "An Hour With Abuelo" treats the distance between generations as something to be expected. My experience contradicts this view, because my grandmother is my good friend.

# Drafting—Get It on Paper

Use your Venn diagram to write your draft. Choose one of the following methods of organization.

► **Block Method** Present all the details about one topic first, and then present all the details about the second topic. The block method works well if you are writing about different types of details.

► **Point-by-Point Method** Discuss one aspect of both subjects, then another, and so on. For example, if you are comparing a truck to a car, you might first discuss the size of each one, then their prices, and so on.

### Block Method

A. "An Hour With Abuelo"
  1. Grandfather is an immigrant
  2. Abuelo and Arturo are distant
  3. Abuelo's past
B. My experience
  1. Grandmother is an immigrant
  2. My grandmother and I are close
  3. My grandmother's stories

### Point-by-Point Method

A. Immigrant grandparents
  1. Abuelo
  2. My grandmother
B. Relationships between generations
  1. Abuelo and Arturo are distant.
  2. My grandmother and I are close.
C. Sharing experience
  1. Abuelo's past
  2. My grandmother's stories

**Clarify relationships.** Use **transition words** that clearly state the relationship between ideas.

| Words That Show Contrasts | *although, but, however, whereas, while* |
|---|---|
| Words That Show Comparisons | *also, just as, like, similarly* |

Write two sentences, the first with a transition word showing a contrast, the second with a transition word showing a comparison.

**1** Contrast: _____

**2** Comparison: _____

# Revising—Make It Better

Review your draft to make sure there is consistency in your structure, evidence, style, and voice.

***Peer Review***  Ask for a friend's, an adult's, or a group's response to your essay. Use the feedback to make revisions.

***Directions***  Read this student essay as a model for your own.

**Student Model: Writing**

Go Online

**Student Model**
Visit: PHSchool.com
Web Code: exr-7601

*Mackenzie Ames, Daytona Beach, FL*

## Stage vs. Set

Theater or television? If you are under eighteen, you more than likely said "television." Have you ever stopped to consider what the magical world of theater has to offer?

Anyone who has been to the theater can tell you that there is nothing like the feeling of sitting and watching people perform. Actors get something special out of theater, too. Knowing that hundreds of people are watching your every move creates a special kind of excitement.

There's also variety. In live theater, every show is different. When you watch a rerun on television, it's the exact same thing every time. With theater, you get a different experience every night. You can go to see the same show with a different cast or director and the performance will be totally different. Even if you go to a show with the same cast and director, it will be different. An actor might forget a line and improvise or suddenly decide to change the way he or she is playing a character in a scene. The audience never knows exactly what will happen.

Theater is also larger than the drama you see on television. I don't care how big a screen your television has, theater will always be BIGGER—the emotion more passionate, the voices louder, and the effect more profound. In theater, you have to project your voice and movements so that they carry to the back rows of the audience. In television, actors just need to be seen and heard by the cameras and microphones....

Next time you're channel surfing and there's nothing good on, why not take some time to check out what's playing in your community playhouse? Who knows? Maybe you'll discover a rising talent. Even better, maybe you'll decide you want to become an actor or actress after you see how thrilling a live production really is.

In the first paragraph, the writer introduces the comparison in a way that grabs the reader's attention. She compares things that are alike yet different.

The writer develops her argument by including examples and explanations, using the point-by-point method of organization.

In the final paragraph, the writer offers a strong conclusion that challenges the reader to accept her point of view.

# Editing—Be Your Own Language Coach

Before you hand in your essay, review it for language convention errors and spelling mistakes. Pay attention to hyphens, dashes, colons, and commas when listing items in a series and organizing ideas for emphasis.

# Publishing—Share It!

When you publish a work, you produce it for a specific audience. Consider the following idea to share your writing.

**Publish a newsletter.** Ask your classmates to submit their essays. Publish them in a newsletter and distribute it in your community.

# Reflecting On Your Writing

**Respond** On a separate sheet of paper, answer the following questions and hand it in with your final draft. What new things did you learn about your topic after writing this essay? What did you do well? What do you need to work on?

**Rubric for Self-Assessment** Assess your essay. For each question, circle a rating.

| CRITERIA | RATING SCALE | | | | |
|---|---|---|---|---|---|
| **IDEAS** Is your paper clear and focused, with rich details? | NOT VERY 1 | 2 | 3 | 4 | VERY 5 |
| **ORGANIZATION** How well do you employ a clear and logical organization? | 1 | 2 | 3 | 4 | 5 |
| **VOICE** Is your writing lively and engaging, drawing the reader in? | 1 | 2 | 3 | 4 | 5 |
| **WORD CHOICE** How appropriate is the language for your audience? | 1 | 2 | 3 | 4 | 5 |
| **SENTENCE FLUENCY** How varied is your sentence structure? | 1 | 2 | 3 | 4 | 5 |
| **CONVENTIONS** How correct is your grammar, especially your use of punctuation and capitalization? | 1 | 2 | 3 | 4 | 5 |

## Reading Skills: Compare and Contrast

Read the following passage. Then answer the questions.

---

The fastball is one of a baseball pitcher's most important tools. It is basically a pitch that is thrown extremely fast, making it difficult to hit. Some fastballs are thrown straight across the plate, while others tend to "move." The difference is in the way the pitcher grips the ball.

You grip a four-seam fastball by placing your index and middle fingers across the wide part of the seams while resting your thumb gently on the bottom of the ball. Holding the ball loosely allows you to release it quickly. This quick release lets you throw the pitch straight across the plate.

The two-seam fastball is known for its "movement"—the way it moves sideways or sinks down as it crosses the plate. With a two-seam fastball, you rest your thumb on the bottom of the ball, just as you do with a four-seam fastball. However, you place your index and middle fingers over the narrow part of the seams, and you grip the ball more tightly than you do with a four-seam fastball. This tighter grip creates friction, giving the ball its movement. The two-seam fastball is about 1 to 3 mph slower than the four-seam fastball.

---

**1** What do these two pitches have in common?

   A. They are equally fast.

   B. They are both easy to hit.

   C. They are both thrown straight.

   D. They are both thrown fast.

**2** Which word or phrase in the third paragraph helps you identify a difference between the pitches?

   F. just as

   G. however

   H. because

   J. tends to

**3** What is one difference between the two-seam and four-seam fastball?

_____

_____

# The Research Process

Read the following passage. Then answer the questions.

The Zunis are a Native American people who live in what is now the southwestern United States. Historically, they grew crops in the desert. The men hunted, made tools, and created jewelry. The women gathered and grew the food, cared for the children, and made pottery and baskets. Both men and women built and took care of the houses. If children wanted to join in the work, no one objected. The children were welcomed, for that was how the Zunis could rely on being able to pass along traditional skills to the younger generation.

Over the years, some traditional skills and cultural activities faded away, as European practices took their place. Many Zuni people have since worked hard to revive their native culture. Jewelry, pottery, and sculpture are some of the art forms practiced by the Zunis. Their sculptures are carved from stones and minerals and represent grasshoppers, bears, skunks, and other animals.

**4** This source is probably an excerpt from _____ .

A. a novel or short story

B. an encyclopedia article

C. a magazine article

D. a diary or journal

**5** If a student wanted to take notes on this information, what is the BEST way to avoid plagiarism?

F. use direct quotations

G. summarize

H. cite the source

J. paraphrase

**6** Which of the following is a primary source a student could use to research the Zunis?

A. an autobiography by a Zuni

B. a biography of a Zuni leader

C. a travel article

D. a book about Native Americans

**7** To find reliable information about contemporary Zuni culture, which source could a student use?

F. a Web site promoting tourism

G. a class Web site for an elementary school research project

H. the homepage of a Zuni potter

J. a university Web site

## Timed Writing: Evaluation (Critical Stance)

**Directions** Think of a selection or book you have read in which a character in the book struggles against his or her community in some way. Which is more important, the character or the community? Use details to support your answer. (20 minutes)

# 6-10 **Reading Skills**
*Summarizing*

In learning new reading skills, you will use special academic vocabulary. Knowing the right words will help you demonstrate your understanding.

## Academic Vocabulary

| Word | Meaning | Example Sentence |
|---|---|---|
| **summarize** *v.*<br>*Related words:*<br>summary, summarizing | to sum up | Will you *summarize* the article? |
| **focus** *v.*<br>*Related words:*<br>focused, focusing | to look closely at; to concentrate on | The lesson today *focuses* on how to write sentences. |
| **sequence** *n.*<br>*Related word:*<br>sequential | one thing after another in chronological order | The timeline shows the *sequence* of events that led to the war. |

A **summary** is a brief passage that presents only the main idea and most important details. A summary is a helpful tool. It allows you to review the important information without having to reread the entire selection.

## How to Summarize

**As you read,** pause occasionally to recall what you have read so far.

▶ **Focus** on the main point of each paragraph or section, noting it in the margin.

▶ Distinguish important details from unimportant details. Ask yourself questions, such as "Is this detail necessary to understanding what I have read?"

**After reading,** restate what you have read.

▶ Write your summary in paragraph form. Describe the main idea and the **sequence** of important details or events. Make sure you use your own words to restate the essential information.

▶ When you have finished, reread your summary for sense and to make sure it includes all the key ideas, facts, and events. Summarizing is a great tool to self-monitor your comprehension.

**Directions** Read the following excerpt. Then, answer the questions.

Link to Science

## Maglev Trains: Speeding into the Future

There are new trains coming, ones that have no wheels and float on air. No, they are not science fiction. They are Magnetically Levitated Trains, or Maglevs for short.

These high-tech trains have no need for wheels because a strong magnetic field suspends them just ten millimeters above the track, or guideway. Changes in the magnetic field propel the floating trains forward. Without any contact between the trains and the guideway to slow them down, Maglevs can reach speeds much greater than normal trains. The Japanese-built MLX-01 Maglev train has reached nearly 350 miles per hour—faster than many single-propeller airplanes!

Due to high costs and changing technology, there are only a few Maglevs in operation today. However, the speed and efficiency of these amazing machines will simplify transportation in the future.

**1** **Identify** What is the topic of this passage?

_____

**2** **Describe** To effectively summarize, what questions could you ask about the passage as you read?

_____

_____

**3** Summarize the passage's main points in the chart below.

|  | **Main Point** |
|---|---|
| **Paragraph 1** |  |
| **Paragraph 2** |  |
| **Paragraph 3** |  |

Now that you have learned about summarizing, practice the skill with the following article. *Guiding Question:* **How does the passage show the importance of community among the Anasazi people?**

As you read the article, stop after each section and jot its main point on a separate sheet of paper.

Link to Social Studies

# The Ancient Ones

ALMOST 2,000 YEARS AGO, THE PEOPLE LIVING IN THE AMERICAN SOUTHWEST FREQUENTLY MOVED FROM PLACE TO PLACE IN SEARCH OF FOOD. WHEN THEY LEARNED TO GROW CROPS, HOWEVER, THEY BEGAN TO SETTLE INTO PERMANENT HOMES. ONE GROUP SETTLED IN WHAT IS TODAY SOUTHERN COLORADO. NO ONE KNOWS WHAT THESE EARLY PEOPLE CALLED THEMSELVES. TODAY WE CALL THEM THE ANASAZI, FROM A NAVAJO WORD MEANING "THE ANCIENT ONES."

## Changing Ways of Life

When the Anasazi first settled in the region, small family groups lived in rock alcoves, or shallow recesses. Because these early settlers made finely crafted baskets, archaeologists named them the Basket Makers. The tightly woven baskets were used for carrying and storing food and water and even for cooking. Stones heated in a fire were dropped into a basket containing water and food. The hot stones made the water boil, which then cooked the food. However, this method was slow and often cooked the food unevenly.

About A.D. 550, some Anasazi moved to Mesa Verde. There they began to build permanent houses.

Archaeologists call these structures pithouses because the floors were formed by digging shallow pits in the ground. The sloping walls and the roof were made of wooden poles covered with mud. Archaeologists have found the remains of several pithouses close together.

Another important change during this time was that the people learned to make pottery. Clay pots and bowls improved the way food was cooked. Unlike baskets, which burn, clay containers could be placed directly over a fire. Thus food could be cooked more quickly and thoroughly than before.

**Above:** Anasazi coiled basket
**Background:** Anasazi settlement in Chapin Mesa, called Cliff Palace

The Anasazi's way of life changed again in about A.D. 750. Instead of pithouses, they began building square rooms with vertical walls. These rooms were often connected to form a small community of homes. This type of building is called a pueblo, from the Spanish word for "village." Pueblos at Mesa Verde were constructed on top of the mesa. A mesa is a raised, flat land form often found in the Southwest.

In about 1100, small villages began to join together to form large towns. Pueblos were built with many connected rooms used for sleeping, storage, and social gatherings. The people stored water in ditches and reservoirs for drier times.

In front of each pueblo was a single room dug into the ground, much like the earlier pithouses. This room, called a kiva, was used for community meetings and religious ceremonies. People would gather in the kiva to conduct healing ceremonies and to pray for rain, a good harvest, and success in hunting.

Between 1150 and 1200, the Anasazi began building their pueblos in large alcoves in the canyon walls. Many pueblos consisted of hundreds of rooms built in rows on top of one another. The roof of one room formed a porch for the room above it. The families who lived in the upper rooms had to climb ladders to reach them.

A major disadvantage of the cliff pueblos was that the people had to climb up and down the steep cliff walls to tend their fields on the mesa top and in the canyon below. Perhaps, some archaeologists suggest, the Anasazi moved to the cliffs because pueblos there would be easier to defend in case of an enemy attack. During their final years at Mesa Verde, the Anasazi began to build towers, which may have been used for sending signals or watching for approaching enemies.

**Above:** Anasazi cliff dwelling in Utah
**Left:** A mummified Anasazi person

# Daily Life

The Anasazi planted and tended fields of corn, squash, and beans. They gathered wild plants—roots, berries, nuts, seeds, and fruits—and hunted deer, rabbits, and other animals. They also raised turkeys, but not for food. Instead, the feathers were wrapped around fibers used to weave warm robes and blankets for the chilly nights and cold winters. Animal skins also provided coverings. Fibers from the yucca plant were twisted into cords to make baskets, sandals, ropes, and snares for catching small animals.

Although some tasks, such as harvesting crops, were shared by all the people, men and women generally had different roles in Anasazi society. Women were responsible for preparing and cooking food. They also cared for the young children. Babies were tucked snugly into cradleboards that their mothers wore on their backs or propped up nearby as they worked. Girls learned how to prepare food, weave baskets, and make clothing, while boys practiced hunting with smaller versions of the men's bows and arrows.

Men were responsible for clearing land and building houses and other structures. They cut logs with stone axes to make wooden supports for floors and roofs. The axes were also used to chip large sandstone chunks into rectangular blocks for building.

# Thinking About the Selection

## The Ancient Ones

**1** **Identify** In informational texts, authors frequently organize their ideas around key vocabulary. In this reading, words like "Anasazi" and "pueblo" are essential to the text's meaning. Use the space below to identify the key words. Group related words together.

_____

_____

_____

**2** **Summarize** In one or two paragraphs, summarize each of the following sections from the article.

**Changing Ways of Life**

_____

_____

_____

_____

_____

_____

_____

**Daily Life**

_____

_____

_____

**Write** Answer the following questions in your Reader's Journal.

**3** **Draw Conclusions** How does the passage show the importance of community among Anasazi people?

**4** **Summarize** Choose a chapter from your Anchor Book. Summarize it in one or two paragraphs, including only the main idea and most important details.

**Ready for a Free-Choice Book?** _Your teacher may ask you if you would like to choose another book to read on your own. Select a book that fits your interest and that you'll enjoy. As you read, think about how your new book compares with your Anchor Book._

# 6-11 The Research Process
## Drafting

Now that you've gathered information, you're ready to begin drafting your report. In your first draft, your goal is to get your thoughts down on paper. You can refine them later.

## Step 1: Write a Thesis Statement

while reading your anchor book

▶ Your main **purpose** in writing a research report is to **inform** readers about a topic. However, you may also have another purpose. For example, if you were writing a report on whales, you might try to **convince** readers that more efforts should be made to protect endangered whale species. In other words, you would be trying to get readers to accept your **perspective,** or point of view.

▶ Once you have identified your purpose and perspective, you need to consider your **audience.** Understanding your readers' backgrounds will help you decide what kind of information to include—and how to present your ideas. For knowledgeable readers, you can include complex explanations and specialized vocabulary. For readers who are new to your topic, you will need simple explanations and clear definitions.

**1** **Identify** Identify your purpose, perspective, and audience.

| Purpose | Perspective | Audience |
|---------|-------------|----------|
|         |             |          |

Suppose someone asked, "What's your research report about?" Could you sum it up in a sentence? This summary is called a **thesis statement.** A good thesis statement is clear and focused.

**Too Broad** Whales are mammals that live in the ocean.
**Too Narrow** There are two kinds of whales: toothed whales and baleen whales.
**Clear Focus** A whale's physical features help it to survive and meet the challenges of its environment.

**2** **Synthesize** Write a thesis statement for your research report. Revise it based on feedback from a partner and your teacher.

# Step 2: Organize Your Ideas

Now that you have written a thesis statement, your next step is to choose how you will present the information you have gathered. Choose a **method of organization** that suits your topic and is easy to follow.

Begin by organizing your information into **main points.** Then, make sure each main point is backed up by **supporting details**—facts, details, and examples that develop the point. Each main point and its supporting details should go in a paragraph or group of related paragraphs.

In addition to grouping main points and details, you can choose another organizational structure. Here are two options.

- ▶ **Chronological order** presents events in the order in which they occur. This method works best for topics that include a narrative sequence, such as historical subjects.

- ▶ **Ordering by type** organizes information into categories. Choose this structure when your topic includes ideas that are equally important—for example, topics that present information about different kinds of animals or places.

Other methods of organization include **cause-and-effect** and **compare-and-contrast.** How do you choose which method to use? Usually, your topic will help you decide. Try sorting your notes into piles. Can you group them into separate categories, or do they sort better by sequence? Your thesis statement might also point you in the right direction.

**1** **Evaluate** Which method of organization works best for your topic? Why?

_____

_____

**2** **Explain** How could you use this method of organization to structure your paper?

_____

_____

# Step 3: Create an Outline

Before you begin your draft, you need to make an **outline.** An outline is a detailed plan for writing a paper. It maps out what you will cover in each paragraph and how you will arrange those paragraphs. Spending time on your outline will help your writing flow more smoothly.

# Graphic Organizer Method

Some writers like to create a visual plan of how their ideas fit together. They write information in a graphic organizer, and then use this loose plan to create a more detailed, traditional outline. Here is one type of graphic organizer you could use. Remember that every main point should support your thesis statement.

**Directions** Using your research notes, plan your paper by filling in the graphic organizer.

while reading your anchor book

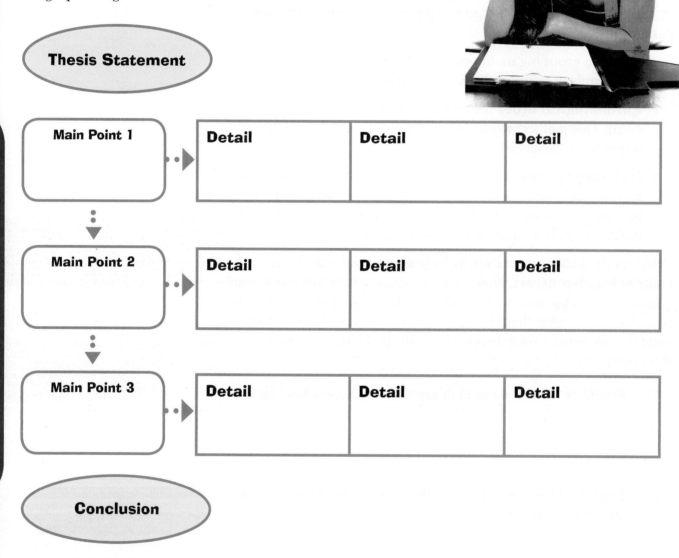

# Formal Outline Method

Whether or not you begin with a graphic organizer, you will need to create an outline. Here is the most common method.

▶ Use a Roman numeral (I, II, III) for each main point.

▶ Under each Roman numeral, use capital letters (A, B, C) for the most important supporting details.

▶ Use Arabic numbers (1, 2, 3) for minor details.

If your report is organized by type, use Roman numerals for categories, capital letters for main points, and regular numbers for supporting details.

**Directions** Study the outline for the first part of a research report on whales. Then answer the questions.

**Student Model: Outline**

I. Introduction

    Thesis Statement: A whale's physical features help it to survive and meet the challenges of its environment.

II. Baleen whales

  A. What baleen looks like

    1. Long, narrow plates that stretch between jaws

    2. Has tiny spaces between each plate

  B. How baleen works

    1. Whale lets in water through open mouth

    2. Whale strains plankton and krill through baleen

  C. Why baleen is important

    1. Feeding method lets whales eat tons of food daily

    2. Helps baleen whales grow to immense sizes

III. Toothed whales

  A. How they feed

    1. Beluga and narwhal shoot jets of water at ocean bottom to stir up prey in sand

    2. Flexible necks help them scan ocean floor for food

  B. Why teeth are important

    1. Allow whales to eat chewy food such as squid and octopus

    2. Amount and type of food in diet leads to smaller size (except sperm whale)

**1**    **Identify** Which method of outlining has the student used? Explain.

**2**    **Synthesize** Look through your research notes. Which method of outlining will work best for your report? Why?

# Step 4: Write Your Rough Draft

Now it's time to draft your report. Keep your outline and research notes handy. Your outline will help you stick to your plan, and your notes will help you develop your ideas.

Use the following checklist as you write your draft.

❏ My introduction includes a focused thesis statement.

❏ Each paragraph covers a main point and supporting details.

❏ All my main points, supporting details, and citations support my thesis statement. I have not included irrelevant information.

❏ My main points are in an order that makes sense for my topic.

❏ I use transitions like *because*, *then*, *in addition*, and *however* to connect paragraphs and sentences.

❏ My conclusion restates my thesis and includes a final comment.

❏ I have included source information in parentheses after every quotation and idea that needs to be credited.

**Directions** Read the student draft below. Then, answer the questions.

(1) The bowhead uses its gigantic head, which is about 40 percent of its total body length, to punch through sheets of ice up to 12 inches thick. (2) This kind of whale is beautiful to look at. (3) Bowheads need to do this to create an airhole in the ice. (4) Sperm whales have a distinctive physical feature: a cavity in the head called the spermaceti organ, which is a large area of tubes filled with a kind of yellow wax. (5) This organ is thought to keep sperm whales afloat and to focus their sonar clicks. (Whales in Danger)

**1** **Analyze** Which sentence in the draft contains an irrelevant detail? Why doesn't it belong?

_____

_____

**2** **Evaluate** Where could the writer have used a transition? Explain your answer, and suggest a transition.

_____

_____

# Thinking About the Research Process

## Drafting

**1** **Apply** Suppose you were writing a paper about whales to be read by members of a whale-watching club. What would you choose as a focus? What type of information would you include? Explain your answers.

**2** **Apply** Which method of organization would you use for a report entitled, "A Day on a Whale-Watch Boat"? Why?

## Research

Now think about your own research paper.

**3** **Apply** Look through your research notes and find one main point for your report. Create a section of an outline that shows how you will cover this point. If you find it helpful, start your planning by creating a graphic organizer on a separate sheet of paper.

**4** **Apply** Write a one-paragraph draft using your main point and the outline you created for the question above.

**Write** Answer the following question in your Reader's Journal.

**5** **Analyze** How is your Anchor Book organized? Why do you think the author chose this structure? Do you think it fits the topic? Explain.

# 6-12 The Research Process
## *Revising Your Research Report*

Even published authors don't accomplish everything in the first draft. That's where revision comes in. At this stage in the writing process, you can review your draft and make changes that improve your organization, flow of ideas, and word choice.

A checklist is a good tool for helping you keep track of your revisions. Put a √ next to each item as you make your revision.

## Revising Checklist

### Overall Organization

❑ The structure of my draft matches the structure of my outline (or improves upon it).

❑ All my paragraphs and details develop my thesis statement.

❑ The paragraphs flow in a logical order and include transitions to show connections between ideas.

### Paragraph Structure

❑ Each paragraph contains one main point that is expressed in a topic sentence.

❑ All the details in a paragraph support the main point.

❑ Each paragraph presents sufficient details to explain the main point.

❑ There is no missing, conflicting, or unnecessary information.

❑ I use transitions to show connections between sentences.

### Sentence Structure and Word Choice

❑ My writing contains a variety of sentence types.

❑ I use vivid, precise language and avoid overused words.

❑ I use active verbs to enliven my writing and avoid using passive voice.

**Directions** Read the following excerpt from the rough draft of a research report on whales. Read the student's revision ideas. Then, answer the questions that follow.

**Student Model: Revising**

*Victoria Gomez, Cincinnati, Ohio*

# Built to Survive: Whales

Whales live in all the oceans of the earth, both in the shallow and deep waters as well as in Arctic and tropical waters. All whales are aquatic mammals of the Cetacean order. They are separated into two groups: the baleen and the toothed. Whales range in body size from the largest mammal in the world (the blue whale) at over 100 feet long, to whales the size of a human—about six feet.

> First paragraph needs a thesis statement.

Instead of teeth, baleen whales have a unique physical feature. It is called baleen. This grows down from their jaw in long, narrow plates with tiny spaces between them. Whales use their baleen to feed by opening their mouths to let in lots of water. Then, they spit out the water through the baleen, leaving plankton and krill, or tiny shrimp, in their mouths. Using the baleen for feeding allows this kind of whale to eat up to four tons of krill a day. It makes sense that baleen whales such as the blue whale, the fin whale, the bowhead whale, the humpback whale, and the sei whale (to name just a few) grow to immense sizes (Carwardine, 19–21). A whale's physical features help it to survive and meet the challenges of its environment.

> Choppy— combine these 3 sentences into 1.

> Needs a transition here to show why it makes sense.

> Move thesis statement to opening paragraph.

On the other hand, the toothed whales such as the beluga, the narwhal, the Baird's beaked whale, and the orca are smaller in size. The sperm whale is an exception, growing up to 59 feet long (Whales in Danger). Having teeth allows these whales to eat chewy foods such as squid and octopus, which are abundant in the waters they inhabit. The blue whale has grooves running from under its chin to partway along the length of its underbelly. As in some other whales, these grooves expand and allow even more food and water to be taken in (Ellis, 18–21). Several of the toothed whales, such as the beluga and the narwhal, shoot a jet of water at the ocean floor to stir up prey hiding in the sand. These whales also have very flexible necks that help them scan the ocean floor for food.

> These details about blue whales belong in the previous paragraph about baleen whales.

Other characteristics can help a whale live in a harsh environment. The bowhead, for instance, has several interesting physical features that allow it to live in the Arctic all the time. The first characteristic is the one from which this species gets its name. The bowhead uses its big head, which is about 40 percent of its total body length, to punch through sheets of ice up to 12 inches thick. Bowheads need to do this to create an airhole in the ice. In addition, their layer of blubber, which is over 2 feet thick, allows them to live in very cold waters (Whales in Danger).

Sperm whales also have a distinctive physical feature: a cavity in the head called the spermaceti organ, which is a large area full of tubes filled with a kind of yellow wax. This layer is thought to keep sperm whales afloat and to focus their sonar clicks (Whales in Danger).

Whales are beautiful, gentle creatures in spite of their enormous size. They are also a critical part of the ocean ecology.

> Replace *big* and *very* with more precise words.

> Final paragraph needs to restate the main idea.

▼ **Good to Know**
Tables, charts, graphs, drawings, and diagrams like this one help support main ideas and enhance the appearance of documents.

**A** humpback whale
**B** beluga whale
**C** orca
**D** narwhal

# Thinking About the Research Process

## Revising

**1** **Apply** Review the comment that identifies the choppy sentences in paragraph 2. Write a sentence that suggests how the writer could combine the highlighted sentences into one that reads more smoothly.

_____

_____

_____

**2** **Apply** Write a transition sentence that the writer could add to connect the ideas in paragraphs 3 and 4.

_____

_____

**3** **Analyze** What should the writer do to determine what information to add to paragraph 5?

_____

_____

_____

**4** **Synthesize** What other revisions could the writer make to this draft? Revise one sentence or section, and explain your reasoning.

_____

_____

_____

_____

## Research

Now think about your own research paper.

**5** **Revise** Trade papers with a partner for peer review. Use a checklist to help you keep an eye out for specific points. Then, use self-stick notes to mark areas for revision and make suggestions. On a separate sheet of paper, write overall comments.

**Write** Answer the following question in your Reader's Journal

**6** **Evaluate** Choose a passage from your Anchor Book that you think can be better. Explain how you would revise it, and why. Then, rewrite the revised passage.

# 6-13 **The Research Process**
*Sources and Publishing*

You're ready for the final stage of revision: proofreading. Your previous revisions focused on **content**—refining your ideas and presentation. When proofreading, you will review details in **mechanics** like grammar and spelling and ensure you have correctly cited your sources.

## Cite Your Sources

**Citations** document where you found the information presented in your report. Citing your sources is important for two reasons.

► to show that your report has a solid foundation

► to guide readers if they wish to research the topic further

You must cite the following information in your report.

► direct quotations

► facts that are not common knowledge

► ideas that are not your own

**How do you cite a source?** You can cite a source using a footnote or an internal citation. An **internal citation** includes source information directly in the body of your report. Include an internal citation at the end of the sentence that contains the relevant information.

> According to biologists who have studied the whale's survival mechanisms, whale blubber, which often exceeds a thickness of 12 inches, helps whales in northern waters exist in cold temperatures (Whales in Danger, 36).

> Enclose the author name or source followed by the page number, if available, in parentheses *before* the closing period. If several sentences contain information from the same source, insert the citation at the end of the last one.

In addition to internal citations, you will need to present complete information about each source in the "works cited" list or bibliography at the end of your report. Create this list in alphabetical order. Follow these guidelines when citing sources in a works cited list. Refer to the works cited list on the following page for further examples.

**To cite a book, play, film, work of art, or long musical piece:**

Author's last name, author's first name. *Title* (in italics). City of publication: publisher, date of publication.

> **Example:** Ellis, Richard. *Men and Whales.* New York: Knopf, 1991.

**To cite a magazine or newspaper article, short story, song, or poem:**

Author's last name, author's first name. "Title." *Title of magazine or newspaper, story or song collection, or poetry anthology* (in italics) Date of publication: page number.

> **Example:** Mello, Felicia. "Ancient harpoon lends clues to whale's age." *The Boston Globe* June 12, 2007: B1

**To cite a Web site:**

Author if given. "Title"(in quotes). Sponsor of Web site. Date of article Web site address. (on its own line, if possible)

> **Example:** Marker, Marjorie. "Baleen Whales." Whale Studies. January 3, 2007
> http://www.wildlife.gov/oceanicorganisms/cetaceans.

## Reviewing Details

Many writers find it difficult to spot spelling and grammar errors while refining a paper's ideas and structure. A checklist can help you keep track of the details.

## Proofreading Checklist

❑ Review for correct spelling.

❑ Capitalize first words in sentences, proper nouns, and titles.

❑ Review punctuation for missing, unnecessary, or misplaced marks.

❑ Check for errors in grammar and usage, such as sentence fragments and subject-verb agreement.

## Publishing Your Work

Now that you've proofread your work, it's time to publish it. In addition to written format, you can present your findings in a variety of ways. Here are some suggestions.

**Create a multimedia presentation.** You might present your report to a student club, community organization, or national group. Create a visually appealing design for your report using a variety of graphics. Consider elements of spacing and design.

**Directions** Study the final draft of the student model on whales. Then, answer the questions.

**Student Model: Final Draft**

*Victoria Gomez, Cincinnati, Ohio*

## Built to Survive: Whales

Whales live in all the oceans of the earth, both in the shallow and deep waters as well as in Arctic and tropical waters. A whale's physical features help it to survive and meet the challenges of its environment. All whales are aquatic mammals of the Cetacean order. They are separated into two groups: the baleen and the toothed. Whales range in body size from the largest mammal in the world (the blue whale) at over 100 feet long, to whales the size of a human—about six feet (Carwardine, 14–19).

Instead of teeth, baleen whales have a unique physical feature called baleen, which grows down from their jaw in long, narrow plates with tiny spaces between them. Whales use their baleen to feed by opening their mouths to let in lots of water (Marker). Then, they spit out the water through the baleen, leaving plankton and krill, or tiny shrimp, in their mouths. Using the baleen for feeding allows this kind of whale to eat up to four tons of krill a day. Therefore, it makes sense that baleen whales such as the blue whale, the fin whale, the bowhead whale, the humpback whale, and the sei whale (to name just a few) grow to immense sizes (Carwardine, 19–21). The blue whale has grooves running from under its chin to partway along the length of its underbelly. As in some other whales, these grooves expand and allow even more food and water to be taken in (Ellis, 18–21).

On the other hand, the toothed whales such as the beluga, the narwhal, the Baird's beaked whale, and the orca are smaller in size. The sperm whale is an exception, growing up to 59 feet long (Whales in Danger). Having teeth allows these whales to eat chewy foods such as squid and octopus, which are abundant in the waters they inhabit (Carwardine, 68–69). Several of the toothed whales, such as the beluga

The thesis statement has been moved to the opening paragraph.

The author shows how the physical features of whales fit their environment—a major focus of the report.

The author organizes the report by type, discussing each major whale group in turn.

The author uses the phrases "on the other hand" and "smaller in size" to connect this paragraph to the previous one.

*while reading your anchor book*

and the narwhal, shoot a jet of water at the ocean floor to stir up prey hiding in the sand. These whales also have very flexible necks that help them scan the ocean floor for food (Carwardine, 190–191).

Other characteristics can help a whale survive in a harsh environment. The bowhead, for instance, has several interesting physical features that allow it to live in the Arctic all the time. The first characteristic is the one from which this species gets its name. The bowhead uses its gigantic head, which is about 40 percent of its total body length, to punch through sheets of ice up to 12 inches thick. Bowheads need to do this to create an airhole in the ice. In addition, their layer of blubber, which is over 2 feet thick, allows them to live in extremely cold water (Whales in Danger).

> This paragraph discusses a single main point: the unusual features of the bowhead whale.

Sperm whales also have a distinctive physical feature: a cavity in the head called the spermaceti organ, which is a large area full of tubes filled with a kind of yellow wax. This layer is thought to keep sperm whales afloat and to focus their sonar clicks (Whales in Danger).

Whales have many special features that make them well adapted to all of the oceans of the world. They are beautiful, gentle creatures in spite of their enormous size. They are also a critical part of the ocean ecology, living peacefully in their watery world.

> In the conclusion, the author restates the main idea of his report, emphasizing the appeal of her topic.

## Bibliography

Carwardine, Mark, Erich Hoyt, R. Ewan Fordyce, and Peter Gill. *The Nature Company Guides: Whales, Dolphins, & Porpoises.* New York: Time-Life Books, 1998.

Marker, Marjorie. "Baleen Whales." Whale Studies. January 3, 2007 http://www.wildlife.gov/oceanicorganisms/cetaceans.

Ellis, Richard. *Men and Whales.* New York: Knopf, 1991.

Whales in Danger. "Discovering Whales." http://whales.magna.com.au/DISCOVER

# Thinking About the Research Process
## Built to Survive: Whales

**1**  **Identify**  Name two types of citation methods used in the report. How are they different?

_____

_____

_____

**2**  **Apply**  Proofread and revise the following book citation.

Bruce MacMillan. "Going on a Whale Watch." Scholastic, Inc. New York, 1992.

_____

_____

**3**  **Analyze**  Find an internal citation in the student's report. Write it on the lines, noting the paragraph and page number. Why do you think the student decided to cite the source here?

_____

_____

_____

_____

**4**  **Respond**  What questions did the student's report raise that could be answered by additional details or further research? Write at least two other questions below.

_____

_____

_____

**5**  **Analyze**  What types of sources did this student use to research her topic? How do you know?

_____

_____

_____

_____

# Research

Now think about your own research paper.

**6** **Communicate** Review your lead—the first few sentences of your paper. Does it draw your readers in, leading them to want to read more? Consider revising your lead so that it raises a question, presents a vivid description, or quotes an exciting statement. Write your new lead below.

_____

_____

_____

**7** **Communicate** Reread your conclusion. Ask yourself, _Does it restate my thesis? Does it summarize my research? Does it connect my topic to other important issues?_ Revise your conclusion below.

_____

_____

_____

_____

**8** **Evaluate** Name two revisions you made in your final draft. How did these changes help strengthen your report? Explain.

_____

_____

_____

**9** **Apply** Consider what other ways you might publish and share your findings. List three methods below. Then, choose one. Explain why you chose this method and describe how you might prepare and publish your materials.

_____

_____

_____

_____

**Write** Answer the following question in your Reader's Journal.

**10** **Evaluate** Consider the title of your Anchor Book. Is it an appropriate title? Explain your answer. Now reread the introductory paragraph of your Anchor Book. Is it convincing and effective? Why or why not?

# 6-14 Listening and Speaking Workshop
## *Analyzing Media Messages*

Companies that are trying to market a product have many different media outlets to choose from—television, newspapers, magazines, the Internet, posters, and billboards, to name a few. In this workshop, you and your group will create a presentation comparing and contrasting two different types of advertisements for the same product.

## Your Tasks

Work with your group to choose one product and two different types of advertisements for it.

▶ Analyze the advertisements and think about which type seems most effective.

▶ Deduce the reasons for choosing two of the media to advertise the same product.

▶ Present your analysis to the class.

## Organize and Present Your Analysis

**1** **Choose a product and two types of advertisements.** Work with your group to choose a popular product that is likely to be advertised through more than one medium.

**2** **Research and analyze the messages.** Consider how both media messages balance fact and opinion. Evaluate both for use of propaganda and persuasive techniques. Consider how these messages impact their audience. Look carefully at how information is communicated through the graphics, color, sound, and motion in both media messages. Use a graphic organizer to compare and contrast their advantages and disadvantages. Use visual aids.

**3** **Create a visual for your audience.** Have an example of each advertisement. If the ad is small, consider gluing it to a piece of poster board and passing it around the room. Check with your teacher about a way to play any recording.

**4** **Plan and practice your delivery.** All members must be speaking participants. Create transitions so that everyone knows when to speak and the presentation flows smoothly. Remember that your tone, volume, pitch, and pace affect each word's meaning.

## 5 Give your presentation.

- Speak clearly and use appropriate grammar, tone, and word choice.
- Make sure the advertisements are visible.

## 6 Respond to your audience.
Follow up with a question-and-answer session.

## SPEAK: Rubric for Oral Interpretation

**Directions** Assess your performance. For each question, circle a rating.

| CRITERIA | RATING SCALE |
|---|---|
| | NOT VERY        VERY |
| **CONTENT** How well did the group analyze the two different types of media messages? | 1  2  3  4  5 |
| **ORGANIZATION** How organized was the group when presenting their scene? Did everyone seem to know when to speak? | 1  2  3  4  5 |
| **DELIVERY** How well did the group explain the similarities and differences between the two types of advertisements? | 1  2  3  4  5 |
| **COOPERATION** How well did the group work together? | 1  2  3  4  5 |

## LISTEN: Rubric for Audience Self-Assessment

**Directions** Assess your role as an audience. For each question, circle a rating.

| CRITERIA | RATING SCALE |
|---|---|
| | NOT VERY        VERY |
| **ACTIVE LISTENING** How well did you focus your attention on the speakers and listen for their analysis of each media message? | 1  2  3  4  5 |
| **ACTIVE LISTENING** How well did you demonstrate active listening with appropriate silence, responses, and body language? | 1  2  3  4  5 |

## Word Choice

When writing, good word choice can mean the difference between an engaging paragraph and one that is not enjoyable to read. Enliven your writing! Choose the right word.

**Go Online**

**Learn More**
Visit: PHSchool.com
Web Code: exp-7603

**Choosing the Better Word**

Read the following two sentences.

> **On his walk, the man saw many animals.**

> **On his daily hike through the forest, the ranger spotted a brown bear, a horned owl, and a rattlesnake.**

These two sentences address the same subject, but the second one uses better word choice, giving the reader a vivid description of the ranger's experiences.

When choosing words in your writing, remember the following.

*Author's Craft*

Reread the section "Changing Ways of Life" from "The Ancient Ones" on page 496. How does the author's word choice help the reader get a clear picture of the types of dwellings in which the Anasazi lived?

| Be creative. | Use modifiers and strong action verbs that will engage the reader. Rather than writing *the man ran out of the house,* write *the architect dashed out of the crumbling old mansion.* |
|---|---|
| Be specific. | Use words that tell exactly what happens or what something is. Don't describe something as an airplane if it's really a supersonic jet! |
| Be accurate. | Use the right word for the sentence. Describing someone as *angry* rather than *upset* will change the meaning of a sentence. Check the dictionary to ensure your word choice matches the definition you need. If it does not, revise your choice. |

**Directions** Rewrite the following sentences, using better word choices to create stronger sentences.

**1** After the movie, we went to a diner and we each ordered some food.

_____

_____

**2** She was happy because she won the contest.

_____

**3** Lin and Mohammed are doing a project for class.

_____

# Using Resources for Better Word Choice

When you can't think of a word that will strengthen your writing, or if you have a word but are not sure of its exact definition, use resources to assist you.

Go Online
**Learn More**
Visit: PHSchool.com
Web Code: exp-7604

- A **thesaurus** can help you find synonyms of a word you have in mind, helping you with your creativity and accuracy. When you find a synonym, be sure it has the connotation and denotation you intend.

- A **dictionary** provides you with the exact definition of a word.

- A **glossary** also provides exact definitions. They are usually more convenient to use than a dictionary, but their content is limited.

- Digital tools, such as an **online dictionary** or a word-processing program's **thesaurus,** can be used for the same purpose as a regular dictionary or thesaurus.

**Directions** To strengthen the following sentences, use one or more of the references above to improve upon the dull words in boldface.

**1** With the **help** of our science teacher, our class **made** a radio.

**2** The clown **walked** into the circus ring and **entertained** the audience.

**3** The pelican might not be **good-looking** on land, but it is **pretty** when it **flies** over the ocean.

**Directions** Revise the following paragraph, replacing dull or general words with ones that strengthen the writing.

**4** Yesterday was fun. In the morning we had a good breakfast and then went outside to play. Around noon, the sky got dark and it began to rain, so we went inside. There were some art supplies, so we decided to make face masks. Each of us made a mask. The power went out in the evening, and we used some candles to light our home. We wore our masks and took turns telling stories to one another.

A **multimedia presentation** presents information through a variety of media, including text, slides, photographs, recorded music and sound effects, and digital imaging. With a partner, use the steps outlined in this workshop to create a multimedia report about a topic that interests you.

Your multimedia presentation should include the following elements.

- A focused topic that can be covered in the time allotted
- A clear organization that presents a main idea
- Audio and visual features from a variety of sources
- Use of formatting and presentation techniques for visual appeal
- Effective pacing with smooth transitions between elements
- Error-free writing, including effective word choice

**Purpose** To create a multimedia report about a topic that interests you

**Audience** You, your teacher, and your classmates

## Prewriting—Plan It Out

Work with your partner and review books, Web sites, or magazines that explore areas you find interesting. List promising topics, and then choose one that will be fun to present, as well as interesting to hear.

**Narrow your topic.** Your multimedia presentation should have a manageable topic. Use the following **idea web** to focus your topic. Write your topic in the center and subtopics in the ovals around it. Choose one of the subtopics to be your focus.

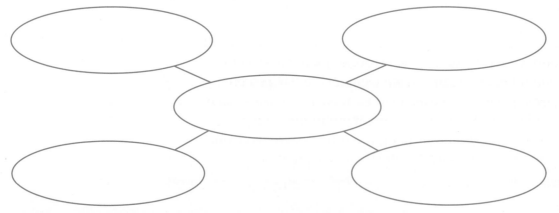

**Gather multimedia materials.** Research your topic, noting creative ways to engage your audience. Check your school or local library and the Internet to find audio and video clips, as well as music, photographs, and art. Keep your content and purpose in mind as you make your selections.

# Drafting—Get It on Paper

Create an **outline** to organize your ideas logically. Every main point and detail should relate to your thesis statement. End with a conclusion that sums up the main points of your presentation. Use the following organizer to outline two main points and their supporting details.

| | |
|---|---|
| **I. Main Point 1** | |
| A. Detail | |
| 1. Supporting Detail | |
| 2. Supporting Detail | |
| B. Detail | |
| 1. Supporting Detail | |
| 2. Supporting Detail | |
| **II. Main Point 2** | |
| A. Detail | |
| 1. Supporting Detail | |
| 2. Supporting Detail | |
| B. Detail | |
| 1. Supporting Detail | |
| 2. Supporting Detail | |

**Provide elaboration.** Use **audio** and **visual aids.** Make certain to avoid using aids as propaganda, but as ethical tools to strengthen your presentation and support your statements. **Audio,** such as interviews or music, can set a mood and provide information. **Visual aids,** such as graphs, charts and diagrams, can organize information.

Use technology, appropriate to your audience and purpose, to display information. Present it on posters, computer monitors, or by using an overhead projector.

## Revising—Make It Better

Use a clear and consistent tone. Look for ways to use words that will have the best impact or effect and reflect your personal style. Replace dull words with precise ones.

***Peer Review*** Ask for a partner's response to your multimedia presentation. Revise it to achieve the reaction you had intended.

**Directions** Read this student multimedia presentation as a model for your own.

**Student Model: Writing**

**Go Online**

**Student Model**
Visit: PHSchool.com
Web Code: exr-7602

*Shane Larkin and Ian Duffy, Williamston, WI*
## Zia

**Slide 1**
**Visual:** Title and Author Slide: *Zia,* by Scott O'Dell
**Script:** This presentation is about the book *Zia* by Scott O'Dell. *Zia* is a sequel to the book *Island of the Blue Dolphins* and shares some of the same characters. Instead of dolphins, though, Zia and her brother see gray whales, like those heard here.

The writers have chosen a topic that can be well covered in the time allotted to their report.

**Slide 2**
**Visual:** Whale
**Sound:** Whale song
**Script:** Reading this book got us very interested in the study of whales and how they adapt to the world around them.

The writers' choice of visuals is both dramatic and appropriate to their topic, audience, and purpose.

**Slide 3**
**Visual:** Setting Slide
**Sound:** Ocean waves crashing against beach
**Script:** The setting of *Zia* is the southern coast of California during the Spanish colonial era. The action takes place in several locations. This is a picture of the California coast.
**Video 1:** Video clip of whale scanning for food.
**Script:** From reading this book and doing a small amount of research, we discovered many ways whales can adapt to these kinds of harsh environments. Several of the toothed whales shoot a jet of water at the ocean floor. They use this jet to stir up prey hiding in the sand. These whales also have very flexible necks that help them scan the ocean floor for food.
**Sound:** Whale song
**Script:** We learned a lot about whales by reading *Zia* and doing our research, but this is only the beginning. This book has inspired us to continue our research to learn more about these amazing creatures and how they adapt to their environment.

The writers use boldface heads and other appropriate formatting to present the organization of their report clearly.

# Editing—Be Your Own Language Coach

Review your draft for language convention errors. Pay attention to sentence structure and word choice, both in spoken and written text.

# Publishing—Share It!

When you publish a work, you produce it for a specific audience. Consider one of the following ways of sharing your writing.

**Present your report.** Perform your multimedia report for your classmates. Ask them to evaluate what they see and hear.

**Share with the community.** Find out if there is a service organization, or another group in your town, that might invite you to share your research.

# Reflecting On Your Writing

**Rubric for Self-Assessment** Assess your script. For each question, circle a rating.

| CRITERIA | RATING SCALE | | | | |
|---|---|---|---|---|---|
| | NOT VERY | | | | VERY |
| IDEAS How clearly do you identify your topic? | 1 | 2 | 3 | 4 | 5 |
| ORGANIZATION How well do you employ a clear and logical organization? | 1 | 2 | 3 | 4 | 5 |
| VOICE Is your writing lively and engaging, drawing the audience in? | 1 | 2 | 3 | 4 | 5 |
| WORD CHOICE How appropriate is the language for your audience? | 1 | 2 | 3 | 4 | 5 |
| SENTENCE FLUENCY How varied is your sentence structure? | 1 | 2 | 3 | 4 | 5 |
| CONVENTIONS How correct is your grammar? | 1 | 2 | 3 | 4 | 5 |
| VISUALS How well do you display information using graphic aids such as posters, photographs, and illustrations? | 1 | 2 | 3 | 4 | 5 |
| OTHER MEDIA How well do you use media elements, including audio and video? | 1 | 2 | 3 | 4 | 5 |
| PRESENTATION How well do you present? | 1 | 2 | 3 | 4 | 5 |

Now that you have finished reading your Anchor Book, get creative!
Complete one of the following projects.

after reading your anchor book

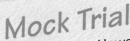
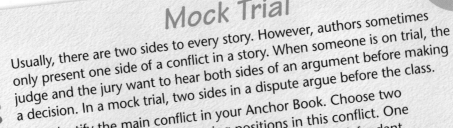

## Mock Trial
**A**

Usually, there are two sides to every story. However, authors sometimes only present one side of a conflict in a story. When someone is on trial, the judge and the jury want to hear both sides of an argument before making a decision. In a mock trial, two sides in a dispute argue before the class.

1. Identify the main conflict in your Anchor Book. Choose two characters who have opposing positions in this conflict. One character is the plaintiff and one character is the defendant.

2. Choose roles. You need: a judge, a defendant, a defense attorney, a plaintiff, a prosecuting attorney, and a witness for each side. The rest of the class will be the jury.

3. Write a script that includes an opening statement presenting your case, questions for both witnesses, and a closing statement that summarizes your position.

4. Present your mock trial in front of the class.

Your mock trial should include the following elements.
- ▶ A discussion about your Anchor Book's conflict
- ▶ A script summarizing your position and main points

## Letter to the Editor
**B**

People write letters to an editor to express their opinion about something printed in a newspaper or magazine. Here's a chance for you to express your opinion about a character or something that occurred in your Anchor Book.

1. Select an important character or event from your Anchor Book.

2. Consider issues, such as why you agree or disagree with what happened and what you would have done differently.

3. Write a letter addressed to the book's editor, discussing your opinion of the character's actions or events in the plot. Be sure to use a business letter format and formal language.

4. Publish your letter by typing it, printing it, and sharing it with your classmates to see if they have the same opinion.

Your letter to the editor should include the following elements.
- ▶ your opinion about a character or event from the book
- ▶ business letter format and formal language

## Multigenre Project C

A multigenre project is a collection of different types (genres) of writing. In this project, you will respond to your Anchor Book through four different genres. Some possibilities are a poem, a recipe, a song, an advertisement, a "Wanted" poster, an essay, a short story, a newspaper interview, a T-shirt, a contract, a computer game, a comic book, a picture book, a travel brochure, a personal ad, a monologue, an action figure ad, a restaurant menu, a home page, a will, and a monologue. Refer to specific details of your Anchor Book in each of your four pieces.

1. Select important details from your Anchor Book and consider how they connect to a central message, or theme.

2. Choose four genres to communicate your understanding of these important details. You can make full use of computers and multimedia.

Your multigenre project should include the following elements.
▶ a theme that unifies the different genres of your project
▶ creation of four different genre pieces
▶ a list of any sources used for details or evidence

## Free-Choice Book Reflection

You have completed your free-choice book. Before you take your test, read the following instructions to write a brief reflection of your book.

My free-choice book is _____ .

The author is _____ .

**1** Would you recommend this book to a friend? Yes _____ No _____

Why or why not? _____

_____

**Write and Discuss** Answer the following question in your Reader's Journal. Then discuss your answer with a partner.

**2 Compare and Contrast** *Community or individual: which is more important?* Compare and contrast how your Anchor Book and free-choice book address this question. Use specific details from both books to support your ideas. To extend the discussion, consider how a historian, a journalist, a politician, or an artist might answer the question.

Answer the questions below to check your understanding of this unit's skills.

## Reading Skills: Compare and Contrast

Read this selection. Then answer the questions that follow.

---

The first governing document of the United States was called the Articles of Confederation. It was ratified, or approved, by the states on March 1, 1781. The Articles remained in effect until the U. S. Constitution was ratified by the ninth state on June 21, 1788. Many of the same people signed both the Articles of Confederation and the Constitution. Both documents formed a congress and called the nation "the United States of America." Unlike the Constitution, however, the Articles of Confederation did not include a president or an executive branch to carry out the nation's laws. In addition, they did not give Congress the power to tax individuals. Instead, Congress had to collect taxes from each state and had no power to enforce its requests for money.

---

**1** What is one similarity between the Articles of Confederation and the Constitution?

    **A.** Both documents included an executive branch.

    **B.** Both documents gave Congress the power to tax individuals.

    **C.** Both documents gave the President the power to tax the states.

    **D.** Both documents established a congress.

**2** Which phrase helps you identify a difference between the Articles of Confederation and the Constitution?

    **F.** in effect until

    **G.** same people

    **H.** unlike the Constitution

    **J.** both documents

## Reading Skills: Summarizing

Read this selection. Then write a summary in your own words.

---

You probably know that frogs are amphibians, but did you know that salamanders are, too? Salamanders come in many shapes and sizes, from

---

the tiny *Thorius arboreus* to the Chinese giant salamander, which can grow to six feet long! Salamanders live in many regions of the world—such as North and South America, Asia, and Europe—but one thing that all salamanders have in common is their love of moisture. In fact, moist places such as damp forest floors and rocky streams help salamanders survive by preventing their skin from drying out. Some salamanders even breathe through their skin and need moisture to keep their bodies working properly. Unfortunately, as land is cleared for development, pollution and habitat destruction threaten the future of these amazing creatures.

**3**

## The Research Process

Read this excerpt from a research report. Then, answer the questions.

The lighthouse at Alexandria, Egypt, known as Pharos, was one of the Seven Wonders of the Ancient World. Completed around 270 B.C., the lighthouse was built to help sailors navigate the treacherous waters around Alexandria (Silverberg, 105).

Estimates of its height vary, but Pharos is generally believed to have stood more than 350 feet high. The only taller man-made structures of that time period would have been the pyramids of Giza, also in Egypt. A fire burned continuously at the top of the enormous lighthouse, and during the day a complex mirror reflected the fire out onto the water (Silverberg, 107). According to legend, the light reflected by the mirror could be seen for 300 miles.

During the 13th and 14th centuries, a series of earthquakes destroyed most of the lighthouse at Alexandria. In 1480, the stones from the base of the once mighty Pharos were incorporated into the wall of a castle and fortress built on the site of the ruin (Silverberg, 111).

**4** Which of the following would most likely be the author's intended **audience?**

A. readers of a daily newspaper

B. architects interested in modern skyscrapers

C. readers interested in ancient history

D. scientists interested in the uses of light and mirrors

**5** Which of the following is the **main idea** of the passage?

F. The lighthouse at Alexandria was called Pharos.

G. Pharos was destroyed by earthquakes.

H. Pharos guided ships to safety near Alexandria, Egypt.

J. Pharos was an enormous ancient structure that served as a lighthouse.

**6** In several of the **internal citations,** "Silverberg" refers to _____ .

A the title of the cited source

B. the author of the cited source

C. the title of the research report

D. the author of the research report

**7** The passage is a **secondary source** because it _____ .

F. was written by a person who was not a participant or an eyewitness

G. provides a first-hand account of the author's experiences

H. does not contain direct quotations

J. directly quotes a primary source

## Language Skills: Vocabulary

Choose the best answer.

**8** A word's **etymology** is its _____ .

A. history

B. part of speech

C. definition

D. pronunciation

**9** In addition to providing a word's definition, a dictionary tells you _____ .

F. how often the word is used

G. the word's part of speech

H. homonyms of the word

J. better word choices

**10** Which online resource would best help you locate a word's etymology?

A. a Web site on word origins

B. a Web site that analyzes media messages

C. an online thesaurus

D. an online encyclopedia

**11** Knowing a word's etymology strengthens your vocabulary by _____ .

F. helping with pronunciation

G. showing that the word has its origin in another language

H. giving the word's part of speech

J. helping you understand the meaning of other, similar words

# Language Skills: Grammar

Choose the best answer.

**12** Hyphens are used to link _____.

    **A.** some suffixes to words

    **B.** an adverb and a verb

    **C.** some prefixes to words

    **D.** a noun and a verb

**13** Which of the following shows the correct use of hyphens?

    **F.** Two-thirds of the class voted for Julianne.

    **G.** Julianne won by a two-thirds majority.

    **H.** Julianne is well-liked by everyone in the class.

    **J.** Julianne is an ex member of the student-council.

**14** Which of the following shows correct capitalization style?

    **A.** Putnam county, New York

    **B.** the civil war

    **C.** the Nineteenth Century

    **D.** World War II

**15** Which words in the following sentence should be capitalized?

we visited florence, italy, and saw paintings and sculptures of the renaissance.

    **F.** We, Florence, Italy, Renaissance

    **G.** We, Florence, Italy, Paintings

    **H.** We, Italy, Paintings, Sculptures

    **J.** Florence, Italy, Renaissance

**16** **Revision** Revise the following paragraph, replacing dull or general words with more vivid and precise language.

> My camp is so awesome! Everyone is super nice, and we do the coolest activities. One of my favorite things about camp is the lake. The water is so clear. Even though it is really cold, my friends and I go right into the water just about the minute we get to camp. I really love that they have about a million sailboats and really great sailing teachers. The only thing I don't love about camp is the bugs! They are so bad, especially at night.

# English and Spanish Glossary

## A

**abominable** (ə bäm' ə nə bəl) *adj.* hateful; disagreeable
  **abominable** odioso; desagradable

**acquainted** (ə kwānt' ed) *adj.* familiar
  **conocido** familiar

**acquire** (ə kwīr') *v.* to obtain; to gain through one's own efforts or actions
  **adquirir** obtener; conseguir por medio de esfuerzos o acciones propias

**adversaries** (ad' vər ser'ēz) *n.* opponents or enemies
  **adversario** oponentes o enemigos

**advocate** (ad' və kit) *v.* to support, argue in favor of
  **defender** apoyar, discutir a favor de

**affect** (ə fekt') *v.* to influence
  **afectar** influir

**ammunition** (am' yu nish' ən) *n.* explosive material fired from a gun; any material used to attack or defend a position
  **munición** material explosivo disparado de un arma de fuego; argumento defender una posición

**analyze** (an' ə līz) *v.* to examine something in great detail
  **analizar** examinar algo en detalle

**ancestral** (an ses' trəl) *adj.* relating to former generations
  **ancestral** relacionado a generaciones anteriores

**anecdotes** (an' ik dōt's) *n.* stories
  **anécdotas** historias

**apply** (ə plī') *v.* to put something to practical or specific use
  **aplicar** poner algo en práctica o en uso específico

**assassinated** (ə sas' ə nāt' ed) *v.* murdered (usually an important person) for political reasons
  **asesinado** matado por razones políticas (usualmente se refiere a una persona importante)

**assess** (ə ses') *v.* judge, measure
  **estimar** juzgar, medir

**assume** (ə sōōm') *v.* to suppose something to be a fact
  **asumir** suponer que algo es un hecho

**audible** (ô də bəl) *adj.* able to be heard
  **audible** que se puede oír

## B

**barren** (bar'ən) *adj.* empty; lacking vegetation
  **baldío** vacío; sin vegetación

**beckon** (bek' ən) *v.* to signal or call by using a motion or gesture
  **llamar por señas** señalar o llamar a alguien usando movimientos o gestos

**benefactor** (ben' ə fak' tar) *n.* someone who gives aid, especially financial assistance
  **benefactor** alguien que presta ayuda, especialmente económicamente

**bigots** (big' əts) *n.* narrow-minded, prejudiced people
  **intolerantes** gente prejuiciosa, de mente cerrada

**boycott** (boi' kät) *v.* an act of protest in which a group of people refuse to buy a product or use a service in order to force a change in policy
  **boicotear** un acto de protesta en el que un grupo rehúsa comprar un producto o usar un servicio para forzar un cambio de política

## C

**categorize** (kat' ə gə riz') *v.* to put into categories
  **categorizar** organizar en categorías

**characteristic** (kar' ək tar is' tik) *n.* a feature that describes a person, place, or thing
  **característica** algo que describe a una persona, lugar o cosa

**clarify** (klar' ə fī') *v.* to make clearer
  **clarificar** aclarar

**classify** (klas' ə fī') *v.* to arrange or group according to some system
  **clasificar** ordenar o agrupar de acuerdo a un sistema

**coils** (koilz) *n.* curled, wound-up sections
  **espirales** secciones enrolladas

**colander** (kul'ən dər) *n.* a type of strainer or sieve
  **colador** tipo de cernedor o tamiz

**collision** (kə lizh' ən) *n.* a violent, direct impact
  **choque** un impacto directo y violento

**commercial program** (kə mur' shəl) *n.* business or technology course
  **programa comercial** curso de negocio o tecnología

**communicate** (kə myōō'ni kāt') *v.* to convey information
  **comunicar** transmitir información

**compare** (kəm per') *v.* to show how things are alike
  **comparar** demostrar cómo cosas se asemejan

**concentration** (kän'sən trā' shən ) *n.* close or fixed attention
  **concentración** enfoque o atención fija

**conclude** (kən klo̅o̅d′) *v.* to decide by reasoning
  **concluir** decidir bajo razonamiento

**condemning** (kən dem′ i[ng]) *adj.* strongly
disapproving of
  **condenador** que desaprueba fuertemente

**connect** (kə nekt′) *v.* to bring two or more things
together to make a different or new whole
  **conectar** vincular dos o más cosas para completar
o formar algo nuevo

**context** (kän tekst′) *n.* the part of a text or statement that
surrounds a word
  **contexto** texto o afirmación que forma el entorno de
una palabra

**contraption** (kən trap′ shən) *n.* machine or device
considered strange
  **artilugio** mecanismo o aparato que se considera
extraño

**contrast** (kən trast′) *v.* to look at how things are different
  **contrastar** ver cómo cosas son diferentes

**convince** (kən vins′) *v.* to cause someone to agree
  **convencer** hacer que una persona esté de acuerdo

**coveted** (kuv′ it ed) *v.* desired
  **codicieron** desearon

**create** (kre′ āt′) *v.* to make or design
  **crear** hacer o diseñar

**credibility** (kred′ ə bil ə tē ) *n.* believability
  **credibilidad** verosimilitud

**credible** (kred′ ə bəl) *n.* believable
  **creíble** verosímil

**critique** (kri tēk′) *v.* to review or discuss critically
  **criticar** revisar o discutir críticamente

## D

**deduce** (dē do̅o̅s′) *v.* to use reasoning to draw something
out
  **deducir** razonar para llegar a una conclusión

**define** (dē fīn′) *v.* to identify the meaning of something
  **definir** identificar el significado de algo

**demolition** (dem′ə lish′ on) *n.* process of destroying or
wrecking something
  **demolición** el proceso de destruir o dañar algo

**describe** (di skrīb′) *v.* to give an account of or represent
something in words
  **describir** detallar o representar en palabras

**detect** (dē tekt′) *v.* to notice or discover something
  **detectar** notar o descubrir algo

**dilemma** (di lem′ ə) *n.* a situation that requires a choice
to be made
  **dilema** una situación en la que se requiere tomar una
decisión

**diluted** (di lo̅o̅t′ ed) *v.* made thinner or weaker, as by
adding a liquid such as water
  **diluido** disuelto o debilitado al agregar un líquido tal
como agua

**discreet** (di skrēt) *adj.* careful about what one says or
does
  **discreto** cuidadoso en lo que dice o hace

**discuss** (di skus′) *v.* to consider and talk about something
  **discutir** considerar y hablar de un tema

**disheveled** (di shev′ əld) *adj.* messy
  **desaliñado** desordenado

**dispel** (di spel′) *v.* to get rid of
  **disipar** deshacerse de algo

**dispersed** (di spʉrs′ d) *adj.* scattered in different
directions
  **dispersado** esparcido en diferentes direcciones

**distinguish** (di sti[ng]′gwish) *v.* to demonstrate the
difference between two or more elements
  **distinguir** demostrar la diferencia entre dos o
más elementos

**diverse** (di vurs′) *adj.* varied
  **diverso** variado

**downy** (dou′ nē) *adj.* soft and fluffy
  **suave** blando y acolchado

## E

**effect** (e fekt′) *n.* result or outcome
  **efecto** resultado o consecuencia

**eloquent** (el′ ə kwənt) *adj.* vividly expressive
  **elocuente** intensamente expresivo

**emphasize** (em′ fə sīz′) *v.* to give special attention; stress
  **enfatizar** dar atención especial; estresar

**enable** (en ā′ bəl) *v.* to allow or facilitate
  **permitir** dejar o facilitar

**establish** (e stab′ lish) *v.* to prove or create
  **establecer** probar o crear

**evaluate** (ē val′yo̅o̅ āt′) *v.* to decide the value of
  **evaluar** decidir el valor de algo

**evolved** (ē vôlv′ d) *v.* developed
**evolucionó** desarrolló

**examine** (eg zam′ən) *v.* to study carefully
**examinar** estudiar cuidadosamente

**explain** (ek splān′) *v.* make clear or understandable
**explicar** aclarar o elucidar

**exploitation** (eks′ ploi tā′ shən) *n.* the act of using another person for selfish purposes
**explotación** el acto de usar a otra persona de manera egoísta

**extension** (ek sten′ shən) *n.* extra period of time to pay something or do something
**extensión** tiempo adicional para hacer un pago o una actividad

## F

**fluent** (flōō′ ənt) *adj.* able to write or speak a language easily and smoothly
**elocuente** que puede escribir o hablar un idioma con facilidad y delicadeza

**focus** (fō′ kəs) *v.* to look closely at; to concentrate on
**enfocar** mirar de cerca; concentrarse en algo

**formulate** (fôr′myōō lāt′) *v.* to devise, to develop
**formular** idear o desarrollar

**fundamental** (fun′də ment′ l) *adj.* essential
**fundamental** esencial

## G

**generalize** (jen′ ər əl iz′) *v.* to draw inferences or a general conclusion (from)
**generalizar** inferir o concluir en general

**glutinous** (glōōt′ n əs) *adj.* gluey; sticky
**glutinoso** pegajoso; engomado

## H

**harness** (här′ nis) *v.* to control and direct the force of
**regir** controlar y dirigir la fuerza

**harrowing** (har′ ō i[ng]) *adj.* dangerous; intense
**angustioso** peligroso; intenso

**haul** (hôl) *v.* to pull
**halar** tirar con fuerza

**haunches** (hōnch′ ez) *n.* the loins and legs of an animal
**ancas** los lomos y piernas de un animal

## I

**identify** (ī den′ tə fī′) *v.* to recognize or point out
**identificar** reconocer o indicar

**illustrate** (il′ ə strāt′) *v.* to make clear or give examples
**ilustrar** aclarar o dar ejemplos

**imply** (im plī′) *v.* to indicate or suggest without stating exactly
**insinuar** indicar o sugerir sin decir explícitamente

**incentive** (in sent′ iv) *n.* reason to do something
**incentiva** razón para hacer algo

**incredulous** (in krej′ oo ləs) *adj.* skeptical; disbelieving
**incrédulo** escéptico; sin fe

**indicate** (in′di kāt′) *v.* to show or point out
**indicar** mostrar o enseñar

**infer** (in fur′) *v.* to draw conclusions based on facts
**inferir** concluir a base de hechos

**integration** (in′ tə grā′ shən) *n.* the bringing together of people of all races and ethnic groups without restrictions
**integración** la incorporación de personas de razas y grupos étnicos diferentes sin restricciones

**interpret** (in tur′prət) *v.* to explain or provide the meaning of
**interpretar** explicar o proveer el significado de algo

**investigate** (in ves′ tə gāt′) *v.* to study closely
**investigar** estudiar cuidadosamente

**irrational** (i rash′ə nəl) *adj.* not using reason
**irracional** que no usa la razón

## J

**justify** (jus′tə fī′) *v.* to prove or show to be deserved, right, or reasonable
**justificar** probar o demostrar que se merece, es correcto o razonable

## L

**laconically** (lə kän′ i klē) *adv.* using few words
**lacónicamente** usando pocas palabras

**lava** (lä′ və) *n.* molten rock from a volcano
**lava** roca incandescente de un volcán

**legacy** (leg′ əsē) *n.* something inherited or handed down
**legado** algo heredado o usado

**legislation** (lej′is lä′ shən) *n.* law or laws
**legislación** ley o leyes

**liberation** (lib′ ə rā′ shən) *n.* being set free
**liberación** que se deja libre

**luster** (lus′tər) *n.* shine
**lustro** brillo

## M

**massive** (mas′ iv) *adj.* huge
**masivo** enorme

**mazy** (mā′ zē) *n.* resembling a maze
**serpenteado** parecido a un laberinto

**modify** (mäd′ə fī′) *v.* to change
**modificar** cambiar

**murmurs** (mʉr′ mərz) *v.* makes a soft, low sound
**murmurar** que hace un sonido suave y bajo

## N

**nonchalant** (nän′ shə länt′) *adj.* casual or offhand
**indiferente** casual o desinteresado

## O

**obscured** (əb skoor′ d) *v.* made dim or indistinct
**oscurecido** opacado o impreciso

**obstinately** (äb′ stə nət′ lē) *adv.* stubbornly
**obstinadamente** tercamente

**optimist** (äp′ tə mist) *n.* one who tends to expect the best outcome
**optimista** el que tiende a esperar el mejor resultado

**organize** (ôr′gə nīz′) *v.* to arrange in a logical order
**organizar** arreglar en un orden lógico

## P

**palled** (pôld) *v.* bored; dulled
**agobió** aburrió

**parchment** (pärch′ mənt) *n.* strong, tough, and somewhat translucent paper
**pergamino** papel fuerte y resistente de apariencia translúcida

**penetrates** (pen′ i trāts) *v.* enters into
**penetra** adentra

**philosophizing** (fi läs ə fīz′ i[ng]) *v.* speculating about what might happen
**filosofando** especulando sobre lo que pueda pasar

**pitch** (pich) *v.* to fall forward
**caer** descender hacia delante

**plaited** (plāt′ ed) *n.* braided
**plegado** trenzado

**predict** (prē dikt′) *v.* make a logical guess about future events
**predecir** hacer una estimación lógica sobre un evento que ocurrirá en el futuro

**presently** (prez′ənt lē) *adv.* soon
**ahora** pronto

**procession** (prō sesh′ ən ) *n.* group moving in an orderly way
**procesión** grupo que se moviliza de manera ordenada

**prominence** (präm′ ə nəns) *n.* fame; being well-known; importance
**prominencia** fama; ser conocido; importancia

**propeller** (prə pel′ ər) *n.* device for moving an airplane or boat, consisting of rotating blades
**hélice** mecanismo para mover aviones o botes, consiste de aletas que rotan

**prospect** (präs pekt′) *n.* something expected; possibility
**prospecto** lo esperado; una posibilidad

## R

**radiant** (rā dē ənt) *adj.* glowing; beaming
**radiante** luminoso; brillante

**recall** (ri kôl′) *v.* to remember
**recordar** acordarse

**refer** (ri fʉr′) *v.* to consult a source for information; mention a source for information
**referir** consultar o mencionar una fuente de información

**reflect** (ri flekt′) *v.* to express a thought or opinion resulting from careful consideration
**reflexionar** expresar un pensamiento u opinión después de extensa consideración

**research** (rē′surch′) *v.* to carefully investigate or study
**investigar** investigar cuidadosamente o estudiar

**resolutely** (rez′ə lo͞ot lē ) *adv.* firmly; in a determined manner
**resueltamente** estrictamente; de una manera determinada

**respond** (ri spänd′) *v.* to say or do something in reply or reaction
**responder** decir o hacer algo al contestar o reaccionar

**restate** (rē stāt′) *v.* to say something again; summarize
**reformular** decir algo de nuevo; resumir

**reveal** (ri vēl′) *v.* to make known to others
**revelar** divulgar

**revelation** ( rev′e lā′ shen) *n.* something not previously known
**revelación** algo que no se sabía previamente

**revise** (ri vīz′) *v.* to change something based on new ideas and information
**revisar** cambiar algo basado en nuevas ideas o información

## S

**sarcastically** (sär kas′ tik lē) *adv.* mockingly; bitingly
**sarcásticamente** en tono de burla; mordazmente

**sequence** (sē′kwəns) *n.* one thing after another in chronological order
**secuencia** una cosa seguida de otra en orden cronológico

**skim** (skim) *v.* to read quickly to note only important information
**hojear** leer apresuradamente, notando solo de información importante

**sluggish** (slug′ ish) *adj.* slow; inactive
**letárgico** lento; inactivo

**solemn** (säl′ əm) *adj.* serious
**solemne** serio

**solitude** (säl′ ə to͞od′) *n.* the state of being alone
**soledad** la condición de estar solo

**specify** (spes′ ə fī) *v.* to mention or state definitely
**especificar** mencionar o afirmar definitivamente

**speculate** (spek′yə lāt′) *v.* to make a prediction
**especular** hacer una predicción

**squabbled** (skwäb′ əld) *v.* argued
**riñeron** discutieron

**succession** (sək sesh′ ən) *n.* a row, series
**sucesión** fila, serie

**summarize** (sum′ə rīz′) *v.* to sum up
**resumir** reducir a términos breves

**synthesize** (sin′thə sīz′) *v.* to put together elements to form a whole
**sintetizar** agrupar elementos para completar algo

## T

**toiling** (toīl i[ng]) *v.* moving with difficulty; working hard
**afanando** moviendo con dificultad; trabajando arduamente

**tolerant** (täl′ər ənt) *adj.* open-minded; able to accept the ideas and behavior of others
**tolerante** de mente abierta; que acepta las ideas o comportamientos de otros

**tomb** (to͞om) *n.* a vault or chamber for burial of the dead
**tumba** cripta o bóveda donde se entierran los muertos

**translucent** (trans′ lo͞o sənt) *adj.* allowing light to pass through, but not clearly
**translúcido** dejar que traspace la luz, pero no claramente

**trite** (trīt) *adj.* overused; clichéd
**trillado** utilizado en exceso; cliché

## V

**verify** (ver′ ə fī′) *v.* to confirm
**verificar** confirmar

## W

**wielding** (wēld i[ng]) *v.* holding
**esgrimiendo** manejando con destrez

**wince** (wins) *v.* to draw back from or flinch as if in pain
**estremecerse** retirarse o hacer una mueca a causa de dolor

# Index of Skills

## Literary Analysis

Allusion, 340–343
Analogies, 125, 304
Author's perspective, 266–267
Author's purpose, 54–59, 244, 245, 246
Author's style/voice, 204–211
Autobiography, 212–229
Biography, 212–229
Character, 6, 18, 60–71, 100
  antagonist, 60
  dynamic character, 60
  emotions, 154
  flat character, 60
  major characters, 60
  minor characters, 60
  protagonist, 60
  round characters, 60
  static character, 60
  traits, 60, 154
Characterization, 154–155, 158–165, 410
  direct characterization, 154
  in drama, 382
  indirect characterization, 154
Character motivation, 410–423
  external motivation, 410
  internal motivation, 410
Comedy, 373
Comparing literary works
  author's style, 204–205
  characters, 61
  character motivation, 410–423
  conflict, 168, 373
  drama and dramatization, 424, 426–433
  figurative language, 280, 304–309
  heroes, 373
  historical and cultural perspective, 212
  imagery, 72–79, 280, 288–289, 291–303
  meter, 327
  poetic forms, 344–351
  primary and secondary sources, 478–483
  rhyme, 326–327
  rhythm, 326–327
  setting and mood, 72–79
  sound devices, 326–339
  symbolism, 340–343
  theme, 166–171, 395
  tone, 204–205, 290–303
Conflict, 6, 18, 30–41, 373
  external conflict, 30
  internal conflict, 30
Connotation, 286, 290
Context

cultural, 162–164, 171, 212, 308, 413
  historical, 212, 431
  science, 337, 408
  social studies, 27, 36, 394, 431
Denotation, 286
Descriptive language, 72, 288,
Dialogue, 233, 382–395, 428–432
Diction, 204–205, 290
Drama, 372–373
  comedy, 373
  dramatic reading, 172–173
  playwright, 373
  reading aloud, 434–435
  scenes, 434–435
  stage directions, 382–395, 424
  staging, 384–385, 424
  props, 384, 424
  tragedy, 373
  types, 373
Dramatization, 424–433
English language, changes in, 204
Expository writing, 194, 244–251
Fables, 31, 113
Fiction
  compared to nonfiction, 7
  elements of, 6
  narrative texts, 18
Figurative language, 280, 304–309
  analogy, 304
  hyperbole, 304
  idioms, 287, 304
  metaphor, 304
  personification, 304
  simile, 304
Figures of speech, 304
Flashback, 126–127, 130–135
Folktales, 167
Foreshadowing, 128–135
Graphic features of text, 292
Historical fiction, 6
How-to writing, 84–87, 194
Imagery, 291–296, 298–302
Irony, 156–165
  dramatic irony, 156
  situational irony, 156
  verbal irony, 156
Legend, 334–339
Media accounts, 516–517
Memoirs, 212
Mood, 72–79, 100, 288
Narrative texts, 18–29, 194
  autobiography, 212, 232
  fiction, 6, 18
  nonfiction, 18
  short story, 101
Nonfiction

compared to fiction, 7
  elements of, 7
  expository texts, 194, 244–251
  narrative texts, 18, 194
  organization methods, 195, 244
  persuasive texts, 194
  reflective texts, 194, 202–203, 206–211
  types, 194–195
Novellas, 101
Novels, 100–101
Organizational patterns, 501
  block method, 489
  cause-and-effect, 195, 244, 501
  chronological, 47, 195, 244, 251, 501
  compare-and-contrast, 195, 244, 501
  order of importance, 47
  ordering by type, 501
  point-by-point, 489
  problem-and-solution, 244
  spatial order, 47
Persuasive techniques, 252–253
  logical appeals, 252
  emotional appeals, 252
  ethical appeals, 252
  irony, 263
  propaganda, 252–253
  rhetorical questions, 263
Persuasive writing, 252–257, 262–265
Plays, 372, 462, 511
Plot, 6, 18, 100, 112–125
  climax, 112, 113
  conflict, 112, 373
  exposition, 112, 113
  falling action, 112, 113
  plot diagram, 112, 125
  resolution, 112, 113
  rising action, 112, 113
Poetry, 344–351
  ballad, 344
  compared with prose, 281
  concrete poem, 345
  epic poem, 344
  epigram, 341
  forms, 344–351
  free verse, 344
  haiku, 344
  kinds
    dramatic poetry, 344
    lyric poetry, 344
    narrative poetry, 344
  limerick, 344
  line, 281
  ode, 344
  refrain, 344

# Index of Skills

sound devices, 7
stanza, 281, 326
Point of view, 62–63
    first-person point of view, 62, 292–301
    limited, 62
    omniscient, 62
    third-person point of view, 62
    types, 62
Problem-Solution, evaluating, 198–199
Propaganda, 252–253
    advertisements, 197
    appeal to authority, 263
    celebrity endorsement, 263
    bandwagon technique, 253
    glittering generalities, 253
    testimonials, 253
Prose, 280–281
Reflective writing, 49, 59, 87, 89, 143, 153, 181, 183, 194, 202–203, 206–211
Rhythm, *See also poetry.*
Sensory Language, 280, 288, 303
Setting, 6, 18, 72–79, 100
Short story, 101
Sound devices, 326–339, *See also poetry.*
    alliteration, 326–339
    meter, 327–339
    onomatopoeia, 326–339
    rhyme, 326–339
    rhythm, 326–339, 360
Sources, 510–511, 513
    primary sources, 478–483
    secondary sources, 478–483
Speeches, 258–259, 481–483
Style, *see also author's style/voice*
Symbolism, 340–343
Themes, 100, 162–163, 352, 356–359
    recurring, 183, 361, 395,
    theme version topic, 166
Tone, 204–205, 290–303
Tragedy, 373

## Reading Skills and Strategies

Activating prior knowledge, 102–107, 148–153, 323, 325, 374–376
Adjust reading rate, 375
Asking questions
    about elements of the text, 402
    connect to personal experience, 144–145, 202–203, 402
    connect to real life, 402
    drawing conclusions, 325
    identify cause-and-effect, 407
    interview report, 398, 399
    making inferences about novels, 150

open-ended questions, 266
response to literature, 314–315
set a purpose, 326–339, 374–375, 376
specific and probing questions, 51
Author's perspective, 266–267
Author's purpose, 54–59, 244, 245
Background knowledge, 148
Cause and effect, 406–409
Classify, 31, 383, 483
Compare and contrast, 458–461, 477
    author's style, 204–205
    character behavior and motivation, 165, 171
    characters in the same book, 61, 165
    conflict, 433
    genres, 425
    historical perspective, 229
    literary works, 433
    poetic devices, 79, 309, 333, 339
    theme, 88, 171, 183, 269, 445, 525
    topic, 171, 283
    tone, 297
Connections, 107, 373, 477
Context clues, 8–13
    homonyms, 380
    idioms, 287
    making inferences, 148–149, 153
    word origins, 201
Discussion, 50–51, 89, 144–145, 183, 266–267, 269, 292, 318–319, 361, 402–403, 445, 525
Drawing conclusions, 155, 211, 322–325, 325, 477, 499
Evaluating strategies, 13, 21, 43, 59, 79, 107, 127, 135, 145, 165, 171, 173, 197, 199, 253, 257, 303, 339, 345, 351, 409, 433, 458, 470, 471, 477, 483, 484, 501, 504, 509, 515
Fact and Opinion, 196–199
Fluency, 172–173, 352–353, 434–435, 516–517, 523
Foreshadowing, 128–135
Graphic organizers, 4, 5, 9, 13–15, 21, 29, 46, 72–73, 84, 108–109, 111–112, 125, 128, 140–141, 144, 148–149, 150, 153–154 156, 192–193, 202, 205, 232–233, 238–239, 258, 262–263, 281–282, 286, 288–290, 314–315, 319, 322, 352, 356–357, 371–372, 376, 380, 384, 398402–403, 409–410, 425, 434, 440, 443, 455–456, 459, 461, 463, 465, 471, 473–474, 487–488, 489, 501–503, 506, 509, 511, 521–522
Main idea and supporting details, 238–243
    implied main idea, 240

organizing nonfiction, 195
using self-stick notes to track supporting details, 110–111
Making inferences, 9, 29, 63, 71, 135, 143, 153, 165, 229, 325, 395, 423, 433, 461
Marking the text, 7, 19–21, 22–28, 31–40, 55, 61, 64–69, 73–78, 113–124, 127, 130–134, 149, 155, 158–164, 168–170, 203, 205–210, 213–228, 245–250, 254–256, 289, 291–296, 298–302, 305–307, 323, 327–330, 332, 334–336, 342, 346–350, 383, 385–394, 411–422, 426–432, 479–482
Meanings of words, 14, 108, 200–201, 286–287, 380–381, 462–463
Note-taking, 110–111, 473–474
Prosody, 7, 254, 306, 307, 386, 551–551
Paraphrasing, 282–285
Phonics, 14
Predicting, 61, 102–107, 125, 129, 143
Prereading, 375
Reading aloud, 7, 10, 254, 306, 307, 352–353, 386
Reading across the curriculum, 5–7, 10–12, 27, 36, 55, 89, 105–106, 121, 151, 183, 218, 222, 239, 241–242, 246–250, 253, 269, 284, 308, 361, 377–378, 408, 431, 445, 475–476, 484–485, 495–498, 525
Repair strategies,
    context clues, 8–9
    graphic organizers, 7
    note taking, 473
    predicting, 102
    questioning, 150
    rereading, 7
    summarizing, 494
Scanning, 195, 327
Self-correcting, 90
Self-monitoring, 7
Scanning, 195, 327
Setting a purpose for reading, 374–379
Skimming, 195, 374
Summarizing, 61, 251, 435, 494–499
Text features, using, 7, 102–103, 223, 374, 459, 499
Text organization, 251, 374, 489, 501
    cause-and-effect, 195, 244
    chronological, 195, 244
    compare-and-contrast, 195, 244
    problem-and-solution, 244
Transitions, 244
Unknown words, 8–14
Using a dictionary, 14, 108, 109, 201, 286, 380–381, 439, 462–463, 519
Using footnotes, 223

536

# Index of Skills

## Grammar, Usage, Mechanics

# Index of Skills

## Critical Thinking

# Index of Features

## Informational Texts

## Literature Circles

## Reader's Journal

## Writer's Workshops

## Assessment

## Author Biographies

# Index of Authors and Titles

# Index of Authors and Titles

# Acknowledgments

## Staff Credits

The people who made up *The Reader's Journey* team—representing design, editorial, education technology, manufacturing and inventory planning, market research, marketing services, planning and budgeting, product planning, production services, project office, publishing processes, the business office, and rights and permissions—are listed below. Boldface type denotes the core team members.

Rosalyn Arcilla, **Daniel Bairos,** Suzanne Biron, **Elizabeth Comeau,** Mark Cirillo, Jason Cuoco, Harold Delmonte, Kerry Dunn, Leslie Feierstone Barna, **Shelby Gragg,** Meredith Glassman, Cassandra Heliczer, **Rebecca Higgins,** Karen Holtzman, Sharon Inglis, **Linda Johnson, Angela Kral,** Monisha Kumar, **Margaret LaRaia, Ellen Levinger,** Cynthia Levinson, **Cheryl Mahan, Elise Miley,** Linda Punskovsky, Tracey Randinelli, John Rosta, **Bryan Salacki,** Laura Smyth, Ana Sofia Villaveces, **Heather Wright**

## Additional Credits

Editorial: Chrysalis Publishing Group, Inc.
Page layout, photo research, art acquisition, production: AARTPACK, Inc.

## Text Credits

# Acknowledgments

**HarperCollins Publishers, Inc.**
From "An American Childhood" by Annie Dillard. Copyright © 1987 by Annie Dillard. Reprinted by permission of HarperCollins Publishers. From the novel "Dragonwings" by Laurence Yep. Copyright © 1975 by Laurence Yep. Used by permission of HarperCollins Publishers. "The Landlord's Daughter" from *Red Scarf Girl* by Ji-li Jiang. Copyright © 1997 by Ji-li Jiang. Foreword copyright © 1997 by HarperCollins Publishers. Reprinted by permission of HarperCollins Publishers. "Summer" by Walter Dean Myers from *Brown Angels: An Album of Pictures and Verse.* Copyright © 1993 by Walter Dean Myers. Used by permission of HarperCollins Publishers. From *The Wounded Wolf* by Jean Craighead George. Text copyright © 1978 by Jean Craighead George.

**Harvard University Press**
"Fame Is a bee (#1763)" by Emily Dickinson from *Poems of Emily Dickinson.* Reprinted by permission of the publishers and the Trustees of Amherst College from *The Poems of Emily Dickinson,* Thomas H. Johnson, ed., Cambridge, Mass: The Belknap Press of Harvard University Press, Copyright © 1951, 1955, 1979, 1983 by the President and Fellows of Harvard College.

**Hilgers Bell & Richards Attorneys at Law**
"All Together Now" by Barbara Jordan from *Sesame Street Parents.* Reprinted by permission of Hilgers Bell & Richards Attorneys at Law for the Estate of Barbara Jordan.

**Henry Holt and Company, Inc.**
"Stopping By Woods on a Snowy Evening" by Robert Frost from *The Poetry of Robert Frost,* edited by Edward Connery Lathem. Copyright 1923, 1969 by Henry Holt and Company, copyright 1951 by Robert Frost. Reprinted by permission of Henry Holt and Company, LLC.

**The Estate of Dr. Martin Luther King, Jr. c/o Writer's House LLC**
"The American Dream" by Dr. Martin Luther King, Jr. Reprinted by arrangement with The Heirs to the Estate of Martin Luther King, Jr., c/o Writers House as agent for the proprietor New York, NY. Copyright 1961 Martin Luther King, Jr., copyright renewed 1989 Coretta Scott King.

**Alfred A. Knopf, Inc.**
"Mother to Son" from *The Collected Poems of Langston Hughes,* edited by Arnold Rampersand with David Roessel, Associate Editor, copyright © 1994 by The Estate of Langston Hughes. Used by permission of Alfred Knopf, a division of Random House, Inc. "Two Somewhat Different Epigrams", edited by Arnold Rampersad with David Roessel, Assoc, from *The Collected Poems of Langston Hughes* by Langston Hughes, edited by Arnold Rampersad with David Roessel, Associate Editor, copyright © 1994 by The Estate of Langston Hughes. Used by permission of Alfred Knopf, a division of Random House, Inc.

**Little, Brown and Company, Inc.**
From "Nisei Daughter" by Monica Sone from *Nisei Daughter.* Copyright © 1953 by Monica Sone; Copyright © renewed 1981 by Monica Sone. By permission of Little Brown & Company.

**Liveright Publishing Corporation**
"in Just-" by E. E. Cummings. Copyright 1923, 1951, © 1991 by the Trustees for the E.E. Cummings Trust. Copyright © 1976 by George James Firmage, from Complete Poems, 1904-1962 by E.E. Cummings, edited by George J. Firmage. Used by permission of Liveright Publishing Corporation.

**Milkweed Editions**
From "Museum Indians" by Susan Power, from *Roofwalker* (Minneapolis: Milkweed Editions, 2002). Copyright © 2002 by Susan Power.

**William Morris Agency**
"A Christmas Carol: Scrooge and Marley" by Israel Horovitz. Copyright 1979 by Israel Horovitz. All rights reserved. Israel Horovitz's adaptation of Charles Dickens' *A Christmas Carol: Scrooge and Marley* was first presented at Center Stage in Baltimore, Maryland in December 1978. CAUTION: Professionals and amateurs are hereby warned that *A Christmas Carol: Scrooge and Marley,* being fully protected under the copyright laws of the United States of America, the British Empire, including the Dominion of Canada, and all other countries of the Universal Copyright and Berne Conventions, are subject to royalty. All rights, including professional, amateur, motion picture, recitation, lecturing, public reading, radio and television broadcasting, and the rights of translation into foreign languages, are strictly reserved. Particular emphasis is laid on the question of readings, permission for which must be secured in writing. All inquiries for *A Christmas Carol: Scrooge and Marley* should be addressed to the William Morris Agency, 1325 Avenue of the Americas, New York, NY 10019.

**Lillian Morrison**
"Sidewalk Racer or On the Skateboard" by Lillian Morrison from *WAY TO GO! Sports Poems* by Lillian Morrison. Copyright © 1965, 1967, 1968, 1977, 2001 by Lillian Morrison. Used by permission of Marian Reiner, for the author.

**National Geographic Magazine**
"A Growing Remembrance" by Margaret G. Zackowitz from *National Geographic, August 2005.* Copyright © 2005 National Geographic Society. Used by permission. "After the Tsunami" by Gregory Stone from *National Geographic, December 2005.* Copyright © 2005 National Geographic Society. Used by permission. "Against the Odds" from *National Geographic, November 2005.* Copyright © 2005 National Geographic Society. Used by permission. "Glass" by from *National Geographic, December 1993.* Copyright © 2004 National Geographic Society. Used by permission. "Plants on the Warpath" by Joel Achenbach from *National Geographic, February 2004.* Copyright © 2004 National Geographic Society. Used by permission. "Surfing's Dynamic Duo" by Joel K. Bourne, Jr. from *National Geographic, July 2006.* Copyright © 2006 National Geographic Society. Used by permission.

**New Directions Publishing Corporation**
"Wind and Water and Stone" by Octavio Paz translated by Mark Strand from *A Draft of Shadows,* copyright © 1979 by The New Yorker Magazine, Inc. Reprinted by permission of New Directions Publishing Corp.

**W.W. Norton & Company, Inc.**
"A Child's Painting" from *Frameless Windows, Squares of Light: Poems* by Cathy Song. Copyright © 1988 by Cathy Song. "Who Burns for the Perfection of Paper" from *City of Coughing and Dead Radiators* by Martin Espada. Copyright © 1993 by Martin Espada. Used by permission of W. W. Norton & Company, Inc.

**Harold Ober Associates, Inc.**
"Stolen Day" by Sherwood Anderson from *This Week Magazine.* Reprinted by permission of Harold Ober Associates Incorporated. Copyright 1941 by Sherwood Anderson. Copyright renewed 1968 by Eleanor Copenhaver Anderson.

**Julia O'Faolain Martines**
"The Trout" by Sean O'Faolain from *The Finest Stories of Sean O'Faolain.* Copyright © 1941, 1949, 1953, 1954, 1956, 1957 by Sean O'Faolain. Used by permission.

**Orchard Books**
From "An Island Like You: Stories of the Barrio" by Julia Ortiz Cofer from. Scholastic Inc./Orchard Books. Copyright © 1995 by Judith Ortiz Cofer. Reprinted by permission.

**Pearson Education Inc.**
"DNA Fingerprinting" by from *Science Explorer: Cells and Heredity.* Copyright © 2005 by Pearson Education, Inc., or its affiliates. All rights reserved. "The Ancient Ones" by Nila Banton Smith from *Be a Better Reader Eighth Edition F.* "Making a Difference-Chico Mendes and the Amazon Rain Forest" by Nila Banton Smith from *Be a Better Reader Eighth Edition F.* "What Are Memories Made Of?" by Nila Banton Smith from *Be a Better Reader Eighth Edition B.* "First Aid for the Choking Victim" by Nila Banton Smith from *Be a Better Reader Eighth Edition C.* "No and Kabuki Plays" by Nila Banton Smith from *Be a Better Reader Eighth Edition C.* Copyright © 2003 by Pearson Education, Inc., or its affiliates. All rights reserved. Used by permission.

**Pearson Educational Measurement**
"The Black Blizzards and Dust Bowl Days" by from TAKS April 2006 *Grade 8 Reading Online Test.* Copyright © and trademark TM 2000. All rights reserved for TAKS. Other licensed products might have a different copyright date. Used by permission.

**Penguin Group (USA) Inc.**
From "Working Fire–The Making of a Fireman" by Zac Unger. Copyright © Zac Unger, 2004. All rights reserved.

**Peter Fraser & Dunlop Group**
"I've Had This Shirt" by Michael Rosen from Mind your Own Business (© Michael Rosen 1974) is reproduced by permission of PFD (www.pfd.co.uk) on behalf of Michael Rosen.

**Philomel Books**
From "Travel Team" by Mike Lupica, Copyright © 2004 by Mike Lupica. Used by permission of Philomel Books, A Division of Penguin Young Readers Group, A Member of Penguin Group (USA) Inc., 345 Hudson Street, New York, NY 10014. All rights reserved.

**Puffin Books**
"Seeing the Island" by Joseph Bruchac from *The Heart of a Chief.* Copyright © Joseph Bruchac, 1998. All rights reserved.

**G.P. Putnam's Sons**
"Describe Somebody" by Jacqueline Woodson from *Locomotion.* Copyright © 2003 by Jacqueline Woodson. Used by permission of G.P. Putnam's Sons, A Division of Penguin Young Readers Group, A Member of Penguin Group (USA) Inc., 345 Hudson Street, New York, NY 10014. All rights reserved. "Rules of the Game" by Amy Tan from *The Joy Luck Club.* Copyright © 1989 by Amy Tan. Used by permission of G.P. Putnam Sons, a division of Penguin Putnam, Inc.

# Acknowledgments

**Random House, Inc.**
"Melting Pot" copyright © 1987 by Anna Quindlen, from *Living Out Loud* by Anna Quindlen. Used by permission of Random House, Inc. "The War of the Wall", from *Deep Sightings and Rescue Missions* by Toni Cade Bambara, copyright © 1996 by The Estate of Toni Cade Bambara. Used by permission of Pantheon Books, a division of Random House, Inc.

**Marian Reiner, Literary Agent**
"Haiku" by Matsuo Basho translated by Harry Behn from *Cricket Songs; Japanese Haiku.* Copyright © 1964 by Harry Behn; Copyright renewed 1992 Prescott Behn, Pamela Behn Adam and Peter Behn. Used by permission of Marian Reiner.

**Russell and Volkening, Inc.**
From "Harriet Tubman: Conductor on the Underground Railroad", by Ann Petry. Copyright © 1955 by Ann Petry, renewed in 1983 by Ann Petry. Reprinted by permission of Russell & Volkening as agents for the author. Used by permission of Russell & Volkening as agents for the author.

**Scholastic, Inc.**
From "The Shutout" published in *Black Diamond: The Story of The Negro Baseball Leagues* by Patricia C. McKissack & Fredrick McKissack, Jr. Copyright © 1994 by Patricia C. McKissack and Fredrick McKissack, Jr. Reprinted by permission of Scholastic Inc.

**Virginia Driving Hawk Sneve**
"The Medicine Bag" by Virginia Driving Hawk Sneve from *Boy's Life.* Copyright © 1975 by Virginia Driving Hawk Sneve. Used by permission.

**South Side News Leader**
"Cyber Chitchat" by Cindy Kauffman from *Chocolate for a Teen's Dreams.* Used by permission.

**Literary Estate of May Swenson**
"Analysis of Baseball" by May Swenson from *American Sports Poems.* Used with permission of the Literary Estate of May Swenson.

**University Press of New England**
"The Talk" by Gary Soto from *A Summer Life.* Copyright © 1990 by University Press of New England, Hanover, NH. Reprinted with permission.

**Viking Penguin, Inc.**
"Trombones and Colleges" by Walter Dean Myers from *Fast Sam, Cool Clyde and Stuff.* Copyright © 1975 by Walter Dean Myers. Used by permission of Viking Penguin, a division of Penguin Young Readers Group, a member of Penguin Group (USA) Inc., 345 Hudson Street, New York, NY 10014. All rights reserved.

Note: Every effort has been made to locate the copyright owner of material reproduced on this component. Omissions brought to our attention will be corrected in subsequent editions.

## Cover Design

Judith Krimski

## Art Credits

## Photo Credits

# Photo and Art Credits

# Tips for Improving Reading Fluency

The tips on these pages will help you improve your reading fluency, or your ability to read easily, smoothly, and expressively.

## Keeping Your Concentration

Becoming an active, aware reader will help you get the most from your assignments. Practice using these strategies:

► Cover what you have already read with a note card as you go along. Then, you will not be able to reread without noticing that you are doing it.

► Set a purpose for reading beyond just completing the assignment. Then, read actively by pausing to ask yourself questions about the material as you read.

► Use the Reading Skills instruction pages that appear twice in each unit of this book.

► Stop reading after a specified period of time (for example, five minutes) and summarize what you have read.

## Reading Phrases

Fluent readers read phrases rather than individual words. Reading this way will speed up your reading and improve your comprehension. Here are some useful ideas:

► Experts recommend rereading as a strategy to increase fluency. Choose a passage of text that is neither too hard nor too easy. Read the same passage aloud several times until you can read it smoothly. When you can read the passage fluently, pick another passage and keep practicing.

► Read aloud into a tape recorder. Then, listen to the recording, noting your accuracy, pacing, and expression. You can also read aloud and share feedback with a partner.

## Understanding Key Vocabulary

► If you do not understand some of the words in an assignment, you may miss out on important concepts. Therefore, it is helpful to keep a dictionary nearby when you are reading. Follow these steps:

► Before you begin reading, scan the text for unfamiliar words or terms. Find out what those words mean before you begin reading.

► Use context—the surrounding words, phrases, and sentences—to help you determine the meanings of unfamiliar words.

# Tips for Improving Reading Fluency

▶ If you are unable to understand the meaning through context, refer to the dictionary.

## Paying Attention to Punctuation

When you read, pay attention to punctuation. Commas, periods, exclamation points, semicolons, and colons tell you when to pause or stop. They also indicate relationships between groups of words. When you recognize these relationships you will read with greater understanding and expression. Look at the chart below.

| Punctuation Mark | Meaning |
|---|---|
| comma | brief pause |
| period | pause at the end of a thought |
| exclamation point | pause that indicates emphasis |
| semicolon | pause between related but distinct thoughts |
| colon | pause before giving explanation or examples |

## Using the Reading Fluency Checklist

Use the checklist below each time you read a selection in this textbook. In a journal or notebook, note which skills you need to work on and chart your progress each week.

| Reading Fluency Checklist |
|---|
| ☐ Preview the text to check for difficult or unfamiliar words. |
| ☐ Practice reading aloud. |
| ☐ Read according to punctuation. |
| ☐ Break down long sentences into the subject and its meaning. |
| ☐ Read groups of words for meaning rather than reading single words. |
| ☐ Read with expression (change your tone of voice to add meaning to the word). |

Reading is a skill that can be improved with practice. The key to improving your fluency is to read. The more you read, the better your reading will become.